CONTENTS

page **18**

page **14**

page **30**

HOME PLANS

RESOURCES

Find thousands of plans on-line, visit our website **www.familyhomeplans.com**

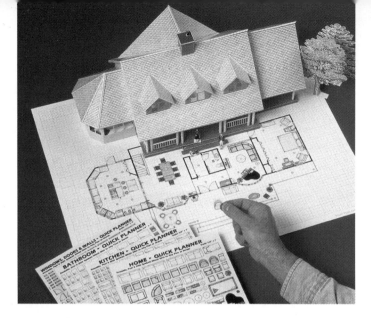

Design, Build and Decorate
Your New Home on Your Kitchen Table

Don't let the frustration of complicated home design software get between you and your dream. Visualize and test your ideas using our proven design systems.

HOME QUICK PLANNER

Design and Decorate Your New Home

Go ahead! Knock down walls and move cabinets, bathroom fixtures, furniture, windows and doors—even whole rooms. 700 pre-cut, reusable peel-and-stick furniture, fixture and architectural symbols. Includes 1/4-in. scale Floor Plan Grid, stairs, outlets, switches, lights, plus design ideas.

Regularly $22.95   Special Offer: $19.95

3-D HOME KIT

"Build" Your New Home

Construct a three-dimensional scale model home of up to 3,000 square feet. (For larger homes, order an extra kit.) A complete assortment of cardboard building materials—from brick, stone, clapboards, roofing and decking to windows, doors, skylights, stairs, bathroom fixtures, kitchen cabinets and more. Includes Floor Plan Grid, interior walls, special Scaled Ruler and Roof Slope Calculator, professional design notes and complete model building instructions.

Regularly $33.95   Special Offer: $29.95

the **Garlinghouse** company

Helping to build dreams since 1907

To order, call
1-800-235-5700

Monday - Friday 8 a.m. - 8 p.m. Eastern Time

404 NARROW LOT HOME PLANS

An Active Interest Media Publication

GARLINGHOUSE, LLC

Art Director	Christopher Berrien
Managing Editor	Debra Cochran
Art Production Manager	Debra Novitch
Production Artist	Cindy King

Exec. Director of Operations	Wade Schmelter
Senior Accountant	Angela West
Director of Home Plan Sales	Sue Lavigne
Director of Sales	Tom Valentino
Accounts Receivable/Payable	Monika Jackson
Telesales Team	Julianna Blamire
	Randolph Hollingsworth
	Renee Johnson
	Barbara Neal
	Carol Patenaude
	Robert Rogala
	Alice Sonski
Fulfillment Supervisor	Audrey Sutton

Advertising Sales
1-800-279-7361

For Plan Orders in Canada
The Garlinghouse Company
102 Ellis Street, Penticton, BC V2A 4L5
1-800-361-7526

For Designer's Submission Information,
e-mail us at dcochran@aimmedia.com

404 NARROW LOT HOME PLANS
Library of Congress: 2004108401   ISBN: 1-893536-16-5

At Garlinghouse, you're buying more than a set of plans.

You're buying a history of exceptional customer service and understanding.

In addition to our experienced staff of sales professionals, The Garlinghouse Company maintains an expert staff of trained house design professionals to help guide you through the complex process of customizing your plans to meet all your needs and expectations.

We don't just want to sell you a plan, we want to partner with you in building your dream home. Some of the many services we offer our customers include:

Answers to Your Questions
If you have technical questions on any plan we sell, give us a call toll-free at 1-800-235-5700.

Customizing Your Stock Plan
Any plan we sell can be modified to become your custom home. For more information, see page 32 and page 343.

Information for Budgeting Your New Home's Construction
A very general cost of building your new home can be arrived at using the so-called National Average Cost to Build, which is $110 per square foot. Based on that average, a 2,400-square-foot home would cost $264,000, including labor and materials, but excluding land, site preparation, windows, doors, cabinets, appliances, etc.

For a more inclusive rough estimate, Garlinghouse offers a Zip Quote estimate for every plan we sell. Based on current prices in your zip code area, we can provide a rough estimate of material and labor costs for the plans you select. See page 344 to learn more.

However, for a more accurate estimate of what it will cost to build your new home, we offer a full materials list, which lists the quantities, dimensions, and specifications for the major materials needed to build your home including appliances. Available at a modest additional charge, the materials list will allow you to get faster, more accurate bids from your contractors and building suppliers—and help you avoid paying for unused materials and waste. Due to differences in regional requirements and homeowner or builder preferences, electrical, plumbing, and heating/air conditioning equipment specifications are not designed specifically for each plan. See page 345 for additional information.

Garlinghouse blueprints have helped create a nation of homeowners, beginning back in 1907. Over the past century, we've made keeping up with the latest trends in floor plan design for new house construction our business. We understand the business of home plans and the real needs and expectations of the home plan buyer. To contact us, call 1-800-235-5700, or visit us on the web at www.familyhomeplans.com.

For America's best home plans.
Trust, value, and experience. Since 1907.

Southern Style

ABOVE: A red standing-seam metal roof with small gabled dormers over a deep covered porch gives authentic Southern cottage appeal to this spacious home.

BELOW: The efficient design packs a lot of counter space and storage into the sunny kitchen.

This attractive home wraps modern amenities within a classic southern farmhouse-style exterior. The foyer is flanked by a coat closet on one side and a powder room on the other. A wide arched doorway opens from the foyer into the soaring two-story great room. To the left of the great room, an open staircase rises to a balcony where a sitting area separates two secondary bedrooms, each with its own full bath. The luxurious master suite takes up the left side of the first floor. To the right of the great room, at the front of the home, is the dining room. Behind that lies the kitchen where every wall is lined with counters or cabinets—or both. The kitchen sink and dishwasher are tucked into a bay window, providing a pleasant and sunny work area. A utility wing stretches out behind the right side of the house to include a large laundry room, screen porch and two-car garage. An apartment with dormered kitchen and dining area and a full bath is above the garage. This home is designed with a crawlspace foundation. ▶

Design 57003

Price Code	Call for pricing
Total Finished	2,438 sq. ft.
First Finished	1,704 sq. ft.
Second Finished	734 sq. ft.
Bonus Unfinished	479 sq. ft.
Dimensions	50'x82'6"
Foundation	Crawlspace
Bedrooms	3
Full Baths	3
Half Baths	1

Please note: The photographed home may have been modified to suit homeowner preferences. If you order plans, have a builder or design professional check them against the photographs to confirm construction details.

SECOND FLOOR

FIRST FLOOR

ABOVE AND BELOW: A great room that lives up to the name. The large space features built-ins, a fireplace, a volume ceiling, and a second floor overlook. The casual look of the exposed brick and natural wood nicely complements the elegant white trim and molding.

Photography: Courtesy of the Designer

ABOVE: A low overhanging roof with large eaves brackets lends an Italianate air to this elegantly modern townhouse.

Maximum
Views

Tall windows and three levels of balconies are designed to make this house one with its setting. The public rooms are all on the second floor, ensuring that the best views are from the rooms you use the most. The great room and dining room take advantage of a double-sided fireplace. The spacious great room features two walls of windows and access to a large porch. The master suite, with private patio and expansive bath shares the first floor with a library, laundry room, and two-car garage. A rec room, bedroom, and storage room make up the lower floor with a convenient elevator tying all the floors together. This house is designed with a basement foundation. ▶

Please note: The photographed home may have been modified to suit homeowner preferences. If you order plans, have a builder or design professional check them against the photographs to confirm construction details.

Design 50066

Price Code	J
Total Finished	3,681 sq. ft.
First Finished	1,423 sq. ft.
Second Finished	1,439 sq. ft.
Lower Finished	819 sq. ft.
Garage Unfinished	423 sq. ft.
Deck Unfinished	281 sq. ft.
Porch Unfinished	139 sq. ft.
Dimensions	41'8"x53'
Foundation	Slab
Bedrooms	3
Full Baths	1
3/4 Baths	2

LOWER FLOOR   **FIRST FLOOR**   **SECOND FLOOR**

Photography: Courtesy of the Designer

Georgian Townhouse

Drawing inspiration from the Georgian townhouses of the 18th and 19th centuries, this handsome home is as impressive from the outside as it is comfortable on the inside. The entry foyer leads past a kitchen lined with counter space to large, open public areas. The dining room flows into the big great room with corner fireplace, an abundance of large windows, and access to a rear porch. A coat closet and powder room are conveniently tucked into the space behind the staircase. On the second floor, a spacious master bedroom with compartmentalized bath and deep walk-in-closet shares space with a secondary bedroom and full bath. The staircase continues up to the third floor where a spacious loft with skylights completes the living area. This home is designed with a basement foundation. ◗

Design 50065

Price Code	C
Total Finished	1,789 sq. ft.
First Finished	770 sq. ft.
Second Finished	755 sq. ft.
Dimensions	20'x40'
Foundation	Basement
Bedrooms	2
Full Baths	2
Half Baths	1

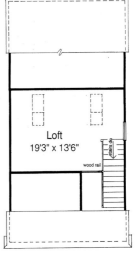

THIRD FLOOR

SECOND FLOOR

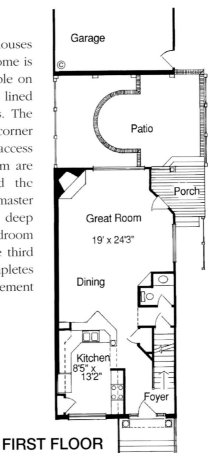

FIRST FLOOR

Photography: Courtesy of the Designer

Stylish Family
Home

ABOVE: The hipped roof and low vertical lines of Prairie style are married to Craftsman-inspired details such as exposed roof beams and rafter tails in this stylish family home.

BELOW: The secluded living room offers a quiet retreat and introduces the Craftsman-style décor that is prevalent throughout the rest of the home.

The appealing entry, sheltered within a small porch, leads into a cozy living room offering a quiet retreat at the front of the home. A wide stair hall leads to the rear of the home, where the space opens up with dramatic impact to a large, open great room/dining room/kitchen space visually separated by varying ceiling heights. The second floor features a sumptuous master suite including plans for a double-sided gas fireplace to be shared by the sitting area and the large whirlpool tub in the master bath. Two secondary bedrooms, a full hall bath, and a convenient laundry room are also on the second floor. The lower level includes a fourth bedroom and large rec room. This home is designed with a basement foundation. ◗

Design 50067

Price Code	F
Total Finished	2,691 sq. ft.
First Finished	1,160 sq. ft.
Second Finished	1,531 sq. ft.
Lower Unfinished	1,160 sq. ft.
Garage Unfinished	465 sq. ft.
Deck Unfinished	339 sq. ft.
Porch Unfinished	75 sq. ft.
Dimensions	37'8"x53'
Foundation	Basement
Bedrooms	3
Full Baths	2
Half Baths	1

Please note: The photographed home may have been modified to suit homeowner preferences. If you order plans, have a builder or design professional check them against the photographs to confirm construction details.

ABOVE: Craftsman-inspired details in the fireplace surround lend authenticity to the open, comfortable space of the great room.

RIGHT: Abundant workspace and attractive cabinetry are highlights of the kitchen. An octagonal dining area creates an intimate space within the larger great room.

LOWER FLOOR

Patio

Rec Room
35'4" x16'4"

FUTURE
WET BAR

Bath

STAIRS UP

Bedroom
13'10" x 13'5"

Unexc.

Unexc.

FIRST FLOOR

Deck

Dining Area
10'6" x 10'8"
8'-2 3/4" CEIL. HGT.
@ DINING AREA

Kitchen

Great Room
37' x 16'4"

STAIRS UP

Bath

Living
Room
13'8" x 13'3"

Garage
19'10" x 28'8"

Foyer

Porch

SECOND FLOOR

WINDOW SEAT

GAS
FIREPLACE

Master
Bath

Master
Bedroom
25'10" X 21'
Irreg.

BUILT-IN TV NICHE

WALK-IN
CLOSET

WALK-IN
CLOSET

WOOD HALL

DOWN

Hall

Bedroom
19' x 12'

WINDOW

CLOSET

Laun.

Bath

Bath

Bedroom
17'5" x 10'

Photography: Courtesy of the Designer

ABOVE: A quartet of gables topping a covered porch adds welcoming detail to this home's facade.

Updated
Four-Square

The period facade of this home harkens back to the early 20th century. Like its predecessors, this floor plan packs a lot of living into its stylized square footage, marrying proven motifs with today's open interiors. Much of the first floor is unobstructed by walls, with arch-and-column configurations serving as the sole delineation for the dining area. The great room and eat-in kitchen are backed by abundant windows, which allow light to stream in unhindered. French doors and custom built-ins characterize the study. The second floor features an expansive, windowed bonus room over the garage, perfect for games, exercise equipment, or home office. ▶

Please note: The photographed home may have been modified to suit homeowner preferences. If you order plans, have a builder or design professional check them against the photographs to confirm construction details.

SECOND FLOOR

Design 81033

Price Code	C
Total Finished	1,946 sq. ft.
First Finished	1,082 sq. ft.
Second Finished	864 sq. ft.
Bonus Unfinished	358 sq. ft.
Garage Unfinished	620 sq. ft.
Porch Unfinished	120 sq. ft.
Dimensions	40'x52'
Foundation	Crawlspace
Bedrooms	3
Full Baths	2
Half Baths	1

FIRST FLOOR

Photography: Courtesy of the Designer

ABOVE: Perfect for a narrow lot, the garage on this home is tucked into the rear, which prevents it from dominating the front facade.

BONUS

OPT. BONUS ROOM
18'-0" X 28'-8"

FIRST FLOOR

GARAGE
20'-0" X 19'-8"

BENCH W/ STORAGE

GRILLING PORCH
8'-0" X 16'-8"
BEADED CEILING

LAU.
6'-0" X 6'-4"

KID'S NOOK

MASTER SUITE
13'-0" X 14'-8"

OPT. 10' BOXED CEILING

BRKFAST ROOM
10'-6" X 9'-0"

COMPUTER CENTER

8" COLUMNS

DINING RM.
12'-8" X 12'-0"

KITCHEN
9'-6" X 14'-0"

DW   RG

PANTRY   REF

GLASS SHWR.   KNEE SPACE

M.BATH
13'-0" X 15'-2"

LIN

WHP TUB

3' GAS FIREPLACE

GREAT ROOM
18'-10" X 17'-8"

BEDROOM 2
13'-0" X 11'-0"

OPT. STAIRS

8' COVERED PORCH
BEADED CEILING

12" COLUMNS

LIN

BED RM. 3 / STUDY
13'-0" X 11'-0"

Please note: The photographed home may have been modified to suit homeowner preferences. If you order plans, have a builder or design professional check them against the photographs to confirm construction details.

Family Spaces

The porch opens directly into the great room, which features a gas fireplace. Directly to the right of the entrance, a short hallway connects the two secondary bedrooms to a full bath. Past the great room is the dining room and large kitchen/breakfast area. The kitchen, almost completely enveloped by counter space, holds a snack bar and built-in computer center. Off the breakfast room are a kid's nook featuring a bench with storage, a laundry room, and access to the grilling porch. The boxed-ceiling master suite takes up half of the right wing and features ample closet space and a luxurious bath with whirlpool tub. On the second floor are 1,191 square feet of bonus space. This home is designed with slab and crawlspace foundation options. ▶

Design 82020

Price Code	C
Total Finished	1,845 sq. ft.
Main Finished	1,845 sq. ft.
Bonus Unfinished	1,191 sq. ft.
Garage Unfinished	496 sq. ft.
Porch Unfinished	465 sq. ft.
Dimensions	41'4"x83'8"
Foundation	Crawlspace Slab
Bedrooms	3
Full Baths	2

Photography: Courtesy of the Designer

ABOVE: Three covered porches, gables, and heavy window trim form a classic country composition.

BELOW: Tall windows form the corners of the family room, casting light over the hardwood floor and through the arched entry to the kitchen.

Elegantly
Efficient

The wraparound porch leads through the main entry into an energy-efficient vestibule. To the left is a secluded study; to the right, the living room, which overlooks the front yard. Beyond the living room is the formal dining area with its own small porch for al fresco dining. This space leads into the kitchen, which is lined with counters and opens on the other end to a casual eating area. Steps away is the family room, which has a fireplace and a corner filled with windows. Beside the staircase, a discrete hallway leads to the laundry room and a powder room.

On the 983-square-foot second floor, a balcony overlooking the living room connects three bedrooms. A walk-in closet fills a corner of the master suite, which has a five-piece bath with a window illuminating the tub. The other two bedrooms have ample closet space, and share a full hall bath. This home is designed with a basement foundation. ▶

Design 65138

Price Code	D
Total Finished	2,257 sq. ft.
First Finished	1,274 sq. ft.
Second Finished	983 sq. ft.
Garage Unfinished	437 sq. ft.
Deck Unfinished	339 sq. ft.
Porch Unfinished	183 sq. ft.
Dimensions	50'x46'
Foundation	Basement
Bedrooms	3
Full Baths	2
Half Baths	1

Please note: The photographed home may have been modified to suit homeowner preferences. If you order plans, have a builder or design professional check them against the photographs to confirm construction details.

ABOVE: An abundance of cabinets and a circular snack bar at the end of the counter make efficient use of space in the galley-style kitchen.

LEFT: An elliptical fanlight tops a lovely arrangement of windows in the living room and repeats the theme of arches found throughout the home from the front porch to the doorways between rooms in the public spaces.

SECOND FLOOR

FIRST FLOOR

Photography: Michael Partenio

Made for
Real Life

ABOVE: The large combination family and dining room is flooded with natural light from three sides.

BELOW: A two-tier peninsula separates the kitchen and dining area. The raised breakfast bar serves three purposes: it provides a perfect spot to share a quick meal, extra counter space, and helps obscure the cooking and cleanup areas from diners.

With three levels and an emphasis on open spaces and storage, this home packs a lot of living into just over 1,600 square feet. One large area combines the window-lined dining and family areas, as opposed to the more formal tradition of isolated eating areas. The kitchen, which is lined with counters, has a peninsula counter to divide the spaces. A cozy secondary bedroom and a separate den round out the 1,022-square-foot first floor.

The entire 580-square-foot second floor is dedicated to the master suite. Storage space surrounds the bedroom, including built-in cedar cabinets, which are located in the exterior kneewalls. The master bath includes a window-lined soaking tub.

The lower floor was created for utility. The large two-car garage has additional space for storage or a workshop. The laundry is conveniently and discretely located at the bottom of the stairs. Another large room serves as a mechanical/storage area. This home is designed with a basement foundation. ▶

Design 32385

Price Code	B
Total Finished	1,602 sq. ft.
First Finished	1,022 sq. ft.
Second Finished	580 sq. ft.
Basement Unfinished	473 sq. ft.
Garage Unfinished	547 sq. ft.
Dimensions	42'x28'
Foundation	Basement
Bedrooms	2
Full Baths	2

Please note: The photographed home may have been modified to suit homeowner preferences. If you order plans, have a builder or design professional check them against the photographs to confirm construction details.

ABOVE: The side elevation shows the small windows that flank the chimney.

LEFT: A central gable flanked by wings comprise the facade.

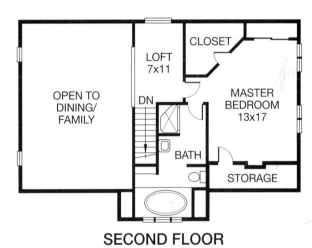

SECOND FLOOR

- OPEN TO DINING/FAMILY
- LOFT 7x11
- CLOSET
- DN
- MASTER BEDROOM 13x17
- BATH
- STORAGE

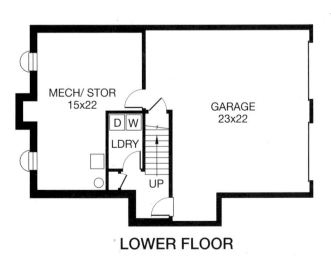

LOWER FLOOR

- MECH/STOR 15x22
- GARAGE 23x22
- D W
- LDRY
- UP

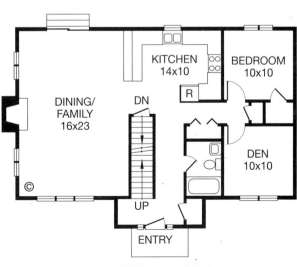

FIRST FLOOR

- KITCHEN 14x10
- BEDROOM 10x10
- DINING/FAMILY 16x23
- DN
- R
- DEN 10x10
- UP
- ENTRY

ABOVE: A gable dormer creates an architecturally interesting cap to the covered porch supported by tapered pillars on brick base.

Room to
Grow

Inside this home, you'll find everything a growing family needs. A den, with an optional closet and alternate door location could easily be converted into a bedroom. Opposite the den, the master suite is secluded for privacy. The kitchen provides plenty of work space, forming one large area with the breakfast and family rooms. On the second floor, two secondary bedrooms share space with a computer loft and 395 square feet of bonus space. This home is designed with a basement foundation. Alternate foundation options available at an additional charge. Please call 800/235-5700 for more information. ▶

Design 68191

Price Code	C
Total Finished	1,924 sq. ft.
First Finished	1,352 sq. ft.
Second Finished	572 sq. ft.
Bonus Unfinished	395 sq. ft.
Basement Unfinished	1,352 sq. ft.
Garage Unfinished	447 sq. ft.
Porch Unfinished	191 sq. ft.
Dimensions	40'x55'8"
Foundation	Basement
Bedrooms	3
Full Baths	3

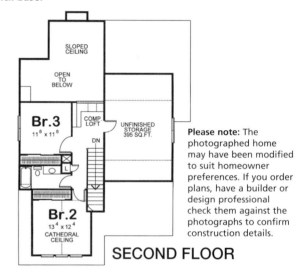

SECOND FLOOR

Please note: The photographed home may have been modified to suit homeowner preferences. If you order plans, have a builder or design professional check them against the photographs to confirm construction details.

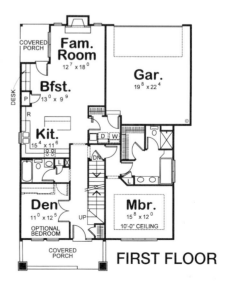

FIRST FLOOR

© William E. Poole Designs

ABOVE: Three-ranked windows balanced with a center paneled door with semi-circular fanlight and elaborated crown and pilasters highlight a mix of Georgian and Adam detailing often found in colonial houses from the late 18th century.

Classic
Colonial

SECOND FLOOR

FIRST FLOOR

This lovely home offers a classic floor plan updated to include all the amenities the modern family requires. The simple elegance of the Georgian entry leads into an updated center-hall style plan. But in this update, the space usually taken up by the hall has been given over to the great room, reducing construction costs while creating a more livable, up-to-date plan. The front-to-back great room has a fireplace and offers rear access to either a patio or deck. To the right of the foyer, a generous dining room at the front of the house leads back to a well-planned L-shape kitchen with center island and breakfast area. Beyond that, a service wing offers a utility room, two-car garage with storage, and rear stairs leading up to bonus space above the garage. This home is designed with a combination basement/crawlspace foundation. ▶

Design 57031

Price Code	Call for pricing
Total Finished	1,871 sq. ft.
First Finished	1,028 sq. ft.
Second Finished	843 sq. ft.
Bonus Unfinished	304 sq. ft.
Dimensions	40'x61'
Foundation	Combo Basement/ Crawlspace
Bedrooms	3
Full Baths	2
Half Baths	1

ABOVE: The two-story porch lets light into the second floor but keeps out the sun during the hottest times of the year. Metal roofing and exposed rafter tails suggest the design's tropical roots.

Tropical
Mix

Created for any climate but steeped in the regional architecture of Key West, Florida, this compact home makes the most of its 1,129 square feet and does it with style. Defining the home is a basic Cape Cod-style shape: a central gable structure with porches front and back. Outside, the home's wide trim, crown moldings, and deep sills create a vintage look. Inside, a sense of spaciousness is projected that reaches beyond the modest-sized home's actual dimensions. To maximize space, hallways are kept at a minimum and the living room, dining area, and kitchen all flow together around a central powder room. Out back is a long screen porch and wraparound deck. On the second floor, a smaller porch leads to a small deck off the rear. The secondary bedroom and master bedroom share the full bath. This home is designed with a crawlspace foundation. ▶

BELOW: Counters and cabinetry surround the kitchen, offering plenty of work space.

Photography: James Yochum Photography

Design 32399

Price Code	A
Total Finished	1,129 sq. ft.
First Finished	576 sq. ft.
Second Finished	553 sq. ft.
Deck Unfinished	230 sq. ft.
Porch Unfinished	331 sq. ft.
Dimensions	36'8x36'
Foundation	Crawlspace
Bedrooms	2
Full Baths	1
Half Baths	1

Please note: The photographed home may have been modified to suit homeowner preferences. If you order plans, have a builder or design professional check them against the photographs to confirm construction details.

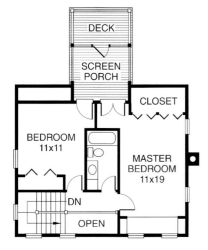

SECOND FLOOR

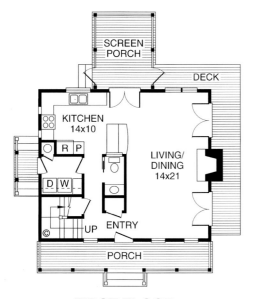

FIRST FLOOR

ABOVE: Set into the longest wall in the open first-floor living and dining space, the fireplace becomes a central focal point. French doors on each side of the fireplace lead to a wraparound deck.

BELOW: Privately nestled into the trees, the first-floor screen porch provides a shaded place to enjoy the backyard.

Photography: James Yochum Photography

ABOVE: A center gable topping the covered porch promotes a sense of balance.

Please note: The photographed home may have been modified to suit homeowner preferences. If you order plans, have a builder or design professional check them against the photographs to confirm construction details.

Farmhouse
Favorite

All the right spaces in all the right places are packed into this efficient beauty, including formal and informal living spaces as well as three bedrooms—all in just 1,550 square feet. A simple footprint makes the design extremely cost-efficient to build. The front porch (not shown on the floor plan) lines the living room, which feels even more spacious because it opens to the dining room. The U-shape kitchen maximizes space and seems larger than it is because it opens into the breakfast area and den, which can include a fireplace. A laundry area, closet and powder room complete the 775-square-foot first floor. On the second floor, double doors open to the master suite. An optional master bath design offers a dual-sink vanity and a third closet. This home is designed with a basement foundation. ▶

Design 32229

Price Code	B
Total Finished	1,550 sq. ft.
First Finished	775 sq. ft.
Second Finished	775 sq. ft.
Basement Unfinished	775 sq. ft.
Deck Unfinished	112 sq. ft.
Porch Unfinished	150 sq. ft.
Dimensions	25'x37'
Foundation	Basement
Bedrooms	3
Full Baths	2
Half Baths	1

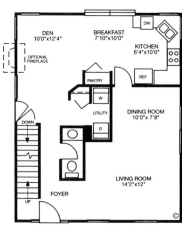

FIRST FLOOR

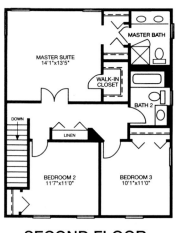

SECOND FLOOR

ABOVE: Dentil cornice molding and a simple paneled door entry give authentic period detail to this modern home.

Design 57030

Price Code	Call for pricing
Total Finished	2,199 sq. ft.
First Finished	1,591 sq. ft.
Second Finished	608 sq. ft.
Bonus Unfinished	414 sq. ft.
Dimensions	41'8"x74'6"
Foundation	Basement
Bedrooms	3
Full Baths	3
Half Baths	1

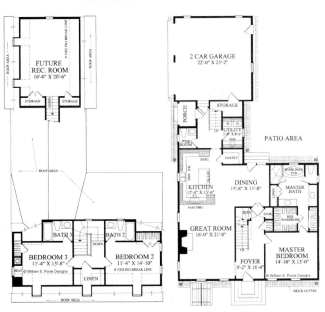

SECOND FLOOR   **FIRST FLOOR**

21ˢᵗ Century
Williamsburg

The classic colonial style with fine Georgian detail of this home might have the look of Colonial Williamsburg on the outside but, on the inside, the layout has been planned with the modern family in mind. A central stair hall offers access to the great room on the left side of the home, the master suite on the right, or the dining room to the rear. Between the great room and the dining room, a U-shape kitchen with center island is lined with work space. A service wing to the rear of the home, housing a powder room, utility room, and two-car garage, creates a sheltered patio space off the dining room. From the service wing, a rear staircase leads to bonus space over the garage. On the second floor of the main part of the home, two secondary bedrooms each have a private bath. This home is designed with a basement foundation. ◗

Photography: Jim Hedrich-Hedrich Blessing

ABOVE: A two-story bay, long and narrow footprint, and covered porch are hallmarks of turn-of-the-century rowhouse architecture, recreated here with very up-to-date interior spaces.

BELOW: The rear deck offers a private retreat without taking up too much space.

Rowhouse
Revival

This home takes what we love about traditional neighborhood architecture and blends it with open and modern spaces to create a hybrid that works for today's families. The entry leads into the spacious open plan of the first floor, composed of the octagonal formal dining room, kitchen/breakfast area, and family room. In the family room, doors leading to the rear deck flank the fireplace. A peninsula bar extending into the breakfast nook separates the family room from the kitchen. A large pantry in the laundry room adds to the kitchen's efficiency. On the 951-square-foot second floor, the master bedroom claims the entire octagonal space within the upper bay. Its large walk-in closet and five-piece master bath round out the suite. Two secondary bedrooms, one with its own walk-in closet, share a full bath. Ideal for a narrow lot, this home packs in a lot of living space. For outdoor enjoyment, it includes a graceful front porch and a rear deck. This home is designed with a basement foundation. ▶

Design 32436

Price Code	A
Total Finished	1,907 sq. ft.
First Finished	956 sq. ft.
Second Finished	951 sq. ft.
Basement Unfinished	965 sq. ft.
Deck Unfinished	112 sq. ft.
Porch Unfinished	126 sq. ft.
Dimensions	28'x48'
Foundation	Basement
Bedrooms	3
Full Baths	2
Half Baths	1

Please note: The photographed home may have been modified to suit homeowner preferences. If you order plans, have a builder or design professional check them against the photographs to confirm construction details.

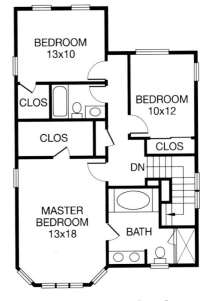

SECOND FLOOR

TOP: French doors leading to the rear deck flank the fireplace, while floor-to-ceiling windows brighten the adjacent wall of the family room.

CENTER: With a few modifications, the homeowner personalized the kitchen with an antique table, which serves as an island, and a raised peninsula counter that's ideal for informal dining.

LEFT: Stained glass surrounds a vanity mirror in the first-floor powder room.

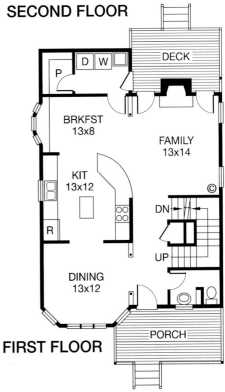

FIRST FLOOR

Photography: Jim Hedrich-Hedrich Blessing

ABOVE: The view from the street is intentionally understated, with the garage and shop buffering the most-used rooms from traffic noise and the hot afternoon sun.

Please note: The photographed home may have been modified to suit homeowner preferences. If you order plans, have a builder or design professional check them against the photographs to confirm construction details.

Personal
Oasis

With a length that's over twice its width and perfect for a narrow lot, this home does not scrimp on space. The entry is located in the courtyard, far from the public eye. Entrances in the garage and studio provide alternative ways of ingress. Walls of windows in the studio, with built-ins, make it comfortably feel as if it is part of the courtyard during all seasons. The master suite also has a wall of windows connecting it to the courtyard.

This home is full of practical features. The living/dining area is one large space, warmed by a fireplace. The kitchen has an island, S-shape counters, and additional counter space next to the pantry. The laundry provides plenty of storage space, as does the shop off the garage. A secondary bedroom sits secluded on the second floor, sharing the space with a full bath and an attic/mechanical room. This home is designed with a slab foundation.

RIGHT: The view from the street is intentionally understated, with the garage and shop buffering the most-used rooms from traffic noise and the hot afternoon sun.

To order blueprints, call **800-235-5700** or visit us on the web, **familyhomeplans.com**

LEFT: Here in the living room, as in the studio (ABOVE), elaborate trusses supported by log pillars add a rustic touch. Natural light from carefully arranged windows is a major design theme throughout this home. The long, narrow footprint with central courtyard maximizes the amount of exterior walls, thereby maximizing the opportunities to capture light through windows.

BOTTOM LEFT: Tall windows and transoms give the master bedroom a view of the courtyard. Built-ins line an adjacent wall, adding practical beauty.

Design 32428

Price Code	H
Total Finished	3,186 sq. ft.
First Finished	2,684 sq. ft.
Second Finished	502 sq. ft.
Garage Unfinished	435 sq. ft.
Dimensions	43'10"x101'5"
Foundation	Slab
Bedrooms	3
Full Baths	2
3/4 Baths	1

SECOND FLOOR

FIRST FLOOR

Snug
Fit

ABOVE & BELOW: Designing a home to be built within setbacks on a tight lot doesn't mean sacrificing style.

Please note: The photographed home may have been modified to suit homeowner preferences. If you order plans, have a builder or design professional check them against the photographs to confirm construction details.

Designed to take advantage of every inch of a small site, this plan achieves an open, even soaring, look with loads of style. The exterior is wrapped in richly textured shingle siding mixed with board-and-batten siding, which is common for bungalows and cottages. Not as common are the home's open spaces and light-filled rooms, not to mention its subtle nautical theme—from the living room fireplace built with boatlike angles to the crow's nest of a tower that houses an office. The living room and family room sit just off the entryway, with the dining room conveniently located next to the space-efficient kitchen. The 647-square-foot second floor is given over to the master suite and complementary private spaces, which include a sleeping porch and private deck. There are 877 square feet on the first floor. This home is designed with a crawlspace foundation. ◗

Design 32209

Price Code	B
Total Finished	1,524 sq. ft.
First Finished	877 sq. ft.
Second Finished	647 sq. ft.
Garage Unfinished	281 sq. ft.
Deck Unfinished	141 sq. ft.
Dimensions	44'6"x36'2"
Foundation	Crawlspace
Bedrooms	1
3/4 Baths	2

LEFT: The board-and-batten chimney provides the living room with an appropriately nautical feel thanks to its boatlike angles.

BELOW LEFT: Ample use of recessed lighting in the efficient kitchen ensures that no work space is left in the dark.

BELOW RIGHT: The homeowner modified the plan to include a compact home office set into the soaring light tower.

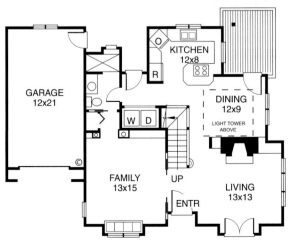

FIRST FLOOR

SECOND FLOOR

© William E. Poole Designs, Inc.

Cape Cod
Styling

ABOVE: Stacked gables, shed dormers, and the gentle slope of the roof over the entry porch project timeless cottage appeal to the neighborhood. The addition of window boxes and a white picket fence, as shown in the rendering, completes the ideal of early 20th century cottage charm, while the floor plan is designed to meet the needs of a 21st century family.

A steep gable roofline punctuated with dormer windows and front facing gables offers a traditional welcome to this family home. The foyer accesses the formal living room through an entry elegantly accented by columns. The dining room has been positioned between the kitchen and the formal living room for an easy transition when entertaining. The kitchen features an island with a convenient snack bar and an L-shaped work area. The kitchen, sunny breakfast room, and family room are all open to each other creating a more spacious feel while varying ceiling heights distinguish the spaces. A second floor balcony overlooks the two-story family room. A secluded master suite offers optimal privacy to the owners. Upstairs three additional bedrooms share a hall bath. There is additional space on the second floor to expand, perhaps for a future recreation room. This home is designed with a crawlspace foundation. ▶

Design 57024

Price Code	Call for pricing
Total Finished	2,410 sq. ft.
First Finished	1,627 sq. ft.
Second Finished	783 sq. ft.
Bonus Unfinished	418 sq. ft.
Dimensions	46'x58'
Foundation	Crawlspace
Bedrooms	4
Full Baths	2
Half Baths	1

FIRST FLOOR

SECOND FLOOR

ABOVE: Elegant columns supporting a double-gallery offer authentic southern charm while high-peak gable roofs make this plan equally ideal for northern climates.

Design 57033

Price Code	Call for pricing
Total Finished	2,318 sq. ft.
First Finished	1,688 sq. ft.
Second Finished	630 sq. ft.
Bonus Unfinished	506 sq. ft.
Dimensions	44'4"x62'4"
Foundation	Crawlspace
Bedrooms	3
Full Baths	3
Half Baths	1

Enchanting
Appeal

With irresistible charm, this home exudes Southern-style curb appeal. Covered porches on the first and second floor recall design themes of another, more gracious era. The foyer is open to the formal dining room and the great room. Both rooms are accented by grand columns at their entries, acting as elegant room dividers while echoing exterior design elements. The kitchen includes a peninsula counter with a snack bar and a swinging door entry into the dining room. Informal meals are served in the breakfast nook. A screen porch expands living space in the warmer weather. The master suite boasts separate shower, whirlpool tub, double vanity and a roomy master closet. Upstairs, there are two bedrooms with private baths. This plan gives the option to finish a fourth bedroom, full bath and recreation room in the future. This home is designed with a crawlspace foundation. ▶

*This home is not to be built within a 100-mile radius of zip code 23451.

SECOND FLOOR

OPEN TO BELOW

STORAGE

FUTURE BEDROOM 4
12'-0" X 12'-0"

BEDROOM 3
12'-0" X 11'-0"

HANDRAIL

BALCONY

HANDRAIL

FUTURE BATH

BEDROOM 2
12'-0" X 13'-0"

BATH 3

DN

FUTURE REC. ROOM
15'-0" X 28'-0"

COVERED PORCH

FIRST FLOOR

SCREEN PORCH

MASTER BEDROOM
14'-0" X 15'-0"

GREAT ROOM
15'-0" X 19'-0"
2 STORY CEILING

BREAKFAST
12'-4" X 10'-0"

LINEN

POW ROOM

BAR

CABINET PANTRY

MASTER BATH

RANGE

KITCHEN
12'-0" X 12'-0"

REFG D/W

WARDROBE
17'-0" X 6'-0"

UP

UTILITY

D W

FOYER
7'-0" X 13'-0"

DINING ROOM
12'-2" X 13'-0"

COVERED PORCH

2 CAR GARAGE
23'-4" X 21'-8"

Photography: Stephen Cridland

Traditional
Details

ABOVE: A mix of clapboard and cedar-shake siding, simple but elegant gables, eave brackets, and tapered pillars establish timeless appeal.

BELOW: The entry to the formal dining room is a mirror image of it's living room counterpart.

Sometimes it's the simple details that make the biggest statement. Such is the case with this house, whose gable roofline, cedar-shake siding accents, and simple but elegant wooden pillars showcase the classic details of traditional design. The garage in the back makes the home suitable for neighborhoods with narrow lots and alley access. The living and dining rooms flank the entry, both providing views to the front. The kitchen features an island with a cooktop and ample pantry storage beneath the U-shape staircase. The second-floor master suite includes a tub, shower, dual-sink vanity, and a walk-in closet. Two additional bedrooms share a full bath. The first floor has 1,211 square feet and the second floor has 867 square feet. This home is designed with a crawlspace foundation. ▶

Design 32049

Price Code	D
Total Finished	2,078 sq. ft.
First Finished	1,211 sq. ft.
Second Finished	867 sq. ft.
Dimensions	40'6"x65'
Foundation	Crawlspace
Bedrooms	3
Full Baths	2
Half Baths	1

Please note: The photographed home may have been modified to suit homeowner preferences. If you order plans, have a builder or design professional check them against the photographs to confirm construction details.

SECOND FLOOR

ABOVE: Half-walls and supporting columns elegantly frame the entry to the living room, where a sense of balance is continued by flanking the central fireplace with windows.

LEFT: The large window and light cabinetry brighten the kitchen. Just beyond the breakfast nook to the right is the door to the laundry room and garage.

BELOW: A double vanity, long mirror, and ample storage space add to the convenience of this shared bathroom.

FIRST FLOOR

Quick and Easy Customizing
Make Changes to Your Home Plan in 4 Easy Steps

Here's an affordable and efficient way to make custom changes to your home plan.

1 Select the house plan that most closely meets your needs. Purchase of a reproducible master (vellum) is necessary to make changes to a plan.

2 Call 800-235-5700 to place your order. Tell the sales representative you're interested in customizing a plan. A $50 refundable consultation fee will be charged. Then you'll need to complete a customization checklist indicating all the changes you wish to make to your plan, attaching sketches if necessary. If you proceed with the custom changes, the $50 will be credited to the total amount charged.

3 Fax the completed customization checklist to our design consultant at 1-866-477-5173 or e-mail blarochelle@drummonddesigns.com. Within 24 to 48* business hours you will be provided with a written cost estimate to modify your plan. Our design consultant will contact you by phone if you wish to discuss any of your changes in greater detail.

4 Once you approve the estimate, a 75% retainer fee is collected and customization work gets underway. Preliminary drawings can usually be completed within 5 to10* business days. Following approval of these preliminary drawings, your design changes are completed within 5 to 10* business days. Your remaining 25% balance due is collected prior to shipment of your completed drawings. You will be shipped five sets of revised blueprints, or a reproducible master.

*Terms are subject to change without notice.

BEFORE

AFTER

Sample Modification Pricing Guide

CATEGORIES	AVERAGE COST
Adding or removing living space (square footage)	Quote required
Adding or removing a garage	Starting at $400
Garage: Front entry to side load or vice versa	Starting at $300
Adding a screened porch	Starting at $280
Adding a bonus room in the attic	Starting at $450
Changing full basement to crawlspace or vice versa	Starting at $220
Changing full basement to slab or vice versa	Starting at $260
Changing exterior building materials	Starting at $200
Changing roof lines	Starting at $360
Adjusting ceiling height	Starting at $280
Adding, moving, or removing an exterior opening	$65 per opening
Adding or removing a fireplace	Starting at $90
Modifying a non-bearing wall or room	$65 per room
Changing exterior walls from 2"x4" to 2"x6"	Starting at $200
Redesigning a bathroom or a kitchen	Starting at $120
Reverse plan right reading	Quote required
Adapting plans for local building code requirements	Quote required
Engineering and Architectural stamping and services	Quote required
Adjust plan for handicapped accessibility	Quote required
Interactive Illustrations (choices of exterior materials)	Quote required
Metric conversion of home plan	Starting at $400

Note: Prices are subject to change according to plan size and style. Please remember that figures shown are average costs. Your quote may be higher or lower depending upon your specific requirements.

Design 10306

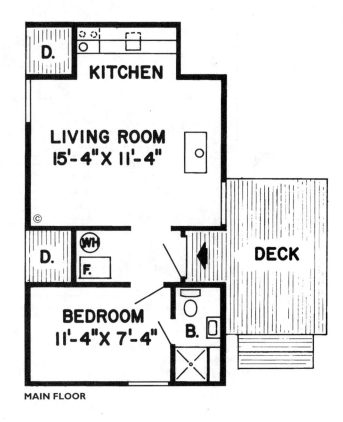

Units	Single
Price Code	A
Total Finished	408 sq. ft.
Main Finished	408 sq. ft.
Dimensions	16'x28'
Foundation	Pier/Post
Bedrooms	1
3/4 Baths	1

D.

KITCHEN

LIVING ROOM
15'-4" X 11'-4"

©

WH

D.

F.

DECK

BEDROOM
11'-4" X 7'-4"

B.

MAIN FLOOR

Design 86008

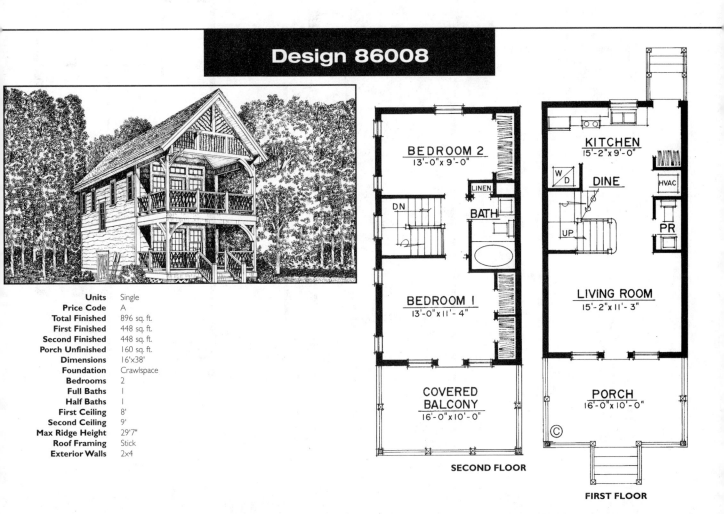

Units	Single
Price Code	A
Total Finished	896 sq. ft.
First Finished	448 sq. ft.
Second Finished	448 sq. ft.
Porch Unfinished	160 sq. ft.
Dimensions	16'x38'
Foundation	Crawlspace
Bedrooms	2
Full Baths	1
Half Baths	1
First Ceiling	8'
Second Ceiling	9'
Max Ridge Height	29'7"
Roof Framing	Stick
Exterior Walls	2x4

BEDROOM 2
13'-0" x 9'-0"

LINEN

DN

BATH

BEDROOM 1
13'-0" x 11'-4"

COVERED BALCONY
16'-0" x 10'-0"

SECOND FLOOR

KITCHEN
15'-2" x 9'-0"

W D

DINE

HVAC

UP

PR

LIVING ROOM
15'-2" x 11'-3"

©

PORCH
16'-0" x 10'-0"

FIRST FLOOR

To order blueprints, call **800-235-5700** or visit us on the web, **familyhomeplans.com**   **33**

Units	Single
Price Code	A
Total Finished	1,400 sq. ft.
First Finished	600 sq. ft.
Second Finished	800 sq. ft.
Garage Unfinished	248 sq. ft.
Dimensions	20'x48'
Foundation	Crawlspace
Bedrooms	3
Full Baths	2
Half Baths	1
First Ceiling	8'
Second Ceiling	8'
Max Ridge Height	23'
Roof Framing	Stick
Exterior Walls	2x6

FIRST FLOOR

GREAT RM
19 X 12
AVG

KIT

DIN RM
9/6 X 9/0
AVG

GST

PDR

2 STORY
FOYER

GARAGE
11/0 X 22/6

COVERED
PORCH

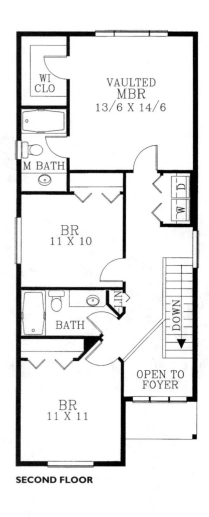

SECOND FLOOR

WI CLO

VAULTED
MBR
13/6 X 14/6

M BATH

W D

BR
11 X 10

BATH

LIN

DOWN

OPEN TO
FOYER

BR
11 X 11

Units	Single
Price Code	A
Total Finished	1,428 sq. ft.
First Finished	684 sq. ft.
Second Finished	744 sq. ft.
Dimensions	20'x41'
Foundation	Crawlspace
Bedrooms	3
Full Baths	1
3/4 Baths	1
Half Baths	1
First Ceiling	9'
Second Ceiling	8'
Max Ridge Height	26'
Roof Framing	Truss
Exterior Walls	2x6

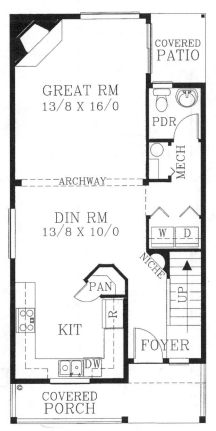

FIRST FLOOR

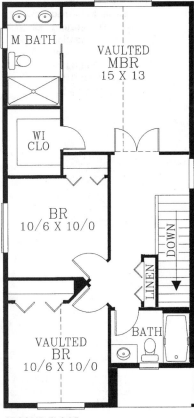

SECOND FLOOR

Units	Single
Price Code	D
Total Finished	2,177 sq. ft.
First Finished	1,374 sq. ft.
Second Finished	803 sq. ft.
Dimensions	20'x96'2"
Foundation	Slab
Bedrooms	3
Full Baths	2
Half Baths	1

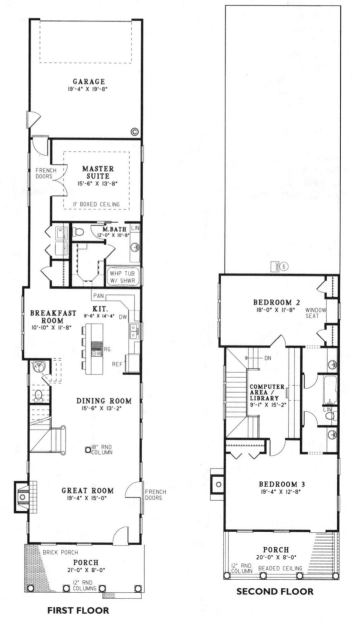

FIRST FLOOR

SECOND FLOOR

Design 65127

Units	Single
Price Code	A
Total Finished	1,002 sq. ft.
First Finished	507 sq. ft.
Second Finished	495 sq. ft.
Dimensions	20'4"x24'4"
Foundation	Basement
Bedrooms	3
Full Baths	1

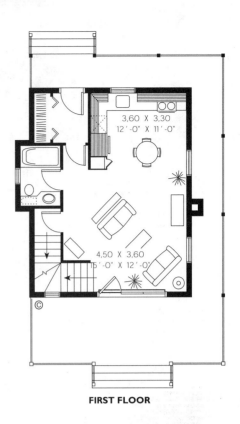

3,60 X 3,30
12'-0" X 11'-0"

4,50 X 3,60
15'-0" X 12'-0"

FIRST FLOOR

3,00 X 3,00
10'-0" X 10'-0"

2,40 X 3,30
8'-0" X 11'-0"

3,60 X 3,60
12'-0" X 12'-0"

SECOND FLOOR

Design 65286

Units	Single
Price Code	A
Total Finished	1,310 sq. ft.
Dimensions	21'x34'
Foundation	Basement
Bedrooms	3
Full Baths	1
Half Baths	1
Roof Framing	Stick
Exterior Walls	2x6

2,80 X 3,30
9'-4" X 11'-0"

3,00 X 2,70
10'-0" X 9'-0"

3,90 X 3,60
13'-0" X 12'-0"

SECOND FLOOR

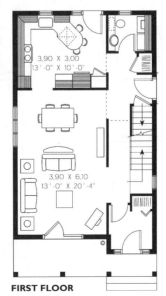

3,90 X 3,00
13'-0" X 10'-0"

3,90 X 6,10
13'-0" X 20'-4"

FIRST FLOOR

Design 24308

Units	Single
Price Code	A
Total Finished	823 sq. ft.
First Finished	660 sq. ft.
Second Finished	163 sq. ft.
Dimensions	22'x33'
Foundation	Crawlspace
Bedrooms	1
3/4 Baths	1
Max Ridge Height	23'
Roof Framing	Stick
Exterior Walls	2x6

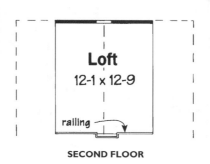

Loft
12-1 x 12-9

railing

SECOND FLOOR

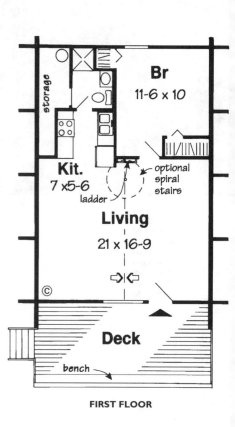

storage

Br
11-6 x 10

Kit.
7 x5-6

optional spiral stairs

ladder

Living
21 x 16-9

Deck

bench

FIRST FLOOR

Design 91031

Units	Single
Price Code	A
Total Finished	880 sq. ft.
First Finished	572 sq. ft.
Second Finished	308 sq. ft.
Dimensions	22'x26'
Foundation	Crawlspace
Bedrooms	2
3/4 Baths	1
Max Ridge Height	20'
Roof Framing	Stick
Exterior Walls	2x6

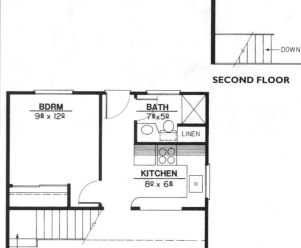

LOFT/BDRM
308 SQ. FT.

DOWN

SECOND FLOOR

BDRM
9² x 12²

BATH
7² x5²

LINEN

KITCHEN
8² x 6²

UP TO
LOFT/BDRM

LIVING/DINING
21³ x 13²

FIRST FLOOR

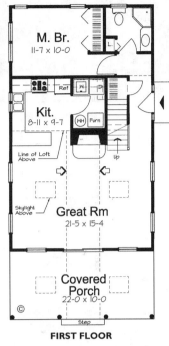

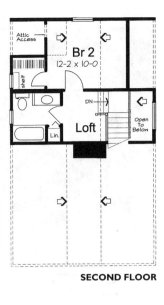

SECOND FLOOR

Units	Single
Price Code	A
Total Finished	1,093 sq. ft.
First Finished	792 sq. ft.
Second Finished	301 sq. ft.
Basement Unfinished	301 sq. ft.
Porch Unfinished	220 sq. ft.
Dimensions	22'x46'
Foundation	Crawlspace
Bedrooms	2
Full Baths	1
3/4 Baths	1
First Ceiling	8'
Second Ceiling	8'
Vaulted Ceiling	16'
Max Ridge Height	22'6"
Roof Framing	Truss
Exterior Walls	2x4

FIRST FLOOR

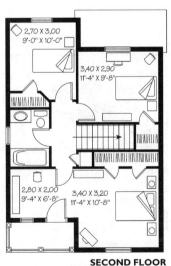

SECOND FLOOR

Units	Single
Price Code	A
Total Finished	1,240 sq. ft.
First Finished	620 sq. ft.
Second Finished	620 sq. ft.
Dimensions	22'x32'
Foundation	Basement
Bedrooms	3
Full Baths	1
Half Baths	1
First Ceiling	8'2"
Second Ceiling	8'2"
Max Ridge Height	28'4"
Roof Framing	Truss
Exterior Walls	2x6

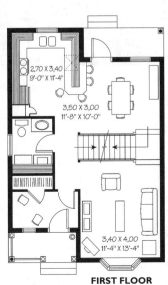

FIRST FLOOR

Design 65003

SECOND FLOOR

Units	Single
Price Code	A
Total Finished	976 sq. ft.
First Finished	593 sq. ft.
Second Finished	383 sq. ft.
Basement Unfinished	593 sq. ft.
Dimensions	22'8"x26'8"
Foundation	Crawlspace
Bedrooms	2
Full Baths	1
3/4 Baths	1
First Ceiling	8'
Second Ceiling	8'
Max Ridge Height	22'8"
Roof Framing	Truss
Exterior Walls	2x6

FIRST FLOOR

Design 65243

SECOND FLOOR

Units	Single
Price Code	A
Total Finished	1,397 sq. ft.
First Finished	696 sq. ft.
Second Finished	701 sq. ft.
Basement Unfinished	696 sq. ft.
Porch Unfinished	210 sq. ft.
Dimensions	22'8"x36'
Foundation	Basement
Bedrooms	3
Full Baths	1
Half Baths	1
First Ceiling	9'
Second Ceiling	8'
Max Ridge Height	38'8"
Roof Framing	Truss
Exterior Walls	2x6

FIRST FLOOR

Units	Single
Price Code	A
Total Finished	1,347 sq. ft.
First Finished	1,040 sq. ft.
Second Finished	307 sq. ft.
Garage Unfinished	263 sq. ft.
Porch Unfinished	48 sq. ft.
Dimensions	22'9½"×60'1½"
Foundation	Slab
Bedrooms	3
Full Baths	2
First Ceiling	8'1⅛"
Second Ceiling	8'1⅛"
Roof Framing	Stick
Exterior Walls	2x4

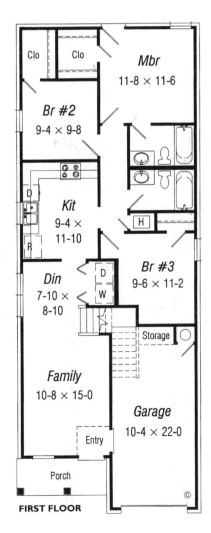

FIRST FLOOR

Clo
Clo
Mbr
11-8 × 11-6
Br #2
9-4 × 9-8
Kit
9-4 × 11-10
D
R
Din
7-10 × 8-10
D W
Br #3
9-6 × 11-2
H
Storage
Family
10-8 × 15-0
Garage
10-4 × 22-0
Entry
Porch

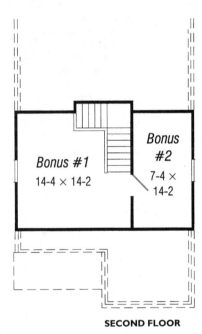

SECOND FLOOR

Bonus #1
14-4 × 14-2
Bonus #2
7-4 × 14-2

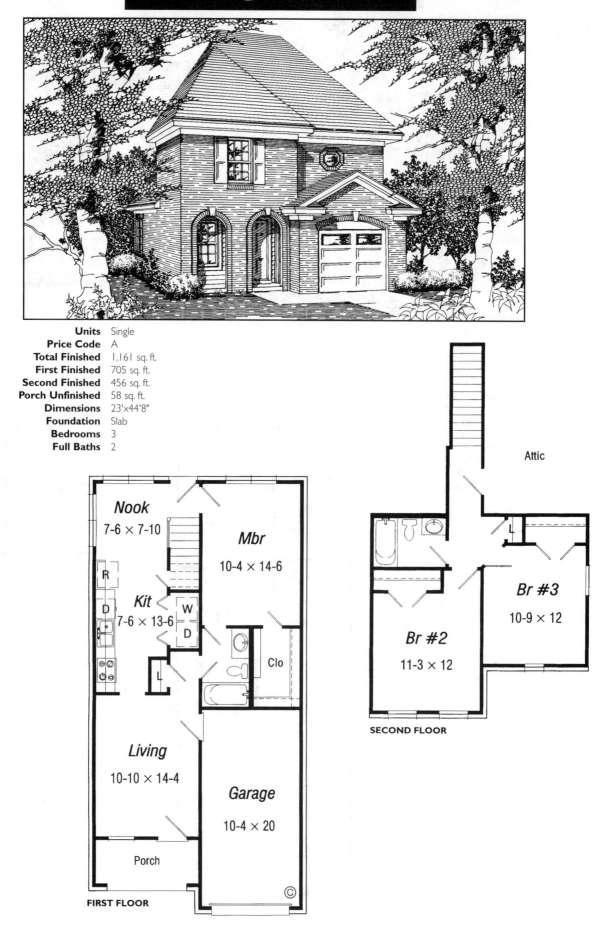

Units Single
Price Code A
Total Finished 1,161 sq. ft.
First Finished 705 sq. ft.
Second Finished 456 sq. ft.
Porch Unfinished 58 sq. ft.
Dimensions 23'x44'8"
Foundation Slab
Bedrooms 3
Full Baths 2

Nook
7-6 × 7-10

Mbr
10-4 × 14-6

R

Kit
7-6 × 13-6

W
D

Clo

Living
10-10 × 14-4

Garage
10-4 × 20

Porch

FIRST FLOOR

Attic

Br #3
10-9 × 12

Br #2
11-3 × 12

SECOND FLOOR

Design 32018

PHOTOGRAPHY: COURTESY OF THE DESIGNER

Units	Single
Price Code	A
Total Finished	663 sq. ft.
Main Finished	663 sq. ft.
Porch Unfinished	206 sq. ft.
Dimensions	23'6"x41'2"
Foundation	Pier/Post
Bedrooms	1
Full Baths	1
Main Ceiling	8'
Max Ridge Height	32'
Roof Framing	Stick
Exterior Walls	2x4

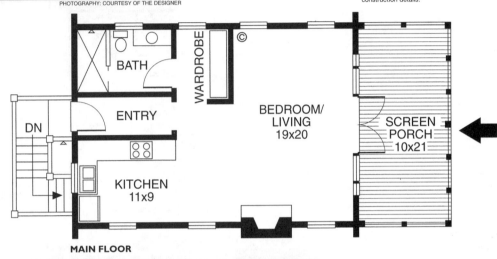

MAIN FLOOR

BATH

WARDROBE

ENTRY

DN

KITCHEN
11x9

BEDROOM/
LIVING
19x20

SCREEN
PORCH
10x21

Design 35009

Units	Single
Price Code	A
Total Finished	1,003 sq. ft.
First Finished	763 sq. ft.
Second Finished	240 sq. ft.
Dimensions	24'x32'
Foundation	Basement
	Crawlspace
	Slab
Bedrooms	1
Full Baths	1
Max Ridge Height	24'
Roof Framing	Stick
Exterior Walls	2x4, 2x6

**OPTIONAL
CRAWLSPACE/SLAB
FOUNDATION**

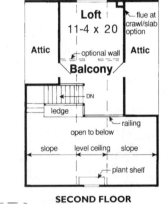

Loft
11-4 x 20

Attic   Attic

Balcony

ledge

open to below

slope   level ceiling   slope

plant shelf

SECOND FLOOR

Br # 1
13-5 x 11

linen

ent. center

UP   DN

Living
13-9 x 11-7
slope   level ceiling   slope

Kit/Dine
9-7 x 17

Deck

DN   DN

FIRST FLOOR

Design 35007

Loft
11-4 x 22

Attic Attic

optional wall

Balcony

flue

DN

ledge

open to below

railing

slope   level ceiling   slope

plant shelf

SECOND FLOOR

Br #2
10-1 x 10-1

Br #1
10-7 X 10-1

D W

DN

ent. center

slope   level ceiling   slope

Living
13-10 x 11-6

Kit/Dine
9-5 x 13-2

DN   DN

Deck

FIRST FLOOR

furn.

w.h.

**OPTIONAL
CRAWLSPACE/SLAB
FOUNDATION**

Units	Single
Price Code	A
Total Finished	1,027 sq. ft.
First Finished	763 sq. ft.
Second Finished	264 sq. ft.
Dimensions	24'x32'
Foundation	Basement
	Crawlspace
	Slab
Bedrooms	2
Full Baths	I
First Ceiling	8'
Max Ridge Height	24'
Roof Framing	Stick
Exterior Walls	2x4, 2x6

Design 65161

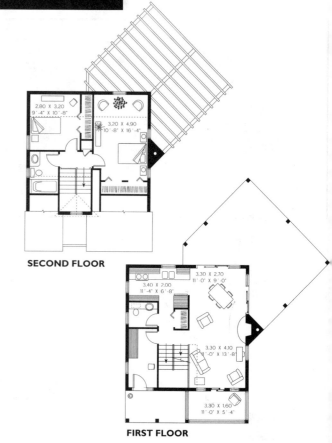

2.80 X 3.20
9'-4" X 10'-8"

3.20 X 4.90
10'-8" X 16'-4"

SECOND FLOOR

3.30 X 2.70
11'-0" X 9'-0"

3.40 X 2.00
11'-4" X 6'-8"

3.30 X 4.10
11'-0" X 13'-8"

3.30 X 1.60
11'-0" X 5'-4"

FIRST FLOOR

Units	Single
Price Code	A
Total Finished	1,056 sq. ft.
First Finished	576 sq. ft.
Second Finished	480 sq. ft.
Basement Unfinished	576 sq. ft.
Deck Unfinished	315 sq. ft.
Porch Unfinished	45 sq. ft.
Dimensions	24'x30'
Foundation	Basement
Bedrooms	2
Full Baths	I
Half Baths	I
First Ceiling	8'
Second Ceiling	8'
Max Ridge Height	23'
Roof Framing	Truss
Exterior Walls	2x6

Design 55007

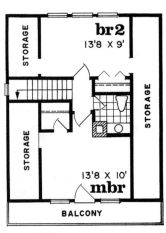

SECOND FLOOR

br2
13'8 X 9'

STORAGE

STORAGE

STORAGE

13'8 X 10'
mbr

BALCONY

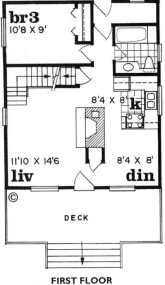

br3
10'8 X 9'

k
8'4 X 8'

11'10 X 14'6
liv

8'4 X 8'
din

DECK

FIRST FLOOR

Units	Single
Price Code	A
Total Finished	1,073 sq. ft.
First Finished	672 sq. ft.
Second Finished	401 sq. ft.
Deck Unfinished	192 sq. ft.
Porch Unfinished	96 sq. ft.
Dimensions	24'x36'
Foundation	Basement
Bedrooms	3
Full Baths	1
Half Baths	1
First Ceiling	8'
Max Ridge Height	24'6"

Design 91002

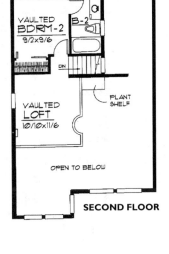

VAULTED
BDRM-2
9/2x9/6

B-2

PLANT
SHELF

VAULTED
LOFT
10/10x11/6

OPEN TO BELOW

SECOND FLOOR

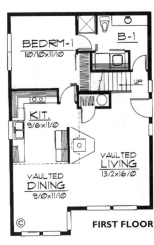

BEDRM-1
10/10x11/10

B-1

UP

KIT.
9/6x11/0

VAULTED
LIVING
13/2x16/0

VAULTED
DINING
9/0x11/10

FIRST FLOOR

Units	Single
Price Code	A
Total Finished	1,096 sq. ft.
First Finished	808 sq. ft.
Second Finished	288 sq. ft.
Dimensions	24'x32'
Foundation	Crawlspace
Bedrooms	2
Full Baths	1
3/4 Baths	1
Max Ridge Height	25'
Roof Framing	Stick
Exterior Walls	2x6

Units	Single
Price Code	A
Total Finished	1,289 sq. ft.
First Finished	768 sq. ft.
Second Finished	521 sq. ft.
Dimensions	24'x32'
Foundation	Slab
Bedrooms	2
Full Baths	1
Half Baths	1
Max Ridge Height	19'
Roof Framing	Stick
Exterior Walls	2x4

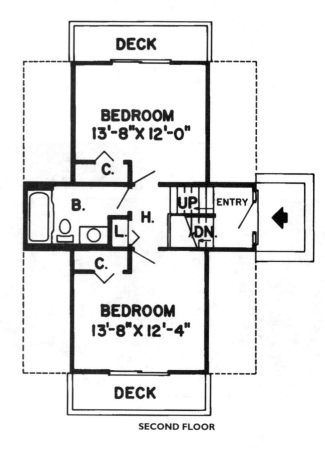

SECOND FLOOR

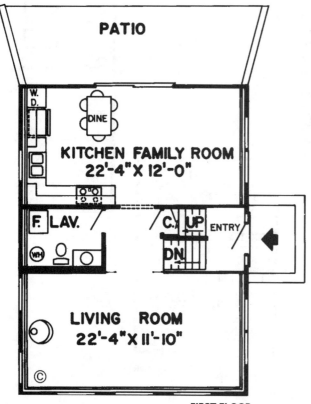

FIRST FLOOR

Units	Single
Price Code	A
Total Finished	996 sq. ft.
Main Finished	996 sq. ft.
Porch Unfinished	66 sq. ft.
Dimensions	24'4"x43'8"
Foundation	Crawlspace
Bedrooms	3
Full Baths	1
Main Ceiling	8'
Max Ridge Height	14'
Roof Framing	Truss
Exterior Walls	2x4

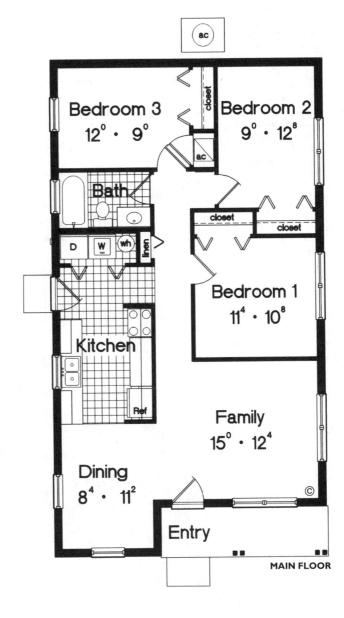

MAIN FLOOR

PHOTOGRAPHY: TRIA GOIVAN

Units	Single
Price Code	B
Total Finished	1,170 sq. ft.
First Finished	988 sq. ft.
Second Finished	182 sq. ft.
Dimensions	26'x38'
Foundation	Pier/Post
Bedrooms	2
Full Baths	2
First Ceiling	8'
Second Ceiling	8'
Max Ridge Height	24'4"
Roof Framing	Stick
Exterior Walls	2x4

Please note: The photographed home may have been modified to suit homeowner preferences. If you order plans, have a builder or design professional check them against the photograph to confirm actual construction details.

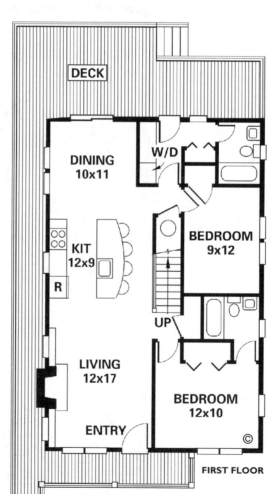

DECK

DINING
10x11

W/D

KIT
12x9

R

BEDROOM
9x12

UP

LIVING
12x17

BEDROOM
12x10

ENTRY

FIRST FLOOR

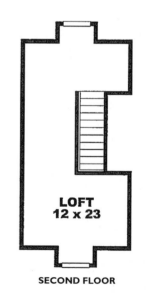

LOFT
12 x 23

SECOND FLOOR

Units	Single
Price Code	A
Total Finished	1,324 sq. ft.
First Finished	737 sq. ft.
Second Finished	587 sq. ft.
Dimensions	26'x33'
Foundation	Basement
Bedrooms	1 or 2
Full Baths	1
Half Baths	1
First Ceiling	8'
Second Ceiling	8'
Max Ridge Height	34'9"
Roof Framing	Truss
Exterior Walls	2x6

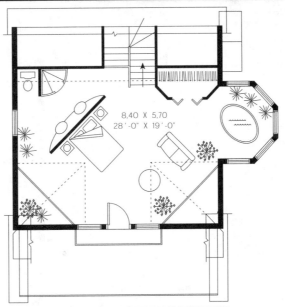

OPTIONAL SECOND FLOOR W/ONE BEDROOM

FIRST FLOOR

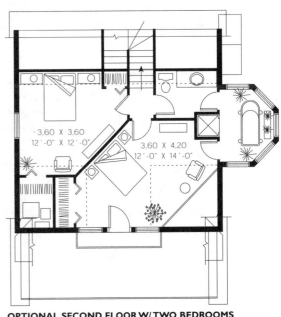

OPTIONAL SECOND FLOOR W/ TWO BEDROOMS

Units	Single
Price Code	A
Total Finished	1,352 sq. ft.
First Finished	676 sq. ft.
Second Finished	676 sq. ft.
Basement Unfinished	676 sq. ft.
Deck Unfinished	32 sq. ft.
Dimensions	26'x26'
Foundation	Basement
Bedrooms	3
Full Baths	I
3/4 Baths	I
First Ceiling	8'
Second Ceiling	8'
Max Ridge Height	28'1"
Roof Framing	Truss
Exterior Walls	2x6

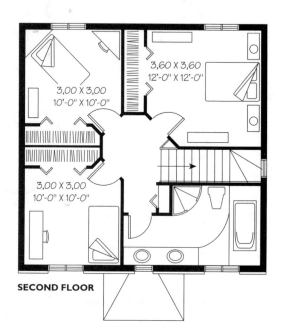

SECOND FLOOR

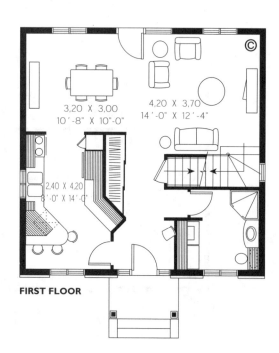

FIRST FLOOR

Design 91026

Units	Single
Price Code	A
Total Finished	1,354 sq. ft.
First Finished	988 sq. ft.
Second Finished	366 sq. ft.
Basement Unfinished	742 sq. ft.
Garage Unfinished	283 sq. ft.
Dimensions	26'x48'
Foundation	Basement
Bedrooms	3
Full Baths	I
3/4 Baths	I
First Ceiling	8'
Vaulted Ceiling	13'6"
Max Ridge Height	32'
Roof Framing	Stick
Exterior Walls	2x6

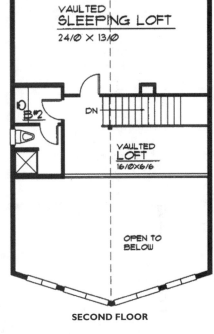

SECOND FLOOR

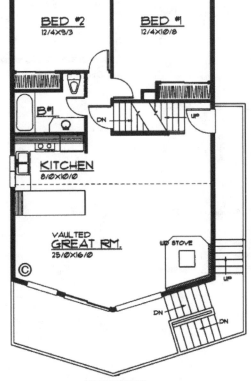

FIRST FLOOR

Units	Single
Price Code	A
Total Finished	1,432 sq. ft.
First Finished	756 sq. ft.
Second Finished	676 sq. ft.
Basement Unfinished	657 sq. ft.
Porch Unfinished	148 sq. ft.
Dimensions	26'x32'
Foundation	Basement
Bedrooms	3
Full Baths	1
3/4 Baths	1
First Ceiling	8'
Second Ceiling	8'
Roof Framing	Truss
Exterior Walls	2x6

FIRST FLOOR

SECOND FLOOR

Units	Single
Price Code	A
Total Finished	1,471 sq. ft.
First Finished	895 sq. ft.
Second Finished	576 sq. ft.
Basement Unfinished	895 sq. ft.
Dimensions	26'x36'
Foundation	Basement
Bedrooms	3
Full Baths	2
First Ceiling	8'2"
Second Ceiling	8'2"
Max Ridge Height	23'8"
Roof Framing	Truss
Exterior Walls	2x6

SECOND FLOOR

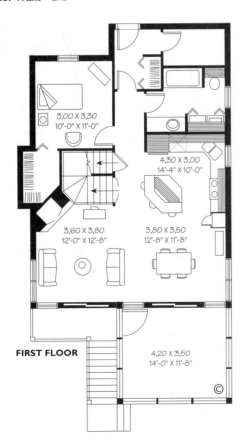

FIRST FLOOR

Design 32162

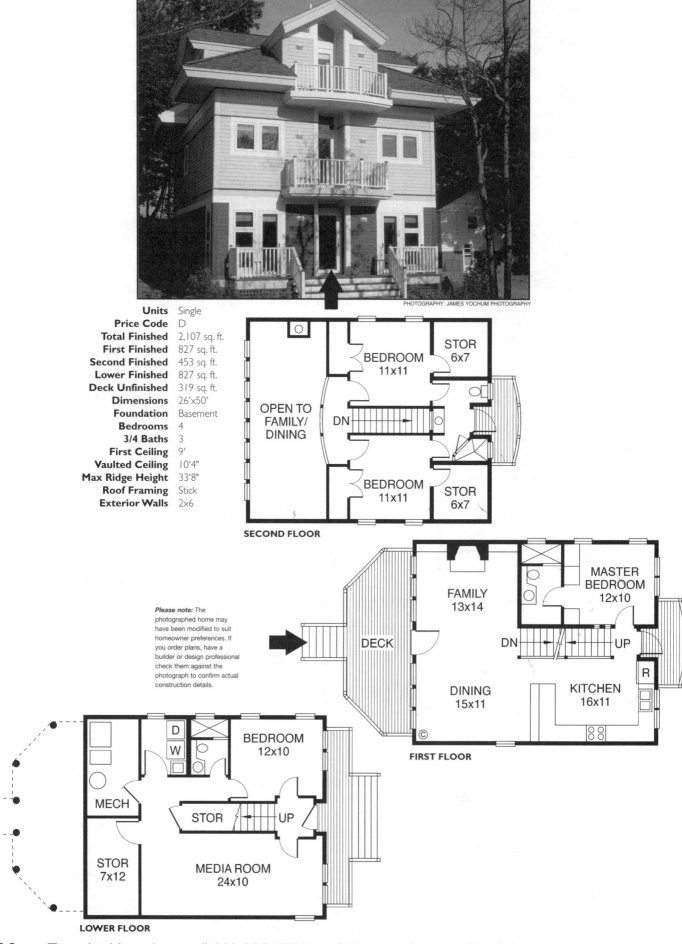

PHOTOGRAPHY: JAMES YOCHUM PHOTOGRAPHY

Units	Single
Price Code	D
Total Finished	2,107 sq. ft.
First Finished	827 sq. ft.
Second Finished	453 sq. ft.
Lower Finished	827 sq. ft.
Deck Unfinished	319 sq. ft.
Dimensions	26'x50'
Foundation	Basement
Bedrooms	4
3/4 Baths	3
First Ceiling	9'
Vaulted Ceiling	10'4"
Max Ridge Height	33'8"
Roof Framing	Stick
Exterior Walls	2x6

SECOND FLOOR

STOR 6x7

BEDROOM 11x11

OPEN TO FAMILY/ DINING

DN

BEDROOM 11x11

STOR 6x7

Please note: The photographed home may have been modified to suit homeowner preferences. If you order plans, have a builder or design professional check them against the photograph to confirm actual construction details.

DECK

FAMILY 13x14

MASTER BEDROOM 12x10

DN   UP

DINING 15x11

KITCHEN 16x11

R

FIRST FLOOR

D
W

BEDROOM 12x10

MECH

STOR   UP

STOR 7x12

MEDIA ROOM 24x10

LOWER FLOOR

Units	Single
Price Code	A
Total Finished	1,450 sq. ft.
First Finished	918 sq. ft.
Second Finished	532 sq. ft.
Basement Finished	918 sq. ft.
Dimensions	26'4"×37'
Foundation	Basement
Bedrooms	3
Full Baths	1
3/4 Baths	1
First Ceiling	8'
Second Ceiling	8'
Max Ridge Height	27'4"
Roof Framing	Truss
Exterior Walls	2x6

FIRST FLOOR

SECOND FLOOR

Units	Single
Price Code	A
Total Finished	1,120 sq. ft.
First Finished	587 sq. ft.
Second Finished	533 sq. ft.
Deck Unfinished	32 sq. ft.
Porch Unfinished	10 sq. ft.
Dimensions	26'8"x24'
Foundation	Slab
Bedrooms	2
Full Baths	1
Half Baths	1
First Ceiling	8'
Second Ceiling	8'
Max Ridge Height	23'10"
Roof Framing	Truss

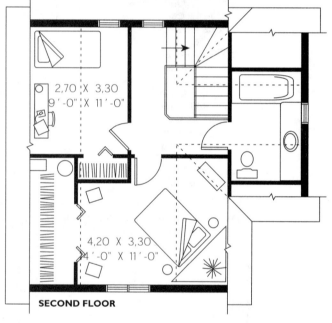

SECOND FLOOR

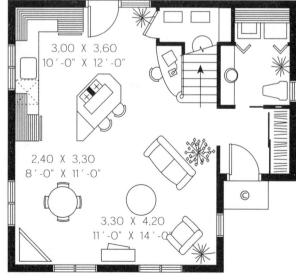

FIRST FLOOR

Units	Single
Price Code	B
Total Finished	1,667 sq. ft.
First Finished	973 sq. ft.
Second Finished	694 sq. ft.
Garage Unfinished	411 sq. ft.
Porch Unfinished	144 sq. ft.
Dimensions	26'5"×64'
Foundation	Slab
Bedrooms	3
Full Baths	2
Max Ridge Height	25'4"
Roof Framing	Stick
Exterior Walls	2x4

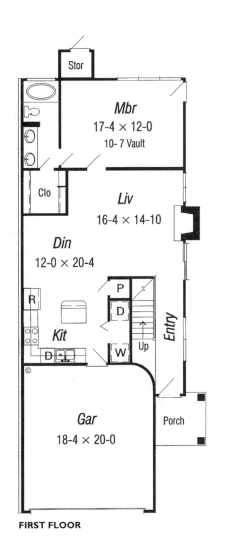

FIRST FLOOR

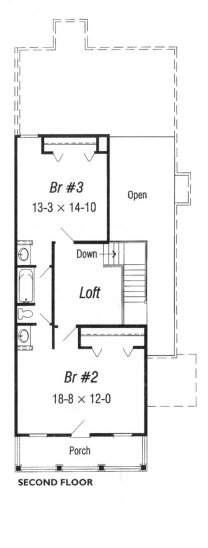

SECOND FLOOR

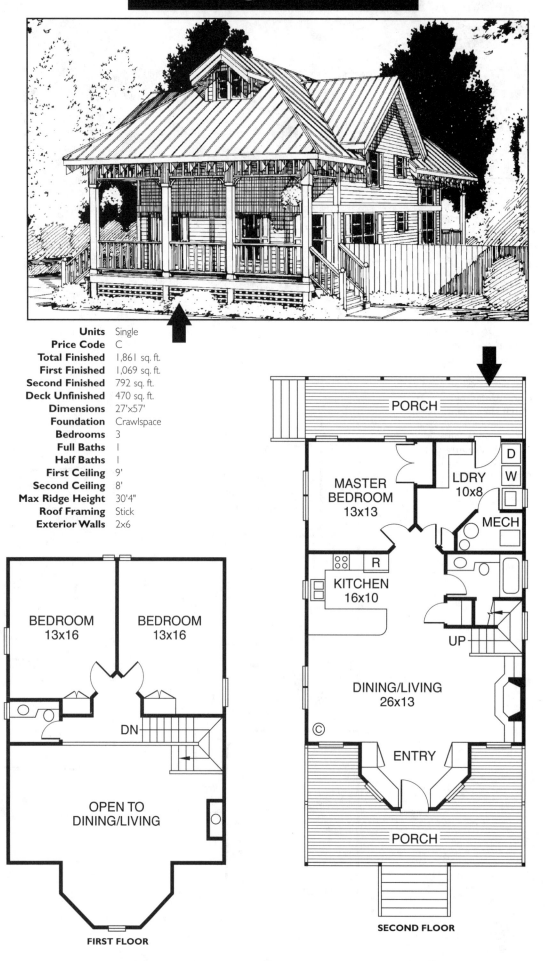

Units	Single
Price Code	C
Total Finished	1,861 sq. ft.
First Finished	1,069 sq. ft.
Second Finished	792 sq. ft.
Deck Unfinished	470 sq. ft.
Dimensions	27'x57'
Foundation	Crawlspace
Bedrooms	3
Full Baths	1
Half Baths	1
First Ceiling	9'
Second Ceiling	8'
Max Ridge Height	30'4"
Roof Framing	Stick
Exterior Walls	2x6

PORCH

MASTER BEDROOM 13x13

LDRY 10x8

D
W

MECH

KITCHEN 16x10

R

UP

DINING/LIVING 26x13

ENTRY

PORCH

SECOND FLOOR

BEDROOM 13x16

BEDROOM 13x16

DN

OPEN TO DINING/LIVING

FIRST FLOOR

Design 65011

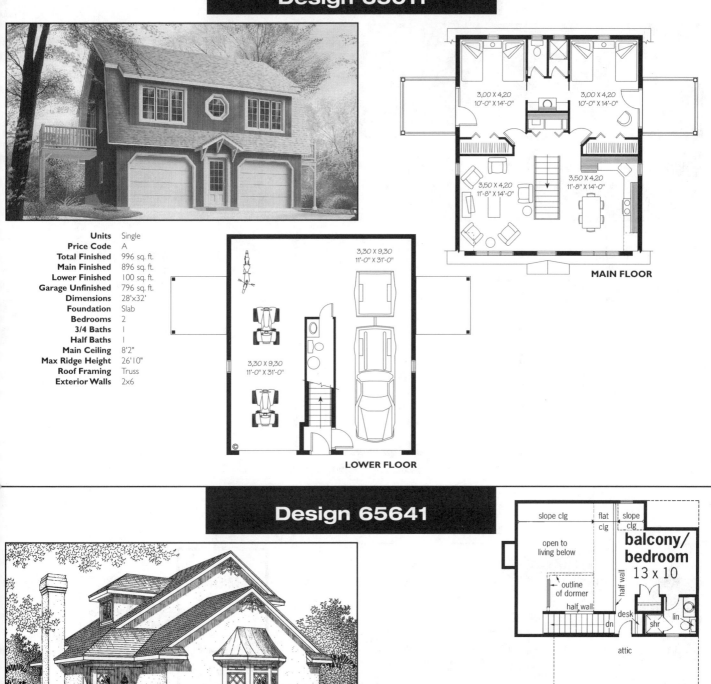

Units	Single
Price Code	A
Total Finished	996 sq. ft.
Main Finished	896 sq. ft.
Lower Finished	100 sq. ft.
Garage Unfinished	796 sq. ft.
Dimensions	28'x32'
Foundation	Slab
Bedrooms	2
3/4 Baths	1
Half Baths	1
Main Ceiling	8'2"
Max Ridge Height	26'10"
Roof Framing	Truss
Exterior Walls	2x6

MAIN FLOOR

LOWER FLOOR

Design 65641

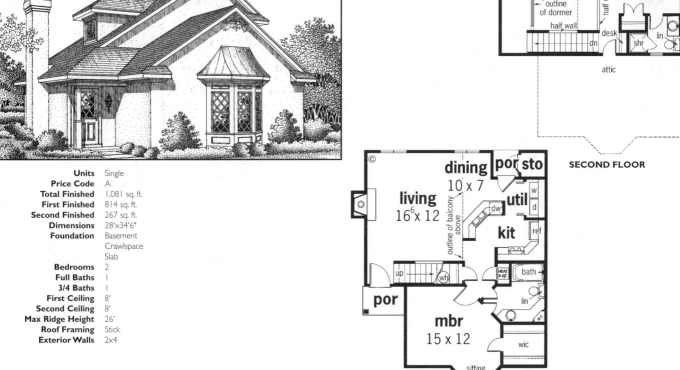

Units	Single
Price Code	A
Total Finished	1,081 sq. ft.
First Finished	814 sq. ft.
Second Finished	267 sq. ft.
Dimensions	28'x34'6"
Foundation	Basement
	Crawlspace
	Slab
Bedrooms	2
Full Baths	1
3/4 Baths	1
First Ceiling	8'
Second Ceiling	8'
Max Ridge Height	26'
Roof Framing	Stick
Exterior Walls	2x4

SECOND FLOOR

FIRST FLOOR

Design 65014

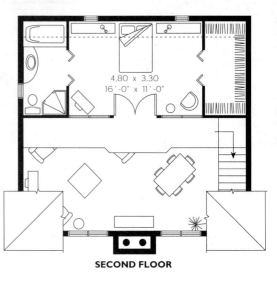

SECOND FLOOR

Units	Single
Price Code	A
Total Finished	1,148 sq. ft.
First Finished	728 sq. ft.
Second Finished	420 sq. ft.
Basement Unfinished	728 sq. ft.
Porch Unfinished	187 sq. ft.
Dimensions	28'x26'
Foundation	Basement
Bedrooms	1
Full Baths	1
Half Baths	1
First Ceiling	8'
Second Ceiling	8'
Max Ridge Height	29'8"
Exterior Walls	2x6

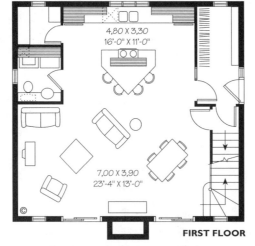

4,80 X 3,30
16'-0" X 11'-0"

7,00 X 3,90
23'-4" X 13'-0"

FIRST FLOOR

Design 24241

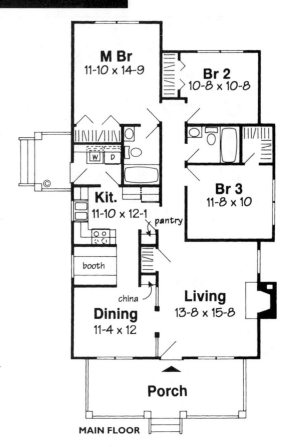

Units	Single
Price Code	A
Total Finished	1,174 sq. ft.
Main Finished	1,174 sq. ft.
Dimensions	28'x54'
Foundation	Crawlspace
Bedrooms	3
Full Baths	2
Max Ridge Height	21'
Roof Framing	Stick
Exterior Walls	2x4

MAIN FLOOR

Design 65134

Units	Single
Price Code	A
Total Finished	1,304 sq. ft.
First Finished	681 sq. ft.
Second Finished	623 sq. ft.
Garage Unfinished	260 sq. ft.
Dimensions	28'x40'
Foundation	Basement
Bedrooms	2
Full Baths	1
Half Baths	1
First Ceiling	8'
Second Ceiling	8'
Roof Framing	Truss
Exterior Walls	2x6

FIRST FLOOR

3.80 X 4.70
12'-8" X 15'-8"

4.20 X 6.00
14'-0" X 20'-0"

3.60 X 5.70
12'-0" X 19'-0"

3.30 X 4.70
11'-0" X 15'-8"

3.00 X 3.30
10'-0" X 11'-0"

SECOND FLOOR

Design 92422

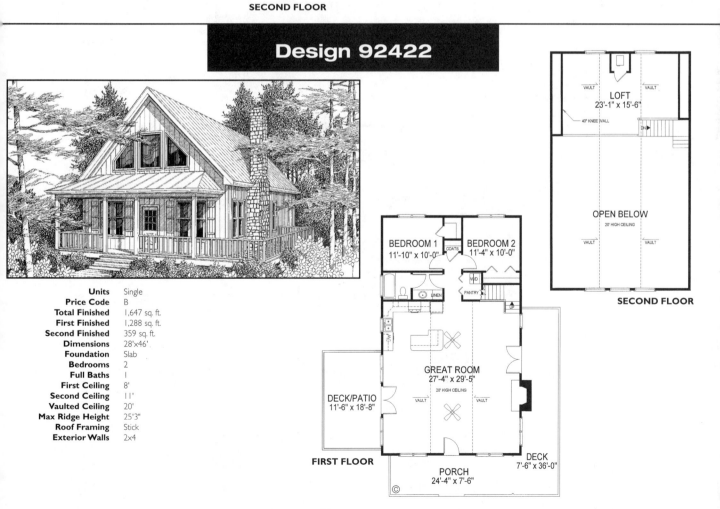

Units	Single
Price Code	B
Total Finished	1,647 sq. ft.
First Finished	1,288 sq. ft.
Second Finished	359 sq. ft.
Dimensions	28'x46'
Foundation	Slab
Bedrooms	2
Full Baths	1
First Ceiling	8'
Second Ceiling	11'
Vaulted Ceiling	20'
Max Ridge Height	25'3"
Roof Framing	Stick
Exterior Walls	2x4

LOFT
23'-1" x 15'-6"

40" KNEE WALL

OPEN BELOW
20' HIGH CEILING

SECOND FLOOR

BEDROOM 1
11'-10" x 10'-0"

BEDROOM 2
11'-4" x 10'-0"

COATS

LINEN

PANTRY

W D

GREAT ROOM
27'-4" x 29'-5"
20' HIGH CEILING

DECK/PATIO
11'-6" x 18'-8"

DECK
7'-6" x 36'-0"

FIRST FLOOR

PORCH
24'-4" x 7'-6"

Design 99914

Units	Single
Price Code	B
Total Finished	1,677 sq. ft.
First Finished	1,064 sq. ft.
Second Finished	613 sq. ft.
Basement Unfinished	1,604 sq. ft.
Deck Unfinished	474 sq. ft.
Porch Unfinished	32 sq. ft.
Dimensions	28'x40'
Foundation	Basement
	Crawlspace
Bedrooms	2
Full Baths	2
First Ceiling	8'
Second Ceiling	8'
Max Ridge Height	26'6"
Roof Framing	Stick
Exterior Walls	2x6

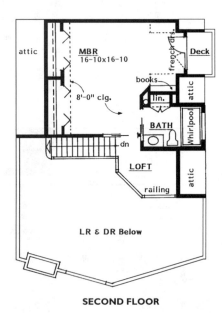

SECOND FLOOR

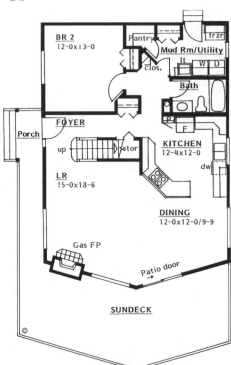

FIRST FLOOR

PHOTOGRAPHY: JOHN EHRENCLOU

Units	Single
Price Code	B
Total Finished	1,710 sq. ft.
First Finished	728 sq. ft.
Second Finished	573 sq. ft.
Lower Finished	409 sq. ft.
Garage Unfinished	244 sq. ft.
Dimensions	28'x32'
Foundation	Basement
Bedrooms	3
Full Baths	2
First Ceiling	8'
Second Ceiling	8'
Max Ridge Height	33'
Roof Framing	Stick
Exterior Walls	2x4, 2x6

Please note: The photographed home may have been modified to suit homeowner preferences. If you order plans, have a builder or design professional check them against the photograph to confirm actual construction details.

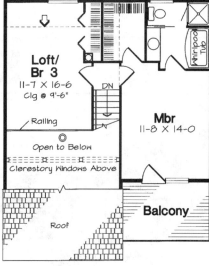

SECOND FLOOR

Loft/
Br 3
11-7 X 16-6
Clg @ 9'-6"

Railing

Open to Below

Clerestory Windows Above

Mbr
11-8 X 14-0

Balcony

Roof

LOWER FLOOR

Util Rm
10-11 X 5-9

Wet Bar

Garage
11-8 X 19-0

Storage

Rec Rm
11-1 X 20-2

Optional Hot Tub

Step

UP

FIRST FLOOR

Broom

Linen

Ref

Kitchen
11-1 X 7-7

Flue

Brkfst Bar

DN

Dining
11-11 X 8-7

DN

Br 1
12-0 X 11-3

Loft Above

Railing

Fireplace

UP

Living
15-1 X 14-10

Deck

Design 65005

Units	Single
Price Code	A
Total Finished	972 sq. ft.
Main Finished	972 sq. ft.
Basement Unfinished	972 sq. ft.
Dimensions	30'x35'
Foundation	Basement
Bedrooms	2
Full Baths	1
Main Ceiling	8'2"
Max Ridge Height	17'6"
Exterior Walls	2x6

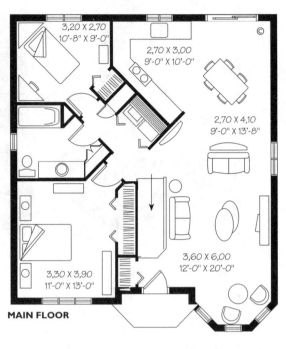

3,20 X 2,70
10'-8" X 9'-0"

2,70 X 3,00
9'-0" X 10'-0"

2,70 X 4,10
9'-0" X 13'-8"

3,30 X 3,90
11'-0" X 13'-0"

3,60 X 6,00
12'-0" X 20'-0"

MAIN FLOOR

Design 63137

Units	Single
Price Code	C
Total Finished	1,118 sq. ft.
Main Finished	1,118 sq. ft.
Dimensions	30'x60'
Foundation	Slab
Bedrooms	3
Full Baths	2
Max Ridge Height	15'11"
Roof Framing	Truss

Covered Patio

Master Bedroom
16° · 16°

Nook

2 Car Garage
21° · 22°

Family Room
17° · 17°

Mstr.
Bath

w.i.c.

Kitchen

Stor.

pan.

Dining Rm.
11° · 11°

L'ndy

Bath 2

Foyer

Study.

Entry

Bedroom 2
10° · 11°

Bedroom 3
12° · 10°

MAIN FLOOR

Design 65140

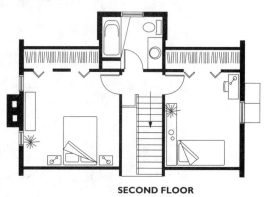

SECOND FLOOR

3,70 x 3,40	12'-4" x 11'-4"
3,20 x 2,60	10'-8" x 8'-8"
4,50 x 3,70	15'-0" x 12'-4"
3,00 x 2,70	10'-0" x 9'-0"

FIRST FLOOR

Units	Single
Price Code	A
Total Finished	1,258 sq. ft.
First Finished	753 sq. ft.
Second Finished	505 sq. ft.
Basement Unfinished	753 sq. ft.
Dimensions	30'x28'
Foundation	Basement
Bedrooms	3
Full Baths	1
Half Baths	1
First Ceiling	8'
Second Ceiling	8'
Max Ridge Height	24'10"
Roof Framing	Truss
Exterior Walls	2x6

Design 26111

PHOTOGRAPHY: JOHN EHRENCLOU

Bedroom	12'-0" x 13'-0"
Bath	
Skylights	
Balcony	
Bedroom	12'-0" x 20'-0"
Open to Living	

SECOND FLOOR

Bedroom/Den	12'-0" x 11'-0"
Bath	
Kitchen	8'-0 x 9'-0
Entry	
Dining Area	12'-0 x 11'-0"
Living	16'-0 x 14'-0
Deck	
Deck	

FIRST FLOOR

Units	Single
Price Code	A
Total Finished	1,341 sq. ft.
First Finished	769 sq. ft.
Second Finished	572 sq. ft.
Basement Unfinished	546 sq. ft.
Dimensions	30'x32'
Foundation	Basement
Bedrooms	3
Full Baths	1
3/4 Baths	1
Roof Framing	Stick
Exterior Walls	2x4, 2x6

Please note: The photographed home may have been modified to suit homeowner preferences. If you order plans, have a builder or design professional check them against the photograph to confirm actual construction details.

Units	Single
Price Code	F
Total Finished	2,520 sq. ft.
First Finished	1,305 sq. ft.
Second Finished	1,215 sq. ft.
Bonus Unfinished	935 sq. ft.
Garage Unfinished	480 sq. ft.
Deck Unfinished	717 sq. ft.
Porch Unfinished	1,434 sq. ft.
Dimensions	30'6"x72'2"
Foundation	Slab
	Pier/Post
Bedrooms	3
Full Baths	2
Half Baths	1
Max Ridge Height	39'6"
Roof Framing	Stick/Truss
Exterior Walls	2x6

* Alternate foundation options available at an additional charge.
Please call 1-800-235-5700 for more information.

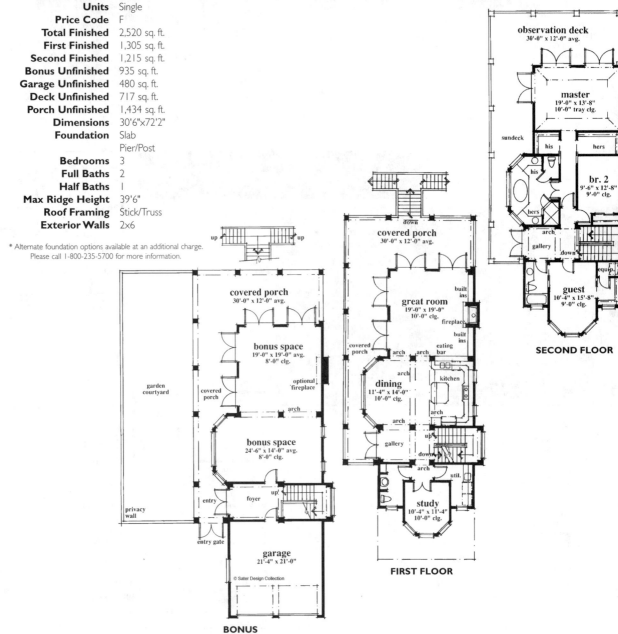

SECOND FLOOR

FIRST FLOOR

BONUS

© Sater Design Collection

Design 65173

SECOND FLOOR

Units	Single
Price Code	A
Total Finished	1,311 sq. ft.
First Finished	713 sq. ft.
Second Finished	598 sq. ft.
Basement Unfinished	713 sq. ft.
Porch Unfinished	158 sq. ft.
Dimensions	30'8"x26'
Foundation	Basement
Bedrooms	2
Full Baths	1
3/4 Baths	1
First Ceiling	8'
Second Ceiling	8'
Max Ridge Height	28'4"
Roof Framing	Truss
Exterior Walls	2x6

FIRST FLOOR

Design 65241

Units	Single
Price Code	A
Total Finished	1,068 sq. ft.
Main Finished	1,068 sq. ft.
Basement Unfinished	1,068 sq. ft.
Garage Unfinished	245 sq. ft.
Dimensions	30'8"x48'
Foundation	Basement
Bedrooms	2
Full Baths	1
Main Ceiling	8'
Max Ridge Height	22'1"
Roof Framing	Truss
Exterior Walls	2x6

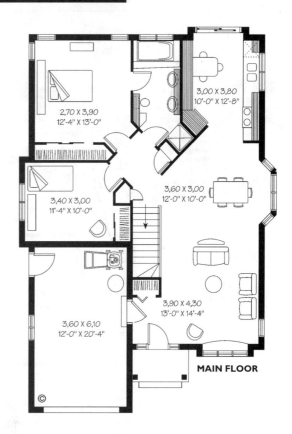

MAIN FLOOR

Design 90433

Units	Single
Price Code	A
Total Finished	928 sq. ft.
Main Finished	928 sq. ft.
Porch Unfinished	230 sq. ft.
Dimensions	32'x29'
Foundation	Crawlspace
	Slab
Bedrooms	2
Full Baths	1
Half Baths	1
Roof Framing	Stick

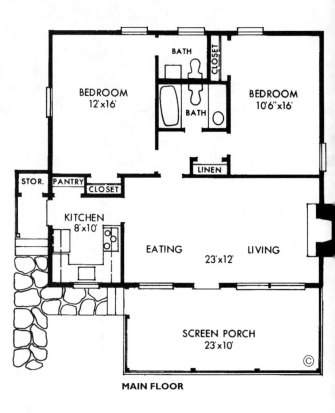

BEDROOM 12'x16'

BATH

CLOSET

BEDROOM 10'6"x16'

BATH

LINEN

STOR. **PANTRY** CLOSET

KITCHEN 8'x10'

EATING 23'x12' **LIVING**

SCREEN PORCH 23'x10'

Ⓒ

MAIN FLOOR

Design 26114

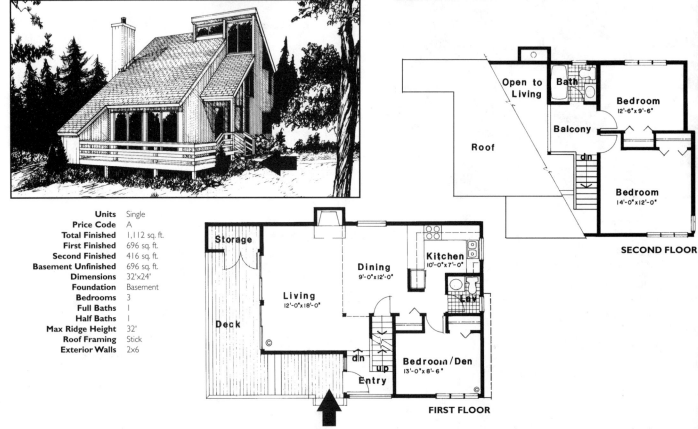

Units	Single
Price Code	A
Total Finished	1,112 sq. ft.
First Finished	696 sq. ft.
Second Finished	416 sq. ft.
Basement Unfinished	696 sq. ft.
Dimensions	32'x24'
Foundation	Basement
Bedrooms	3
Full Baths	1
Half Baths	1
Max Ridge Height	32'
Roof Framing	Stick
Exterior Walls	2x6

Open to Living

Bath

Roof

Balcony

Bedroom 12'-6" x 9'-6"

dn

Bedroom 14'-0" x 12'-0"

SECOND FLOOR

Storage

Dining 9'-0"x12'-0"

Kitchen 10'-0"x7'-0"

Living 12'-0"x18'-0"

Deck

Ⓒ

Lav

dn

up

Entry

Bedroom/Den 13'-0"x8'-6"

Ⓒ

FIRST FLOOR

Design 65001

Units	Single
Price Code	A
Total Finished	1,480 sq. ft.
First Finished	1,024 sq. ft.
Second Finished	456 sq. ft.
Basement Unfinished	1,024 sq. ft.
Dimensions	32'x40'
Foundation	Basement
Bedrooms	2
Full Baths	2
First Ceiling	8'
Second Ceiling	8'
Max Ridge Height	23'8"
Roof Framing	Truss
Exterior Walls	2x6

SECOND FLOOR

2,70 X 3,60
9'-0" X 12'-0"

3,00 X 3,90
10'-0" X 13'-0"

FIRST FLOOR

4,40 X 3,60
14'-8" X 12'-0"

4,20 X 6,80
14'-0" X 22'-8"

4,40 X 3,60
14'-8" X 12'-0"

Design 26112

Units	Single
Price Code	A
Total Finished	1,487 sq. ft.
First Finished	911 sq. ft.
Second Finished	576 sq. ft.
Basement Unfinished	911 sq. ft.
Dimensions	32'x34'
Foundation	Basement
Bedrooms	3
Full Baths	1
Half Baths	1
First Ceiling	9'
Second Ceiling	8'
Max Ridge Height	29'
Roof Framing	Stick
Exterior Walls	2x6

SECOND FLOOR

FIRST FLOOR

To order blueprints, call **800-235-5700** or visit us on the web, **familyhomeplans.com**

Units	Single
Price Code	B
Total Finished	1,519 sq. ft.
First Finished	788 sq. ft.
Second Finished	731 sq. ft.
Garage Unfinished	266 sq. ft.
Dimensions	32'x36'
Foundation	Basement
Bedrooms	3
Full Baths	1
3/4 Baths	1

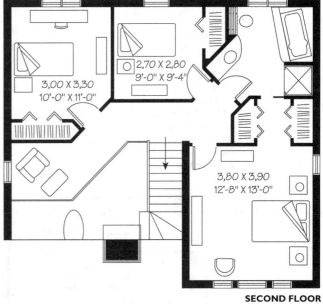

SECOND FLOOR

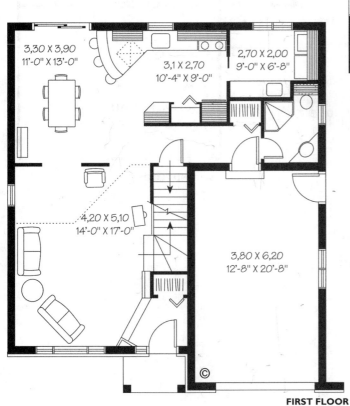

FIRST FLOOR

Units	Single
Price Code	D
Total Finished	2,015 sq. ft.
First Finished	1,280 sq. ft.
Second Finished	735 sq. ft.
Porch Unfinished	80 sq. ft.
Dimensions	32'x40'
Foundation	Crawlspace
Bedrooms	3
Full Baths	2
Half Baths	1
First Ceiling	8'
Second Ceiling	8'
Max Ridge Height	32'
Roof Framing	Stick
Exterior Walls	2x6

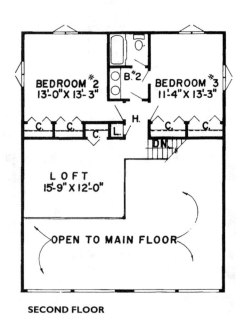

SECOND FLOOR

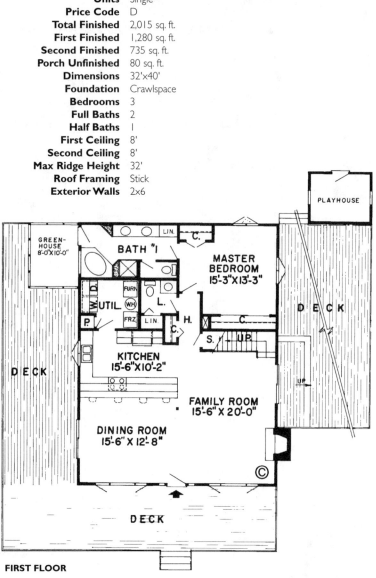

FIRST FLOOR

Units	Single
Price Code	D
Total Finished	2,108 sq. ft.
Main Finished	1,198 sq. ft.
Lower Finished	910 sq. ft.
Garage Unfinished	288 sq. ft
Dimensions	32'x36'
Foundation	Basement
Bedrooms	3
Full Baths	2
Half Baths	1
Exterior Walls	2x4

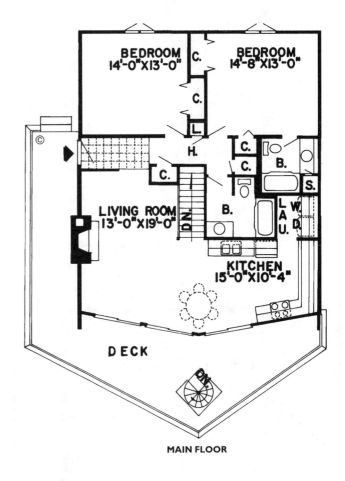

MAIN FLOOR

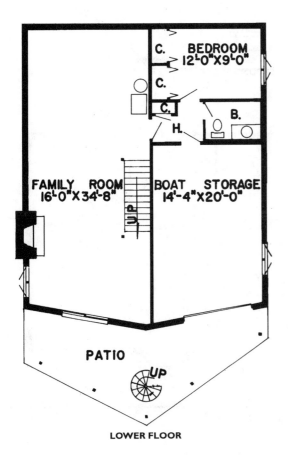

LOWER FLOOR

Design 65207

Units	Single
Price Code	C
Total Finished	1,864 sq. ft.
First Finished	790 sq. ft.
Second Finished	287 sq. ft.
Lower Finished	787 sq. ft.
Dimensions	32'4"x24'4"
Foundation	Basement
Bedrooms	3
Full Baths	1
3/4 Baths	1
Max Ridge Height	29'6'
Roof Framing	Truss

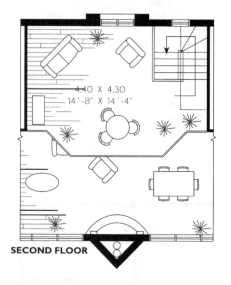

4,40 X 4,30
14'-8" X 14'-4"

SECOND FLOOR

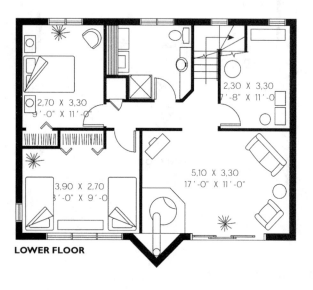

2,70 X 3,30
9'-0" X 11'-0"

2,30 X 3,30
7'-8" X 11'-0"

3,90 X 2,70
13'-0" X 9'-0"

5,10 X 3,30
17'-0" X 11'-0"

LOWER FLOOR

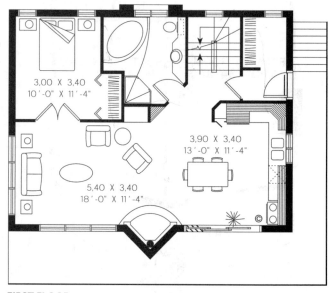

3,00 X 3,40
10'-0" X 11'-4"

3,90 X 3,40
13'-0" X 11'-4"

5,40 X 3,40
18'-0" X 11'-4"

FIRST FLOOR

Units	Single
Price Code	A
Total Finished	984 sq. ft.
Main Finished	984 sq. ft.
Dimensions	33'9"x43'
Foundation	Crawlspace
	Slab
Bedrooms	2
Full Baths	1
3/4 Baths	1
Max Ridge Height	26'
Exterior Walls	2x6

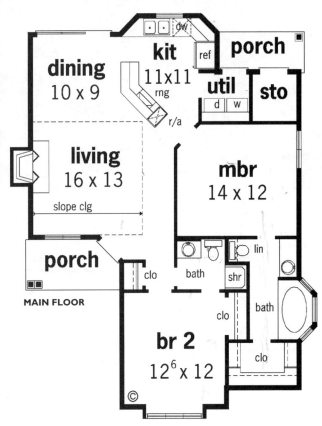

MAIN FLOOR

dining 10 x 9

kit 11x11

porch

util

sto

living 16 x 13
slope clg

mbr 14 x 12

porch

br 2 12⁶ x 12

Units	Single
Price Code	A
Total Finished	1,079 sq. ft.
Main Finished	1,079 sq. ft.
Dimensions	34'x34'
Foundation	Basement
Bedrooms	2
Full Baths	1
Max Ridge Height	22'6"
Roof Framing	Truss
Exterior Walls	2x6

4,00 X 3,60
13'-4" X 12'-0"

5,70 X 3,60
19'-0" X 12'-0"

3,60 X 4,80
12'-0" X 16'-0"

3,30 X 3,00
11'-0" X 10'-0"

MAIN FLOOR

Design 65640

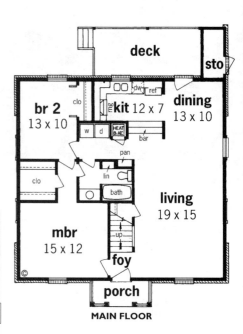

Units	Single
Price Code	A
Total Finished	1,088 sq. ft.
Main Finished	1,088 sq. ft.
Bonus Unfinished	580 sq. ft.
Dimensions	34'x44'
Foundation	Crawlspace
	Slab
Bedrooms	2
Full Baths	1
Main Ceiling	8'
Second Ceiling	8'
Max Ridge Height	30'
Roof Framing	Stick
Exterior Walls	2x6

MAIN FLOOR

br 2 13 x 10
kit 12 x 7
dining 13 x 10
deck
sto
living 19 x 15
mbr 15 x 12
foy
porch

open to kitchen below
br 3 16 x 12
br 4 16 x 12

BONUS

Design 91033

Units	Single
Price Code	A
Total Finished	1,249 sq. ft.
First Finished	952 sq. ft.
Second Finished	297 sq. ft.
Dimensions	34'x28'
Foundation	Basement
	Crawlspace
Bedrooms	2
Full Baths	2
First Ceiling	8'
Max Ridge Height	24'
Roof Framing	Stick
Exterior Walls	2x6

OPTIONAL BASEMENT STAIR LOCATION

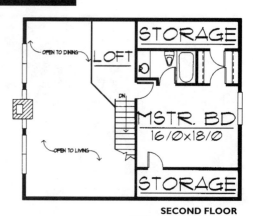

SECOND FLOOR

OPEN TO DINING
LOFT
STORAGE
MSTR. BD 16/0x18/0
STORAGE
OPEN TO LIVING

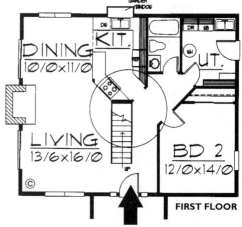

FIRST FLOOR

DINING 10/0x11/0
KIT.
UT.
LIVING 13/6x16/0
BD 2 12/0x14/0
GARDEN WINDOW

Design 20055

Units	Single
Price Code	B
Total Finished	1,701 sq. ft.
First Finished	928 sq. ft.
Second Finished	773 sq. ft.
Basement Unfinished	910 sq. ft.
Garage Unfinished	484 sq. ft.
Dimensions	34'x58'4"
Foundation	Basement
Bedrooms	3
Full Baths	2
Half Baths	1
Max Ridge Height	30'
Roof Framing	Stick
Exterior Walls	2x6

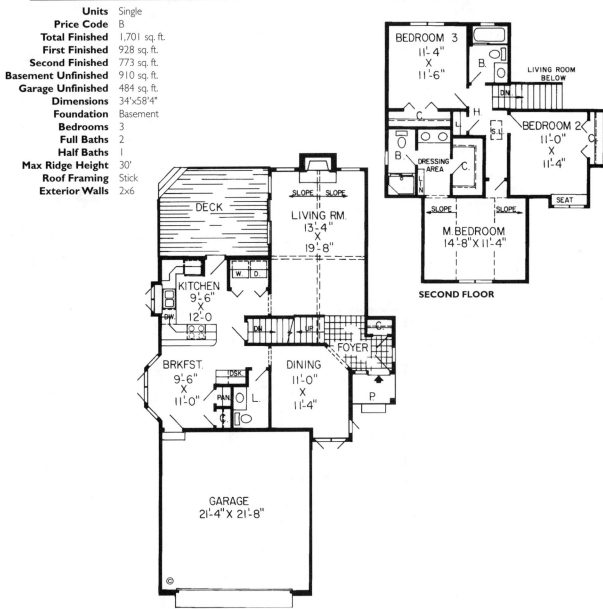

SECOND FLOOR

FIRST FLOOR

Units	Single
Price Code	B
Total Finished	1,702 sq. ft.
First Finished	1,238 sq. ft.
Second Finished	464 sq. ft.
Basement Unfinished	1,175 sq. ft.
Garage Unfinished	484 sq. ft.
Deck Unfinished	509 sq. ft.
Dimensions	34'x56'
Foundation	Basement
Bedrooms	3
Full Baths	1
3/4 Baths	1
First Ceiling	8'
Max Ridge Height	26'6"
Roof Framing	Stick
Exterior Walls	2x6

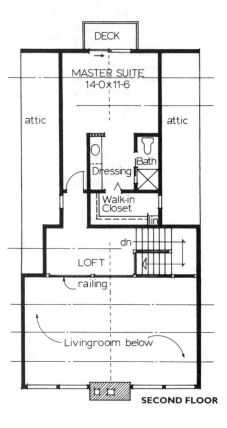

SECOND FLOOR

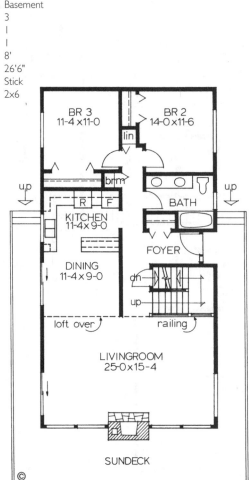

FIRST FLOOR

Units	Single
Price Code	B
Total Finished	1,727 sq. ft.
First Finished	939 sq. ft.
Second Finished	788 sq. ft.
Bonus Unfinished	210 sq. ft.
Basement Unfinished	939 sq. ft.
Garage Unfinished	401 sq. ft.
Porch Unfinished	65 sq. ft.
Dimensions	34'x52'2"
Foundation	Basement
Bedrooms	3
Full Baths	1
3/4 Baths	1
Half Baths	1
First Ceiling	8'
Second Ceiling	8'
Max Ridge Height	27'10"
Roof Framing	Truss
Exterior Walls	2x4

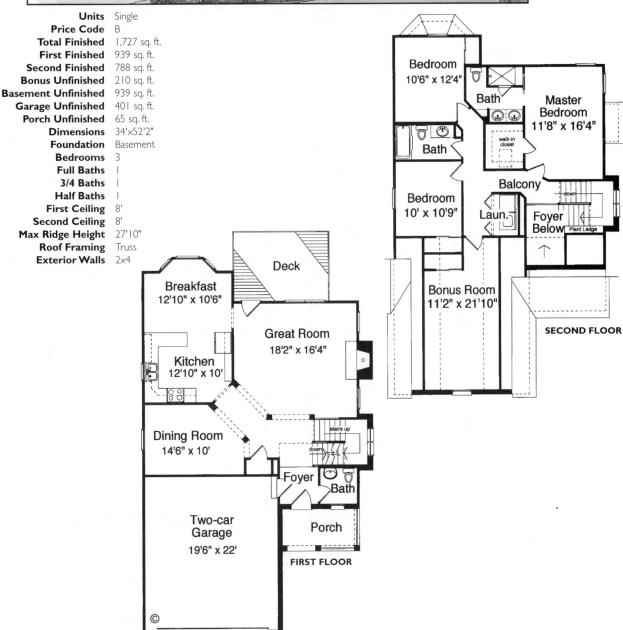

PHOTOGRAPHY: COURTESY OF THE DESIGNER

Units	Single
Price Code	D
Total Finished	2,221 sq. ft.
First Finished	1,307 sq. ft.
Second Finished	914 sq. ft.
Dimensions	34'x44'
Foundation	Pier/Post
Bedrooms	4
Full Baths	3
First Ceiling	9'
Second Ceiling	8'
Max Ridge Height	41'
Roof Framing	Stick
Exterior Walls	2x4

Please note: The photographed home may have been modified to suit homeowner preferences. If you order plans, have a builder or design professional check them against the photograph to confirm actual construction details.

SECOND FLOOR

Study 10'x 10'

Sitting Area 10'9"x 10'

Master Bedroom 12'x 16'

Bedroom 12'4"x 13'

Balcony 21'x 8'

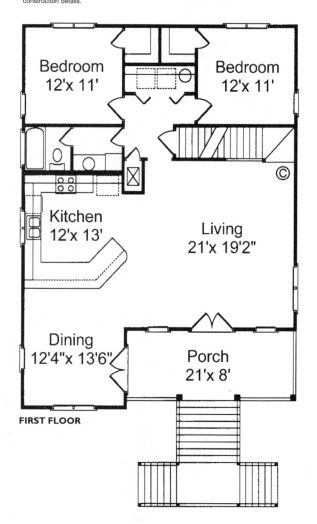

FIRST FLOOR

Bedroom 12'x 11'

Bedroom 12'x 11'

Kitchen 12'x 13'

Living 21'x 19'2"

Dining 12'4"x 13'6"

Porch 21'x 8'

Design 68096

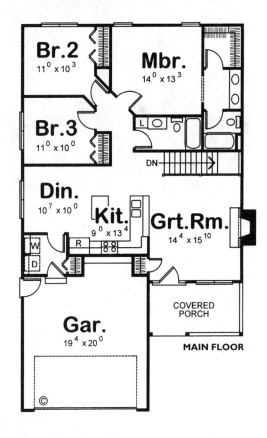

Units	Single
Price Code	A
Total Finished	1,311 sq. ft.
Main Finished	1,311 sq. ft.
Garage Unfinished	439 sq. ft.
Deck Unfinished	112 sq. ft.
Dimensions	34'8"x58'4"
Foundation	Crawlspace
	Slab
Bedrooms	3
Full Baths	2
Main Ceiling	9'
Max Ridge Height	22'6"
Exterior Walls	2x4

* Alternate foundation options available at an additional charge.
Please call 1-800-235-5700 for more information.

Br.2 11⁰ x 10³

Mbr. 14⁰ x 13³

Br.3 11⁰ x 10⁰

Din. 10⁷ x 10⁰

Kit. 9⁰ x 13⁴

Grt.Rm. 14⁴ x 15¹⁰

DN

COVERED PORCH

Gar. 19⁴ x 20⁰

MAIN FLOOR

Design 61093

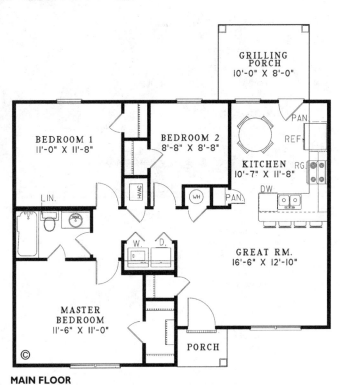

Units	Single
Price Code	A
Total Finished	930 sq. ft.
Main Finished	930 sq. ft.
Porch Unfinished	102 sq. ft.
Dimensions	35'x28'6"
Foundation	Crawlspace
	Slab
Bedrooms	3
Full Baths	1
Main Ceiling	8'
Roof Framing	Stick
Exterior Walls	2x4

GRILLING PORCH 10'-0" X 8'-0"

BEDROOM 1 11'-0" X 11'-8"

BEDROOM 2 8'-8" X 8'-8"

KITCHEN 10'-7" X 11'-8"

LIN.

HVAC

WH

PAN

REF

PAN

DW

W. D.

GREAT RM. 16'-6" X 12'-10"

MASTER BEDROOM 11'-6" X 11'-0"

PORCH

MAIN FLOOR

Design 65015

SECOND FLOOR

3.00 X 3.30
10'-0" X 11'-0"

4.50 X 3.30
15'-0" X 11'-0"

3.60 X 3.60
12'-0" X 12'-0"

6.00 X 4.20
20'-0" X 14'-0"

4.20 X 3.90
14'-0" X 13'-0"

FIRST FLOOR

3.90 X 2.70
13'-0" X 9'-0"

Units	Single
Price Code	A
Total Finished	1,360 sq. ft.
First Finished	858 sq. ft.
Second Finished	502 sq. ft.
Basement Unfinished	858 sq. ft.
Dimensions	35'x29'8"
Foundation	Basement
Bedrooms	3
Full Baths	2
First Ceiling	8'
Second Ceiling	8'
Max Ridge Height	26'6"
Roof Framing	Truss
Exterior Walls	2x6

Design 90847

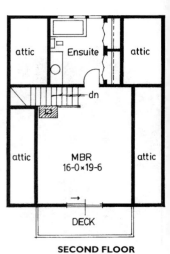

attic Ensuite attic

attic

MBR
16-0×19-6

attic

DECK

SECOND FLOOR

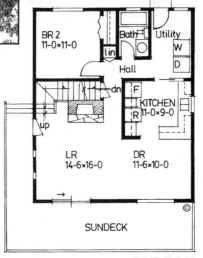

BR 2
11-0×11-0

Bath Utility

lin

Hall

W
D

KITCHEN
11-0×9-0

up

LR
14-6×16-0

DR
11-6×10-0

SUNDECK

FIRST FLOOR

Units	Single
Price Code	A
Total Finished	1,362 sq. ft.
First Finished	864 sq. ft.
Second Finished	498 sq. ft.
Basement Unfinished	864 sq. ft.
Deck Unfinished	340 sq. ft.
Dimensions	35'x40'
Foundation	Basement
	Crawlspace
Bedrooms	2
Full Baths	2
Roof Framing	Stick
Exterior Walls	2x6

Units	Single
Price Code	A
Total Finished	1,427 sq. ft.
Main Finished	1,427 sq. ft.
Garage Unfinished	420 sq. ft.
Deck Unfinished	96 sq. ft.
Porch Unfinished	32 sq. ft.
Dimensions	35'x68'5"
Foundation	Slab
Bedrooms	3
Full Baths	1
3/4 Baths	1
Main Ceiling	8'-10'
Max Ridge Height	23'6"
Roof Framing	Stick
Exterior Walls	2x4

MAIN FLOOR

Units	Single
Price Code	A
Total Finished	1,470 sq. ft.
First Finished	1,035 sq. ft.
Second Finished	435 sq. ft.
Basement Unfinished	1,018 sq. ft.
Deck Unfinished	240 sq. ft.
Porch Unfinished	192 sq. ft.
Dimensions	35'x42'
Foundation	Basement
	Crawlspace
	Slab
Bedrooms	3
Full Baths	2
First Ceiling	8'
Second Ceiling	8'
Max Ridge Height	27'
Roof Framing	Stick
Exterior Walls	2x4, 2x6

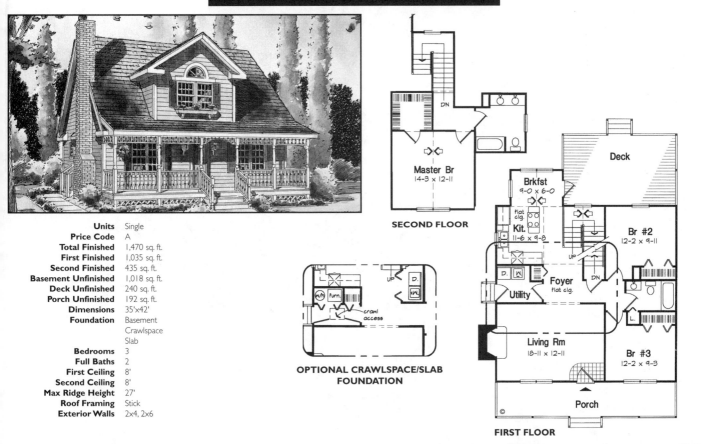

SECOND FLOOR

OPTIONAL CRAWLSPACE/SLAB FOUNDATION

FIRST FLOOR

Design 19191

PHOTOGRAPHY: COURTESY OF THE DESIGNER

Units	Single
Price Code	B
Total Finished	1,533 sq. ft.
First Finished	1,079 sq. ft.
Second Finished	454 sq. ft.
Garage Unfinished	240 sq. ft.
Dimensions	35'x65'
Foundation	Crawlspace
Bedrooms	3
Full Baths	2
First Ceiling	8'
Second Ceiling	8'
Max Ridge Height	24'
Roof Framing	Stick
Exterior Walls	2x6

Please note: The photographed home may have been modified to suit homeowner preferences. If you order plans, have a builder or design professional check them against the photograph to confirm actual construction details.

Units	Single
Price Code	B
Total Finished	1,508 sq. ft.
First Finished	1,050 sq. ft.
Second Finished	458 sq. ft.
Porch Unfinished	233 sq. ft.
Dimensions	35'6"x39'9"
Foundation	Pier/Post
Bedrooms	3
Full Baths	2
Half Baths	I
First Ceiling	9'
Second Ceiling	8'
Max Ridge Height	23'6"
Roof Framing	Stick
Exterior Walls	2x4

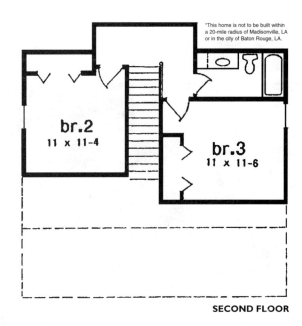

*This home is not to be built within a 20-mile radius of Madisonville, LA or in the city of Baton Rouge, LA.

br.2
11 x 11-4

br.3
11 x 11-6

SECOND FLOOR

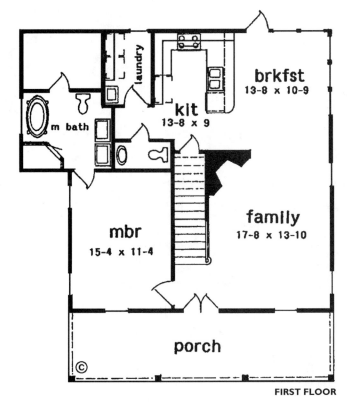

brkfst
13-8 x 10-9

kit
13-8 x 9

laundry

m bath

mbr
15-4 x 11-4

family
17-8 x 13-10

porch

FIRST FLOOR

Design 65170

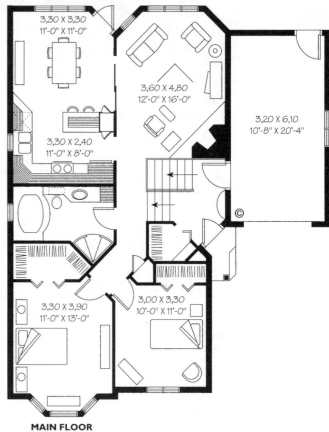

Units	Single
Price Code	A
Total Finished	1,050 sq. ft.
Main Finished	1,050 sq. ft.
Basement Unfinished	1,050 sq. ft.
Dimensions	36'x45'
Foundation	Basement
Bedrooms	2
Full Baths	1
Max Ridge Height	26'4"
Roof Framing	Truss
Exterior Walls	2x6

3.30 X 3.30
11'-0" X 11'-0"

3.60 X 4.80
12'-0" X 16'-0"

3.20 X 6.10
10'-8" X 20'-4"

3.30 X 2.40
11'-0" X 8'-0"

3.30 X 3.90
11'-0" X 13'-0"

3.00 X 3.30
10'-0" X 11'-0"

MAIN FLOOR

Design 92052

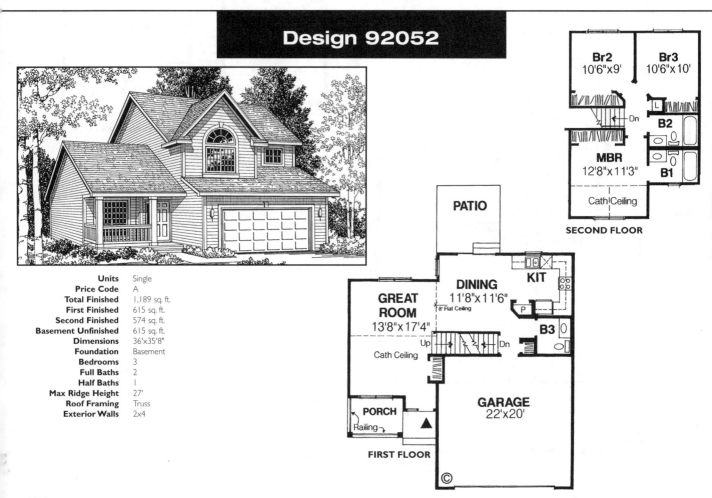

Units	Single
Price Code	A
Total Finished	1,189 sq. ft.
First Finished	615 sq. ft.
Second Finished	574 sq. ft.
Basement Unfinished	615 sq. ft.
Dimensions	36'x35'8"
Foundation	Basement
Bedrooms	3
Full Baths	2
Half Baths	1
Max Ridge Height	27'
Roof Framing	Truss
Exterior Walls	2x4

Br2
10'6"x9'

Br3
10'6"x 10'

B2

MBR
12'8"x 11'3"

B1

Cath Ceiling

SECOND FLOOR

PATIO

DINING
11'8"x 11'6"
8' Flat Ceiling

KIT

GREAT
ROOM
13'8"x 17'4"
Cath Ceiling

Up   Dn

B3

P

GARAGE
22'x20'

PORCH
Railing

FIRST FLOOR

To order blueprints, call **800-235-5700** or visit us on the web, **familyhomeplans.com**

Design 34600

PHOTOGRAPHY: MICHELE EVANS CHRISTY

OPTIONAL CRAWLSPACE/SLAB FOUNDATION

SECOND FLOOR

Units	Single
Price Code	A
Total Finished	1,328 sq. ft.
First Finished	1,013 sq. ft.
Second Finished	315 sq. ft.
Basement Unfinished	1,013 sq. ft.
Dimensions	36'x36'
Foundation	Basement
	Crawlspace
	Slab
Bedrooms	3
Full Baths	2
First Ceiling	8'
Second Ceiling	7'6"
Max Ridge Height	23'6"
Roof Framing	Stick
Exterior Walls	2x4, 2x6

Please note: The photographed home may have been modified to suit homeowner preferences. If you order plans, have a builder or design professional check them against the photograph to confirm actual construction details.

FIRST FLOOR

Design 94314

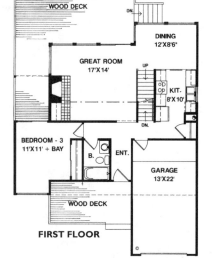

SECOND FLOOR

Units	Single
Price Code	C
Total Finished	1,951 sq. ft.
First Finished	812 sq. ft.
Second Finished	653 sq. ft.
Lower Finished	486 sq. ft.
Garage Unfinished	283 sq. ft.
Deck Unfinished	374 sq. ft.
Dimensions	36'x50'
Foundation	Combo
	Basement/
	Crawlspace
Bedrooms	3
Full Baths	1
3/4 Baths	1
Max Ridge Height	26'
Roof Framing	Stick
Exterior Walls	2x6

LOWER FLOOR

FIRST FLOOR

To order blueprints, call **800-235-5700** or visit us on the web, **familyhomeplans.com**   **87**

Design 94635

Units	Single
Price Code	E
Total Finished	2,473 sq. ft.
First Finished	1,504 sq. ft.
Second Finished	969 sq. ft.
Porch Unfinished	212 sq. ft.
Dimensions	36'x53'
Foundation	Crawlspace
	Slab
Bedrooms	4
Full Baths	2
Half Baths	1
First Ceiling	10'
Second Ceiling	9'
Max Ridge Height	32'6"
Roof Framing	Stick
Exterior Walls	2x4

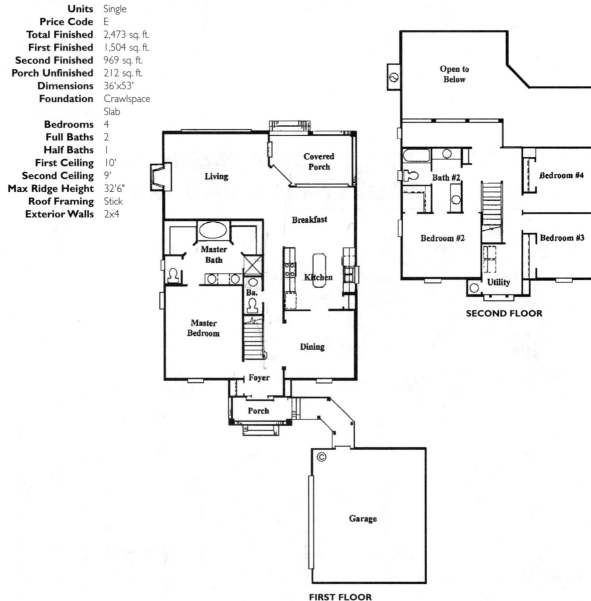

SECOND FLOOR

FIRST FLOOR

Design 65008

Units	Single
Price Code	H
Total Finished	3,072 sq. ft.
First Finished	1,437 sq. ft.
Second Finished	1,635 sq. ft.
Garage Unfinished	474 sq. ft.
Dimensions	36'x62'
Foundation	Slab
Bedrooms	4
Full Baths	3
First Ceiling	8'
Second Ceiling	8'
Max Ridge Height	26'6"
Roof Framing	Truss
Exterior Walls	2x6

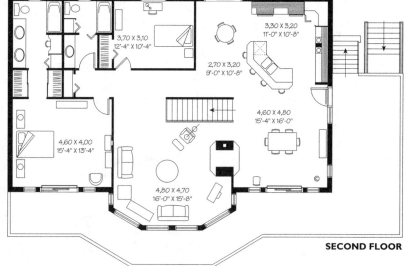

SECOND FLOOR

FIRST FLOOR

Units	Single
Price Code	E
Total Finished	2,453 sq. ft.
First Finished	1,804 sq. ft.
Second Finished	649 sq. ft.
Porch Unfinished	346 sq. ft.
Dimensions	36'6"x65'6"
Foundation	Crawlspace
	Slab
Bedrooms	4
Full Baths	3
First Ceiling	10'
Max Ridge Height	33'6"
Roof Framing	Stick
Exterior Walls	2x4

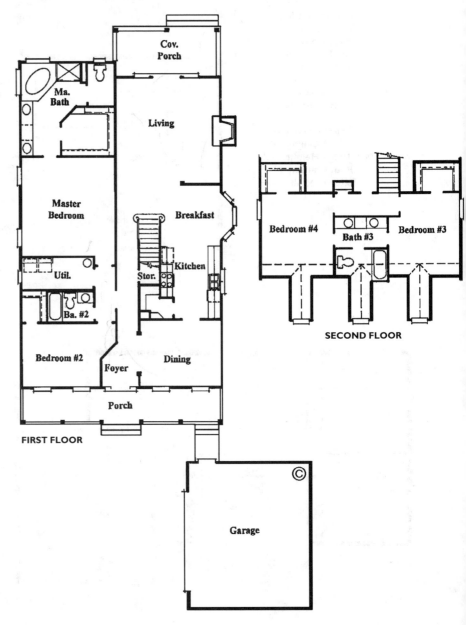

Design 52190

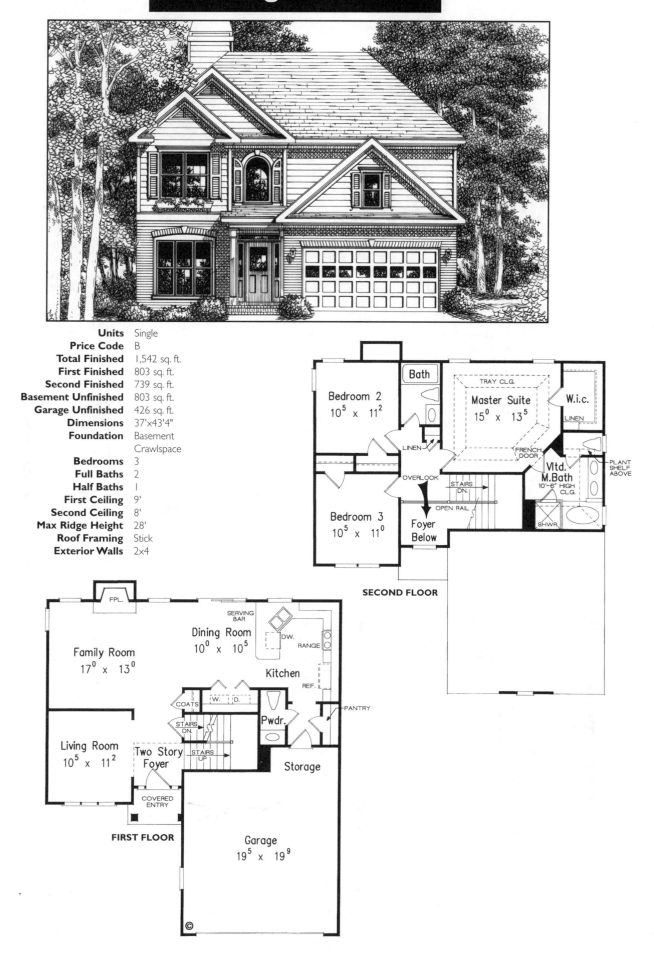

Units	Single
Price Code	B
Total Finished	1,542 sq. ft.
First Finished	803 sq. ft.
Second Finished	739 sq. ft.
Basement Unfinished	803 sq. ft.
Garage Unfinished	426 sq. ft.
Dimensions	37'x43'4"
Foundation	Basement
	Crawlspace
Bedrooms	3
Full Baths	2
Half Baths	1
First Ceiling	9'
Second Ceiling	8'
Max Ridge Height	28'
Roof Framing	Stick
Exterior Walls	2x4

SECOND FLOOR

Bath

Bedroom 2
10⁵ x 11²

TRAY CLG.

Master Suite
15⁰ x 13⁵

W.i.c.

LINEN

LINEN

FRENCH DOOR

PLANT SHELF ABOVE

OVERLOOK

STAIRS DN.

Vltd. M.Bath
10'-6" HIGH CLG.

Bedroom 3
10⁵ x 11⁰

OPEN RAIL

Foyer Below

SHWR.

FIRST FLOOR

FPL.

SERVING BAR

Dining Room
10⁰ x 10⁵

DW.

RANGE

Family Room
17⁰ x 13⁰

Kitchen

REF.

COATS

W. D.

PANTRY

Living Room
10⁵ x 11²

STAIRS DN.

Pwdr.

Two Story Foyer

STAIRS UP

Storage

COVERED ENTRY

Garage
19⁵ x 19⁹

To order blueprints, call **800-235-5700** or visit us on the web, **familyhomeplans.com**   **91**

Design 65141

Units	Single
Price Code	B
Total Finished	1,550 sq. ft.
First Finished	946 sq. ft.
Second Finished	604 sq. ft.
Dimensions	37'x30'8"
Foundation	Basement
Bedrooms	3
Full Baths	2
First Ceiling	8'
Roof Framing	Truss

SECOND FLOOR

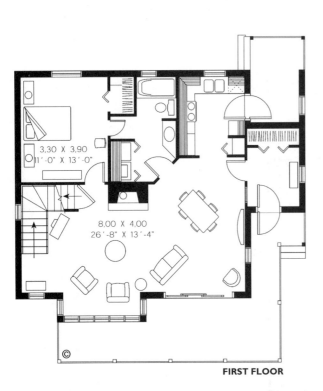

FIRST FLOOR

PHOTOGRAPHY: JAMES SALOMON

Units	Single
Price Code	C
Total Finished	1,913 sq. ft.
First Finished	1,209 sq. ft.
Second Finished	704 sq. ft.
Basement Unfinished	685 sq. ft.
Garage Unfinished	524 sq. ft.
Dimensions	37'x49'
Foundation	Basement
Bedrooms	3
Full Baths	1
3/4 Baths	2
First Ceiling	8'
Second Ceiling	8'
Max Ridge Height	28'
Roof Framing	Stick
Exterior Walls	2x6

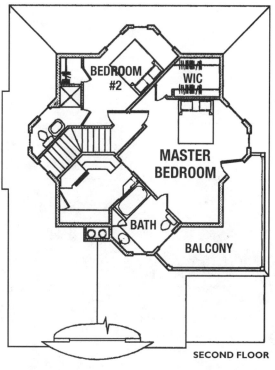

SECOND FLOOR

Please note: The photographed home may have been modified to suit homeowner preferences. If you order plans, have a builder or design professional check them against the photograph to confirm actual construction details.

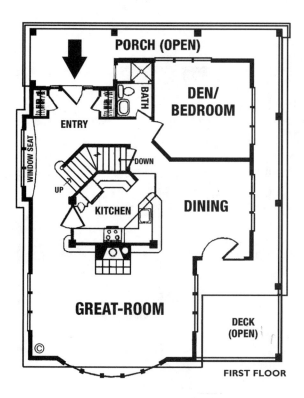

FIRST FLOOR

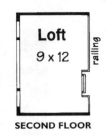

Loft
9 x 12
railing

SECOND FLOOR

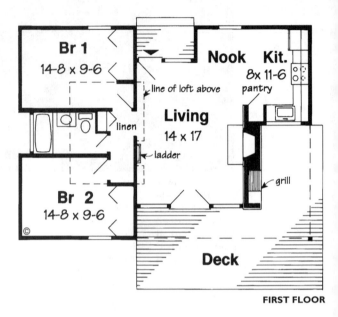

Units	Single
Price Code	A
Total Finished	897 sq. ft.
First Finished	789 sq. ft.
Second Finished	108 sq. ft.
Dimensions	38'x26'
Foundation	Crawlspace
Bedrooms	2
Full Baths	1
First Ceiling	7'9"
Max Ridge Height	21'
Roof Framing	Stick/Truss
Exterior Walls	2x4

Br 1
14-8 x 9-6

Nook Kit.
8x 11-6

line of loft above

pantry

linen

Living
14 x 17

ladder

grill

Br 2
14-8 x 9-6

Deck

FIRST FLOOR

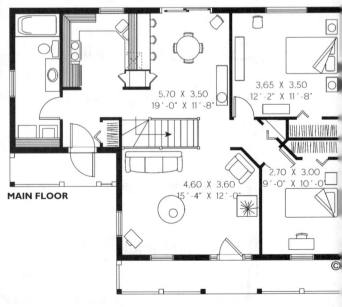

Units	Single
Price Code	A
Total Finished	920 sq. ft.
Main Finished	920 sq. ft.
Porch Unfinished	152 sq. ft.
Dimensions	38'x28'
Foundation	Basement
Bedrooms	2
Full Baths	1
Main Ceiling	8'
Max Ridge Height	20'6"
Roof Framing	Truss
Exterior Walls	2x6

5,70 X 3,50
19'-0" X 11'-8"

3,65 X 3,50
12'-2" X 11'-8"

MAIN FLOOR

2,70 X 3,00
9'-0" X 10'-0"

4,60 X 3,60
15'-4" X 12'-0"

Design 93175

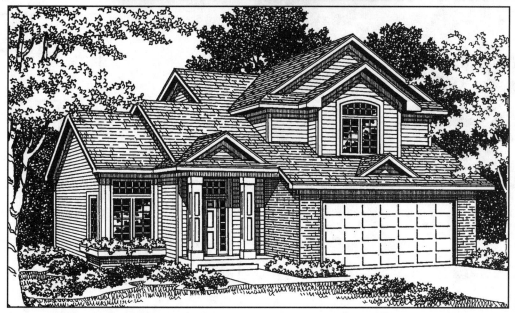

Units	Single
Price Code	B
Total Finished	1,550 sq. ft.
First Finished	804 sq. ft.
Second Finished	746 sq. ft.
Basement Unfinished	804 sq. ft.
Dimensions	38'x38'4"
Foundation	Basement
Bedrooms	3
Full Baths	2
Half Baths	1
Max Ridge Height	26'6"
Roof Framing	Stick
Exterior Walls	2x6

*This home is not to be built within a 20-mile radius of Iowa City, Iowa.

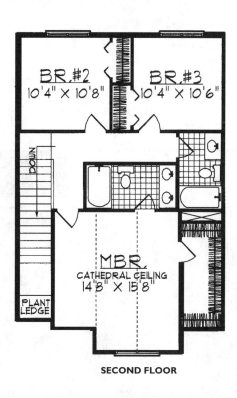

SECOND FLOOR

BR. #2
10'4" X 10'8"

BR. #3
10'4" X 10'6"

DOWN

MBR.
CATHEDRAL CEILING
14'8" X 15'8"

PLANT LEDGE

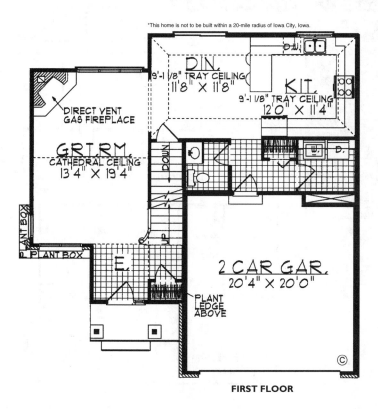

FIRST FLOOR

DIRECT VENT GAS FIREPLACE

GRT. RM.
CATHEDRAL CEILING
13'4" X 19'4"

DIN.
9'-1 1/8" TRAY CEILING
11'8" X 11'8"

KIT.
9'-1 1/8" TRAY CEILING
12'0" X 11'4"

DOWN

UP

PLANT BOX

PLANT BOX

PLANT LEDGE ABOVE

2 CAR GAR.
20'4" X 20'0"

Design 69018

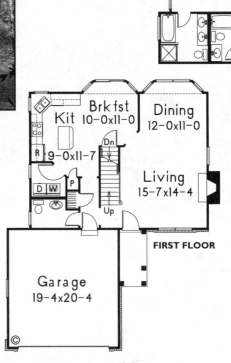

SECOND FLOOR

MBr
12-0x14-8
vaulted clg

Br 2
12-0x11-0

Br 3
12-0x11-3
vaulted clg

plant shelf

Brk fst
10-0x11-0

Kit
9-0x11-7

Dining
12-0x11-0

Living
15-7x14-4

FIRST FLOOR

Garage
19-4x20-4

Units	Single
Price Code	B
Total Finished	1,575 sq. ft.
First Finished	802 sq. ft.
Second Finished	773 sq. ft.
Dimensions	38'x47'
Foundation	Basement
Bedrooms	3
Full Baths	2
Half Baths	1
First Ceiling	8'
Second Ceiling	8'
Max Ridge Height	26'6"
Roof Framing	Truss
Exterior Walls	2x4

Design 92423

STORAGE

BEDROOM 3
15X12

BEDROOM 2
15X12

OPEN TO BELOW

SECOND FLOOR

SKYLIGHT

DINING
12x12

KITCHEN
10x12

MASTER BEDRM
15x13

FAMILY ROOM
18x15

FIRST FLOOR

Units	Single
Price Code	B
Total Finished	1,643 sq. ft.
First Finished	1,064 sq. ft.
Second Finished	579 sq. ft.
Dimensions	38'x34'
Foundation	Basement
Bedrooms	3
Full Baths	2
Half Baths	1
First Ceiling	8'
Second Ceiling	8'
Vaulted Ceiling	14'
Max Ridge Height	21'6"
Exterior Walls	2x4

Units	Single
Price Code	C
Total Finished	1,764 sq. ft.
First Finished	869 sq. ft.
Second Finished	895 sq. ft.
Basement Unfinished	869 sq. ft.
Garage Unfinished	412 sq. ft.
Dimensions	38'x44'4"
Foundation	Basement
	Crawlspace
	Slab
Bedrooms	4
Full Baths	2
Half Baths	1
First Ceiling	8'
Max Ridge Height	25'5"
Roof Framing	Stick
Exterior Walls	2x4

* Alternate foundation options available at an additional charge.
Please call 1-800-235-5700 for more information.

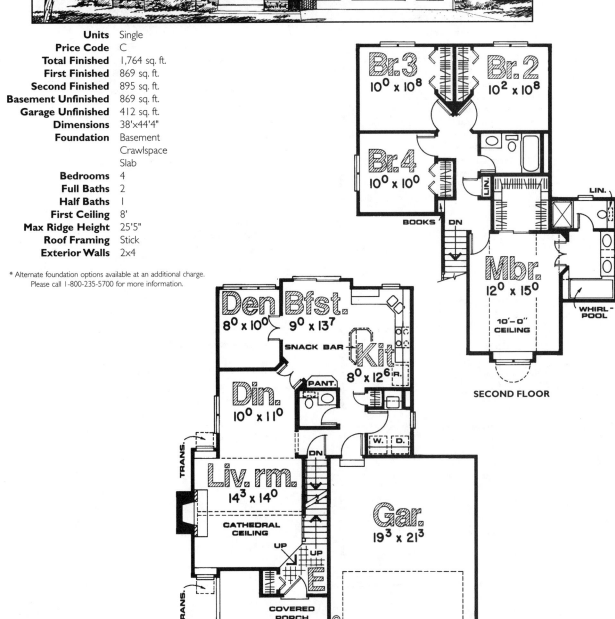

Units	Single
Price Code	C
Total Finished	1,832 sq. ft.
First Finished	1,212 sq. ft.
Second Finished	620 sq. ft.
Basement Unfinished	1,212 sq. ft.
Dimensions	38'x40'
Foundation	Basement
Bedrooms	3
Full Baths	2
First Ceiling	8'
Max Ridge Height	26'4"

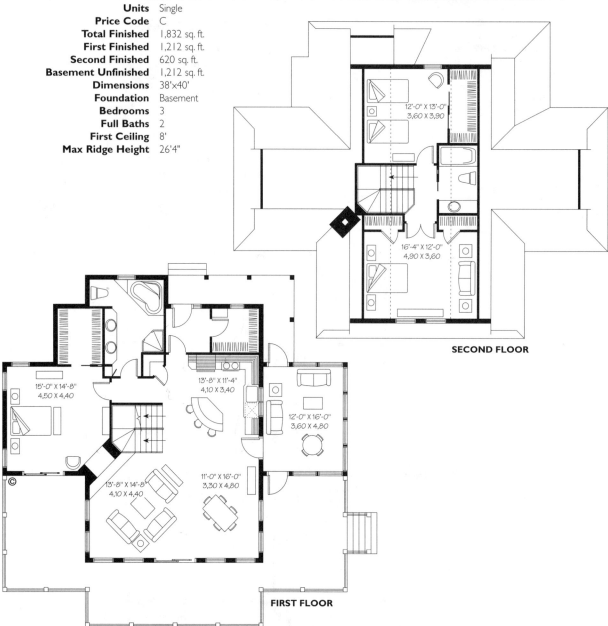

SECOND FLOOR

FIRST FLOOR

To order blueprints, call **800-235-5700** or visit us on the web, **familyhomeplans.com**

Units	Single
Price Code	D
Total Finished	2,146 sq. ft.
First Finished	1,654 sq. ft.
Second Finished	492 sq. ft.
Garage Unfinished	464 sq. ft.
Porch Unfinished	324 sq. ft.
Dimensions	38'10"x70'4"
Foundation	Basement
	Crawlspace
	Slab
Bedrooms	3
Full Baths	2
Half Baths	1
First Ceiling	9'
Second Ceiling	8'
Roof Framing	Stick
Exterior Walls	2x4

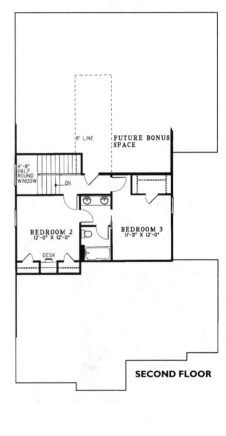

SECOND FLOOR

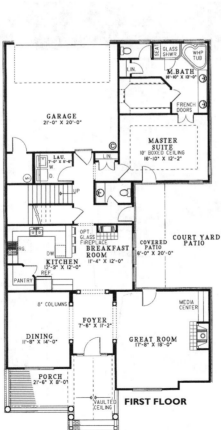

FIRST FLOOR

Design 82003

Units	Single
Price Code	A
Total Finished	1,379 sq. ft.
Main Finished	1,379 sq. ft.
Garage Unfinished	493 sq. ft.
Porch Unfinished	142 sq. ft.
Dimensions	38'4"x68'6"
Foundation	Crawlspace
	Slab
Bedrooms	3
Full Baths	2
Main Ceiling	9'
Roof Framing	Stick
Exterior Walls	2x4

MAIN FLOOR

Design 82015

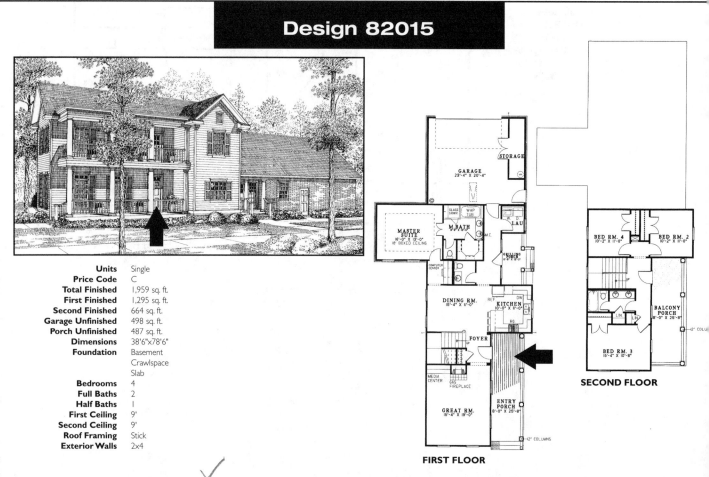

Units	Single
Price Code	C
Total Finished	1,959 sq. ft.
First Finished	1,295 sq. ft.
Second Finished	664 sq. ft.
Garage Unfinished	498 sq. ft.
Porch Unfinished	487 sq. ft.
Dimensions	38'6"x78'6"
Foundation	Basement
	Crawlspace
	Slab
Bedrooms	4
Full Baths	2
Half Baths	1
First Ceiling	9'
Second Ceiling	9'
Roof Framing	Stick
Exterior Walls	2x4

SECOND FLOOR

FIRST FLOOR

PHOTOGRAPHY: JAMES YOCHUM PHOTOGRAPHY

Units	Single
Price Code	D
Total Finished	2,071 sq. ft.
First Finished	1,109 sq. ft.
Second Finished	962 sq. ft.
Basement Unfinished	1,015 sq. ft.
Garage Unfinished	462 sq. ft.
Deck Unfinished	140 sq. ft.
Porch Unfinished	264 sq. ft.
Dimensions	38'6"x56'
Foundation	Basement
Bedrooms	3
Full Baths	2
3/4 Baths	1
First Ceiling	9'
Second Ceiling	8'
Max Ridge Height	28'6"
Roof Framing	Truss
Exterior Walls	2x4

Please note: The photographed home may have been modified to suit homeowner preferences. If you order plans, have a builder or design professional check them against the photograph to confirm actual construction details.

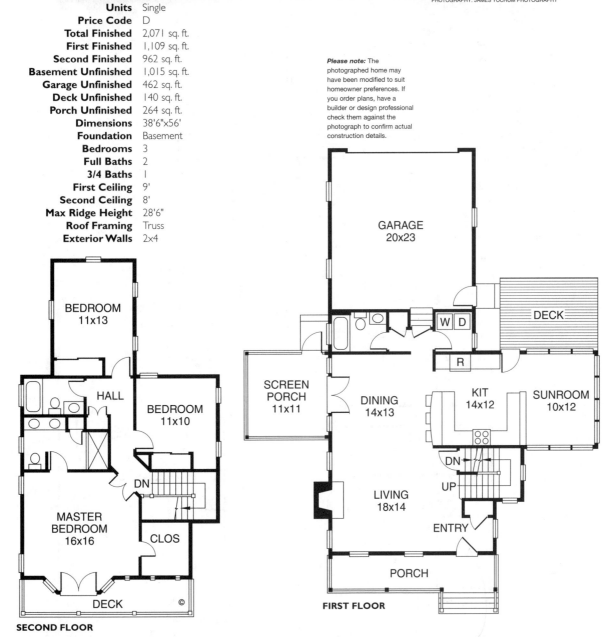

SECOND FLOOR

FIRST FLOOR

PHOTOGRAPHY: JAMES YOCHUM PHOTOGRAPHY

Units	Single
Price Code	E
Total Finished	3,705 sq. ft.
First Finished	1,311 sq. ft.
Second Finished	1,214 sq. ft.
Lower Finished	1,180 sq. ft.
Garage Unfinished	553 sq. ft.
Deck Unfinished	346 sq. ft.
Porch Unfinished	180 sq. ft.
Dimensions	38'8"x70'9"
Foundation	Basement
Bedrooms	6
Full Baths	1
3/4 Baths	2
Half Baths	1
First Ceiling	9'
Second Ceiling	8'
Max Ridge Height	35'8"
Exterior Walls	2x6

SECOND FLOOR

Please note: The photographed home may have been modified to suit homeowner preferences. If you order plans, have a builder or design professional check them against the photograph to confirm actual construction details.

LOWER FLOOR

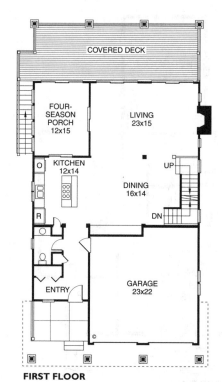

FIRST FLOOR

Design 98434

Units	Single
Price Code	A
Total Finished	1,346 sq. ft.
Main Finished	1,346 sq. ft.
Basement Unfinished	1,358 sq. ft.
Garage Unfinished	395 sq. ft.
Dimensions	39'x51'
Foundation	Basement
	Crawlspace
	Slab
Bedrooms	3
Full Baths	2
Max Ridge Height	21'6"
Roof Framing	Stick
Exterior Walls	2x4

MAIN FLOOR

Design 62073

Units	Single
Price Code	C
Total Finished	1,832 sq. ft.
Main Finished	1,832 sq. ft.
Bonus Unfinished	790 sq. ft.
Dimensions	39'x81'
Foundation	Crawlspace
	Slab
Bedrooms	3
Full Baths	2
Main Ceiling	9'
Second Ceiling	8'
Max Ridge Height	25'8"
Roof Framing	Stick
Exterior Walls	2x4

BONUS

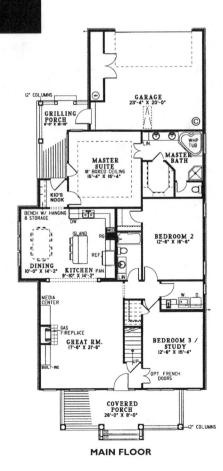

MAIN FLOOR

Design 82022

Units	Single
Price Code	C
Total Finished	1,927 sq. ft.
Main Finished	1,927 sq. ft.
Bonus Unfinished	988 sq. ft.
Garage Unfinished	448 sq. ft.
Porch Unfinished	432 sq. ft.
Dimensions	39'x82'4"
Foundation	Basement
	Crawlspace
	Slab
Bedrooms	3
Full Baths	2
Main Ceiling	10'
Roof Framing	Stick
Exterior Walls	2x4

MAIN FLOOR

Design 52120

CAD FILES AVAILABLE For more information call 800-235-5700

Units	Single
Price Code	D
Total Finished	2,215 sq. ft.
First Finished	1,293 sq. ft.
Second Finished	922 sq. ft.
Bonus Unfinished	235 sq. ft.
Basement Unfinished	1,293 sq. ft.
Garage Unfinished	498 sq. ft.
Dimensions	40'x57'
Foundation	Basement
	Crawlspace
Bedrooms	3
Full Baths	3
First Ceiling	9'
Second Ceiling	8'
Max Ridge Height	32'4"
Roof Framing	Stick
Exterior Walls	2x4

SECOND FLOOR

FIRST FLOOR

Units	Single
Price Code	D
Total Finished	2,001 sq. ft.
Main Finished	2,001 sq. ft.
Basement Unfinished	979 sq. ft.
Garage Unfinished	455 sq. ft.
Deck Unfinished	220 sq. ft.
Porch Unfinished	21 sq. ft.
Dimensions	39'6"x84'10"
Bedrooms	3
Full Baths	2
Main Ceiling	8'
Max Ridge Height	27'7"
Roof Framing	Stick
Exterior Walls	2x4

MASTER BEDROOM
12'-0"x21'-0"

DECK
11'-8"x18'-0"

MR BATH

LIN

WIC

BEDROOM #2
12'-0"x10'-4"

GREAT ROOM
19'-6"x22'-8"

FP

LINEN

BOOKS

DINE

BATH #2

W D

DN

KITCHEN
11'-4"x11'-0"

LAUNDRY

FOYER

STUDY/
BEDROOM #3
12'-0"x10'-7"

NOOK
11'-4"x7'-0"
(+BAY)

MAIN FLOOR

GARAGE
20'-8"x20'-8"

Design 94913

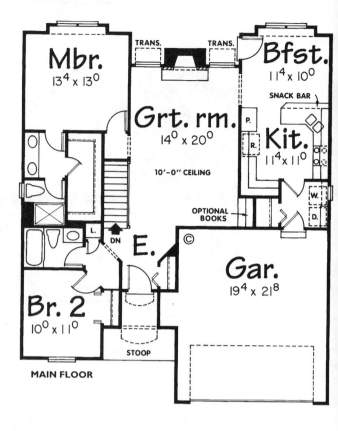

MAIN FLOOR

Units	Single
Price Code	A
Total Finished	1,212 sq. ft.
Main Finished	1,212 sq. ft.
Basement Unfinished	1,212 sq. ft.
Garage Unfinished	448 sq. ft.
Dimensions	40'x47'8"
Foundation	Basement
Bedrooms	2
Full Baths	1
3/4 Baths	1
Main Ceiling	8'
Max Ridge Height	19'
Roof Framing	Stick
Exterior Walls	2x4

* Alternate foundation options available at an additional charge.
Please call 1-800-235-5700 for more information.

Design 92281

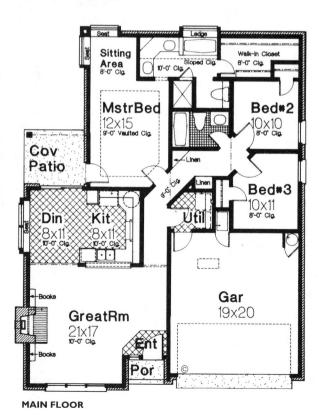

MAIN FLOOR

Units	Single
Price Code	A
Total Finished	1,360 sq. ft.
Main Finished	1,360 sq. ft.
Garage Unfinished	380 sq. ft.
Deck Unfinished	82 sq. ft.
Porch Unfinished	18 sq. ft.
Dimensions	40'x49'10"
Foundation	Slab
Bedrooms	3
Full Baths	2
Max Ridge Height	21'
Roof Framing	Stick
Exterior Walls	2x4

Design 94304

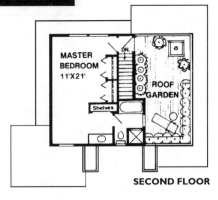

SECOND FLOOR

Units	Single
Price Code	A
Total Finished	1,377 sq. ft.
First Finished	981 sq. ft.
Second Finished	396 sq. ft.
Dimensions	40'x50'
Foundation	Basement
Bedrooms	3
Full Baths	2
First Ceiling	8'
Second Ceiling	8'
Roof Framing	Truss
Exterior Walls	2x4

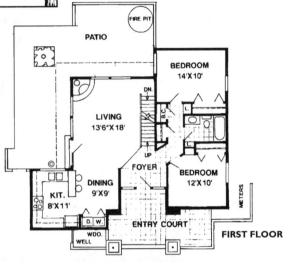

FIRST FLOOR

Design 97652

Units	Single
Price Code	A
Total Finished	1,425 sq. ft.
Main Finished	1,425 sq. ft.
Basement Unfinished	1,425 sq. ft.
Garage Unfinished	394 sq. ft.
Dimensions	40'x53'
Foundation	Basement
	Crawlspace
Bedrooms	3
Full Baths	2
Main Ceiling	8'
Max Ridge Height	24'
Roof Framing	Stick
Exterior Walls	2x4

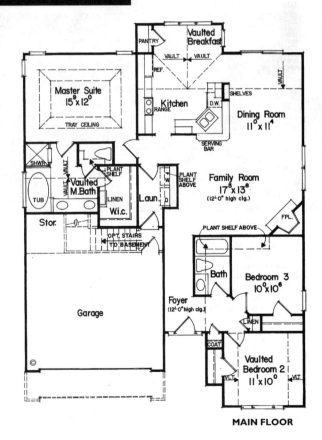

MAIN FLOOR

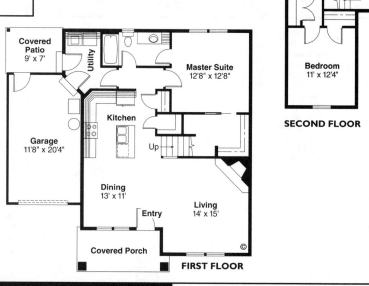

Units	Single
Price Code	A
Total Finished	1,426 sq. ft.
First Finished	983 sq. ft.
Second Finished	443 sq. ft.
Garage Unfinished	246 sq. ft.
Dimensions	40'x38'
Foundation	Crawlspace
Bedrooms	3
Full Baths	1
3/4 Baths	1
First Ceiling	8'
Second Ceiling	8'
Max Ridge Height	22'8"
Roof Framing	Truss
Exterior Walls	2x6

Bedroom 11' x 10'4"

Dn

Bedroom 11' x 12'4"

SECOND FLOOR

Covered Patio 9' x 7'

Utility

Master Suite 12'8" x 12'8"

Kitchen

Garage 11'8" x 20'4"

Up

Dining 13' x 11'

Living 14' x 15'

Entry

Covered Porch

FIRST FLOOR

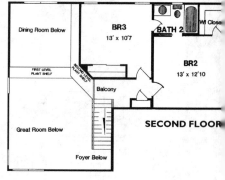

Units	Single
Price Code	A
Total Finished	1,493 sq. ft.
First Finished	973 sq. ft.
Second Finished	520 sq. ft.
Basement Unfinished	973 sq. ft.
Garage Unfinished	462 sq. ft.
Dimensions	40'x41'
Foundation	Basement
Bedrooms	3
Full Baths	2
Half Baths	1
First Ceiling	8'1½"
Second Ceiling	8'1⅛"
Max Ridge Height	24'6"
Roof Framing	Stick/Truss
Exterior Walls	2x4

Dining Room Below

BR3 13' x 10'7"

BATH 2

WI Closet

FIRST LEVEL PLANT SHELF

Balcony

BR2 13' x 12'10"

Great Room Below

SECOND FLOOR

Foyer Below

cath cl'g DIN RM 11'2 x 12'2

KIT 9'6 x 9'2

MBATH

MBR 13' x 13'2

PLANT SHELF ABOVE

cath cl'g GREAT RM 15'2 x 17'2

Entry

Lav

WI Closet

GARAGE 20'4 x 21'8

FIRST FLOOR

Covered Entry

Design 97152

Units	Single
Price Code	B
Total Finished	1,557 sq. ft.
Main Finished	1,557 sq. ft.
Basement Unfinished	1,557 sq. ft.
Garage Unfinished	400 sq. ft.
Dimensions	40'x61'
Foundation	Basement
Bedrooms	3
Full Baths	1
3/4 Baths	1
Max Ridge Height	26'4"
Roof Framing	Truss
Exterior Walls	2x6

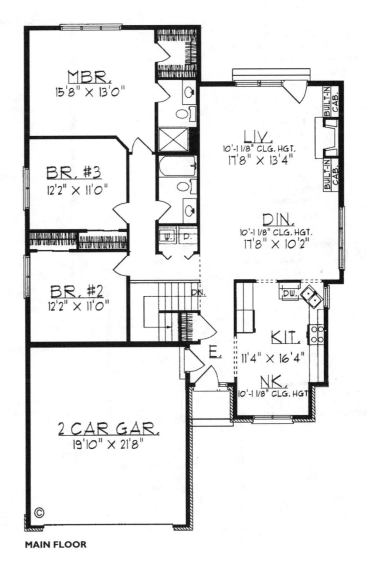

MAIN FLOOR

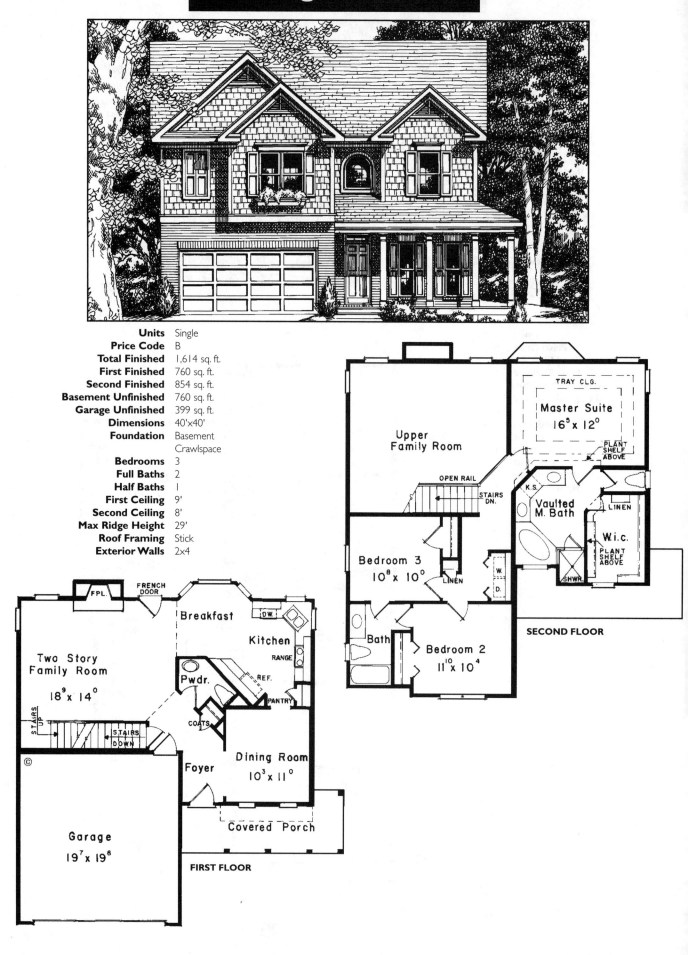

Units	Single
Price Code	B
Total Finished	1,614 sq. ft.
First Finished	760 sq. ft.
Second Finished	854 sq. ft.
Basement Unfinished	760 sq. ft.
Garage Unfinished	399 sq. ft.
Dimensions	40'x40'
Foundation	Basement
	Crawlspace
Bedrooms	3
Full Baths	2
Half Baths	1
First Ceiling	9'
Second Ceiling	8'
Max Ridge Height	29'
Roof Framing	Stick
Exterior Walls	2x4

TRAY CLG.

Master Suite
16⁵ x 12⁰

PLANT SHELF ABOVE

Upper Family Room

OPEN RAIL

STAIRS DN.

K.S.

LINEN

Vaulted M. Bath

W.i.c.

PLANT SHELF ABOVE

SHWR.

Bedroom 3
10⁸ x 10⁰

LINEN

W.

D.

SECOND FLOOR

Bath

Bedroom 2
11¹⁰ x 10⁴

FPL.

FRENCH DOOR

Breakfast

D.W.

Kitchen

RANGE

Two Story Family Room
18⁹ x 14⁰

Pwdr.

REF.

PANTRY

STAIRS UP

STAIRS DOWN

COATS

©

Dining Room
10³ x 11⁰

Foyer

Garage
19⁷ x 19⁸

Covered Porch

FIRST FLOOR

Design 68001

Units	Single
Price Code	B
Total Finished	1,699 sq. ft.
First Finished	964 sq. ft.
Second Finished	735 sq. ft.
Basement Unfinished	964 sq. ft.
Garage Unfinished	452 sq. ft.
Dimensions	40'x46'
Foundation	Basement
	Crawlspace
	Slab
Bedrooms	3
Full Baths	2
Half Baths	1
First Ceiling	8'
Max Ridge Height	25'
Roof Framing	Stick
Exterior Walls	2x4, 2x6

* Alternate foundation options available at an additional charge.
Please call 1-800-235-5700 for more information.

Design 60132

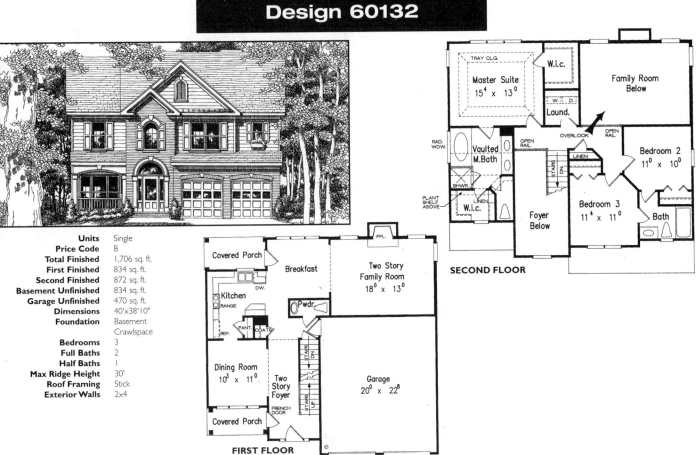

Units	Single
Price Code	B
Total Finished	1,706 sq. ft.
First Finished	834 sq. ft.
Second Finished	872 sq. ft.
Basement Unfinished	834 sq. ft.
Garage Unfinished	470 sq. ft.
Dimensions	40'x38'10"
Foundation	Basement
	Crawlspace
Bedrooms	3
Full Baths	2
Half Baths	1
Max Ridge Height	30'
Roof Framing	Stick
Exterior Walls	2x4

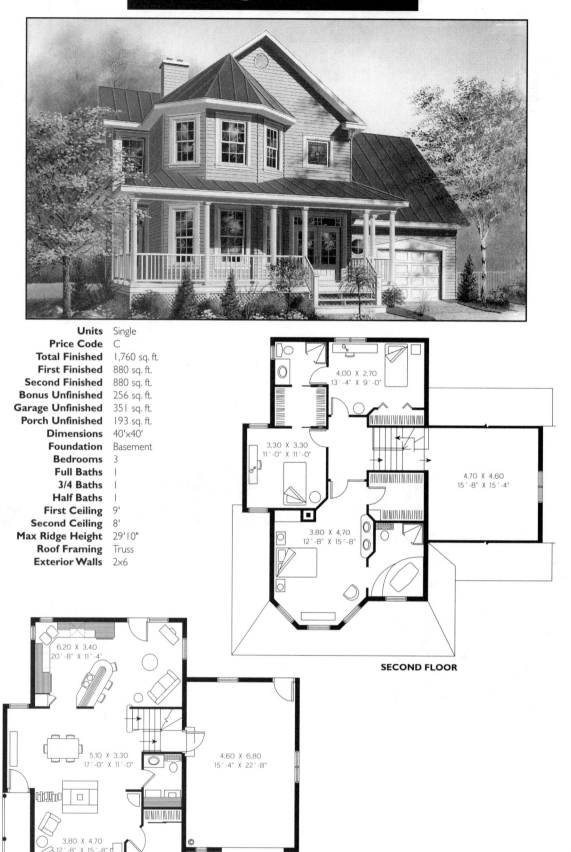

Units	Single
Price Code	C
Total Finished	1,760 sq. ft.
First Finished	880 sq. ft.
Second Finished	880 sq. ft.
Bonus Unfinished	256 sq. ft.
Garage Unfinished	351 sq. ft.
Porch Unfinished	193 sq. ft.
Dimensions	40'x40'
Foundation	Basement
Bedrooms	3
Full Baths	1
3/4 Baths	1
Half Baths	1
First Ceiling	9'
Second Ceiling	8'
Max Ridge Height	29'10"
Roof Framing	Truss
Exterior Walls	2x6

4,00 X 2,70
13'-4" X 9'-0"

3,30 X 3,30
11'-0" X 11'-0"

4,70 X 4,60
15'-8" X 15'-4"

3,80 X 4,70
12'-8" X 15'-8"

SECOND FLOOR

6,20 X 3,40
20'-8" X 11'-4"

5,10 X 3,30
17'-0" X 11'-0"

4,60 X 6,80
15'-4" X 22'-8"

3,80 X 4,70
12'-8" X 15'-8"

FIRST FLOOR

Units	Single
Price Code	C
Total Finished	1,893 sq. ft.
First Finished	1,087 sq. ft.
Second Finished	806 sq. ft.
Garage Unfinished	636 sq. ft.
Dimensions	40'x45'
Foundation	Crawlspace
Bedrooms	3
Full Baths	2
Half Baths	1
First Ceiling	9'
Max Ridge Height	29'
Roof Framing	Stick
Exterior Walls	2x6

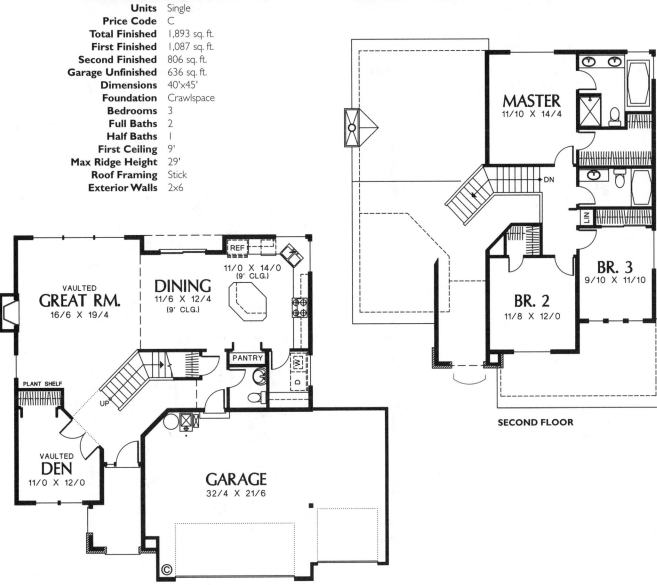

MASTER
11/10 X 14/4

BR. 3
9/10 X 11/10

BR. 2
11/8 X 12/0

SECOND FLOOR

Vaulted
GREAT RM.
16/6 X 19/4

DINING
11/6 X 12/4
(9' CLG.)

REF
11/0 X 14/0
(9' CLG.)

PANTRY

PLANT SHELF

UP

Vaulted
DEN
11/0 X 12/0

GARAGE
32/4 X 21/6

FIRST FLOOR

Units	Single
Price Code	C
Total Finished	1,919 sq. ft.
Main Finished	1,919 sq. ft.
Garage Unfinished	454 sq. ft.
Dimensions	40'x62'
Foundation	Slab
Bedrooms	4
Full Baths	2
Main Ceiling	8'
Max Ridge Height	18'6"
Roof Framing	Stick

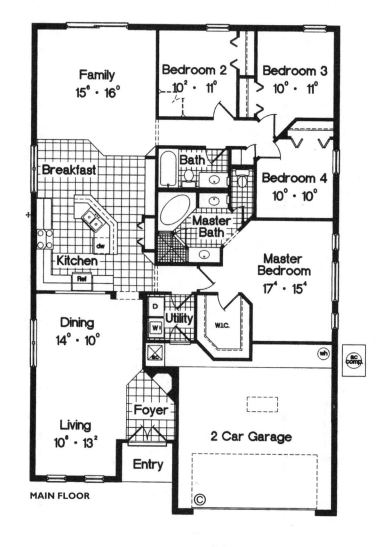

MAIN FLOOR

Units	Single
Price Code	C
Total Finished	1,994 sq. ft.
First Finished	1,112 sq. ft.
Second Finished	882 sq. ft.
Dimensions	40'x43'
Foundation	Crawlspace
Bedrooms	3
Full Baths	2
Half Baths	1
First Ceiling	9'
Second Ceiling	8'
Max Ridge Height	29'
Roof Framing	Truss
Exterior Walls	2x6

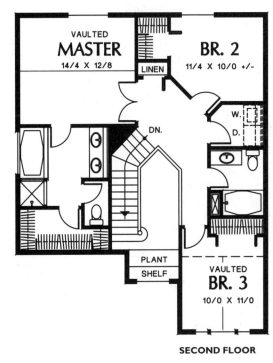

SECOND FLOOR

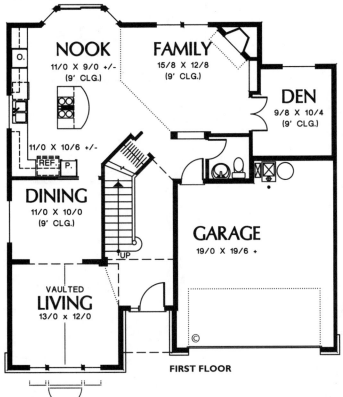

FIRST FLOOR

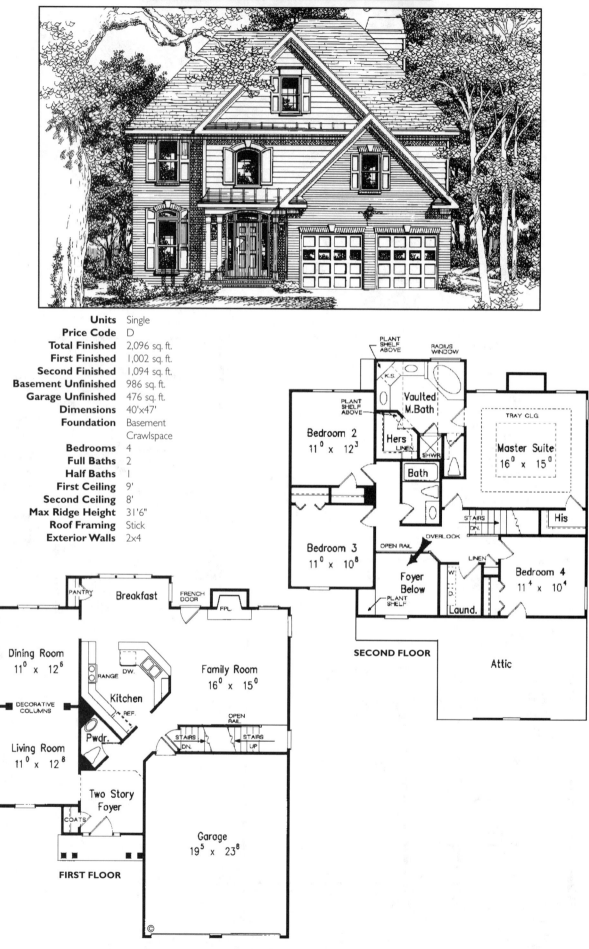

Units	Single
Price Code	D
Total Finished	2,096 sq. ft.
First Finished	1,002 sq. ft.
Second Finished	1,094 sq. ft.
Basement Unfinished	986 sq. ft.
Garage Unfinished	476 sq. ft.
Dimensions	40'x47'
Foundation	Basement
	Crawlspace
Bedrooms	4
Full Baths	2
Half Baths	1
First Ceiling	9'
Second Ceiling	8'
Max Ridge Height	31'6"
Roof Framing	Stick
Exterior Walls	2x4

SECOND FLOOR

Bedroom 2
11⁰ x 12³

Vaulted M.Bath

Hers

Bath

Master Suite
16⁰ x 15⁰

TRAY CLG.

His

STAIRS DN.

Bedroom 3
11⁰ x 10⁸

OPEN RAIL

OVERLOOK

Foyer Below

Bedroom 4
11⁴ x 10⁴

Laund.

Attic

FIRST FLOOR

Breakfast

PANTRY

FRENCH DOOR

FPL

Dining Room
11⁰ x 12⁶

Kitchen

RANGE

DW

Family Room
16⁰ x 15⁰

DECORATIVE COLUMNS

REF.

Living Room
11⁰ x 12⁸

Pwdr.

OPEN RAIL

STAIRS DN.

STAIRS UP

Two Story Foyer

COATS

Garage
19⁵ x 23⁸

Units	Single
Price Code	D
Total Finished	2,154 sq. ft.
First Finished	998 sq. ft.
Second Finished	1,156 sq. ft.
Garage Unfinished	442 sq. ft.
Deck Unfinished	190 sq. ft.
Dimensions	40'x42'
Foundation	Basement
Bedrooms	4
Full Baths	2
Half Baths	I
First Ceiling	9'
Second Ceiling	8'
Max Ridge Height	30'
Roof Framing	Stick
Exterior Walls	2x4

Bdrm.4/ Opt. Mstr. Sitting
10-8 x 13-4

Bdrm.3
11-0 x 11-10

Bdrm.2
11-0 x 13-4

Otp. Opening

Master Bdrm.
14-0 x 17-2

Trav Ceil

Bth.2

Two Story Living Area

Lin.

Ks.

Linen

M.Bath
Flat Ceil 10-6 High

SECOND FLOOR

Sundeck
17-0 x 12-0

Kitchen
11-0 x 13-4

Dining
11-0 x 13-4

Keeping/Brkfst.
17-0 x 13-4

Ref.

Cab.

Stor.
7-4 x 6-0

Lav.

P.

Cts.

Flat Ceil.
Une.

Sh.

Two Story Living Area
16-0 x 15-4

Up

Double Garage
19-4 x 19-8

Porch

FIRST FLOOR

Units	Single
Price Code	D
Total Finished	2,229 sq. ft.
First Finished	1,195 sq. ft.
Second Finished	1,034 sq. ft.
Basement Unfinished	1,195 sq. ft.
Garage Unfinished	469 sq. ft.
Dimensions	40'x52'
Foundation	Basement
	Crawlspace
	Slab
Bedrooms	4
Full Baths	2
Half Baths	I
First Ceiling	8'
Max Ridge Height	27'
Roof Framing	Stick
Exterior Walls	2x4

* Alternate foundation options available at an additional charge.
Please call 1-800-235-5700 for more information.

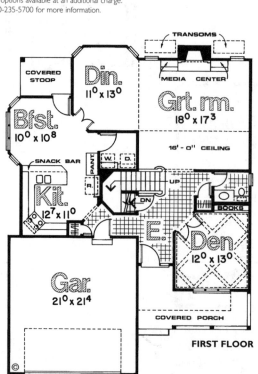

FIRST FLOOR

SECOND FLOOR

Design 86014

SECOND FLOOR

Units	Single
Price Code	B
Total Finished	1,582 sq. ft.
First Finished	949 sq. ft.
Second Finished	633 sq. ft.
Porch Unfinished	415 sq. ft.
Dimensions	40'3"x40'6"
Foundation	Crawlspace
Bedrooms	3
Full Baths	2
First Ceiling	9'
Second Ceiling	8'
Max Ridge Height	30'10"
Roof Framing	Stick
Exterior Walls	2x4

FIRST FLOOR

Design 93219

PHOTOGRAPHY: JOHN EHRENCLOU

Please note: The photographed home may have been modified to suit homeowner preferences. If you order plans, have a builder or design professional check them against the photograph to confirm actual construction details.

Units	Single
Price Code	B
Total Finished	1,668 sq. ft.
First Finished	1,057 sq. ft.
Second Finished	611 sq. ft.
Basement Unfinished	511 sq. ft.
Garage Unfinished	546 sq. ft.
Dimensions	40'4"x38'
Foundation	Basement
Bedrooms	3
Full Baths	2
Half Baths	1
First Ceiling	8'
Second Ceiling	8'
Max Ridge Height	23'
Roof Framing	Stick
Exterior Walls	2x4

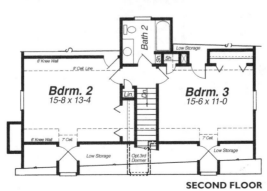

SECOND FLOOR

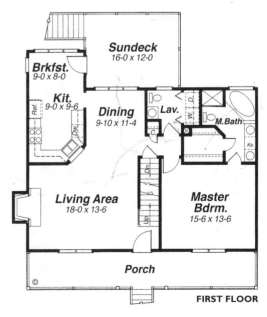

FIRST FLOOR

To order blueprints, call **800-235-5700** or visit us on the web, **familyhomeplans.com**   **119**

Design 93269

PHOTOGRAPHY: JOHN EHRENCLOU

Units	Single
Price Code	B
Total Finished	1,735 sq. ft.
First Finished	1,045 sq. ft.
Second Finished	690 sq. ft.
Basement Unfinished	465 sq. ft.
Garage Unfinished	580 sq. ft.
Dimensions	40'4"×44'
Foundation	Basement
Bedrooms	3
Full Baths	2
Half Baths	1
First Ceiling	8'
Max Ridge Height	23'
Roof Framing	Stick
Exterior Walls	2x4

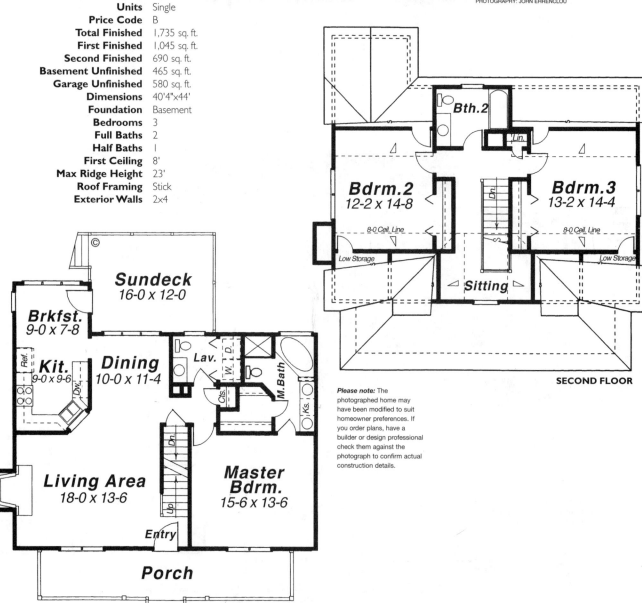

Please note: The photographed home may have been modified to suit homeowner preferences. If you order plans, have a builder or design professional check them against the photograph to confirm actual construction details.

Design 94907

Units	Single
Price Code	C
Total Finished	1,768 sq. ft.
First Finished	905 sq. ft.
Second Finished	863 sq. ft.
Basement Unfinished	905 sq. ft.
Garage Unfinished	487 sq. ft.
Dimensions	40'8"x46'
Foundation	Basement
Bedrooms	3
Full Baths	2
Half Baths	1
First Ceiling	8'
Max Ridge Height	30'6"
Roof Framing	Stick
Exterior Walls	2x4

* Alternate foundation options available at an additional charge.
Please call 1-800-235-5700 for more information.

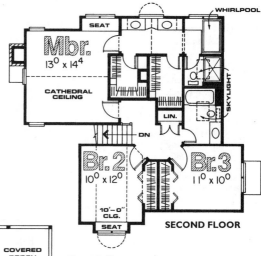

SECOND FLOOR

Please note: The photographed home may have been modified to suit homeowner preferences. If you order plans, have a builder or design professional check them against the photograph to confirm actual construction details.

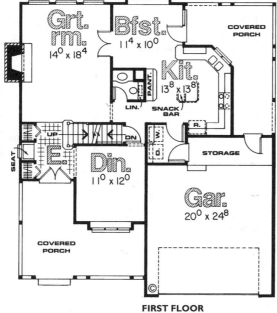

FIRST FLOOR

Units	Single
Price Code	C
Total Finished	1,845 sq. ft.
First Finished	1,327 sq. ft.
Second Finished	518 sq. ft.
Basement Unfinished	1,327 sq. ft.
Garage Unfinished	443 sq. ft.
Dimensions	40'8"x53'
Foundation	Basement
	Crawlspace
Bedrooms	4
Full Baths	2
Half Baths	I
First Ceiling	8'
Max Ridge Height	25'
Roof Framing	Stick
Exterior Walls	2x4

* Alternate foundation options available at an additional charge.
Please call 1-800-235-5700 for more information.

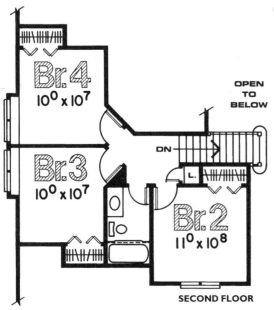

SECOND FLOOR

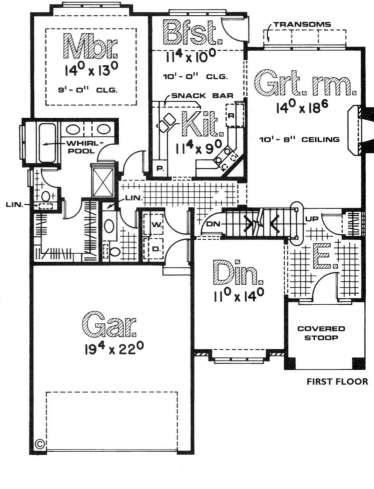

FIRST FLOOR

Units	Single
Price Code	D
Total Finished	2,133 sq. ft.
First Finished	1,099 sq. ft.
Second Finished	1,034 sq. ft.
Basement Unfinished	1,099 sq. ft.
Dimensions	40'8"x44'
Foundation	Basement
Bedrooms	4
Full Baths	2
Half Baths	I
Max Ridge Height	28'
Roof Framing	Truss
Exterior Walls	2x6

BR. #3
11'4" X 10'4"

BR. #2
11'0" X 11'0"

MBR.
13'4" X 15'0"

BR. #4
12'0" X 13'8"

DOWN

OPEN TO
E.

SECOND FLOOR

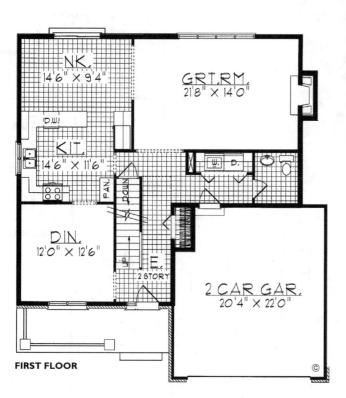

NK.
14'6" X 9'4"

GRT.RM.
21'8" X 14'0"

KIT.
14'6" X 11'6"

D.W.

PAN.

DOWN

UP

E.

2 STORY

DIN.
12'0" X 12'6"

2 CAR GAR.
20'4" X 22'0"

FIRST FLOOR

Design 97201

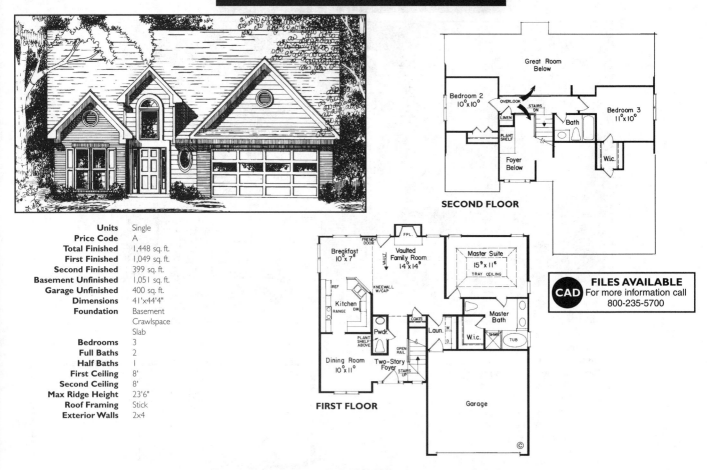

SECOND FLOOR

Great Room Below

Bedroom 2
10⁰x10⁰

OVERLOOK
STAIRS DN

LINEN
PLANT SHELF

Bath

Bedroom 3
11⁰x10⁰

W.i.c.

Foyer Below

Units	Single
Price Code	A
Total Finished	1,448 sq. ft.
First Finished	1,049 sq. ft.
Second Finished	399 sq. ft.
Basement Unfinished	1,051 sq. ft.
Garage Unfinished	400 sq. ft.
Dimensions	41'x44'4"
Foundation	Basement
	Crawlspace
	Slab
Bedrooms	3
Full Baths	2
Half Baths	1
First Ceiling	8'
Second Ceiling	8'
Max Ridge Height	23'6"
Roof Framing	Stick
Exterior Walls	2x4

FPL
FRENCH DOOR

Breakfast
10⁰x7⁰

Vaulted Family Room
14⁰x14⁹

Master Suite
15⁹x11⁶
TRAY CEILING

REF
Kitchen
RANGE
D.W.
KNEEWALL W/CAP

Pwdr.

COATS

Master Bath

PLANT SHELF ABOVE

Laun.
W D

W.i.c.
SHWR
TUB

Dining Room
10⁰x11⁰

Two-Story Foyer

OPEN RAIL

STAIRS UP

FIRST FLOOR

Garage

CAD FILES AVAILABLE For more information call 800-235-5700

Design 97612

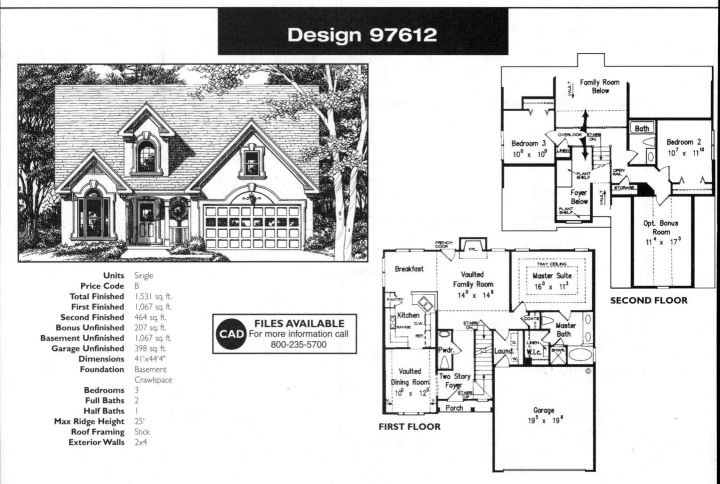

Family Room Below

VAULT

Bedroom 3
10⁰ x 10⁰

OVERLOOK
STAIRS DN

LINEN
PLANT SHELF

Bath

Bedroom 2
10⁷ x 11¹⁰

OPEN RAIL
STORAGE

Foyer Below
VAULT

PLANT SHELF

Opt. Bonus Room
11⁴ x 17⁰

SECOND FLOOR

Units	Single
Price Code	B
Total Finished	1,531 sq. ft.
First Finished	1,067 sq. ft.
Second Finished	464 sq. ft.
Bonus Unfinished	207 sq. ft.
Basement Unfinished	1,067 sq. ft.
Garage Unfinished	398 sq. ft.
Dimensions	41'x44'4"
Foundation	Basement
	Crawlspace
Bedrooms	3
Full Baths	2
Half Baths	1
Max Ridge Height	25'
Roof Framing	Stick
Exterior Walls	2x4

CAD FILES AVAILABLE For more information call 800-235-5700

FRENCH DOOR
FPL

Breakfast

Vaulted Family Room
14⁰ x 14⁹

TRAY CEILING
Master Suite
16⁰ x 11³

PANTRY
Kitchen
RANGE
D.W.
REF.

STAIRS DN

COATS

Master Bath

Pwdr.

Laund.
D W

LINEN
W.i.c.
SHWR

Vaulted Dining Room
10⁰ x 12⁰

Two Story Foyer

STAIRS UP

Porch

Garage
19⁵ x 19⁹

FIRST FLOOR

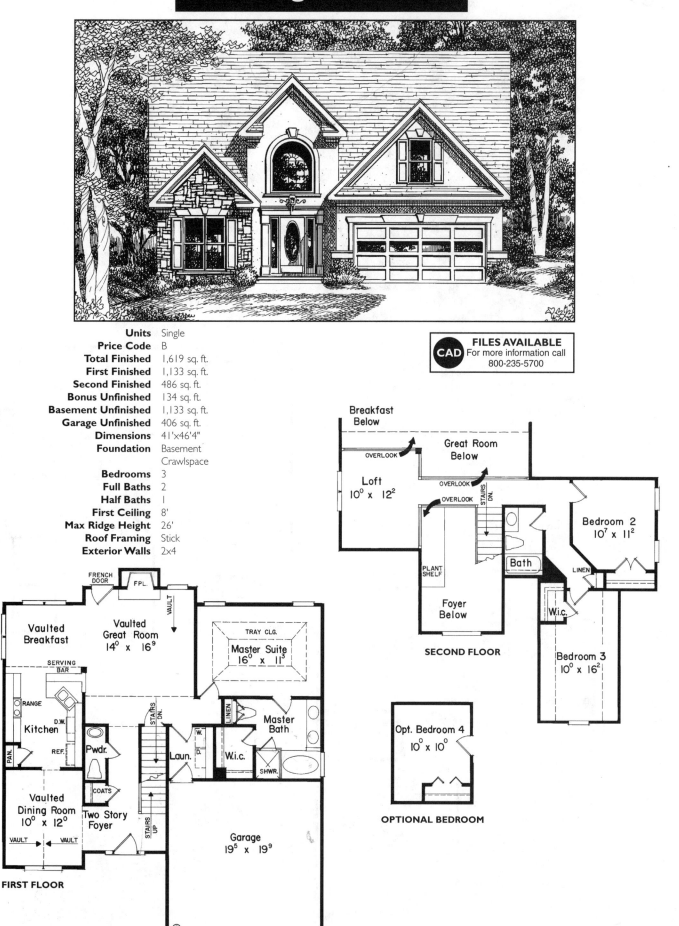

Units	Single
Price Code	B
Total Finished	1,619 sq. ft.
First Finished	1,133 sq. ft.
Second Finished	486 sq. ft.
Bonus Unfinished	134 sq. ft.
Basement Unfinished	1,133 sq. ft.
Garage Unfinished	406 sq. ft.
Dimensions	41'x46'4"
Foundation	Basement Crawlspace
Bedrooms	3
Full Baths	2
Half Baths	1
First Ceiling	8'
Max Ridge Height	26'
Roof Framing	Stick
Exterior Walls	2x4

CAD FILES AVAILABLE
For more information call
800-235-5700

FIRST FLOOR

SECOND FLOOR

OPTIONAL BEDROOM

Design 24268

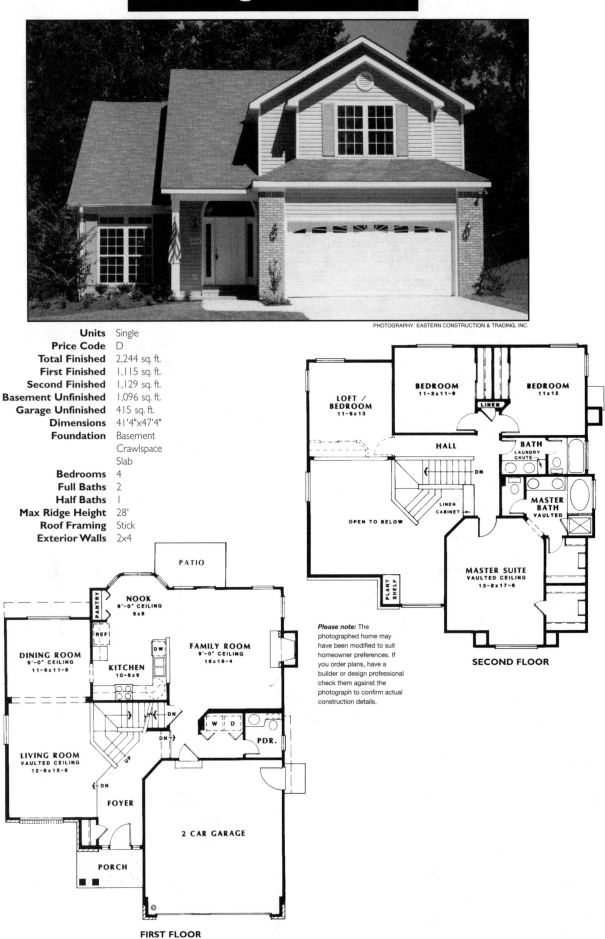

PHOTOGRAPHY: EASTERN CONSTRUCTION & TRADING, INC.

Units	Single
Price Code	D
Total Finished	2,244 sq. ft.
First Finished	1,115 sq. ft.
Second Finished	1,129 sq. ft.
Basement Unfinished	1,096 sq. ft.
Garage Unfinished	415 sq. ft.
Dimensions	41'4"x47'4"
Foundation	Basement Crawlspace Slab
Bedrooms	4
Full Baths	2
Half Baths	1
Max Ridge Height	28'
Roof Framing	Stick
Exterior Walls	2x4

SECOND FLOOR

Please note: The photographed home may have been modified to suit homeowner preferences. If you order plans, have a builder or design professional check them against the photograph to confirm actual construction details.

FIRST FLOOR

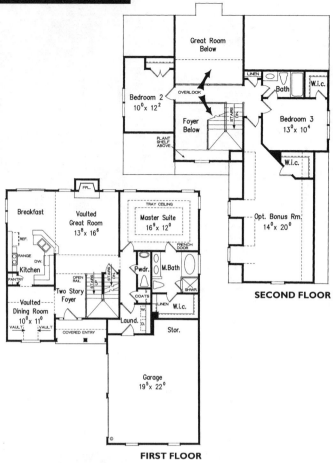

SECOND FLOOR

FIRST FLOOR

Units	Single
Price Code	B
Total Finished	1,639 sq. ft.
First Finished	1,179 sq. ft.
Second Finished	460 sq. ft.
Bonus Unfinished	418 sq. ft.
Basement Unfinished	1,179 sq. ft.
Garage Unfinished	476 sq. ft.
Dimensions	41'6"x54'4"
Foundation	Basement
	Crawlspace
Bedrooms	3
Full Baths	2
Half Baths	1
First Ceiling	9'
Second Ceiling	8'
Max Ridge Height	29'
Roof Framing	Stick
Exterior Walls	2x4

Design 82007

MAIN FLOOR

Units	Single
Price Code	A
Total Finished	1,287 sq. ft.
Main Finished	1,287 sq. ft.
Garage Unfinished	510 sq. ft.
Porch Unfinished	217 sq. ft.
Dimensions	41'10"x59'8"
Foundation	Crawlspace
	Slab
Bedrooms	2
Full Baths	2
Main Ceiling	9'
Roof Framing	Stick
Exterior Walls	2x4

Design 65073

Units	Single
Price Code	A
Total Finished	1,272 sq. ft.
Main Finished	1,272 sq. ft.
Garage Unfinished	274 sq. ft.
Dimensions	42'x42'
Foundation	Basement
Bedrooms	3
Full Baths	1

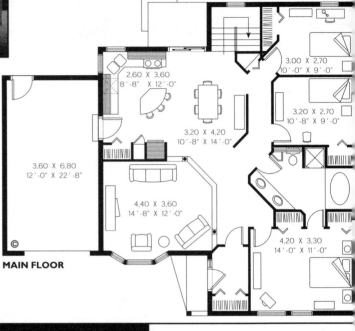

3,60 X 6,80
12'-0" X 22'-8"

2,60 X 3,60
8'-8" X 12'-0"

3,20 X 4,20
10'-8" X 14'-0"

4,40 X 3,60
14'-8" X 12'-0"

3,00 X 2,70
10'-0" X 9'-0"

3,20 X 2,70
10'-8" X 9'-0"

4,20 X 3,30
14'-0" X 11'-0"

MAIN FLOOR

Design 97476

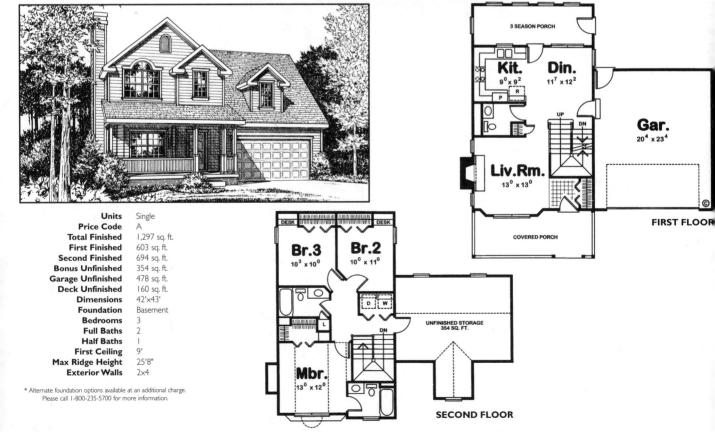

Units	Single
Price Code	A
Total Finished	1,297 sq. ft.
First Finished	603 sq. ft.
Second Finished	694 sq. ft.
Bonus Unfinished	354 sq. ft.
Garage Unfinished	478 sq. ft.
Deck Unfinished	160 sq. ft.
Dimensions	42'x43'
Foundation	Basement
Bedrooms	3
Full Baths	2
Half Baths	1
First Ceiling	9'
Max Ridge Height	25'8"
Exterior Walls	2x4

* Alternate foundation options available at an additional charge.
  Please call 1-800-235-5700 for more information.

3 SEASON PORCH

Kit.
9⁰ x 9²

Din.
11⁷ x 12²

Gar.
20⁴ x 23⁴

UP   DN

Liv.Rm.
13⁰ x 13⁰

COVERED PORCH

FIRST FLOOR

DESK   DESK

Br.3
10³ x 10⁰

Br.2
10⁰ x 11⁰

D W

DN

UNFINISHED STORAGE
354 SQ. FT.

Mbr.
13⁰ x 12⁰

SECOND FLOOR

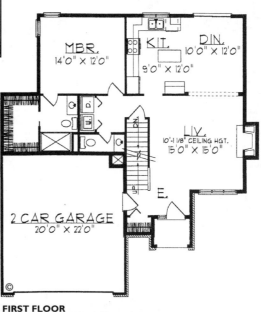

SECOND FLOOR

Units	Single
Price Code	A
Total Finished	1,342 sq. ft.
First Finished	927 sq. ft.
Second Finished	415 sq. ft.
Basement Unfinished	927 sq. ft.
Garage Unfinished	440 sq. ft.
Dimensions	42'x44'
Foundation	Basement
Bedrooms	3
Full Baths	1
3/4 Baths	1
Half Baths	1
First Ceiling	8'
Second Ceiling	8'
Max Ridge Height	25'6"
Roof Framing	Truss
Exterior Walls	2x6

FIRST FLOOR

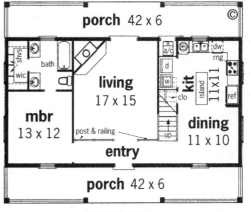

SECOND FLOOR

Units	Single
Price Code	G
Total Finished	1,485 sq. ft.
First Finished	924 sq. ft.
Second Finished	561 sq. ft.
Porch Unfinished	504 sq. ft.
Dimensions	42'x34'
Foundation	Basement
	Crawlspace
	Slab
Bedrooms	3
Full Baths	2
First Ceiling	8'
Second Ceiling	8'
Max Ridge Height	30'
Exterior Walls	2x6

FIRST FLOOR

Design 97999

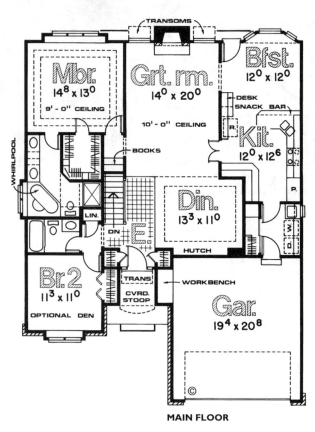

MAIN FLOOR

Units	Single
Price Code	A
Total Finished	1,499 sq. ft.
Main Finished	1,499 sq. ft.
Garage Unfinished	493 sq. ft.
Dimensions	42'x54'
Foundation	Basement
	Crawlspace
	Slab
Bedrooms	2
Full Baths	2
Max Ridge Height	19'7"
Roof Framing	Stick
Exterior Walls	2x4, 2x6

* Alternate foundation options available at an additional charge.
Please call 1-800-235-5700 for more information.

Design 24326

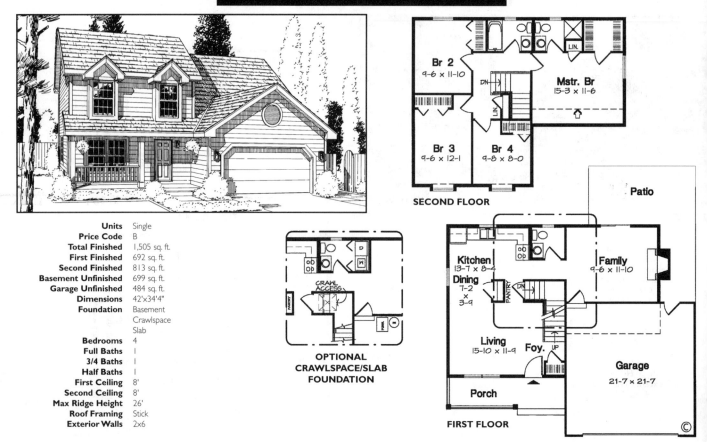

SECOND FLOOR

OPTIONAL CRAWLSPACE/SLAB FOUNDATION

FIRST FLOOR

Units	Single
Price Code	B
Total Finished	1,505 sq. ft.
First Finished	692 sq. ft.
Second Finished	813 sq. ft.
Basement Unfinished	699 sq. ft.
Garage Unfinished	484 sq. ft.
Dimensions	42'x34'4"
Foundation	Basement
	Crawlspace
	Slab
Bedrooms	4
Full Baths	1
3/4 Baths	1
Half Baths	1
First Ceiling	8'
Second Ceiling	8'
Max Ridge Height	26'
Roof Framing	Stick
Exterior Walls	2x6

Design 68032

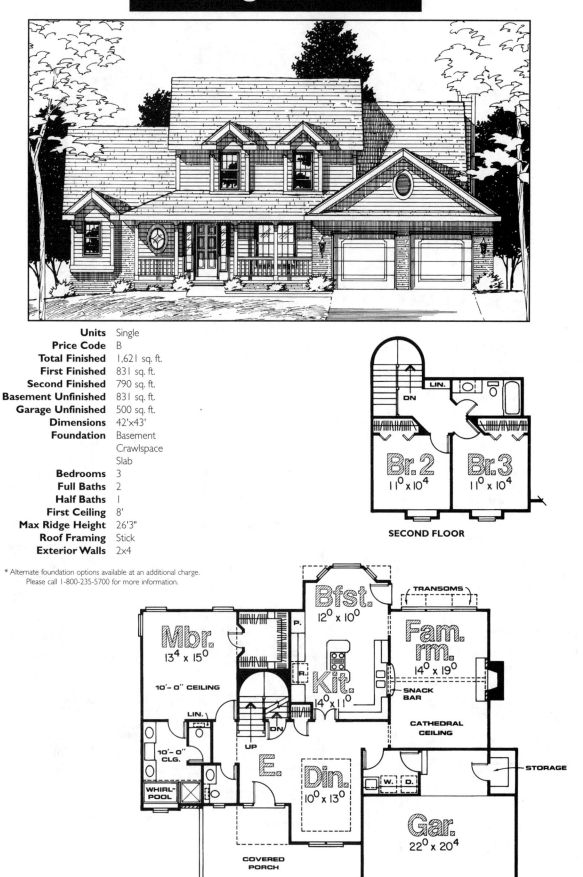

Units	Single
Price Code	B
Total Finished	1,621 sq. ft.
First Finished	831 sq. ft.
Second Finished	790 sq. ft.
Basement Unfinished	831 sq. ft.
Garage Unfinished	500 sq. ft.
Dimensions	42'x43'
Foundation	Basement
	Crawlspace
	Slab
Bedrooms	3
Full Baths	2
Half Baths	1
First Ceiling	8'
Max Ridge Height	26'3"
Roof Framing	Stick
Exterior Walls	2x4

* Alternate foundation options available at an additional charge.
Please call 1-800-235-5700 for more information.

SECOND FLOOR

Br. 2
11⁰ x 10⁴

Br. 3
11⁰ x 10⁴

LIN.

DN

FIRST FLOOR

Mbr.
13⁴ x 15⁰

10'-0" CEILING

10'-0" CLG.

LIN.

WHIRL-POOL

Bfst.
12⁰ x 10⁰

TRANSOMS

Fam. rm.
14⁰ x 19⁰

SNACK BAR

CATHEDRAL CEILING

Kit.
14⁰ x 11⁰

E.

Din.
10⁰ x 13⁰

W.   D.

STORAGE

Gar.
22⁰ x 20⁴

UP   DN

P.

R.

COVERED PORCH

Units	Single
Price Code	C
Total Finished	1,948 sq. ft.
First Finished	1,517 sq. ft.
Second Finished	431 sq. ft.
Basement Unfinished	1,517 sq. ft.
Garage Unfinished	443 sq. ft.
Dimensions	42'x54'
Foundation	Basement
	Crawlspace
	Slab
Bedrooms	4
Full Baths	3
First Ceiling	8'
Max Ridge Height	24'6"
Roof Framing	Stick
Exterior Walls	2x4

* Alternate foundation options available at an additional charge.
Please call 1-800-235-5700 for more information.

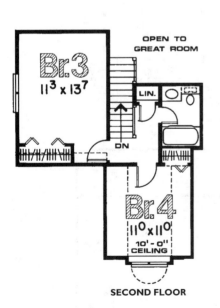

SECOND FLOOR

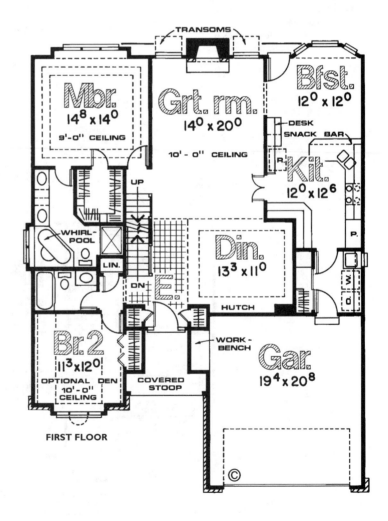

FIRST FLOOR

Design 52197

Units	Single
Price Code	D
Total Finished	2,199 sq. ft.
First Finished	1,053 sq. ft.
Second Finished	1,146 sq. ft.
Basement Unfinished	1,053 sq. ft.
Garage Unfinished	488 sq. ft.
Dimensions	42'x45'4"
Foundation	Basement
	Crawlspace
Bedrooms	4
Full Baths	2
Half Baths	1
First Ceiling	9'
Second Ceiling	8'
Max Ridge Height	31'6"
Roof Framing	Stick
Exterior Walls	2x4

Design 68019

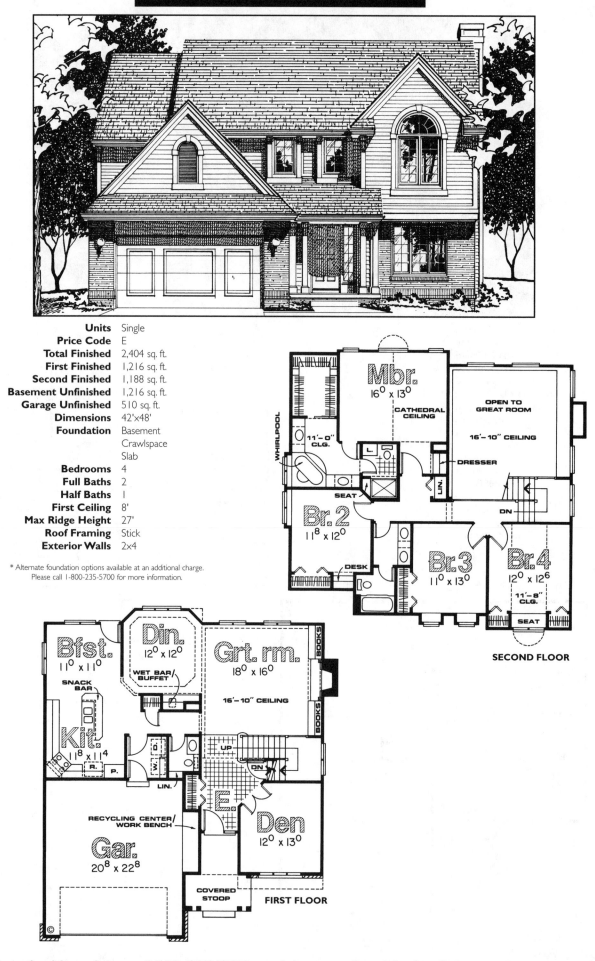

Units	Single
Price Code	E
Total Finished	2,404 sq. ft.
First Finished	1,216 sq. ft.
Second Finished	1,188 sq. ft.
Basement Unfinished	1,216 sq. ft.
Garage Unfinished	510 sq. ft.
Dimensions	42'x48'
Foundation	Basement
	Crawlspace
	Slab
Bedrooms	4
Full Baths	2
Half Baths	1
First Ceiling	8'
Max Ridge Height	27'
Roof Framing	Stick
Exterior Walls	2x4

* Alternate foundation options available at an additional charge.
Please call 1-800-235-5700 for more information.

Mbr.
16⁰ x 13⁰

CATHEDRAL CEILING

OPEN TO GREAT ROOM

16'–10" CEILING

WHIRLPOOL

11'–0" CLG.

DRESSER

LIN.

SEAT

DN

Br. 2
11⁸ x 12⁰

DESK

Br. 3
11⁰ x 13⁰

Br. 4
12⁰ x 12⁶

11'–8" CLG.

SEAT

SECOND FLOOR

Bfst.
11⁰ x 11⁰

Din.
12⁰ x 12⁰

WET BAR/ BUFFET

Grt. rm.
18⁰ x 16⁰

16'–10" CEILING

BOOKS

SNACK BAR

Kit.
11⁸ x 11⁴

UP

DN

D.

W.

LIN.

P.

RECYCLING CENTER/ WORK BENCH

Den
12⁰ x 13⁰

Gar.
20⁸ x 22⁸

COVERED STOOP

FIRST FLOOR

Design 32381

PHOTOGRAPHY: TIM MURPHY, FOTO IMAGERY

Units	Single
Price Code	D
Total Finished	2,699 sq. ft.
First Finished	1,670 sq. ft.
Second Finished	1,029 sq. ft.
Dimensions	42'x60'6"
Foundation	Basement
	Crawlspace
Bedrooms	4
Full Baths	2
3/4 Baths	1
First Ceiling	9'
Second Ceiling	8'
Vaulted Ceiling	29'
Max Ridge Height	31'7"
Exterior Walls	2x6

Please note: The photographed home may have been modified to suit homeowner preferences. If you order plans, have a builder or design professional check them against the photograph to confirm actual construction details.

FIRST FLOOR

MASTER BEDROOM 14x18

BATH

FAMILY 13x14

LIVING 14x12

KIT 9x10

STUDY 14x10

ENTRY

BRKFST 8x10

DINING 10x14

PORCH

SECOND FLOOR

OPEN TO MBR

BEDROOM 11x10

BATH

BEDROOM 13x14

OPEN TO LIVING

LOFT ABOVE

PLAY AREA

OPEN TO STUDY

BEDROOM 17x14

DECK

Design 32045

SECOND FLOOR

Please note: The photographed home may have been modified to suit homeowner preferences. If you order plans, have a builder or design professional check them against the photograph to confirm actual construction details.

Units	Single
Price Code	G
Total Finished	2,980 sq. ft.
First Finished	1,480 sq. ft.
Second Finished	1,500 sq. ft.
Lower Unfinished	760 sq. ft.
Garage Unfinished	720 sq. ft.
Dimensions	42'x41'
Foundation	Basement
Bedrooms	4
Full Baths	2
Half Baths	1
Max Ridge Height	43'
Roof Framing	Stick
Exterior Walls	2x4

LOWER FLOOR

FIRST FLOOR

Design 52192

Units	Single
Price Code	B
Total Finished	1,652 sq. ft.
First Finished	1,192 sq. ft.
Second Finished	460 sq. ft.
Basement Unfinished	1,192 sq. ft.
Garage Unfinished	440 sq. ft.
Dimensions	42'4"x52'
Foundation	Basement
	Crawlspace
Bedrooms	3
Full Baths	2
Half Baths	1
First Ceiling	9'
Second Ceiling	8'
Max Ridge Height	23'6"
Roof Framing	Stick
Exterior Walls	2x4

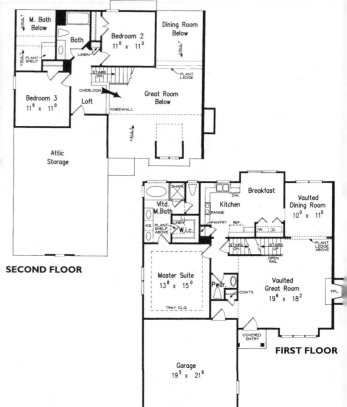

SECOND FLOOR

FIRST FLOOR

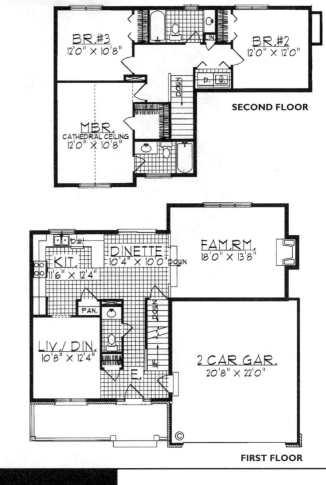

SECOND FLOOR

Units	Single
Price Code	B
Total Finished	1,722 sq. ft.
First Finished	864 sq. ft.
Second Finished	858 sq. ft.
Basement Unfinished	864 sq. ft.
Dimensions	42'8"x36'8"
Foundation	Basement
Bedrooms	3
Full Baths	2
Half Baths	1
Max Ridge Height	24'4"
Roof Framing	Stick
Exterior Walls	2x6

FIRST FLOOR

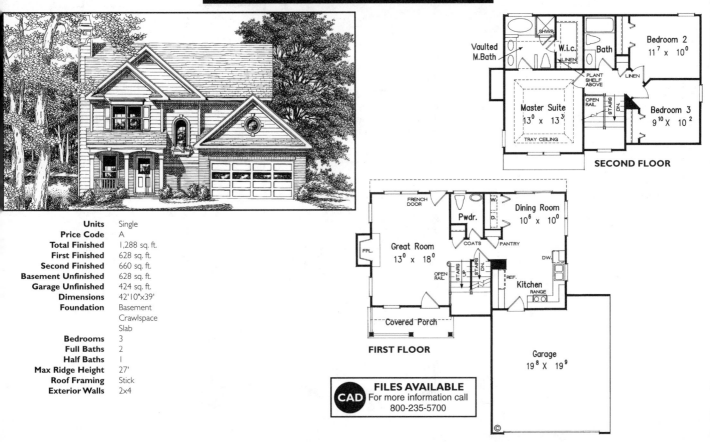

Units	Single
Price Code	A
Total Finished	1,288 sq. ft.
First Finished	628 sq. ft.
Second Finished	660 sq. ft.
Basement Unfinished	628 sq. ft.
Garage Unfinished	424 sq. ft.
Dimensions	42'10"x39'
Foundation	Basement
	Crawlspace
	Slab
Bedrooms	3
Full Baths	2
Half Baths	1
Max Ridge Height	27'
Roof Framing	Stick
Exterior Walls	2x4

SECOND FLOOR

FIRST FLOOR

CAD FILES AVAILABLE
For more information call
800-235-5700

Design 94671

Units	Single
Price Code	G
Total Finished	2,807 sq. ft.
First Finished	2,441 sq. ft.
Second Finished	366 sq. ft.
Garage Unfinished	545 sq. ft.
Porch Unfinished	116 sq. ft.
Dimensions	42'10"x92'11"
Foundation	Slab
Bedrooms	3
Full Baths	2
First Ceiling	9'
Second Ceiling	8'
Max Ridge Height	29'7"
Roof Framing	Stick
Exterior Walls	2x4

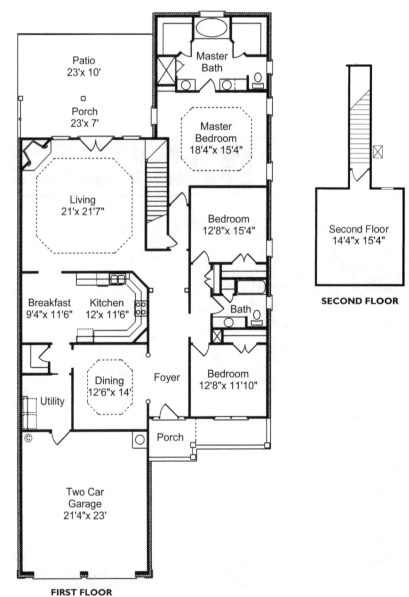

Patio 23'x 10'

Master Bath

Porch 23'x 7'

Master Bedroom 18'4"x 15'4"

Living 21'x 21'7"

Bedroom 12'8"x 15'4"

Breakfast 9'4"x 11'6"

Kitchen 12'x 11'6"

Bath

Dining 12'6"x 14'

Foyer

Bedroom 12'8"x 11'10"

Utility

Porch

Two Car Garage 21'4"x 23'

FIRST FLOOR

Second Floor 14'4"x 15'4"

SECOND FLOOR

Design 96511

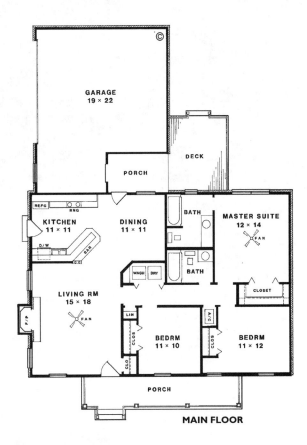

Units	Single
Price Code	A
Total Finished	1,247 sq. ft.
Main Finished	1,247 sq. ft.
Garage Unfinished	512 sq. ft.
Dimensions	43'x60'
Foundation	Crawlspace
	Slab
Bedrooms	3
Full Baths	2
Main Ceiling	8'
Max Ridge Height	19'
Roof Framing	Stick
Exterior Walls	2x4

MAIN FLOOR

GARAGE 19 × 22
DECK
PORCH
REFG / RNG
KITCHEN 11 × 11
DINING 11 × 11
BATH
MASTER SUITE 12 × 14
FAN
D/W BAR
CLOSET
WASH DRY
BATH
LIVING RM 15 × 18
F/P FAN
LIN
BEDRM 11 × 10
CLOS
CLOS
BEDRM 11 × 12
PORCH

Design 93447

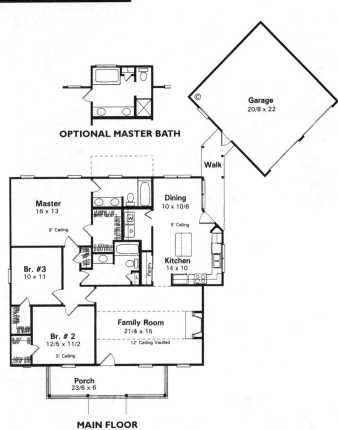

Units	Single
Price Code	A
Total Finished	1,474 sq. ft.
Main Finished	1,474 sq. ft.
Garage Unfinished	454 sq. ft.
Deck Unfinished	72 sq. ft.
Porch Unfinished	142 sq. ft.
Dimensions	43'x42'6"
Foundation	Crawlspace
	Slab
Bedrooms	3
Full Baths	2
Main Ceiling	9'
Max Ridge Height	22'
Roof Framing	Stick
Exterior Walls	2x4

OPTIONAL MASTER BATH

Garage 20/8 x 22
Walk
Master 16 x 13
9' Ceiling
Dining 10 x 10/6
9' Ceiling
Br. #3 10 x 11
Kitchen 14 x 10
Pantry
Family Room 21/4 x 15
12' Ceiling Vaulted
Br. # 2 12/5 x 11/2
9' Ceiling
Porch 23/6 x 6

MAIN FLOOR

Design 93416

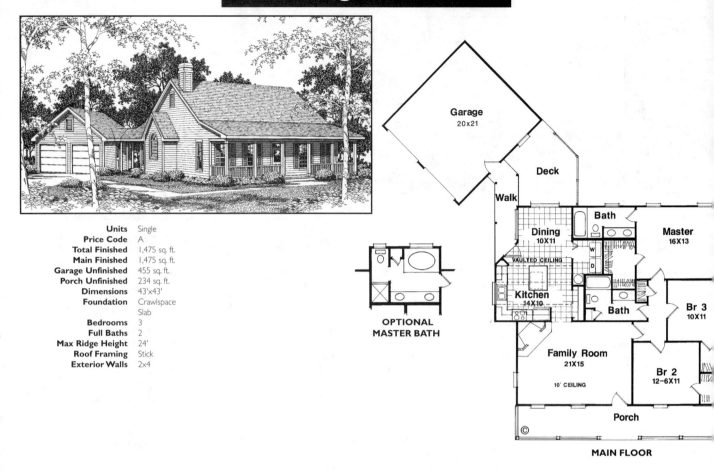

Units	Single
Price Code	A
Total Finished	1,475 sq. ft.
Main Finished	1,475 sq. ft.
Garage Unfinished	455 sq. ft.
Porch Unfinished	234 sq. ft.
Dimensions	43'x43'
Foundation	Crawlspace
	Slab
Bedrooms	3
Full Baths	2
Max Ridge Height	24'
Roof Framing	Stick
Exterior Walls	2x4

Garage 20x21

Deck

Walk

Bath

Dining 10X11

VAULTED CEILING

Kitchen 14X10

Master 16X13

Bath

Br 3 10X11

Family Room 21X15

10' CEILING

Br 2 12-6X11

Porch

OPTIONAL MASTER BATH

MAIN FLOOR

Design 32194

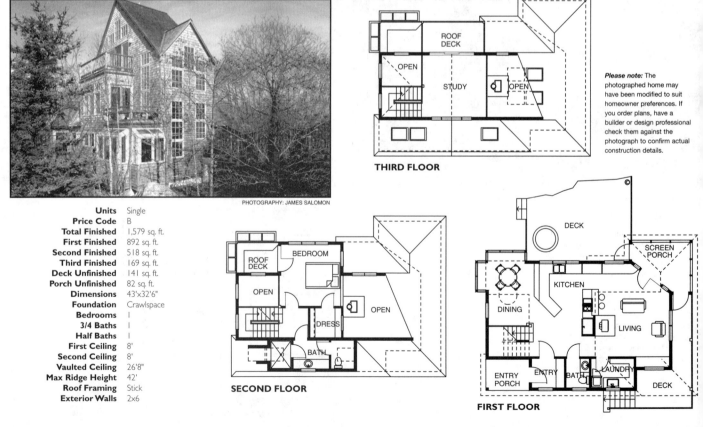

PHOTOGRAPHY: JAMES SALOMON

Units	Single
Price Code	B
Total Finished	1,579 sq. ft.
First Finished	892 sq. ft.
Second Finished	518 sq. ft.
Third Finished	169 sq. ft.
Deck Unfinished	141 sq. ft.
Porch Unfinished	82 sq. ft.
Dimensions	43'x32'6"
Foundation	Crawlspace
Bedrooms	1
3/4 Baths	1
Half Baths	1
First Ceiling	8'
Second Ceiling	8'
Vaulted Ceiling	26'8"
Max Ridge Height	42'
Roof Framing	Stick
Exterior Walls	2x6

ROOF DECK

OPEN

STUDY

OPEN

THIRD FLOOR

Please note: The photographed home may have been modified to suit homeowner preferences. If you order plans, have a builder or design professional check them against the photograph to confirm actual construction details.

ROOF DECK

BEDROOM

OPEN

OPEN

DRESS

BATH

SECOND FLOOR

DECK

SCREEN PORCH

KITCHEN

DINING

LIVING

ENTRY PORCH

ENTRY

BATH

LAUNDRY

DECK

FIRST FLOOR

To order blueprints, call **800-235-5700** or visit us on the web, **familyhomeplans.com**

Design 20093

PHOTOGRAPHY: JOHN EHRENCLOU

Units	Single
Price Code	D
Total Finished	2,001 sq. ft.
First Finished	1,027 sq. ft.
Second Finished	974 sq. ft.
Basement Unfinished	978 sq. ft.
Garage Unfinished	476 sq. ft.
Dimensions	43'x56'
Foundation	Basement
Bedrooms	3
Full Baths	2
Half Baths	1
Max Ridge Height	34'
Roof Framing	Stick
Exterior Walls	2x6

Please note: The photographed home may have been modified to suit homeowner preferences. If you order plans, have a builder or design professional check them against the photograph to confirm actual construction details.

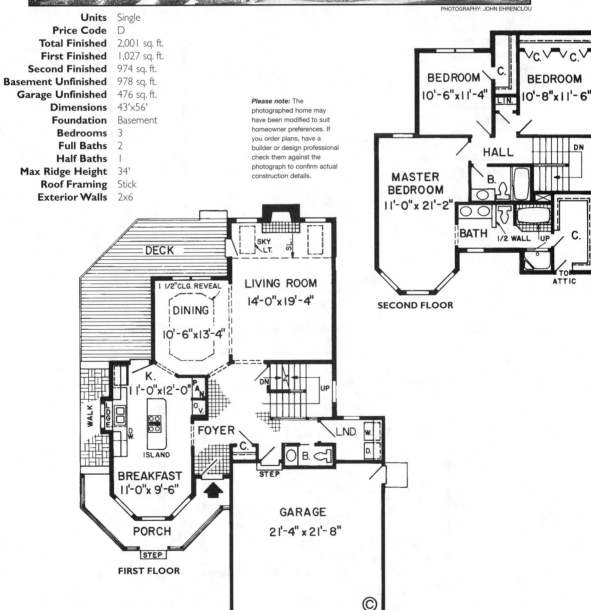

Design 91592

PHOTOGRAPHY: BOB GREENSPAN, BOB GREENSPAN PHOTOGRAPHY

Units	Single
Price Code	E
Total Finished	2,287 sq. ft.
First Finished	1,371 sq. ft.
Second Finished	916 sq. ft.
Garage Unfinished	427 sq. ft.
Porch Unfinished	864 sq. ft.
Dimensions	43'x69'
Foundation	Crawlspace
Bedrooms	3
Full Baths	2
Half Baths	1
Max Ridge Height	35'
Roof Framing	Stick
Exterior Walls	2x6

SECOND FLOOR

BR. 3
10/6 X 13/0

PLANT SHELF

FAMILY BELOW

BR. 2
12/4 X 11/0

LINEN

DN.

VAULTED
MASTER
12/0 X 15/0 +

Please note: The photographed home may have been modified to suit homeowner preferences. If you order plans, have a builder or design professional check them against the photograph to confirm actual construction details.

GARAGE
21/4 X 20/0

NOOK
10/6 X 13/0
(9' CLG.)

W   D.

REF.

10/6 X 13/0

FAMILY
15/0 X 16/4 +/-
(9' CLG.)

DESK

DINING
12/0 X 10/0
(9' CLG.)

UP

FOYER

LIVING
14/0 X 11/0 +/-
(9' CLG.)

DEN
14/0 X 10/0 +
(9' CLG.)

FIRST FLOOR

Design 98931

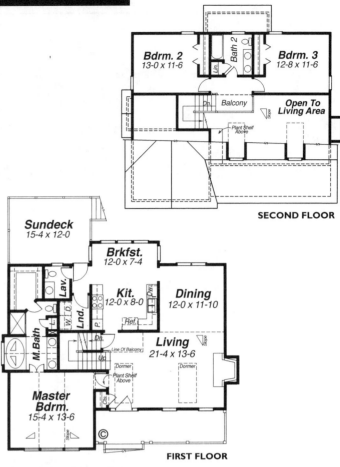

SECOND FLOOR

Bdrm. 2
13-0 x 11-6

Bath 2

Bdrm. 3
12-8 x 11-6

Dn. Balcony

Open To
Living Area

Plant Shelf
Above

Sundeck
15-4 x 12-0

Brkfst.
12-0 x 7-4

Lav.

Kit.
12-0 x 8-0

Dining
12-0 x 11-10

Ref.

W.D.

Lnd.

P.

Dn.

Line Of Balcony

Living
21-4 x 13-6

M.Bath

Up

Dormer

Dormer

Plant Shelf
Above

Master
Bdrm.
15-4 x 13-6

FIRST FLOOR

Units	Single
Price Code	C
Total Finished	1,765 sq. ft.
First Finished	1,210 sq. ft.
Second Finished	555 sq. ft.
Garage Unfinished	612 sq. ft.
Deck Unfinished	184 sq. ft.
Porch Unfinished	144 sq. ft.
Dimensions	43'4"x37'
Foundation	Basement
Bedrooms	3
Full Baths	2
Half Baths	1
Max Ridge Height	27'
Roof Framing	Stick
Exterior Walls	2×6

Design 34003

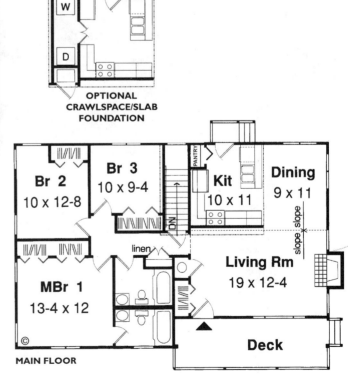

W

D

**OPTIONAL
CRAWLSPACE/SLAB
FOUNDATION**

Br 2
10 x 12-8

Br 3
10 x 9-4

PANTRY

Kit
10 x 11

Dining
9 x 11

DN

linen

slope slope

MBr 1
13-4 x 12

Living Rm
19 x 12-4

Deck

MAIN FLOOR

Units	Single
Price Code	A
Total Finished	1,146 sq. ft.
Main Finished	1,146 sq. ft.
Dimensions	44'x28'
Foundation	Basement
	Crawlspace
	Slab
Bedrooms	3
Full Baths	2
Main Ceiling	8'
Max Ridge Height	16'
Roof Framing	Stick
Exterior Walls	2x4, 2x6

Design 65638

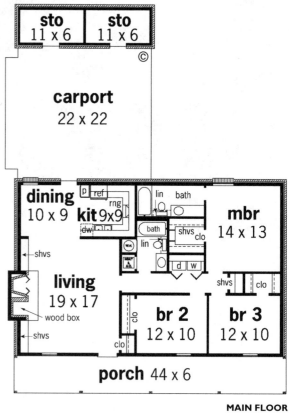

Units	Single
Price Code	A
Total Finished	1,244 sq. ft.
Main Finished	1,244 sq. ft.
Dimensions	44'x62'
Foundation	Crawlspace
	Slab
Bedrooms	3
Full Baths	2
Main Ceiling	8'
Max Ridge Height	26'
Roof Framing	Stick
Exterior Walls	2x6

sto 11 x 6 **sto** 11 x 6

carport 22 x 22

dining 10 x 9 **kit** 9x9 **mbr** 14 x 13

bath bath lin lin

living 19 x 17 wood box

br 2 12 x 10 **br 3** 12 x 10

porch 44 x 6

MAIN FLOOR

Design 98549

Units	Single
Price Code	A
Total Finished	1,431 sq. ft.
Main Finished	1,431 sq. ft.
Garage Unfinished	410 sq. ft.
Deck Unfinished	110 sq. ft.
Dimensions	44'x57'1"
Foundation	Slab
Bedrooms	3
Full Baths	2
Max Ridge Height	23'2"
Roof Framing	Stick
Exterior Walls	2x4

Patio

MstrBed 12 x15 Cathedral Clg.

Walk-in Closet Sloped Clg.

Din 11 x 9 Cathedral Clg.

LivRm 19x17 10'-0" Clg.

Bed#3 11 x11

Kit 11x10 Cathedral Clg.

Util Pantry

T.V. Linen

Bed#2 12 x11 Sloped Clg. From 8'-0" to 10'-0"

Stoop **Por.**

Gar 19x21 8'-4" Clg.

MAIN FLOOR

Units	Single
Price Code	A
Total Finished	1,492 sq. ft.
First Finished	856 sq. ft.
Second Finished	636 sq. ft.
Dimensions	44'x26'
Foundation	Basement
Bedrooms	3
Full Baths	1
Half Baths	1
Max Ridge Height	31'9"
Roof Framing	Stick
Exterior Walls	2x6

SECOND FLOOR

FIRST FLOOR

Design 94938

PHOTOGRAPHY: COURTESY OF THE DESIGNER

Units	Single
Price Code	B
Total Finished	1,650 sq. ft.
First Finished	891 sq. ft.
Second Finished	759 sq. ft.
Basement Unfinished	891 sq. ft.
Garage Unfinished	484 sq. ft.
Dimensions	44'x40'
Foundation	Basement
Bedrooms	3
Full Baths	2
Half Baths	1
Max Ridge Height	25'6"
Roof Framing	Stick
Exterior Walls	2x4

* Alternate foundation options available at an additional charge.
Please call 1-800-235-5700 for more information.

Please note: The photographed home may have been modified to suit homeowner preferences. If you order plans, have a builder or design professional check them against the photograph to confirm actual construction details.

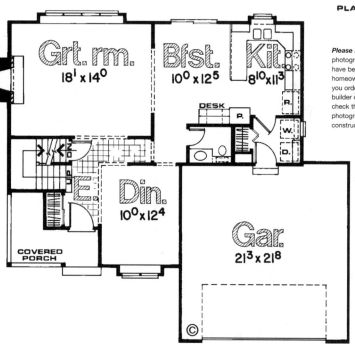

FIRST FLOOR

SECOND FLOOR

Design 91418

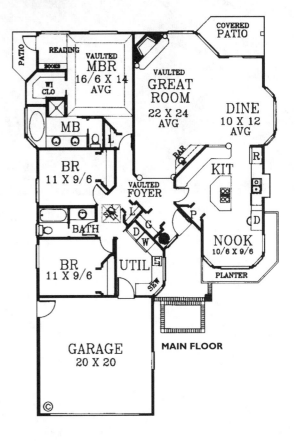

MAIN FLOOR

Units	Single
Price Code	B
Total Finished	1,665 sq. ft.
Main Finished	1,665 sq. ft.
Dimensions	44'x65'
Foundation	Basement
	Crawlspace
	Slab
Bedrooms	3
Full Baths	2
Max Ridge Height	21'
Roof Framing	Stick/Truss
Exterior Walls	2x6

OPTIONAL BASEMENT STAIR LOCATION

Design 93298

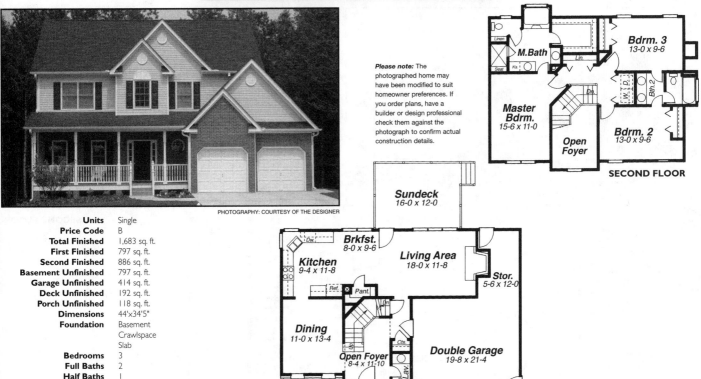

PHOTOGRAPHY: COURTESY OF THE DESIGNER

Please note: The photographed home may have been modified to suit homeowner preferences. If you order plans, have a builder or design professional check them against the photograph to confirm actual construction details.

SECOND FLOOR

FIRST FLOOR

Units	Single
Price Code	B
Total Finished	1,683 sq. ft.
First Finished	797 sq. ft.
Second Finished	886 sq. ft.
Basement Unfinished	797 sq. ft.
Garage Unfinished	414 sq. ft.
Deck Unfinished	192 sq. ft.
Porch Unfinished	118 sq. ft.
Dimensions	44'x34'5"
Foundation	Basement
	Crawlspace
	Slab
Bedrooms	3
Full Baths	2
Half Baths	1
Max Ridge Height	29'
Roof Framing	Stick
Exterior Walls	2x4

Design 99491

PHOTOGRAPHY: COURTESY OF THE DESIGNER

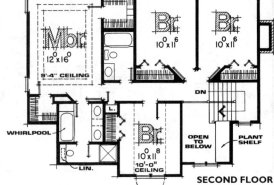

SECOND FLOOR

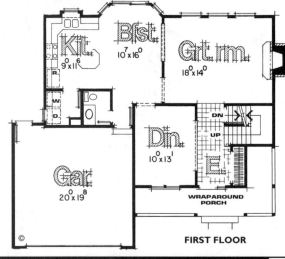

FIRST FLOOR

Units	Single
Price Code	C
Total Finished	1,846 sq. ft.
First Finished	919 sq. ft.
Second Finished	927 sq. ft.
Garage Unfinished	414 sq. ft.
Dimensions	44'x40'
Foundation	Basement
	Slab
Bedrooms	4
Full Baths	2
Half Baths	1
Max Ridge Height	26'10"
Roof Framing	Stick
Exterior Walls	2x4

* Alternate foundation options available at an additional charge.
Please call 1-800-235-5700 for more information.

Please note: The photographed home may have been modified to suit homeowner preferences. If you order plans, have a builder or design professional check them against the photograph to confirm actual construction details.

Design 94248

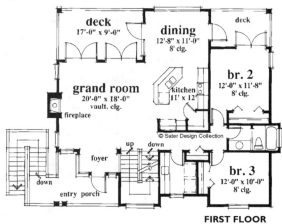

SECOND FLOOR

FIRST FLOOR

Units	Single
Price Code	D
Total Finished	1,853 sq. ft.
First Finished	1,342 sq. ft.
Second Finished	511 sq. ft.
Garage Unfinished	1,740 sq. ft.
Dimensions	44'x40'
Foundation	Pier/Post
Bedrooms	3
Full Baths	2
First Ceiling	8'
Second Ceiling	8'
Max Ridge Height	37'
Roof Framing	Stick
Exterior Walls	2x6

* Alternate foundation options available at an additional charge.
Please call 1-800-235-5700 for more information.

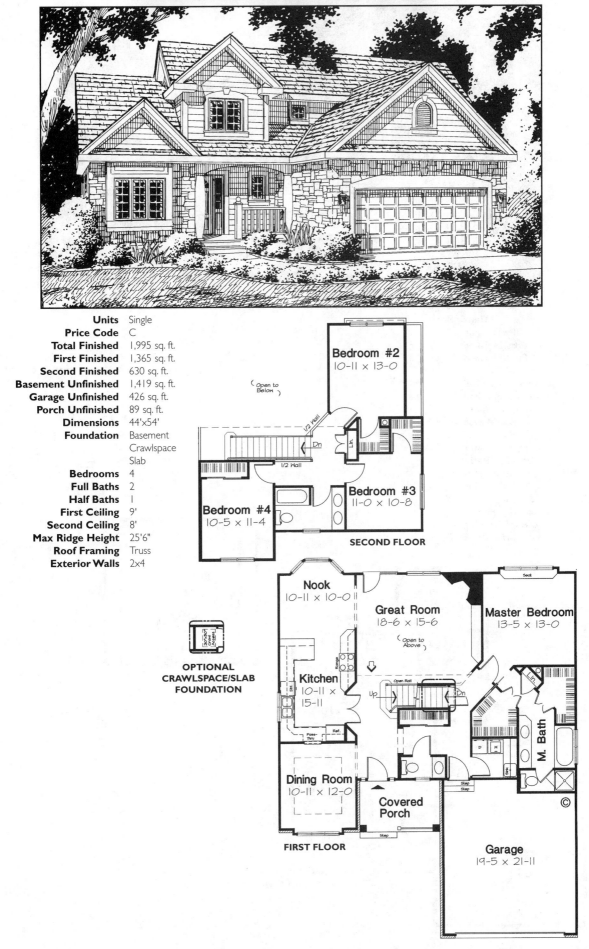

Units	Single
Price Code	C
Total Finished	1,995 sq. ft.
First Finished	1,365 sq. ft.
Second Finished	630 sq. ft.
Basement Unfinished	1,419 sq. ft.
Garage Unfinished	426 sq. ft.
Porch Unfinished	89 sq. ft.
Dimensions	44'x54'
Foundation	Basement
	Crawlspace
	Slab
Bedrooms	4
Full Baths	2
Half Baths	1
First Ceiling	9'
Second Ceiling	8'
Max Ridge Height	25'6"
Roof Framing	Truss
Exterior Walls	2x4

OPTIONAL
CRAWLSPACE/SLAB
FOUNDATION

Bedroom #2
10-11 x 13-0

Open to Below

Dn

Ln.

Bedroom #4
10-5 x 11-4

Bedroom #3
11-0 x 10-8

SECOND FLOOR

Nook
10-11 x 10-0

Great Room
18-6 x 15-6

Master Bedroom
13-5 x 13-0

Open to Above

Kitchen
10-11 x 15-11

Up

Dn

M. Bath

Ln.

Dining Room
10-11 x 12-0

Covered Porch

Garage
19-5 x 21-11

FIRST FLOOR

Units	Single
Price Code	D
Total Finished	2,082 sq. ft.
First Finished	1,218 sq. ft.
Second Finished	864 sq. ft.
Garage Unfinished	472 sq. ft.
Porch Unfinished	118 sq. ft.
Dimensions	44'x51'
Foundation	Crawlspace
	Slab
Bedrooms	3
Full Baths	2
Half Baths	1
First Ceiling	9'
Second Ceiling	8'
Max Ridge Height	28'
Roof Framing	Truss
Exterior Walls	2x4

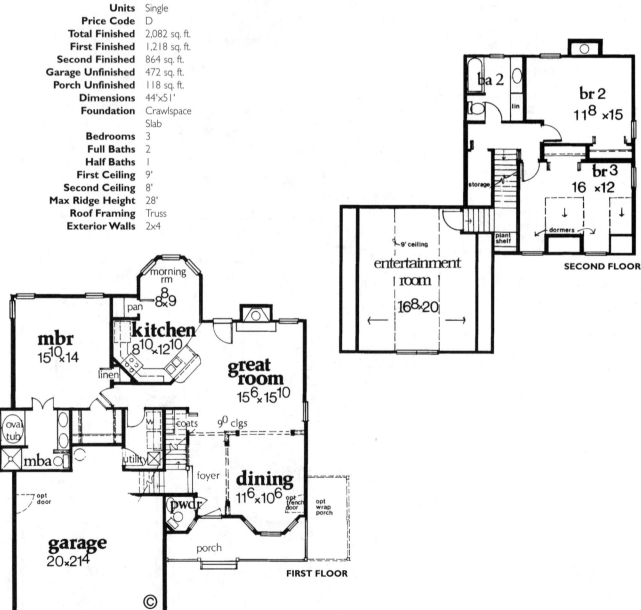

Design 65131

Units	Duplex
Price Code	D
Total Finished	2,172 sq. ft.
First Finished	1,086 sq. ft.
Second Finished	1,086 sq. ft.
Dimensions	44'x28'8"
Foundation	Basement
Bedrooms	3
Full Baths	1
Half Baths	1
First Ceiling	8'
Second Ceiling	8'
Max Ridge Height	25'11"
Roof Framing	Truss
Exterior Walls	2x6

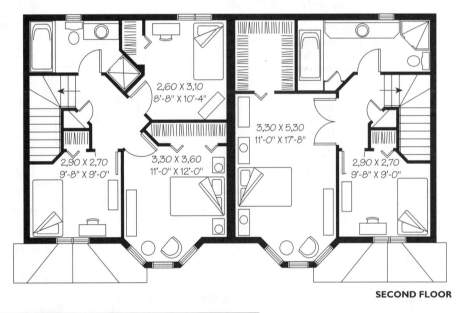

SECOND FLOOR

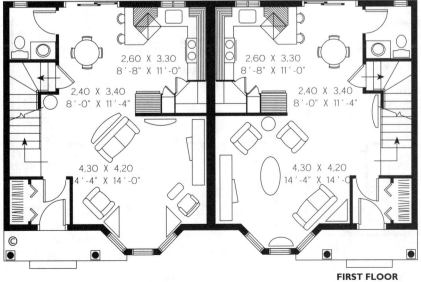

FIRST FLOOR

Units	Single
Price Code	H
Total Finished	2,374 sq. ft.
First Finished	1,510 sq. ft.
Second Finished	864 sq. ft.
Basement Unfinished	1,290 sq. ft.
Deck Unfinished	275 sq. ft.
Porch Unfinished	275 sq. ft.
Dimensions	44'x49'
Foundation	Basement
Bedrooms	3
Full Baths	3
Half Baths	I
Max Ridge Height	43'4"
Roof Framing	Truss
Exterior Walls	2x6

* Alternate foundation options available at an additional charge.
Please call 1-800-235-5700 for more information.

SECOND FLOOR

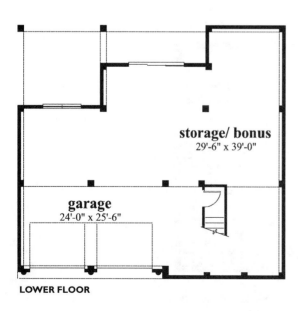

LOWER FLOOR

FIRST FLOOR

Units	Single
Price Code	H
Total Finished	2,374 sq. ft.
First Finished	1,510 sq. ft.
Second Finished	864 sq. ft.
Bonus Unfinished	1,290 sq. ft.
Deck Unfinished	275 sq. ft.
Porch Unfinished	275 sq. ft.
Dimensions	44'x49'
Foundation	Basement
Bedrooms	3
Full Baths	3
Half Baths	1
Max Ridge Height	43'4"
Roof Framing	Truss
Exterior Walls	2x6

*Alternate foundation options available at an additional charge.
Please call 1-800-235-5700 for more information.*

SECOND FLOOR

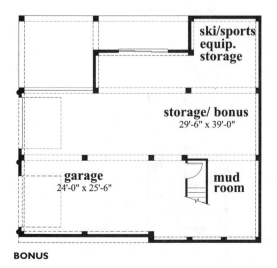

BONUS

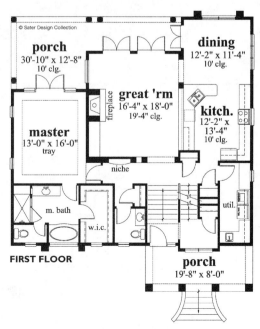

FIRST FLOOR

Design 91107

MAIN FLOOR

Units	Single
Price Code	A
Total Finished	1,199 sq. ft.
Main Finished	1,199 sq. ft.
Garage Unfinished	484 sq. ft.
Porch Unfinished	34 sq. ft.
Dimensions	44'2"x42'6¾"
Foundation	Slab
Bedrooms	3
Full Baths	2
Main Ceiling	8'
Vaulted Ceiling	11'
Max Ridge Height	18'
Roof Framing	Stick
Exterior Walls	2x4

Floor plan labels: Closet, Bath, Books, Mbr 12-0 × 13-0 11'-0" Ceiling Ht., F/P, Din 9-4 × 9-2, Liv 15-2 × 18-6 11'-0" Ceiling Ht., Snack bar, Pot Shelf Above, Kit 9-0 × 9-0, Ref, DW, Pan, Cl, Br #3 10-0 × 10-0, Entry, Hall, Bath, Lin, W D, Porch, Storage, Gar 20-0 × 23-0, Optional Side Load, Br #2 11-0 × 10-6

Design 93413

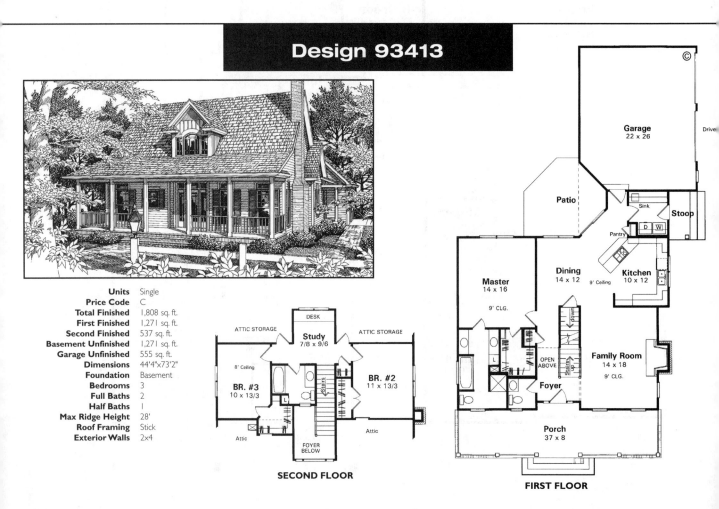

SECOND FLOOR

FIRST FLOOR

Units	Single
Price Code	C
Total Finished	1,808 sq. ft.
First Finished	1,271 sq. ft.
Second Finished	537 sq. ft.
Basement Unfinished	1,271 sq. ft.
Garage Unfinished	555 sq. ft.
Dimensions	44'4"x73'2"
Foundation	Basement
Bedrooms	3
Full Baths	2
Half Baths	1
Max Ridge Height	28'
Roof Framing	Stick
Exterior Walls	2x4

Second floor labels: ATTIC STORAGE, DESK, Study 7/8 × 9/6, ATTIC STORAGE, 8' Ceiling, BR. #3 10 × 13/3, Stairs, BR. #2 11 × 13/3, Attic, Attic, FOYER BELOW

First floor labels: Garage 22 x 26, Drive, Patio, Sink, Stoop, Pantry, D W, Master 14 x 16 9' CLG., Dining 14 x 12 9' ceiling, Kitchen 10 x 12, Down, Up, Open Above, Stairs, Foyer, Family Room 14 x 18 9' CLG., Porch 37 x 8

Design 68031

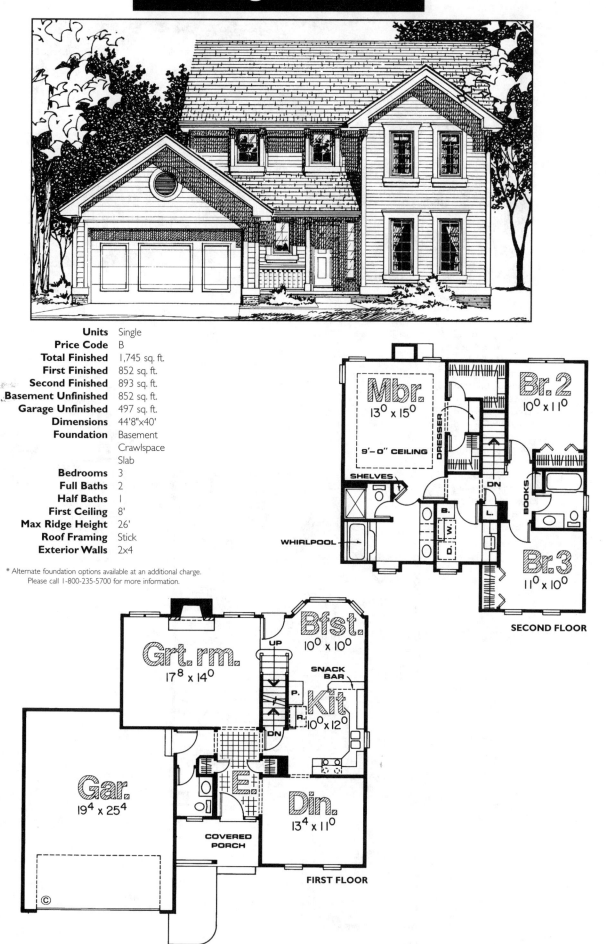

Units	Single
Price Code	B
Total Finished	1,745 sq. ft.
First Finished	852 sq. ft.
Second Finished	893 sq. ft.
Basement Unfinished	852 sq. ft.
Garage Unfinished	497 sq. ft.
Dimensions	44'8"x40'
Foundation	Basement
	Crawlspace
	Slab
Bedrooms	3
Full Baths	2
Half Baths	1
First Ceiling	8'
Max Ridge Height	26'
Roof Framing	Stick
Exterior Walls	2x4

* Alternate foundation options available at an additional charge.
   Please call 1-800-235-5700 for more information.

SECOND FLOOR

Mbr. 13⁰ x 15⁰ 9'-0" CEILING SHELVES WHIRLPOOL DRESSER B. D. W. DN L. BOOKS

Br. 2 10⁰ x 11⁰

Br. 3 11⁰ x 10⁰

Grt. rm. 17⁸ x 14⁰

Bfst. 10⁰ x 10⁰ SNACK BAR

Kit. 10⁰ x 12⁰

Gar. 19⁴ x 25⁴

Din. 13⁴ x 11⁰

COVERED PORCH

FIRST FLOOR

UP DN P. R.

Units	Single
Price Code	D
Total Finished	2,088 sq. ft.
Main Finished	2,088 sq. ft.
Bonus Unfinished	320 sq. ft.
Garage Unfinished	520 sq. ft.
Deck Unfinished	140 sq. ft.
Porch Unfinished	42 sq. ft.
Dimensions	44'10"x79'10"
Foundation	Slab
Bedrooms	3
Full Baths	2
Main Ceiling	9'-10'
Max Ridge Height	27'6"
Roof Framing	Stick
Exterior Walls	2x4

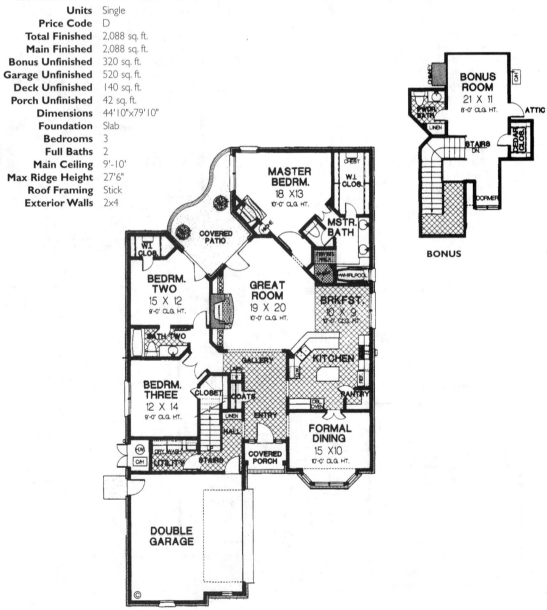

Design 66050

Units	Single
Price Code	D
Total Finished	2,168 sq. ft.
Main Finished	2,168 sq. ft.
Bonus Unfinished	308 sq. ft.
Garage Unfinished	472 sq. ft.
Deck Unfinished	85 sq. ft.
Dimensions	44'10"x79'10"
Foundation	Slab
Bedrooms	3
Full Baths	2
Main Ceiling	9'
Second Ceiling	10'
Max Ridge Height	24'6"
Roof Framing	Stick
Exterior Walls	2x4

BONUS

MAIN FLOOR

Design 93265

Units	Single
Price Code	A
Total Finished	1,325 sq. ft.
Main Finished	1,269 sq. ft.
Lower Finished	56 sq. ft.
Bonus Unfinished	382 sq. ft.
Garage Unfinished	598 sq. ft.
Deck Unfinished	140 sq. ft.
Dimensions	45'x36'
Foundation	Basement
Bedrooms	3
Full Baths	2
Max Ridge Height	16'
Roof Framing	Stick/Truss
Exterior Walls	2x4

LOWER FLOOR

Design 82005

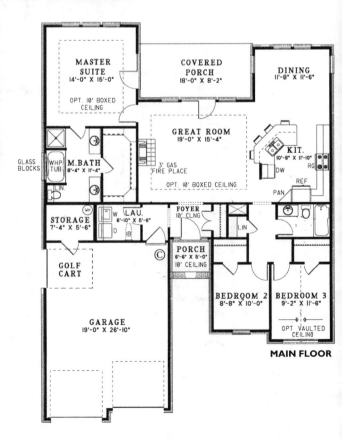

Units	Single
Price Code	A
Total Finished	1,472 sq. ft.
Main Finished	1,472 sq. ft.
Garage Unfinished	510 sq. ft.
Porch Unfinished	231 sq. ft.
Dimensions	45'x60'4"
Foundation	Crawlspace
	Slab
Bedrooms	3
Full Baths	2
Main Ceiling	9'
Roof Framing	Stick
Exterior Walls	2x4

Design 99168

SECOND FLOOR

BR. #2
10'10" × 12'0"

BR. #3
12'2" × 10'8"

LIN.

Units	Single
Price Code	B
Total Finished	1,556 sq. ft.
First Finished	1,126 sq. ft.
Second Finished	430 sq. ft.
Basement Unfinished	1,126 sq. ft.
Garage Unfinished	469 sq. ft.
Dimensions	45'x46'
Foundation	Basement
Bedrooms	3
Full Baths	2
Half Baths	1
Max Ridge Height	29'8"
Roof Framing	Truss
Exterior Walls	2x6

MBR.
14'8" × 14'0"

KIT.
10'0" × 12'0"

DIN.
10'-1 1/8" CLG. HGT.
11'0" × 12'0"

LIV.
10'-1 1/8" CLG. HGT.
17'0" × 14'8"

E.
10'-1 1/8" CLG. HGT.

2 CAR GAR.
20'6" × 21'6"

FIRST FLOOR

Design 96524

SECOND FLOOR

BED RM.
12x11

BATH

BED RM.
12x11

LANDING

BED RM.
13x11

CLOSET

ACCESS

DOWN

Units	Single
Price Code	B
Total Finished	1,705 sq. ft.
First Finished	1,056 sq. ft.
Second Finished	649 sq. ft.
Garage Unfinished	562 sq. ft.
Porch Unfinished	162 sq. ft.
Dimensions	45'x45'
Foundation	Crawlspace
	Slab
Bedrooms	4
Full Baths	2
Half Baths	1
First Ceiling	8'
Second Ceiling	8'
Max Ridge Height	25'
Exterior Walls	2x4

PORCH

KITCHEN
10x11

BATH
WHIRLPOOL

MASTER SUITE
13x14

DINING
12x11

RANGE

CLOSET

BATH

GREAT RM.
15 x 18

STOR.

WASH DRY

STORAGE

FIREPLACE

FOYER

GARAGE
23x23

PORCH

FIRST FLOOR

Design 63114

Units	Single
Price Code	C
Total Finished	1,868 sq. ft.
Main Finished	1,868 sq. ft.
Garage Unfinished	400 sq. ft.
Dimensions	45'×66'
Foundation	Slab
Bedrooms	4
Full Baths	2
Max Ridge Height	19'10"
Roof Framing	Truss

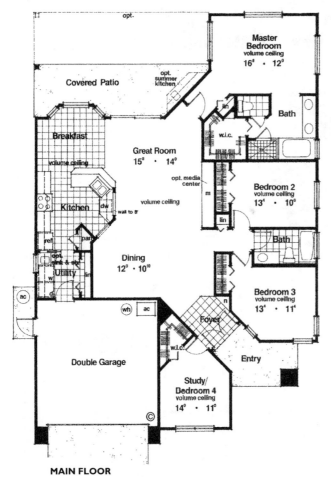

MAIN FLOOR

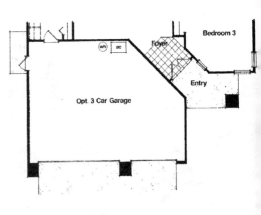

3-CAR GARAGE OPTION

Design 63030

Units	Single
Price Code	F
Total Finished	2,616 sq. ft.
First Finished	1,447 sq. ft.
Second Finished	1,169 sq. ft.
Bonus Unfinished	254 sq. ft.
Garage Unfinished	383 sq. ft.
Porch Unfinished	181 sq. ft.
Dimensions	45'x76'
Foundation	Slab
Bedrooms	3
Full Baths	1
3/4 Baths	1
Half Baths	1
First Ceiling	10'
Second Ceiling	8'
Max Ridge Height	38'6"
Roof Framing	Truss
Exterior Walls	2x4

FIRST FLOOR

SECOND FLOOR

Units	Single
Price Code	G
Total Finished	2,894 sq. ft.
First Finished	1,751 sq. ft.
Second Finished	1,143 sq. ft.
Dimensions	45'x69'6"
Foundation	Crawlspace
Bedrooms	4
Full Baths	3
Half Baths	1
Max Ridge Height	35'6"
Roof Framing	Stick
Exterior Walls	2x4

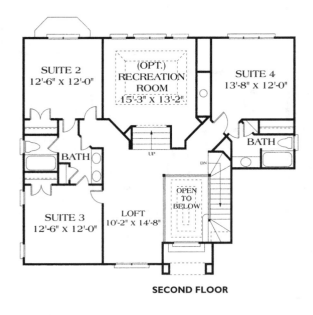

SECOND FLOOR

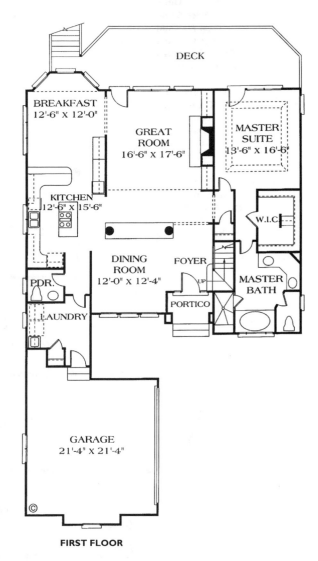

FIRST FLOOR

Design 67024

Units	Single
Price Code	E
Total Finished	2,293 sq. ft.
First Finished	1,001 sq. ft.
Second Finished	1,292 sq. ft.
Dimensions	45'3"x34'2"
Foundation	Slab
Bedrooms	3
Full Baths	2
Half Baths	1
Roof Framing	Stick
Exterior Walls	2x4

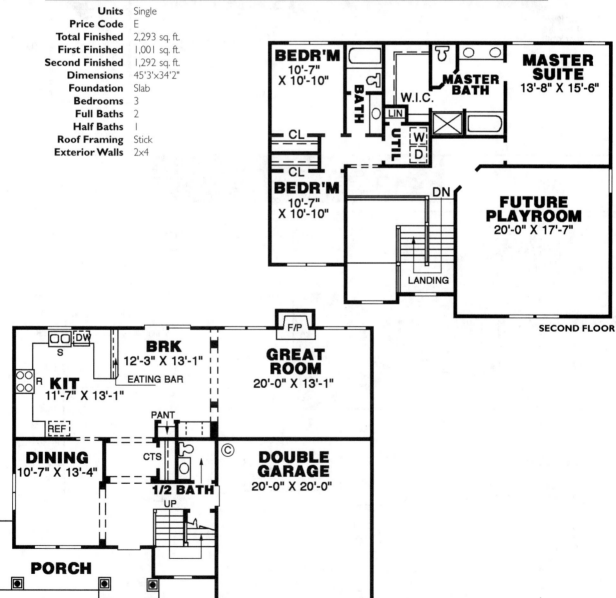

BEDR'M 10'-7" X 10'-10"

BATH

MASTER BATH

MASTER SUITE 13'-8" X 15'-6"

W.I.C.

LIN

UTIL

W D

CL

CL

BEDR'M 10'-7" X 10'-10"

DN

FUTURE PLAYROOM 20'-0" X 17'-7"

LANDING

SECOND FLOOR

F/P

DW

S

BRK 12'-3" X 13'-1"

EATING BAR

GREAT ROOM 20'-0" X 13'-1"

R

KIT 11'-7" X 13'-1"

REF

PANT

DINING 10'-7" X 13'-4"

CTS

©

DOUBLE GARAGE 20'-0" X 20'-0"

1/2 BATH

UP

PORCH

FIRST FLOOR

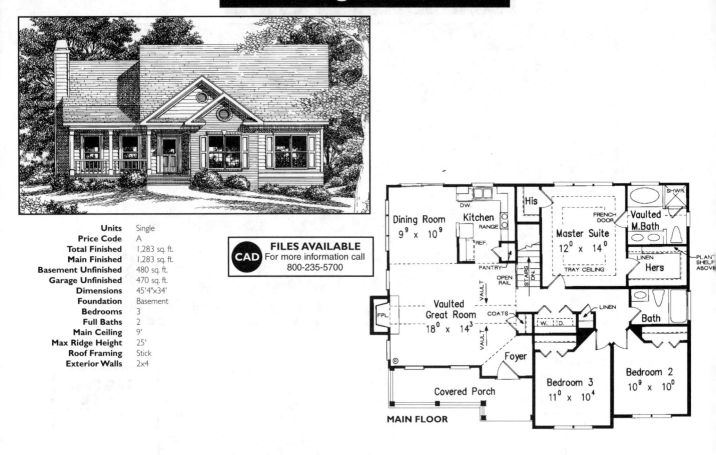

Units	Single
Price Code	A
Total Finished	1,283 sq. ft.
Main Finished	1,283 sq. ft.
Basement Unfinished	480 sq. ft.
Garage Unfinished	470 sq. ft.
Dimensions	45'4"x34'
Foundation	Basement
Bedrooms	3
Full Baths	2
Main Ceiling	9'
Max Ridge Height	25'
Roof Framing	Stick
Exterior Walls	2x4

CAD FILES AVAILABLE For more information call 800-235-5700

MAIN FLOOR

Units	Single
Price Code	F
Total Finished	2,672 sq. ft.
First Finished	1,574 sq. ft.
Second Finished	1,098 sq. ft.
Garage Finished	522 sq. ft.
Dimensions	45'4"x52'4"
Foundation	Basement
	Crawlspace
	Slab
Bedrooms	4
Full Baths	3
Max Ridge Height	27'
Roof Framing	Stick
Exterior Walls	2x4

FIRST FLOOR

SECOND FLOOR

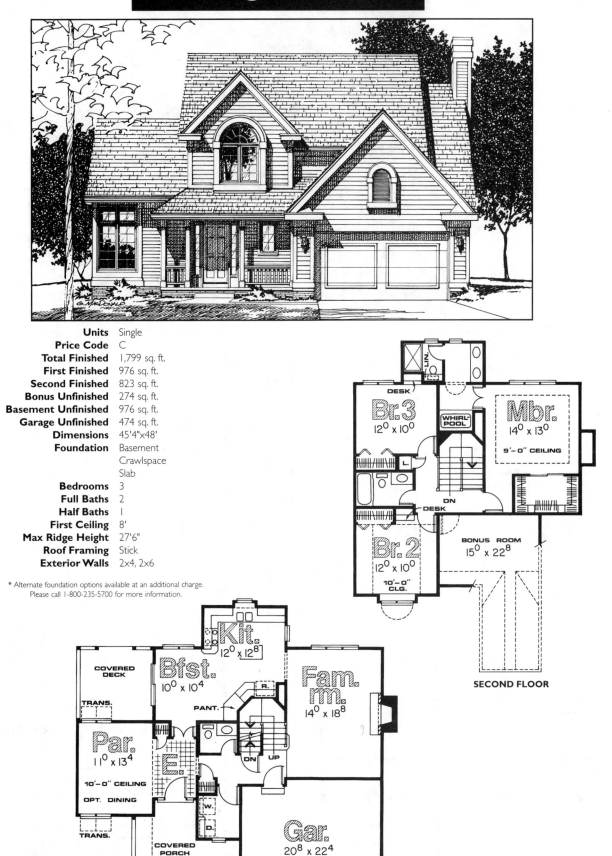

Units	Single
Price Code	C
Total Finished	1,799 sq. ft.
First Finished	976 sq. ft.
Second Finished	823 sq. ft.
Bonus Unfinished	274 sq. ft.
Basement Unfinished	976 sq. ft.
Garage Unfinished	474 sq. ft.
Dimensions	45'4"x48'
Foundation	Basement
	Crawlspace
	Slab
Bedrooms	3
Full Baths	2
Half Baths	1
First Ceiling	8'
Max Ridge Height	27'6"
Roof Framing	Stick
Exterior Walls	2x4, 2x6

* Alternate foundation options available at an additional charge.
Please call 1-800-235-5700 for more information.

SECOND FLOOR

FIRST FLOOR

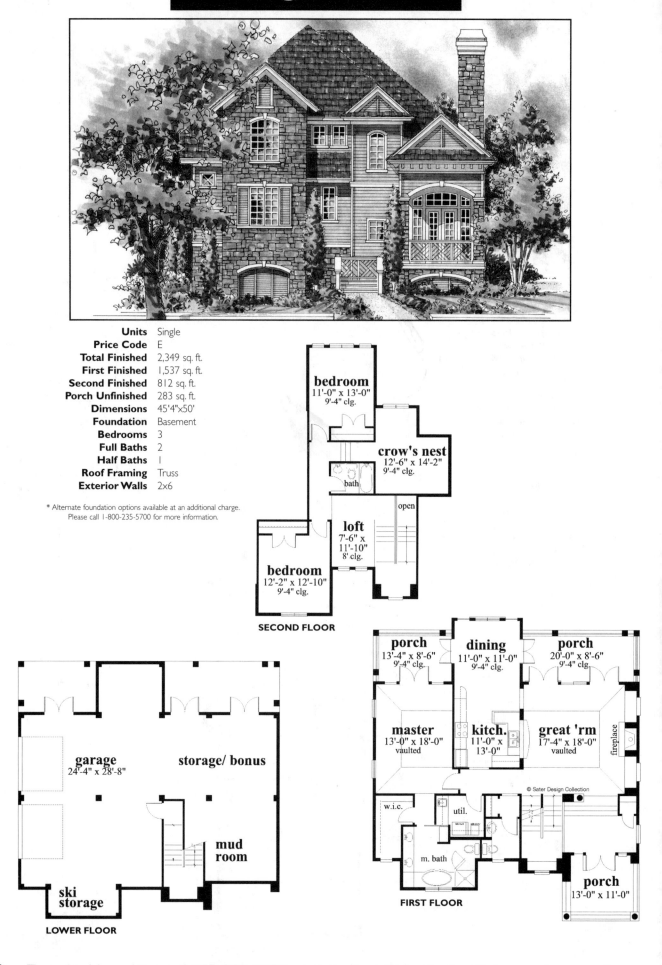

Units	Single
Price Code	E
Total Finished	2,349 sq. ft.
First Finished	1,537 sq. ft.
Second Finished	812 sq. ft.
Porch Unfinished	283 sq. ft.
Dimensions	45'4"x50'
Foundation	Basement
Bedrooms	3
Full Baths	2
Half Baths	1
Roof Framing	Truss
Exterior Walls	2x6

* Alternate foundation options available at an additional charge.
Please call 1-800-235-5700 for more information.

SECOND FLOOR

bedroom
11'-0" x 13'-0"
9'-4" clg.

crow's nest
12'-6" x 14'-2"
9'-4" clg.

bath

open

loft
7'-6" x
11'-10"
8' clg.

bedroom
12'-2" x 12'-10"
9'-4" clg.

LOWER FLOOR

garage
24'-4" x 28'-8"

storage/ bonus

mud
room

ski
storage

FIRST FLOOR

porch
13'-4" x 8'-6"
9'-4" clg.

dining
11'-0" x 11'-0"
9'-4" clg.

porch
20'-0" x 8'-6"
9'-4" clg.

master
13'-0" x 18'-0"
vaulted

kitch.
11'-0" x
13'-0"

great 'rm
17'-4" x 18'-0"
vaulted

fireplace

w.i.c.

util.

m. bath

© Sater Design Collection

porch
13'-0" x 11'-0"

Design 24705

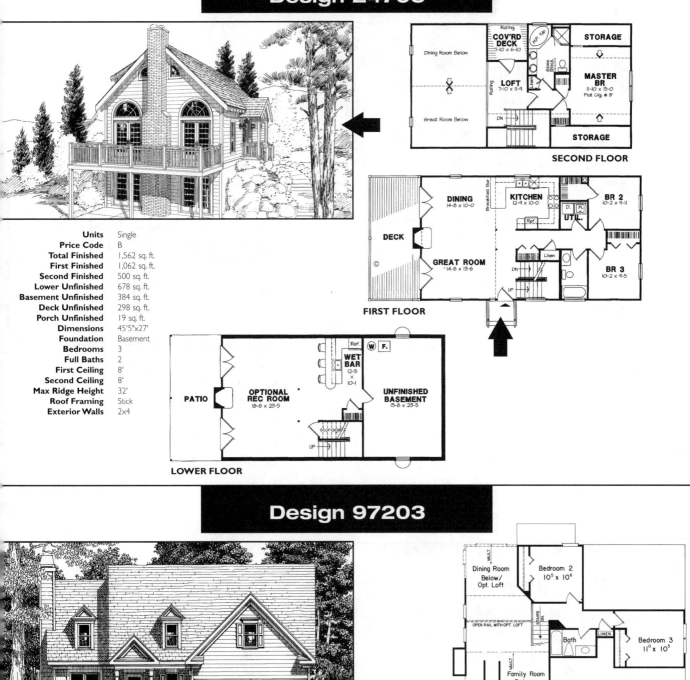

SECOND FLOOR

- COV'RD DECK 7-10 x 6-10
- Dining Room Below
- LOFT 7-10 x 11-4
- Great Room Below
- STORAGE
- MASTER BR 11-10 x 15-0 Flat Clg. @ 8'
- STORAGE
- DN

FIRST FLOOR

- DINING 14-8 x 10-0
- KITCHEN 12-4 x 10-0
- BR 2 10-2 x 4-11
- UTIL.
- Ref.
- DECK
- GREAT ROOM 14-8 x 13-6
- BR 3 10-2 x 4-5
- Linen
- DN
- UP

LOWER FLOOR

- PATIO
- OPTIONAL REC ROOM 18-8 x 23-5
- WET BAR 12-5 x 10-1
- UNFINISHED BASEMENT 15-8 x 23-5
- storage
- UP
- W F. Ref.

Units	Single
Price Code	B
Total Finished	1,562 sq. ft.
First Finished	1,062 sq. ft.
Second Finished	500 sq. ft.
Lower Unfinished	678 sq. ft.
Basement Unfinished	384 sq. ft.
Deck Unfinished	298 sq. ft.
Porch Unfinished	19 sq. ft.
Dimensions	45'5"x27'
Foundation	Basement
Bedrooms	3
Full Baths	2
First Ceiling	8'
Second Ceiling	8'
Max Ridge Height	32'
Roof Framing	Stick
Exterior Walls	2x4

Design 97203

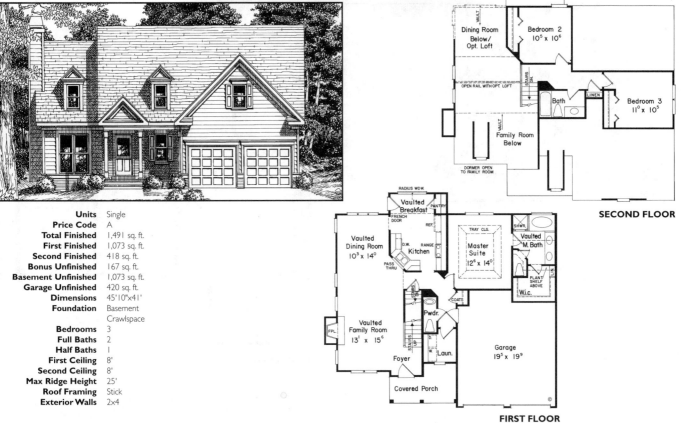

SECOND FLOOR

- Dining Room Below/ Opt. Loft
- Bedroom 2 10⁵ x 10⁶
- OPEN RAIL WITH OPT. LOFT
- STAIRS DN
- Bath
- LINEN
- Bedroom 3 11⁰ x 10⁵
- Family Room Below
- VAULT
- DORMER OPEN TO FAMILY ROOM

FIRST FLOOR

- RADIUS WDW.
- Vaulted Breakfast
- PANTRY
- FRENCH DOOR
- REF.
- D.W.
- RANGE
- Vaulted Dining Room 10³ x 14⁰
- Kitchen
- TRAY CLG.
- Master Suite 12⁶ x 14⁰
- SHWR.
- Vaulted M. Bath
- PASS THRU
- PLANT SHELF ABOVE
- W.i.c.
- STAIRS UP
- COATS
- Pwdr.
- FPL.
- Vaulted Family Room 13' x 15⁶
- W. Laun.
- Garage 19⁵ x 19⁹
- Foyer
- Covered Porch

Units	Single
Price Code	A
Total Finished	1,491 sq. ft.
First Finished	1,073 sq. ft.
Second Finished	418 sq. ft.
Bonus Unfinished	167 sq. ft.
Basement Unfinished	1,073 sq. ft.
Garage Unfinished	420 sq. ft.
Dimensions	45'10"x41'
Foundation	Basement Crawlspace
Bedrooms	3
Full Baths	2
Half Baths	1
First Ceiling	8'
Second Ceiling	8'
Max Ridge Height	25'
Roof Framing	Stick
Exterior Walls	2x4

Design 94307

Units	Single
Price Code	A
Total Finished	786 sq. ft.
Main Finished	786 sq. ft.
Deck Unfinished	580 sq. ft.
Dimensions	46'x22'
Foundation	Crawlspace
Bedrooms	2
3/4 Baths	2
Main Ceiling	8'
Vaulted Ceiling	16'
Max Ridge Height	18'6"
Roof Framing	Truss
Exterior Walls	2x6

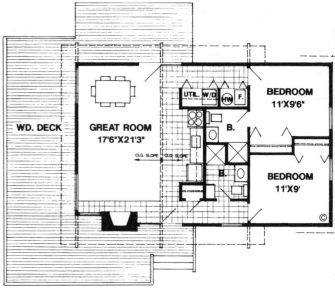

MAIN FLOOR

Design 65093

Units	Single
Price Code	A
Total Finished	1,087 sq. ft.
Main Finished	1,087 sq. ft.
Dimensions	46'x40'4"
Foundation	Basement
Bedrooms	2
Full Baths	1

MAIN FLOOR

Design 91340

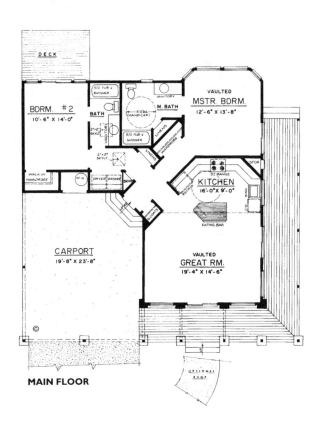

Units	Single
Price Code	A
Total Finished	1,111 sq. ft.
Main Finished	1,111 sq. ft.
Dimensions	46'x44'
Foundation	Crawlspace
	Slab
Bedrooms	2
Full Baths	2
Max Ridge Height	18'
Roof Framing	Stick
Exterior Walls	2x4

OPTIONAL BATH

MAIN FLOOR

Design 92431

OPTIONAL MASTER BATH

Units	Single
Price Code	A
Total Finished	1,296 sq. ft.
Main Finished	1,296 sq. ft.
Basement Unfinished	1,336 sq. ft.
Garage Unfinished	380 sq. ft.
Dimensions	46'x42'
Foundation	Basement
	Crawlspace
	Slab
Bedrooms	3
Full Baths	2
Main Ceiling	8'
Vaulted Ceiling	12'
Max Ridge Height	17'6"
Roof Framing	Truss
Exterior Walls	2x4

MAIN FLOOR

Design 98807

Units	Single
Price Code	A
Total Finished	1,487 sq. ft.
Main Finished	1,487 sq. ft.
Basement Unfinished	1,480 sq. ft.
Garage Unfinished	427 sq. ft.
Dimensions	46'x50'
Foundation	Basement
Bedrooms	2
Full Baths	2
Main Ceiling	8'
Max Ridge Height	19'11"
Roof Framing	Truss
Exterior Walls	2x6

MAIN FLOOR

Design 97923

PHOTOGRAPHY: COURTESY OF THE DESIGNER

Please note: The photographed home may have been modified to suit homeowner preferences. If you order plans, have a builder or design professional check them against the photograph to confirm actual construction details.

SECOND FLOOR

Units	Single
Price Code	B
Total Finished	1,700 sq. ft.
First Finished	904 sq. ft.
Second Finished	796 sq. ft.
Garage Unfinished	509 sq. ft.
Dimensions	46'x41'4"
Foundation	Basement
	Crawlspace
	Slab
Bedrooms	3
Full Baths	2
Half Baths	1
First Ceiling	8'
Max Ridge Height	25'6"
Roof Framing	Stick
Exterior Walls	2x4, 2x6

* Alternate foundation options available at an additional charge.
Please call 1-800-235-5700 for more information.

FIRST FLOOR

Design 94204

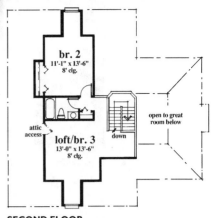

SECOND FLOOR

br. 2
11'-1" x 13'-6"
8' clg.

loft/br. 3
13'-6" x 13'-6"
8' clg.

attic access

down

open to great room below

Please note: The photographed home may have been modified to suit homeowner preferences. If you order plans, have a builder or design professional check them against the photograph to confirm actual construction details.

PHOTOGRAPHY: COURTESY OF THE DESIGNER

Units	Single
Price Code	C
Total Finished	1,764 sq. ft.
First Finished	1,189 sq. ft.
Second Finished	575 sq. ft.
Bonus Unfinished	581 sq. ft.
Garage Unfinished	658 sq. ft.
Dimensions	46'x44'6"
Foundation	Pier/Post
Bedrooms	3
Full Baths	2
Half Baths	1
Max Ridge Height	36'
Roof Framing	Stick/Truss
Exterior Walls	2x6

* Alternate foundation options available at an additional charge. Please call 1-800-235-5700 for more information.

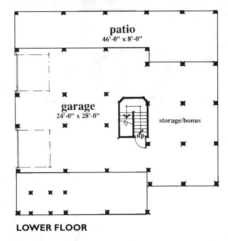

patio
46'-0" x 8'-0"

garage
24'-0" x 28'-0"

storage/bonus

up

LOWER FLOOR

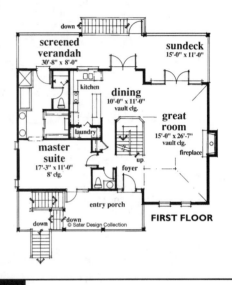

down

screened verandah
30'-8" x 8'-0"

sundeck
15'-0" x 11'-0"

kitchen

dining
10'-0" x 11'-0"
vault clg.

great room
15'-0" x 26'-7"
vault clg.
fireplace

laundry

master suite
17'-3" x 11'-0"
8' clg.

up

foyer

entry porch

down

down

© Sater Design Collection

FIRST FLOOR

Design 34800

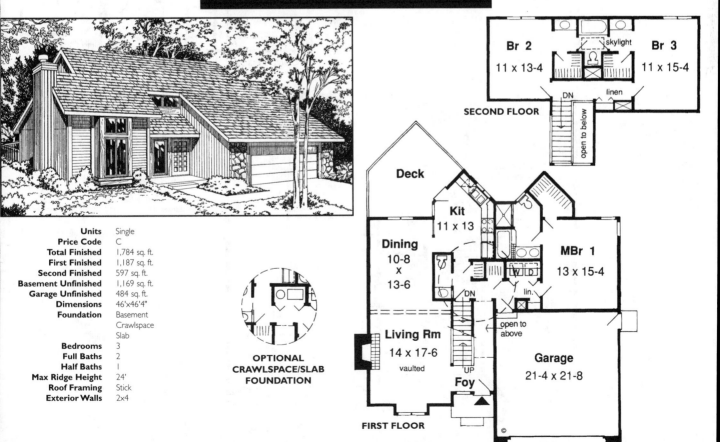

SECOND FLOOR

Br 2
11 x 13-4

skylight

Br 3
11 x 15-4

DN

linen

Units	Single
Price Code	C
Total Finished	1,784 sq. ft.
First Finished	1,187 sq. ft.
Second Finished	597 sq. ft.
Basement Unfinished	1,169 sq. ft.
Garage Unfinished	484 sq. ft.
Dimensions	46'x46'4"
Foundation	Basement
	Crawlspace
	Slab
Bedrooms	3
Full Baths	2
Half Baths	1
Max Ridge Height	24'
Roof Framing	Stick
Exterior Walls	2x4

OPTIONAL CRAWLSPACE/SLAB FOUNDATION

Deck

Kit
11 x 13

Dining
10-8 x 13-6

MBr 1
13 x 15-4

open to below

up

Living Rm
14 x 17-6
vaulted

DN

lin.

open to above

Garage
21-4 x 21-8

Foy

UP

FIRST FLOOR

©

Design 94936

PHOTOGRAPHY: COURTESY OF THE DESIGNER

Units	Single
Price Code	D
Total Finished	2,078 sq. ft.
First Finished	1,113 sq. ft.
Second Finished	965 sq. ft.
Basement Unfinished	1,113 sq. ft.
Garage Unfinished	486 sq. ft.
Dimensions	46'x41'5"
Foundation	Basement
Bedrooms	4
Full Baths	2
Half Baths	1
First Ceiling	8'
Second Ceiling	8'
Max Ridge Height	25'5"
Roof Framing	Stick
Exterior Walls	2x4

* Alternate foundation options available at an additional charge.
Please call 1-800-235-5700 for more information.

Please note: The photographed home may have been modified to suit homeowner preferences. If you order plans, have a builder or design professional check them against the photograph to confirm actual construction details.

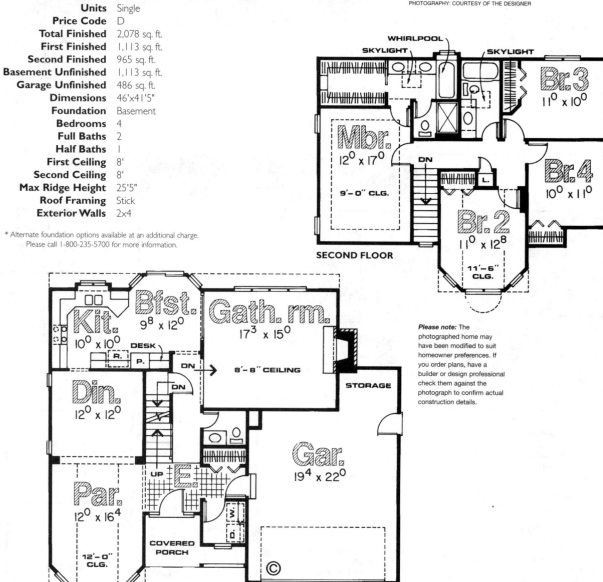

PHOTOGRAPHY: COURTESY OF THE DESIGNER

Units	Single
Price Code	E
Total Finished	2,270 sq. ft.
First Finished	1,150 sq. ft.
Second Finished	1,120 sq. ft.
Basement Unfinished	1,150 sq. ft.
Garage Unfinished	457 sq. ft.
Dimensions	46'x48'
Foundation	Basement
Bedrooms	4
Full Baths	2
Half Baths	1
First Ceiling	8'
Second Ceiling	8'
Tray Ceiling	9'4"
Max Ridge Height	28'
Roof Framing	Stick
Exterior Walls	2x4

* Alternate foundation options available at an additional charge.
Please call 1-800-235-5700 for more information.

SECOND FLOOR

WHIRLPOOL

Mbr.
16⁰ x 14⁰
9'- 4" CEILING

Br.2
11² x 11⁶

LIN.

LINEN

DN

PLANT SHELF

OPEN TO BELOW

Br.3
11⁰ x 12⁰
10'- 0" CEILING

Br.4
11⁰ x 11⁴

DESK

Please note: The photographed home may have been modified to suit homeowner preferences. If you order plans, have a builder or design professional check them against the photograph to confirm actual construction details.

Grt. rm.
20⁰ x 16⁰

Bfst.
11⁰ x 11⁰

DESK

Kit.
10⁰ x 11³

Hrth.
11⁸ x 10⁰

ENT. CENTER

DN

UP

Din.
12⁰ x 13⁰

HUTCH

Gar.
20⁷ x 21⁸

COVERED PORCH

FIRST FLOOR

Units	Single
Price Code	E
Total Finished	2,403 sq. ft.
First Finished	1,688 sq. ft.
Second Finished	715 sq. ft.
Bonus Unfinished	251 sq. ft.
Basement Unfinished	1,688 sq. ft.
Garage Unfinished	484 sq. ft.
Dimensions	46'x55'4"
Foundation	Basement
	Crawlspace
	Slab
Bedrooms	4
Full Baths	2
Half Baths	1
First Ceiling	8'
Max Ridge Height	26'
Roof Framing	Stick
Exterior Walls	2x4

* Alternate foundation options available at an additional charge.
Please call 1-800-235-5700 for more information.

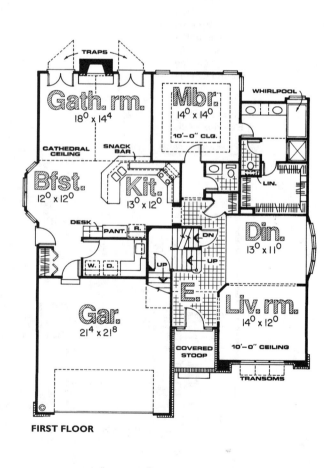

FIRST FLOOR

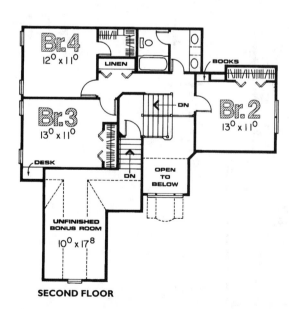

SECOND FLOOR

© William E. Poole Designs, Inc.

Units	Single
Price Code	Call for pricing
Total Finished	2,410 sq. ft.
First Finished	1,627 sq. ft.
Second Finished	783 sq. ft.
Bonus Unfinished	418 sq. ft.
Dimensions	46'x58'6"
Foundation	Crawlspace
Bedrooms	4
Full Baths	2
Half Baths	1
Max Ridge Height	31'
Roof Framing	Stick
Exterior Walls	2x4

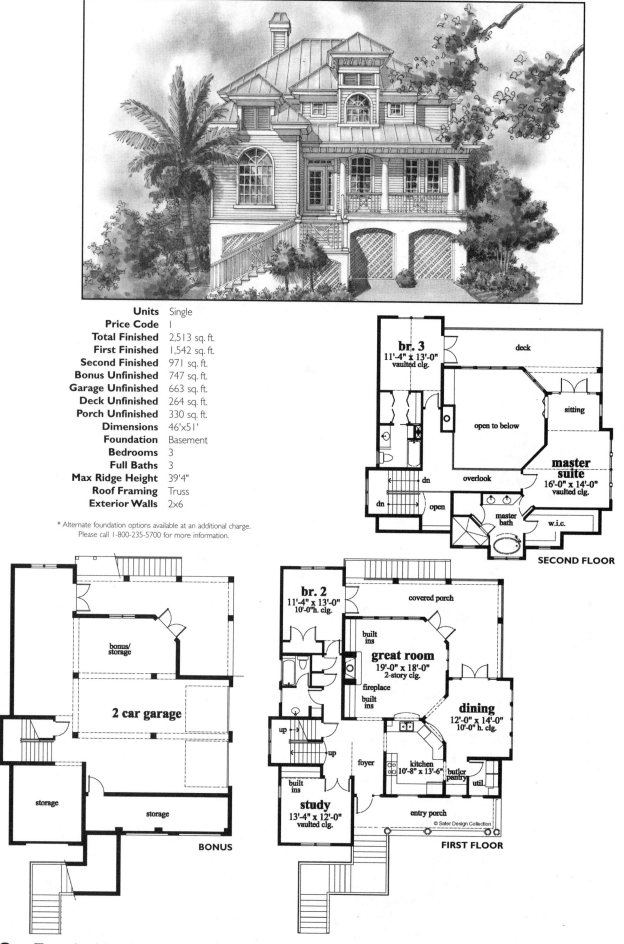

Units	Single
Price Code	I
Total Finished	2,513 sq. ft.
First Finished	1,542 sq. ft.
Second Finished	971 sq. ft.
Bonus Unfinished	747 sq. ft.
Garage Unfinished	663 sq. ft.
Deck Unfinished	264 sq. ft.
Porch Unfinished	330 sq. ft.
Dimensions	46'x51'
Foundation	Basement
Bedrooms	3
Full Baths	3
Max Ridge Height	39'4"
Roof Framing	Truss
Exterior Walls	2x6

* Alternate foundation options available at an additional charge.
Please call 1-800-235-5700 for more information.

SECOND FLOOR

br. 3
11'-4" x 13'-0"
vaulted clg.

deck

open to below

sitting

overlook

master
suite
16'-0" x 14'-0"
vaulted clg.

dn

dn

open

master
bath

w.i.c.

BONUS

bonus/
storage

2 car garage

storage

storage

FIRST FLOOR

br. 2
11'-4" x 13'-0"
10'-0"h. clg.

covered porch

built
ins

great room
19'-0" x 18'-0"
2-story clg.

fireplace

built
ins

dining
12'-0" x 14'-0"
10'-0" h. clg.

up

up

foyer

kitchen
10'-8" x 13'-6"

butler
pantry

util.

built
ins

study
13'-4" x 12'-0"
vaulted clg.

entry porch

© Sater Design Collection

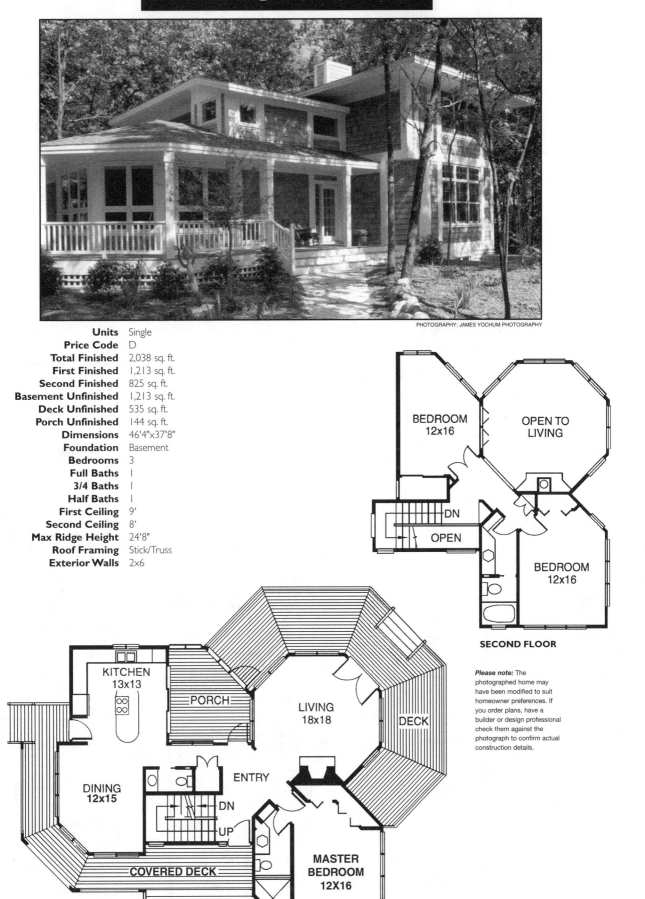

PHOTOGRAPHY: JAMES YOCHUM PHOTOGRAPHY

Units	Single
Price Code	D
Total Finished	2,038 sq. ft.
First Finished	1,213 sq. ft.
Second Finished	825 sq. ft.
Basement Unfinished	1,213 sq. ft.
Deck Unfinished	535 sq. ft.
Porch Unfinished	144 sq. ft.
Dimensions	46'4"x37'8"
Foundation	Basement
Bedrooms	3
Full Baths	1
3/4 Baths	1
Half Baths	1
First Ceiling	9'
Second Ceiling	8'
Max Ridge Height	24'8"
Roof Framing	Stick/Truss
Exterior Walls	2x6

BEDROOM 12x16

OPEN TO LIVING

DN

OPEN

BEDROOM 12x16

SECOND FLOOR

Please note: The photographed home may have been modified to suit homeowner preferences. If you order plans, have a builder or design professional check them against the photograph to confirm actual construction details.

KITCHEN 13x13

PORCH

LIVING 18x18

DECK

DINING 12x15

ENTRY

DN

UP

COVERED DECK

MASTER BEDROOM 12X16

FIRST FLOOR

Units	Single
Price Code	G
Total Finished	2,801 sq. ft.
First Finished	1,651 sq. ft.
Second Finished	1,150 sq. ft.
Dimensions	46'4"x79'1"
Foundation	Crawlspace
	Slab
Bedrooms	5
Full Baths	3
First Ceiling	9'
Second Ceiling	8'
Roof Framing	Stick
Exterior Walls	2x4

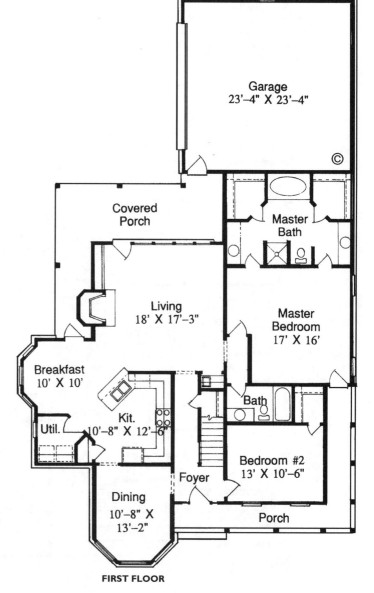

Garage
23'–4" X 23'–4"

Covered
Porch

Master
Bath

Living
18' X 17'–3"

Master
Bedroom
17' X 16'

Breakfast
10' X 10'

Bath

Util.

Kit.
10'–8" X 12'–6"

Bedroom #2
13' X 10'–6"

Foyer

Dining
10'–8" X
13'–2"

Porch

FIRST FLOOR

Bedroom #3

Gameroom
17' X 10'–10"

Ba.

Bedroom #4
14'–4" X 13'

Bedroom #5
17' X 12'

SECOND FLOOR

Design 98478

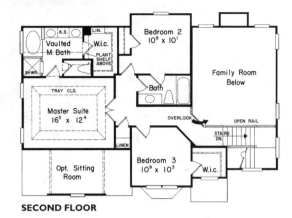

SECOND FLOOR

Units	Single
Price Code	B
Total Finished	1,663 sq. ft.
First Finished	840 sq. ft.
Second Finished	823 sq. ft.
Bonus Unfinished	80 sq. ft.
Basement Unfinished	840 sq. ft.
Garage Unfinished	494 sq. ft.
Dimensions	46'6"x32'10"
Foundation	Basement Crawlspace
Bedrooms	3
Full Baths	2
Half Baths	1
Max Ridge Height	29'6"
Roof Framing	Stick
Exterior Walls	2x6

FIRST FLOOR

Design 32341

PHOTOGRAPHY: SUSAN GILMORE

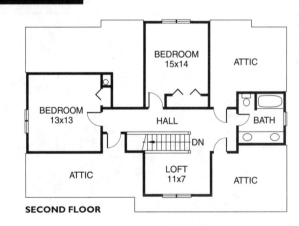

SECOND FLOOR

Units	Single
Price Code	E
Total Finished	2,282 sq. ft.
First Finished	1,427 sq. ft.
Second Finished	855 sq. ft.
Dimensions	46'6"x35'
Foundation	Crawlspace
Bedrooms	3
Full Baths	2
First Ceiling	8'
Second Ceiling	8'
Max Ridge Height	30'8"
Roof Framing	Stick
Exterior Walls	2x4

Please note: The photographed home may have been modified to suit homeowner preferences. If you order plans, have a builder or design professional check them against the photograph to confirm actual construction details.

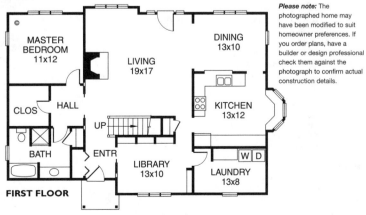

FIRST FLOOR

Design 24610

SECOND FLOOR

Br 2
11-6 x 11-4

Br 3
11 x 11-4

linen

open to below

1/2 wall

railing

DN

Mstr Br
13-4 x 15

FIRST FLOOR

Dining
12-1 x 11-4

Kitchen
13 x 11-4

pantry

Great Rm
14 x 21-8

open to above

UP

DN

Garage
22 x 23-4

Units	Single
Price Code	C
Total Finished	1,785 sq. ft.
First Finished	891 sq. ft.
Second Finished	894 sq. ft.
Basement Unfinished	891 sq. ft.
Garage Unfinished	534 sq. ft.
Dimensions	46'8"x35'8"
Foundation	Basement
	Crawlspace
	Slab
Bedrooms	3
Full Baths	1
3/4 Baths	1
Half Baths	1
First Ceiling	8'
Second Ceiling	8'
Max Ridge Height	28'
Roof Framing	Stick
Exterior Walls	2x4

Design 96803

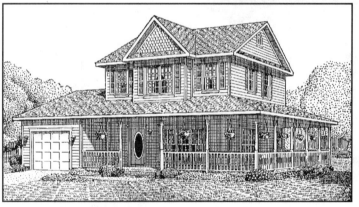

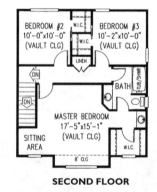

SECOND FLOOR

BEDROOM #2
10'-0"x10'-0"
(VAULT CLG)

BEDROOM #3
10'-2"x10'-0"
(VAULT CLG)

W.I.C.

W.I.C.

LINEN

BATH

TUB/SHWR

MASTER BEDROOM
17'-5"x15'-1"
(VAULT CLG)

SITTING
AREA

W.I.C.

8' CLG

DN

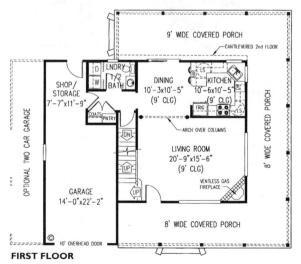

FIRST FLOOR

9' WIDE COVERED PORCH

CANTILEVERED 2nd FLOOR

OPTIONAL TWO CAR GARAGE

LNDRY

1/2
BATH

SHOP/
STORAGE
7'-7"x11'-9"

COATS

PNTRY

DINING
10'-3"x10'-5"
(9' CLG)

KITCHEN
10'-6x10'-5"
(9' CLG)

FRIG

ARCH OVER COLUMNS

LIVING ROOM
20'-9"x15'-6"
(9' CLG)

VENTLESS GAS
FIREPLACE

GARAGE
14'-0"x22'-2"

8' WIDE COVERED PORCH

8' WIDE COVERED PORCH

10' OVERHEAD DOOR

Units	Single
Price Code	A
Total Finished	1,399 sq. ft.
First Finished	732 sq. ft.
Second Finished	667 sq. ft.
Basement Unfinished	732 sq. ft.
Garage Unfinished	406 sq. ft.
Dimensions	46'9"x43'6"
Foundation	Basement
	Crawlspace
	Slab
Bedrooms	3
Full Baths	1
Half Baths	1
First Ceiling	9'
Second Ceiling	8'2"
Max Ridge Height	25'9"
Roof Framing	Truss
Exterior Walls	2x4

Design 32122

PHOTOGRAPHY: JAMES SALOMON

Units	Single
Price Code	A
Total Finished	1,112 sq. ft.
Main Finished	1,112 sq. ft.
Basement Unfinished	484 sq. ft.
Deck Unfinished	280 sq. ft.
Porch Unfinished	152 sq. ft.
Dimensions	47'x45'6"
Foundation	Basement
	Crawlspace
Bedrooms	2
Full Baths	1
Main Ceiling	9'
Vaulted Ceiling	18'9"
Max Ridge Height	24'9"
Roof Framing	Stick
Exterior Walls	2x6

SCREEN PORCH

DECK

UP

LIVING
15x16

BEDROOM
15x11

HALL

KITCHEN
15x8

W
D
R

ENTRY

BEDROOM
16x10

MAIN FLOOR

Design 97272

Units	Single
Price Code	A
Total Finished	1,354 sq. ft.
Main Finished	1,354 sq. ft.
Basement Unfinished	1,390 sq. ft.
Garage Unfinished	434 sq. ft.
Dimensions	47'x46'
Foundation	Basement
	Crawlspace
Bedrooms	3
Full Baths	2
Main Ceiling	9'
Max Ridge Height	24'9"
Roof Framing	Stick
Exterior Walls	2x4

CAD FILES AVAILABLE
For more information call
800-235-5700

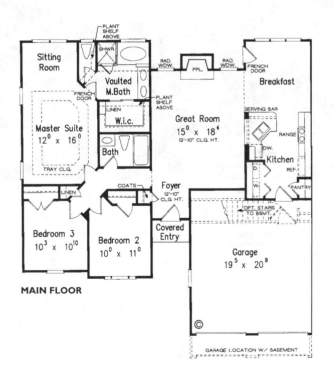

PLANT SHELF ABOVE

Sitting Room

SHWR

Vaulted M.Bath

RAD. WDW.

FPL.

RAD. WDW.

FRENCH DOOR

Breakfast

FRENCH DOOR

LINEN

PLANT SHELF ABOVE

Master Suite
12⁰ x 16⁰

W.i.c.

Great Room
15⁰ x 18⁴
12'-10" CLG. HT.

SERVING BAR

RANGE

Bath

DW.

Kitchen

REF.

TRAY CLG.

LINEN

COATS

Foyer
12'-10" CLG. HT.

PANTRY

OPT. STAIRS TO BSMT.

Bedroom 3
10³ x 10¹⁰

Bedroom 2
10⁰ x 11⁰

Covered Entry

Garage
19⁵ x 20⁹

MAIN FLOOR

GARAGE LOCATION W/ BASEMENT

Design 97224

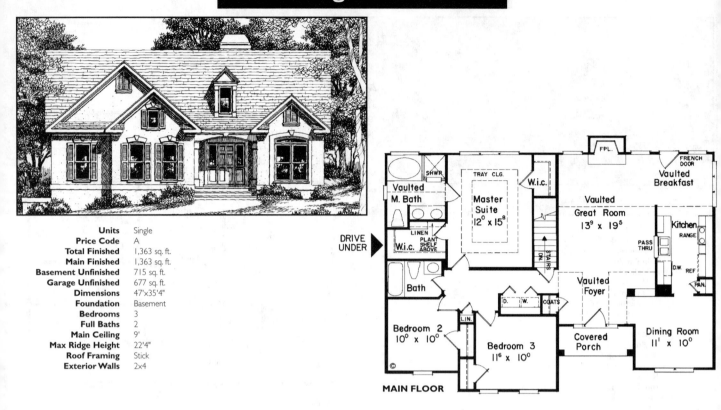

Units	Single
Price Code	A
Total Finished	1,363 sq. ft.
Main Finished	1,363 sq. ft.
Basement Unfinished	715 sq. ft.
Garage Unfinished	677 sq. ft.
Dimensions	47'x35'4"
Foundation	Basement
Bedrooms	3
Full Baths	2
Main Ceiling	9'
Max Ridge Height	22'4"
Roof Framing	Stick
Exterior Walls	2x4

DRIVE UNDER ▶

MAIN FLOOR

Design 66008

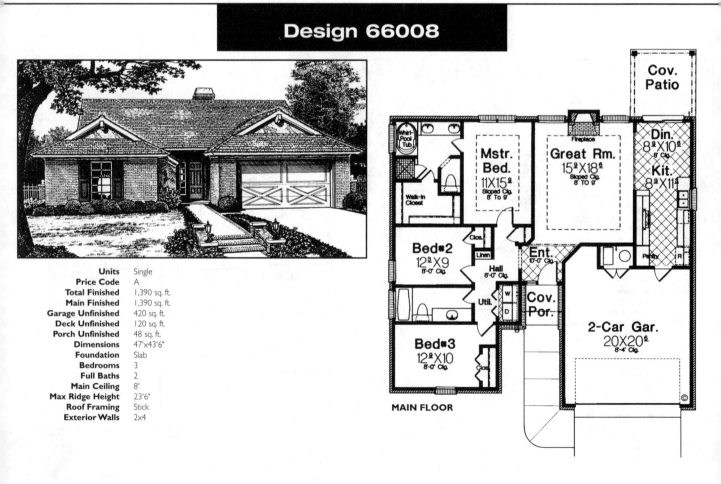

Units	Single
Price Code	A
Total Finished	1,390 sq. ft.
Main Finished	1,390 sq. ft.
Garage Unfinished	420 sq. ft.
Deck Unfinished	120 sq. ft.
Porch Unfinished	48 sq. ft.
Dimensions	47'x43'6"
Foundation	Slab
Bedrooms	3
Full Baths	2
Main Ceiling	8'
Max Ridge Height	23'6"
Roof Framing	Stick
Exterior Walls	2x4

MAIN FLOOR

Design 82010

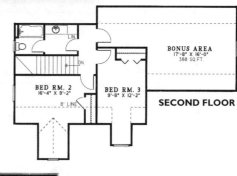

SECOND FLOOR

- BED RM. 2 16'-4" X 9'-2"
- BED RM. 3 9'-8" X 12'-2"
- BONUS AREA 17'-8" X 16'-0" 380 SQ.FT.

- MASTER BATH
- WHP TUB
- GRILLING PORCH 14'-0" X 6'-0"
- KITCHEN 11'-0" X 10'-0"
- NOOK 7'-0" X 9'-0"
- LAU.
- STORAGE 10'-0" X 6'-0"
- MASTER SUITE 11'-6" X 14'-0"
- ISLAND
- GARAGE 19'-8" X 19'-4"
- 8' COLUMNS
- GREAT RM. 15'-6" X 16'-0"
- DINING 10'-2" X 14'-0"
- FOYER
- PRCH

FIRST FLOOR

Units	Single
Price Code	B
Total Finished	1,684 sq. ft.
First Finished	1,155 sq. ft.
Second Finished	529 sq. ft.
Bonus Unfinished	380 sq. ft.
Garage Unfinished	400 sq. ft.
Porch Unfinished	164 sq. ft.
Dimensions	47'x50'
Foundation	Basement
	Crawlspace
	Slab
Bedrooms	3
Full Baths	2
Half Baths	1
First Ceiling	9'
Second Ceiling	8'
Roof Framing	Stick
Exterior Walls	2x4

Design 10785

SECOND FLOOR

- Br 2 10-4 x 14
- Br 3 11 x 14
- Balcony
- skylight
- open to below
- slope
- DN
- plant ledge

OPTIONAL CRAWLSPACE/SLAB FOUNDATION

FIRST FLOOR

- Optional Deck
- Living Rm 13 x 19-6
- Ldry
- Kitchen 11 x 12
- wood stove
- MBr 1 13-6 x 14
- Dining Rm 12-10 x 13-6
- DN
- Foyer

Units	Single
Price Code	C
Total Finished	1,907 sq. ft.
First Finished	1,269 sq. ft.
Second Finished	638 sq. ft.
Basement Unfinished	1,269 sq. ft.
Dimensions	47'x39'
Foundation	Basement
	Crawlspace
	Slab
Bedrooms	3
Full Baths	2
Half Baths	1
First Ceiling	8'
Second Ceiling	8'
Max Ridge Height	24'
Roof Framing	Stick
Exterior Walls	2x6

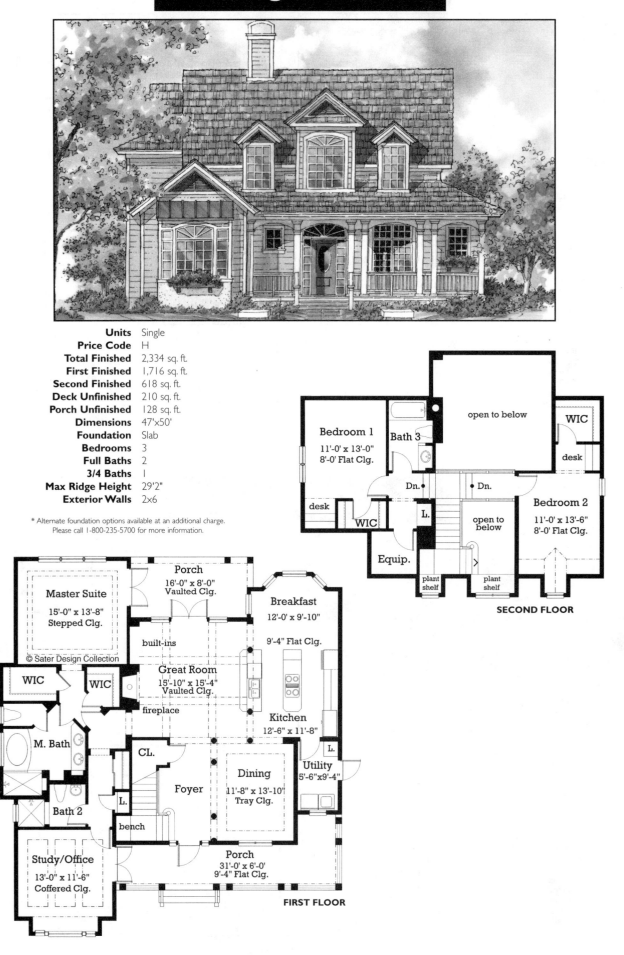

Units	Single
Price Code	H
Total Finished	2,334 sq. ft.
First Finished	1,716 sq. ft.
Second Finished	618 sq. ft.
Deck Unfinished	210 sq. ft.
Porch Unfinished	128 sq. ft.
Dimensions	47'×50'
Foundation	Slab
Bedrooms	3
Full Baths	2
3/4 Baths	1
Max Ridge Height	29'2"
Exterior Walls	2x6

* Alternate foundation options available at an additional charge.
Please call 1-800-235-5700 for more information.

SECOND FLOOR

Bedroom 1
11'-0" x 13'-0"
8'-0" Flat Clg.

Bath 3

open to below

WIC

desk

Dn.   Dn.

desk

WIC

L.

open to below

Bedroom 2
11'-0' x 13'-6"
8'-0' Flat Clg.

Equip.

plant shelf   plant shelf

FIRST FLOOR

Master Suite
15'-0" x 13'-8"
Stepped Clg.

© Sater Design Collection

WIC   WIC

M. Bath

Bath 2

L.

bench

Study/Office
13'-0" x 11'-6"
Coffered Clg.

Porch
16'-0" x 8'-0"
Vaulted Clg.

built-ins

Breakfast
12'-0' x 9'-10"
9'-4" Flat Clg.

Great Room
15'-10" x 15'-4"
Vaulted Clg.

fireplace

Kitchen
12'-6" x 11'-8"

CL.

Foyer

Dining
11'-8" x 13'-10"
Tray Clg.

Utility
5'-6"x9'-4"

L.

Porch
31'-0" x 6'-0'
9'-4" Flat Clg.

Design 63060

Units	Single
Price Code	E
Total Finished	2,441 sq. ft.
First Finished	1,226 sq. ft.
Second Finished	1,215 sq. ft.
Garage Unfinished	638 sq. ft.
Dimensions	47'x60'8"
Foundation	Slab
Bedrooms	4
Full Baths	2
Half Baths	1
First Ceiling	8'
Second Ceiling	8'
Max Ridge Height	28'4"
Roof Framing	Truss
Exterior Walls	2x4

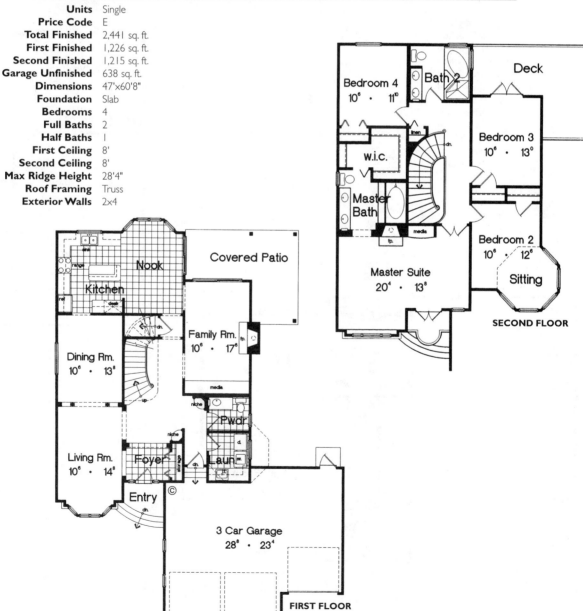

Design 98463

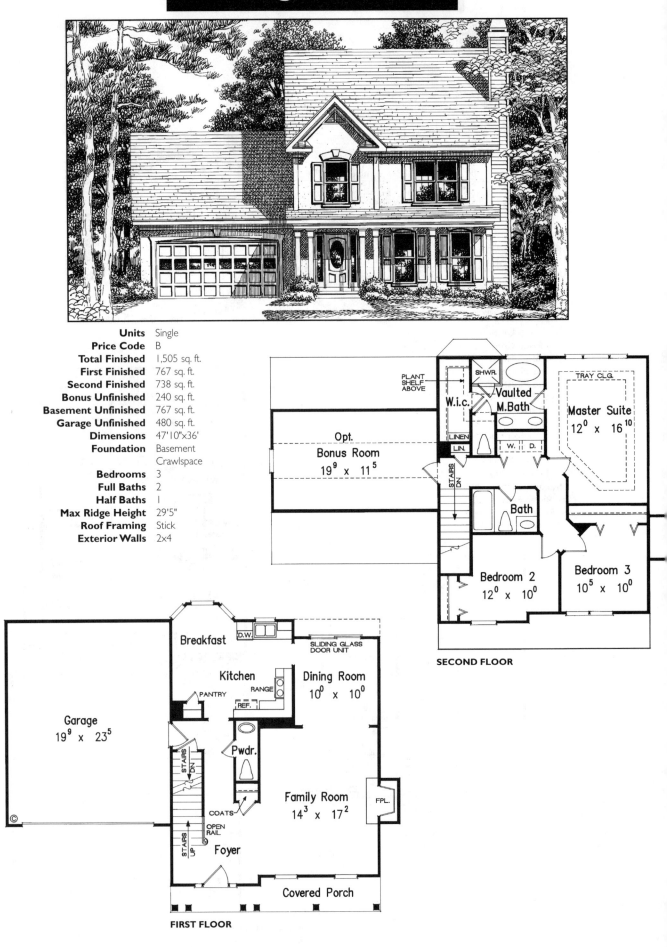

Units	Single
Price Code	B
Total Finished	1,505 sq. ft.
First Finished	767 sq. ft.
Second Finished	738 sq. ft.
Bonus Unfinished	240 sq. ft.
Basement Unfinished	767 sq. ft.
Garage Unfinished	480 sq. ft.
Dimensions	47'10"x36'
Foundation	Basement
	Crawlspace
Bedrooms	3
Full Baths	2
Half Baths	1
Max Ridge Height	29'5"
Roof Framing	Stick
Exterior Walls	2x4

SECOND FLOOR

Opt. Bonus Room 19⁹ x 11⁵

PLANT SHELF ABOVE

W.i.c.

SHWR.

Vaulted M.Bath

TRAY CLG.

Master Suite 12⁰ x 16¹⁰

LINEN

LIN.

W. D.

STAIRS DN

Bath

Bedroom 2 12⁰ x 10⁰

Bedroom 3 10⁵ x 10⁰

FIRST FLOOR

Garage 19⁹ x 23⁵

Breakfast

D.W.

SLIDING GLASS DOOR UNIT

Kitchen

RANGE

REF.

PANTRY

Dining Room 10⁰ x 10⁰

STAIRS DN

Pwdr.

COATS

Family Room 14³ x 17²

FPL.

OPEN RAIL

STAIRS UP

Foyer

Covered Porch

Units	Single
Price Code	B
Total Finished	1,633 sq. ft.
Main Finished	1,633 sq. ft.
Bonus Unfinished	285 sq. ft.
Basement Unfinished	1,633 sq. ft.
Garage Unfinished	433 sq. ft.
Dimensions	47'6"x54'4"
Foundation	Basement
	Crawlspace
Bedrooms	3
Full Baths	2
Main Ceiling	9'
Second Ceiling	8'
Max Ridge Height	23'
Roof Framing	Stick
Exterior Walls	2x4

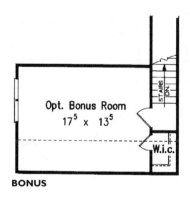

Opt. Bonus Room
17⁵ x 13⁵

W.i.c.

BONUS

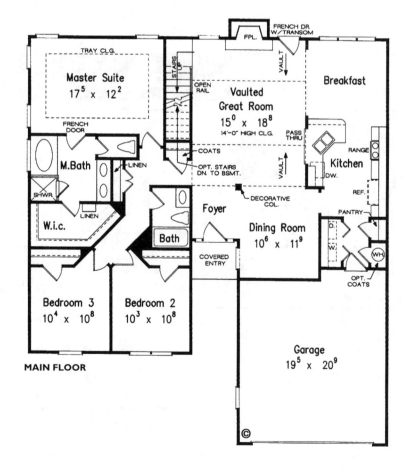

MAIN FLOOR

Design 65136

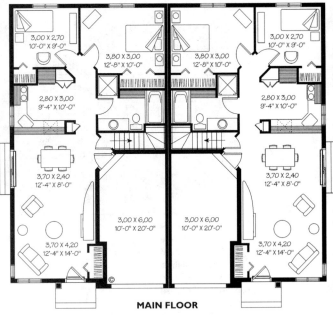

Units	Duplex
Price Code	A
Total Finished	834 sq. ft. (per unit)
Main Finished	834 sq. ft. (per unit)
Garage Unfinished	208 sq. ft. (per unit)
Dimensions	48'x44'
Foundation	Basement
Bedrooms	2 (per unit)
Full Baths	1 (per unit)
Main Ceiling	8'
Max Ridge Height	20'5"
Exterior Walls	2x6

MAIN FLOOR

Design 24304

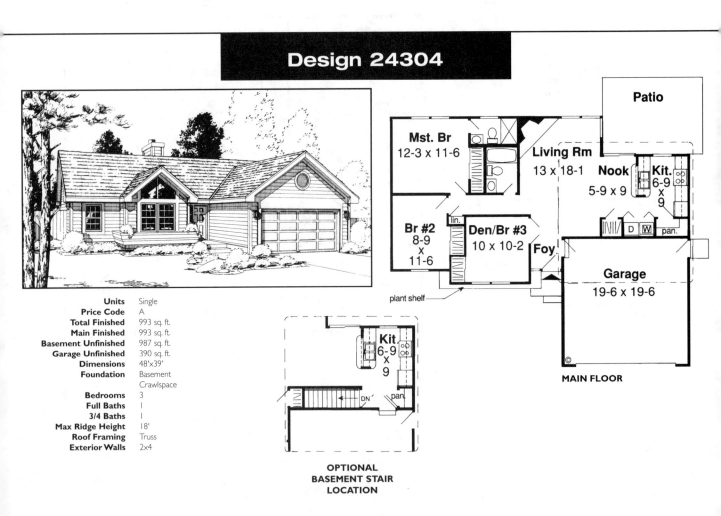

Units	Single
Price Code	A
Total Finished	993 sq. ft.
Main Finished	993 sq. ft.
Basement Unfinished	987 sq. ft.
Garage Unfinished	390 sq. ft.
Dimensions	48'x39'
Foundation	Basement
	Crawlspace
Bedrooms	3
Full Baths	1
3/4 Baths	1
Max Ridge Height	18'
Roof Framing	Truss
Exterior Walls	2x4

OPTIONAL BASEMENT STAIR LOCATION

MAIN FLOOR

Design 65642

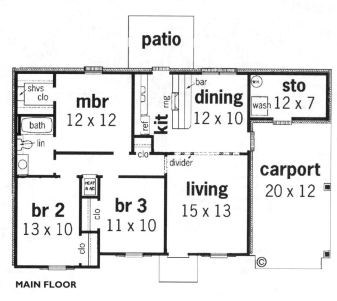

patio

shvs clo

mbr 12 x 12

bath

lin

clo

kit rng ref

bar

dining 12 x 10

W.H. wash

sto 12 x 7

divider

HEAT & AC

br 2 13 x 10

clo

clo

br 3 11 x 10

living 15 x 13

carport 20 x 12

©

MAIN FLOOR

Units	Single
Price Code	A
Total Finished	998 sq. ft.
Main Finished	998 sq. ft.
Dimensions	48'x29'
Foundation	Crawlspace Slab
Bedrooms	3
Full Baths	1
Main Ceiling	8'
Max Ridge Height	26'
Roof Framing	Stick
Exterior Walls	2x4

Design 93222

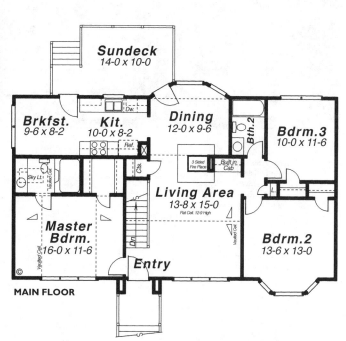

Sundeck 14-0 x 10-0

Brkfst. 9-6 x 8-2

Dw.

Kit. 10-0 x 8-2

Ref.

Dining 12-0 x 9-6

Bth.2

Bdrm.3 10-0 x 11-6

Sky Lt.

3 Sided Fire Place

Built in Cab

Living Area 13-8 x 15-0
Flat Ceil. 12-9 High

Vaulted Ceil.

Master Bdrm. 16-0 x 11-6

Vaulted Ceil.

Dn.

Vaulted Ceil.

Bdrm.2 13-6 x 13-0

©

Entry

MAIN FLOOR

Units	Single
Price Code	A
Total Finished	1,292 sq. ft.
Main Finished	1,276 sq. ft.
Lower Finished	16 sq. ft.
Basement Unfinished	392 sq. ft.
Garage Unfinished	728 sq. ft.
Dimensions	48'x38'
Foundation	Basement
Bedrooms	3
Full Baths	2
Main Ceiling	8'
Max Ridge Height	16'
Roof Framing	Stick
Exterior Walls	2x4

Design 99673

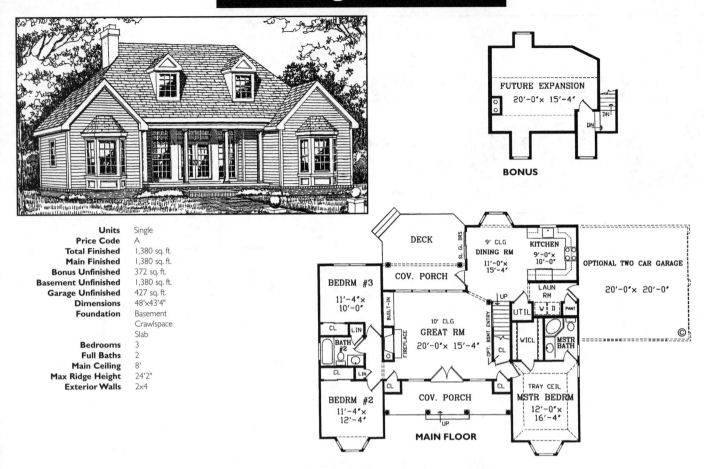

FUTURE EXPANSION
20'-0" x 15'-4"

BONUS

Units	Single
Price Code	A
Total Finished	1,380 sq. ft.
Main Finished	1,380 sq. ft.
Bonus Unfinished	372 sq. ft.
Basement Unfinished	1,380 sq. ft.
Garage Unfinished	427 sq. ft.
Dimensions	48'x43'4"
Foundation	Basement
	Crawlspace
	Slab
Bedrooms	3
Full Baths	2
Main Ceiling	8'
Max Ridge Height	24'2"
Exterior Walls	2x4

DECK

DINING RM 9' CLG 11'-0" x 15'-4"

KITCHEN 9'-0" x 10'-0"

COV. PORCH

OPTIONAL TWO CAR GARAGE 20'-0" x 20'-0"

BEDRM #3 11'-4" x 10'-0"

LAUN RM

GREAT RM 10' CLG 20'-0" x 15'-4"

UTIL

MSTR BATH

BATH #2

WICL

BEDRM #2 11'-4" x 12'-4"

COV. PORCH

MSTR BEDRM TRAY CEIL 12'-0" x 16'-4"

MAIN FLOOR

Design 93279

Units	Single
Price Code	A
Total Finished	1,388 sq. ft.
Main Finished	1,388 sq. ft.
Garage Unfinished	400 sq. ft.
Dimensions	48'x46'
Foundation	Crawlspace
	Slab
Bedrooms	3
Full Baths	2
Main Ceiling	8'
Max Ridge Height	18'
Roof Framing	Truss
Exterior Walls	2x4

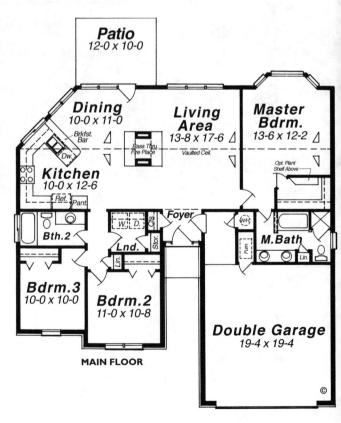

Patio 12-0 x 10-0

Dining 10-0 x 11-0

Living Area 13-8 x 17-6

Master Bdrm. 13-6 x 12-2

Kitchen 10-0 x 12-6

Opt. Plant Shelf Above

Foyer

Bth.2

Lnd.

M.Bath

Bdrm.3 10-0 x 10-0

Bdrm.2 11-0 x 10-8

Double Garage 19-4 x 19-4

MAIN FLOOR

Design 97113

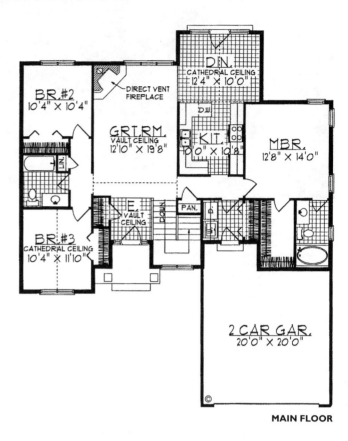

MAIN FLOOR

Units	Single
Price Code	A
Total Finished	1,416 sq. ft.
Main Finished	1,416 sq. ft.
Basement Unfinished	1,416 sq. ft.
Dimensions	48'x55'4"
Foundation	Basement
Bedrooms	3
Full Baths	2
Max Ridge Height	21'8"
Roof Framing	Truss
Exterior Walls	2x6

Design 82009

MAIN FLOOR

Units	Single
Price Code	A
Total Finished	1,452 sq. ft.
Main Finished	1,452 sq. ft.
Garage Unfinished	480 sq. ft.
Porch Unfinished	197 sq. ft.
Dimensions	48'x63'4"
Foundation	Crawlspace
	Slab
Bedrooms	3
Full Baths	2
Main Ceiling	9'
Roof Framing	Stick
Exterior Walls	2x4

Design 93165

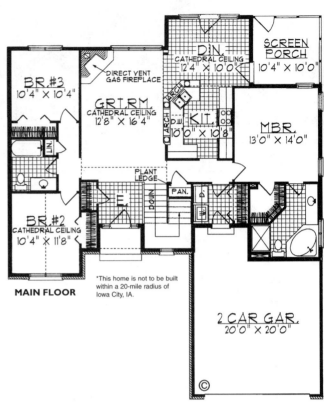

Units	Single
Price Code	A
Total Finished	1,472 sq. ft.
Main Finished	1,472 sq. ft.
Basement Unfinished	1,472 sq. ft.
Garage Unfinished	424 sq. ft.
Dimensions	48'x56'4"
Foundation	Basement
Bedrooms	3
Full Baths	2
Max Ridge Height	19'8"
Roof Framing	Stick
Exterior Walls	2x6

BR. #3
10'4" X 10'4"

DIRECT VENT GAS FIREPLACE

DIN.
CATHEDRAL CEILING
12'4" X 10'0"

SCREEN PORCH
10'4" X 10'0"

GRT. RM.
CATHEDRAL CEILING
12'8" X 16'4"

KIT.
10'0" X 10'8"

MBR.
13'0" X 14'0"

BR. #2
CATHEDRAL CEILING
10'4" X 11'8"

PLANT LEDGE

DOWN

PAN.

MAIN FLOOR

*This home is not to be built within a 20-mile radius of Iowa City, IA.

2 CAR GAR.
20'0" X 20'0"

Design 99106

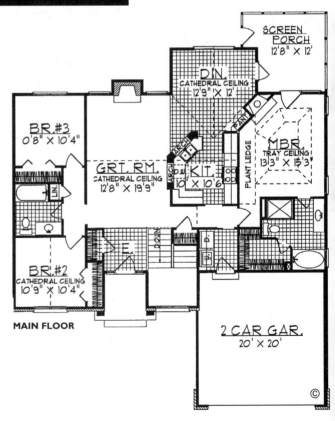

Units	Single
Price Code	A
Total Finished	1,495 sq. ft.
Main Finished	1,495 sq. ft.
Basement Unfinished	1,495 sq. ft.
Dimensions	48'x58'8"
Foundation	Basement
Bedrooms	3
Full Baths	2
Max Ridge Height	20'6"
Roof Framing	Truss
Exterior Walls	2x4

SCREEN PORCH
12'8" X 12'

BR. #3
0'8" X 10'4"

DIN.
CATHEDRAL CEILING
12'9" X 12'

MBR.
TRAY CEILING
13'3" X 15'3"

GRT. RM.
CATHEDRAL CEILING
12'8" X 19'9"

KIT.
10'3" X 10'6"

PLANT LEDGE

DOWN

BR. #2
CATHEDRAL CEILING
10'9" X 10'4"

MAIN FLOOR

2 CAR GAR.
20' X 20'

Design 66044

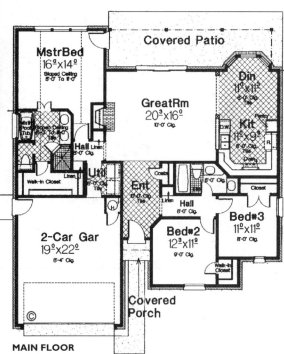

Units	Single
Price Code	B
Total Finished	1,573 sq. ft.
Main Finished	1,573 sq. ft.
Dimensions	48'x51'
Foundation	Slab
Bedrooms	3
Full Baths	2
Main Ceiling	8'-10'
Max Ridge Height	24'
Roof Framing	Stick
Exterior Walls	2x4

Covered Patio

MstrBed
16⁰x14⁰
Sloped Ceiling
8'-0" To 11'-0"

GreatRm
20³x16⁰
10'-0" Clg.

Din
11⁰x11²
9'-0" Clg.

Kit
11⁰x9⁸

Hall
8'-0" Clg.

Linen

Util
8'-0" Tile

Walk-in Closet

Ent
9'-0" Clg.
Tile

Hall
8'-0" Clg.

Bed#3
11⁰x11⁰
8'-0" Clg.

Bed#2
12³x11⁹
9'-0" Clg.

Walk-in Closet

2-Car Gar
19⁰x22⁰
8'-4" Clg.

Closet

Covered Porch

MAIN FLOOR

Design 81009

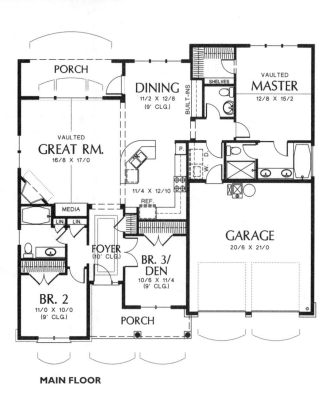

Units	Single
Price Code	B
Total Finished	1,580 sq. ft.
Main Finished	1,580 sq. ft.
Garage Unfinished	452 sq. ft.
Dimensions	48'x50'
Foundation	Crawlspace
Bedrooms	3
Full Baths	2
Half Baths	1

PORCH

DINING
11/2 X 12/8
(9' CLG.)

SHELVES

VAULTED
MASTER
12/8 X 15/2

BUILT-INS

VAULTED
GREAT RM.
16/8 X 17/0

11/4 X 12/10

REF.

MEDIA

LIN. LIN.

FOYER
(10' CLG.)

BR. 3/
DEN
10/6 X 11/4
(9' CLG.)

W. D.

P.

GARAGE
20/6 X 21/0

BR. 2
11/0 X 10/0
(9' CLG.)

PORCH

MAIN FLOOR

Units	Single
Price Code	B
Total Finished	1,595 sq. ft.
Main Finished	1,595 sq. ft.
Basement Unfinished	1,589 sq. ft.
Garage Unfinished	409 sq. ft.
Deck Unfinished	279 sq. ft.
Dimensions	48'x51'4"
Foundation	Basement
Bedrooms	3
Full Baths	2
Main Ceiling	8'
Vaulted Ceiling	14'
Max Ridge Height	24'6"
Roof Framing	Truss
Exterior Walls	2x4

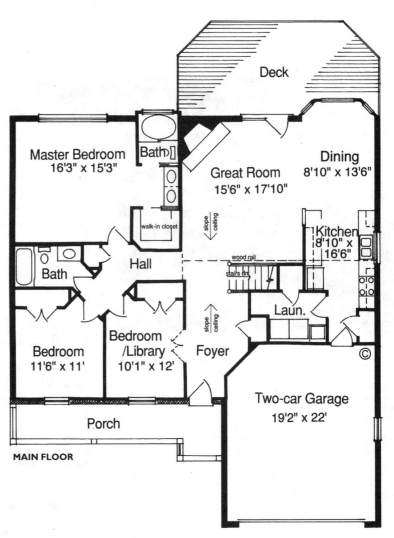

MAIN FLOOR

Design 92238

Units	Single
Price Code	B
Total Finished	1,664 sq. ft.
Main Finished	1,664 sq. ft.
Basement Unfinished	1,600 sq. ft.
Garage Unfinished	440 sq. ft.
Dimensions	48'x63'
Foundation	Basement
	Crawlspace
	Slab
Bedrooms	3
Full Baths	2
Max Ridge Height	22'6"
Roof Framing	Stick
Exterior Walls	2x4

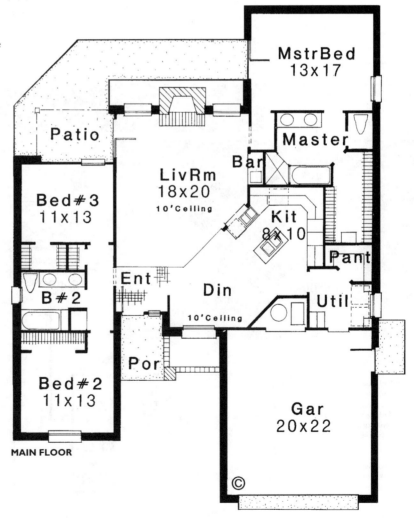

MAIN FLOOR

Design 66002

Units	Single
Price Code	B
Total Finished	1,673 sq. ft.
Main Finished	1,673 sq. ft.
Garage Unfinished	425 sq. ft.
Deck Unfinished	104 sq. ft.
Porch Unfinished	62 sq. ft.
Dimensions	48'x63'
Foundation	Basement
	Crawlspace
	Slab
Bedrooms	3
Full Baths	2
Main Ceiling	8'-10'
Max Ridge Height	22'6"
Roof Framing	Stick
Exterior Walls	2x4

PATIO AREA

COVERED PATIO

MSTR.BDRM. 17 X 13
COFFER CLG. 8" TO 10"

MSTR BATH

W-I CLO.

BDRM.3 12⁸ X 10⁶
8" CLG.

LIVING RM. 17⁶X20
10' CLG.

WET BAR

HALL

CLO.

ENT 10' CLG.

HALL

KITCHEN /DINING 18³ X 18³
10' CLG.

ISLAND

PANTRY

UT.

W. D.

COVERED POR.

BDRM.2 12X12
8' CLG.

DOUBLE GARAGE 20X21⁶
8' CLG.

MAIN FLOOR

Design 34901

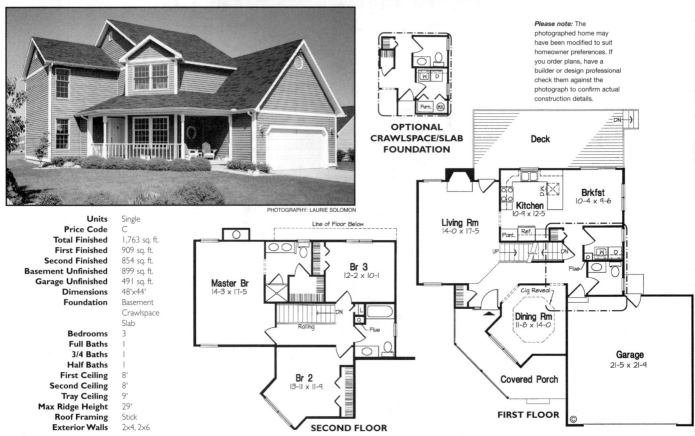

PHOTOGRAPHY: LAURIE SOLOMON

OPTIONAL CRAWLSPACE/SLAB FOUNDATION

Units	Single
Price Code	C
Total Finished	1,763 sq. ft.
First Finished	909 sq. ft.
Second Finished	854 sq. ft.
Basement Unfinished	899 sq. ft.
Garage Unfinished	491 sq. ft.
Dimensions	48'x44'
Foundation	Basement
	Crawlspace
	Slab
Bedrooms	3
Full Baths	1
3/4 Baths	1
Half Baths	1
First Ceiling	8'
Second Ceiling	8'
Tray Ceiling	9'
Max Ridge Height	29'
Roof Framing	Stick
Exterior Walls	2x4, 2x6

Line of Floor Below

Master Br 14-3 x 17-5

Br 3 12-2 x 10-1

DN

Railing

Flue

Br 2 13-11 x 11-9

SECOND FLOOR

DN

Deck

Kitchen 10-4 x 12-5

Brkfst 10-4 x 9-6

Living Rm 14-0 x 17-5

Pant.

Ref.

UP

Flue

DN

Clg Reveal

Dining Rm 11-8 x 14-0

Covered Porch

Garage 21-5 x 21-4

FIRST FLOOR

Design 68030

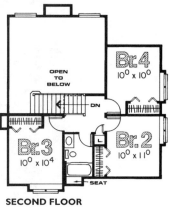

SECOND FLOOR

Br. 4
10⁰ x 10⁰

Br. 3
10⁰ x 10⁴

Br. 2
10⁰ x 11⁰

OPEN TO BELOW

DN

SEAT

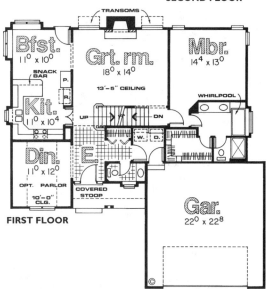

FIRST FLOOR

Bfst.
11⁰ x 10⁰

Grt. rm.
18⁰ x 14⁰
13'-5" CEILING

Mbr.
14⁴ x 13⁰

WHIRLPOOL

SNACK BAR

Kit.
11⁰ x 10⁴

UP

DN

W. D.

Din.
11⁰ x 12⁰

E.

COVERED STOOP

Gar.
22⁰ x 22⁸

OPT. PARLOR
10'-0" CLG.

TRANSOMS

Units	Single
Price Code	C
Total Finished	1,783 sq. ft.
First Finished	1,265 sq. ft.
Second Finished	518 sq. ft.
Basement Unfinished	1,265 sq. ft.
Garage Unfinished	499 sq. ft.
Dimensions	48'x48'
Foundation	Basement
	Crawlspace
	Slab
Bedrooms	4
Full Baths	2
Half Baths	1
First Ceiling	8'
Max Ridge Height	25'8"
Roof Framing	Stick
Exterior Walls	2x4

* Alternate foundation options available at an additional charge.
Please call 1-800-235-5700 for more information.

Design 62052

SECOND FLOOR

4' WALL

BED RM. 2
11'-0" X 10'-8"

BED RM. 3
9'-3" X 11'-0"

ATTIC STORAGE

FIRST FLOOR

GLASS BLOCKS

WHP TUB

SEAT SHWR

M. BATH

KNEE SPACE LIN

STRG.
6'-0" X 4'-0"

LAU.
7'-2" X 6'-0"

MASTER SUITE
15'-0" X 13'-3"

MEDIA CENTER

GREAT RM.
18'-2" X 18'-0"

GARAGE
19'-0" X 20'-0"

KITCHEN
9'-10" X 11'-0"

REF

RG

DW

PAN

FOYER
10' CLNG

BRKFAST RM.
9'-10" X 8'-0"

8" COLUMNS

DINING RM.
10' CLNG
11'-6" X 12'-6"

PRCH

Units	Single
Price Code	C
Total Finished	1,797 sq. ft.
First Finished	1,356 sq. ft.
Second Finished	441 sq. ft.
Dimensions	48'x43'
Foundation	Basement
	Crawlspace
	Slab
Bedrooms	3
Full Baths	2
Half Baths	1

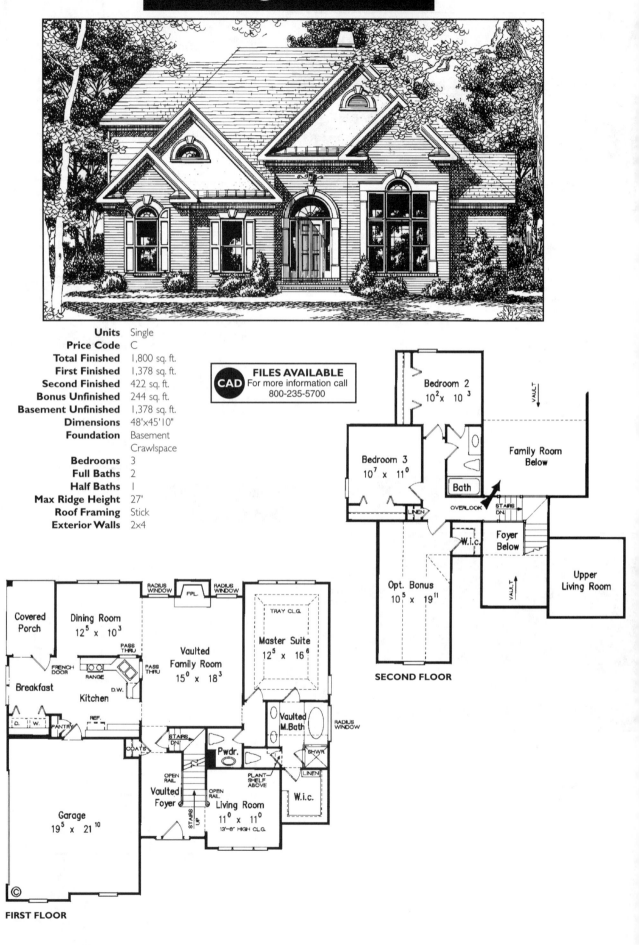

Units	Single
Price Code	C
Total Finished	1,800 sq. ft.
First Finished	1,378 sq. ft.
Second Finished	422 sq. ft.
Bonus Unfinished	244 sq. ft.
Basement Unfinished	1,378 sq. ft.
Dimensions	48'x45'10"
Foundation	Basement
	Crawlspace
Bedrooms	3
Full Baths	2
Half Baths	1
Max Ridge Height	27'
Roof Framing	Stick
Exterior Walls	2x4

CAD FILES AVAILABLE
For more information call
800-235-5700

SECOND FLOOR

Bedroom 2 10^2 x 10^3

Bedroom 3 10^7 x 11^0

Bath

Family Room Below

OVERLOOK

STAIRS DN.

VAULT

LINEN

W.i.c.

Foyer Below

Opt. Bonus 10^5 x 19^{11}

VAULT

Upper Living Room

FIRST FLOOR

Covered Porch

Dining Room 12^5 x 10^3

RADIUS WINDOW   FPL.   RADIUS WINDOW

Vaulted Family Room 15^0 x 18^3

TRAY CLG.

Master Suite 12^5 x 16^6

PASS THRU

PASS THRU

RANGE

D.W.

FRENCH DOOR

Breakfast

Kitchen

REF.

D. W.   PANTRY

COATS

STAIRS DN.

Pwdr.

Vaulted M.Bath

RADIUS WINDOW

SHWR.

LINEN

Vaulted Foyer

OPEN RAIL

OPEN RAIL

STAIRS UP

PLANT SHELF ABOVE

Living Room 11^0 x 11^0 13'-6" HIGH CLG.

W.i.c.

Garage 19^5 x 21^{10}

©

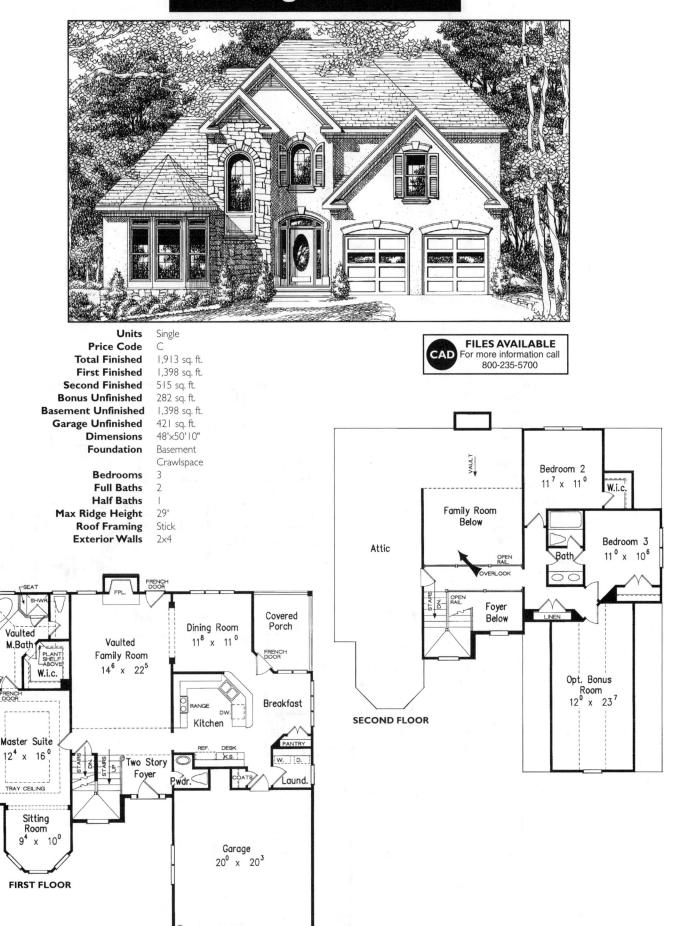

Units	Single
Price Code	C
Total Finished	1,913 sq. ft.
First Finished	1,398 sq. ft.
Second Finished	515 sq. ft.
Bonus Unfinished	282 sq. ft.
Basement Unfinished	1,398 sq. ft.
Garage Unfinished	421 sq. ft.
Dimensions	48'x50'10"
Foundation	Basement
	Crawlspace
Bedrooms	3
Full Baths	2
Half Baths	1
Max Ridge Height	29'
Roof Framing	Stick
Exterior Walls	2x4

CAD FILES AVAILABLE
For more information call
800-235-5700

SECOND FLOOR

Attic

VAULT

Bedroom 2
11⁷ x 11⁰

W.i.c.

Family Room
Below

Bath

Bedroom 3
11⁰ x 10⁶

OPEN RAIL

OVERLOOK

STAIRS DN.

OPEN RAIL

Foyer
Below

LINEN

Opt. Bonus
Room
12⁰ x 23⁷

FIRST FLOOR

SEAT

SHWR

FPL.

FRENCH DOOR

Vaulted
M.Bath

PLANT SHELF ABOVE

W.i.c.

LINEN

FRENCH DOOR

Vaulted
Family Room
14⁶ x 22⁵

Dining Room
11⁸ x 11⁰

Covered
Porch

FRENCH DOOR

RANGE

DW

Kitchen

Breakfast

PANTRY

Master Suite
12⁴ x 16⁰

STAIRS DN.

STAIRS UP

Two Story
Foyer

REF. DESK

K.S.

W. D.

Pwdr.

COATS

Laund.

TRAY CEILING

Sitting
Room
9⁴ x 10⁰

Garage
20⁰ x 20³

Units	Single
Price Code	E
Total Finished	2,336 sq. ft.
First Finished	1,189 sq. ft.
Second Finished	1,147 sq. ft.
Garage Unfinished	530 sq. ft.
Dimensions	48'x49'
Foundation	Basement
Bedrooms	4
Full Baths	2
3/4 Baths	1
Half Baths	1
First Ceiling	9'
Second Ceiling	8'
Max Ridge Height	30'8"
Roof Framing	Stick
Exterior Walls	2x4

* Alternate foundation options available at an additional charge.
Please call 1-800-235-5700 for more information.

SECOND FLOOR

FIRST FLOOR

Units	Single
Price Code	E
Total Finished	2,478 sq. ft.
First Finished	1,883 sq. ft.
Second Finished	595 sq. ft.
Basement Unfinished	617 sq. ft.
Garage Unfinished	675 sq. ft.
Deck Unfinished	157 sq. ft.
Porch Unfinished	429 sq. ft.
Dimensions	48'x42'
Foundation	Basement
Bedrooms	3
Full Baths	2
Max Ridge Height	36'
Exterior Walls	2x6

* Alternate foundation options available at an additional charge.
Please call 1-800-235-5700 for more information.

SECOND FLOOR

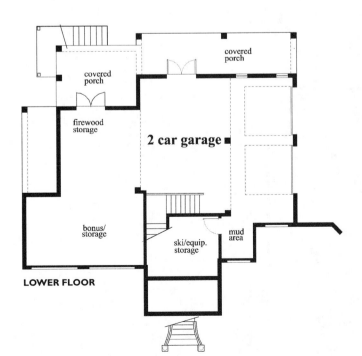

LOWER FLOOR

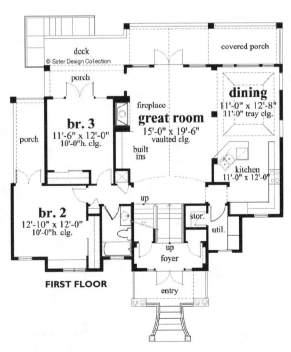

FIRST FLOOR

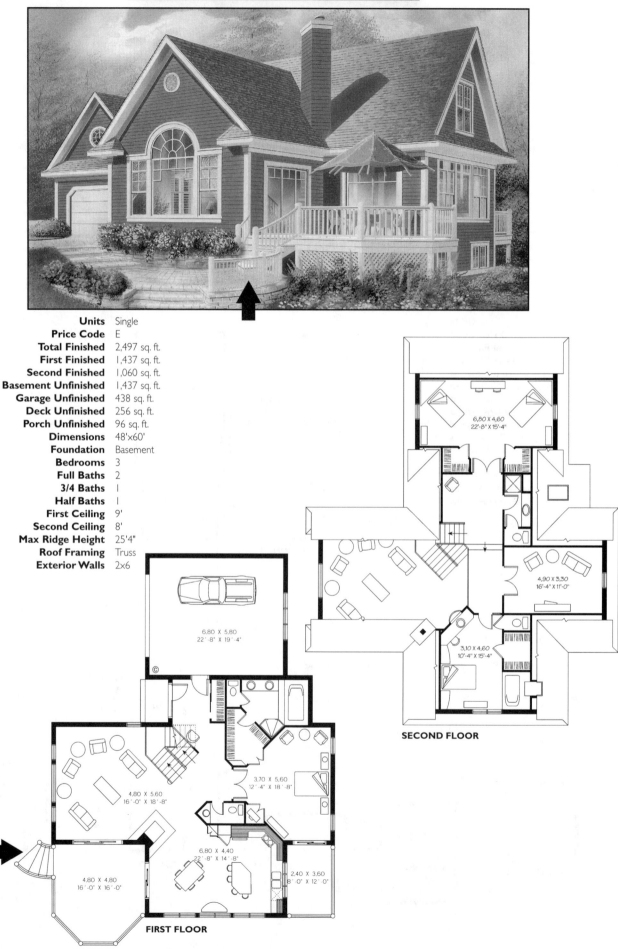

Units	Single
Price Code	E
Total Finished	2,497 sq. ft.
First Finished	1,437 sq. ft.
Second Finished	1,060 sq. ft.
Basement Unfinished	1,437 sq. ft.
Garage Unfinished	438 sq. ft.
Deck Unfinished	256 sq. ft.
Porch Unfinished	96 sq. ft.
Dimensions	48'x60'
Foundation	Basement
Bedrooms	3
Full Baths	2
3/4 Baths	1
Half Baths	1
First Ceiling	9'
Second Ceiling	8'
Max Ridge Height	25'4"
Roof Framing	Truss
Exterior Walls	2x6

SECOND FLOOR

FIRST FLOOR

Units	Single
Price Code	F
Total Finished	2,663 sq. ft.
First Finished	1,332 sq. ft.
Second Finished	1,331 sq. ft.
Basement Unfinished	1,332 sq. ft.
Dimensions	48'x42'
Foundation	Basement
Bedrooms	4
Full Baths	3
Half Baths	1
First Ceiling	9'
Second Ceiling	8'
Vaulted Ceiling	10'
Tray Ceiling	10'
Max Ridge Height	33'
Roof Framing	Stick
Exterior Walls	2x4

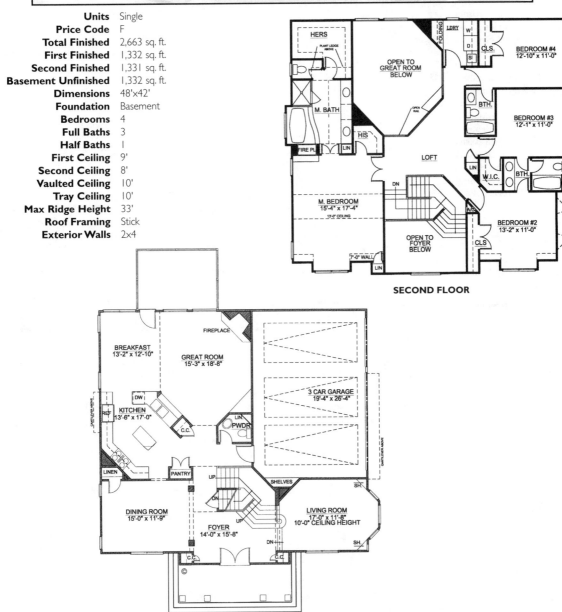

SECOND FLOOR

FIRST FLOOR

Units	Single
Price Code	C
Total Finished	1,966 sq. ft.
First Finished	1,409 sq. ft.
Second Finished	557 sq. ft.
Garage Unfinished	548 sq. ft.
Porch Unfinished	316 sq. ft.
Dimensions	48'2"x67'5"
Foundation	Basement
Bedrooms	3
Full Baths	2
Half Baths	1
Max Ridge Height	25'8"
Roof Framing	Stick
Exterior Walls	2x4

SECOND FLOOR

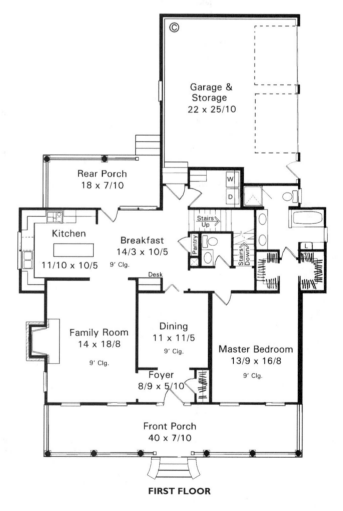

FIRST FLOOR

Design 19410

PHOTOGRAPHY: MIKE MORELAND

Units	Single
Price Code	D
Total Finished	2,175 sq. ft.
First Finished	1,600 sq. ft.
Second Finished	575 sq. ft.
Lower Unfinished	1,509 sq. ft.
Garage Unfinished	413 sq. ft.
Dimensions	48'4"x60'
Foundation	Basement
Bedrooms	4
Full Baths	2
Half Baths	1
First Ceiling	8'4"
Second Ceiling	8'4"
Roof Framing	Stick
Exterior Walls	2x4

Please note: The photographed home may have been modified to suit homeowner preferences. If you order plans, have a builder or design professional check them against the photograph to confirm actual construction details.

SECOND FLOOR

ATTIC

OPEN TO LIVING/DINING

LOFT OR BEDRM 15x12½

CLOS

DN

BATH

BEDRM 12x14

ATTIC

LOWER FLOOR

STORAGE 10½x25

RECREATION 15½x26½

BEDRM 14½x19

CLOS

BATH

UP

STORAGE 15x13½

FIRST FLOOR

DECK

BRKFST 10½x9

LIVING 14x22

LIBRARY OR BEDRM 12x11

DECK

KIT 10½x15

PWDR

DN

BEDRM 12x20½

W/D

DINING 11x12

UP

BATH

GARAGE 19½x20½

ENTRY

CLOS

Units	Single
Price Code	A
Total Finished	1,500 sq. ft.
Main Finished	1,500 sq. ft.
Garage Unfinished	417 sq. ft.
Porch Unfinished	57 sq. ft.
Dimensions	48'6"x48'4"
Foundation	Crawlspace
	Slab
Bedrooms	3
Full Baths	2
Main Ceiling	8'
Roof Framing	Stick
Exterior Walls	2x4

MAIN FLOOR

- GLASS SHWR
- LIN
- M. BATH 8'-0" X 18'-0"
- WHP TUB
- MASTER SUITE 9' PAN CEILING 13'-0" X 14'-0"
- GREAT ROOM 15'-4" X 19'-8" 9' BOXED CEILING
- DINING 11'-6" X 10'-6"
- BAR
- KIT. 10'-6" X 10'-0"
- RG
- REF
- DW
- BEDROOM 3 12'-4" X 10'-8"
- LAU. 9'-4" X 5'-6"
- D
- W
- PAN
- BATH
- PRCH
- BEDROOM 2 10'-8" X 12'-0"
- VAULTED CEILING
- GARAGE 20'-10" X 20'-0"

Units	Single
Price Code	A
Total Finished	1,416 sq. ft.
Main Finished	1,416 sq. ft.
Garage Unfinished	480 sq. ft.
Deck Unfinished	160 sq. ft.
Porch Unfinished	48 sq. ft.
Dimensions	49'x49'10"
Foundation	Crawlspace
	Slab
Bedrooms	3
Full Baths	2
Max Ridge Height	22'
Exterior Walls	2x4

- MSTR. BDRM. 16X12 SLOPED CLG. 8' TO 11'
- COVERED PATIO
- DIN. 10X11 8' CLG.
- GREAT ROOM 18X16 10' CLG.
- MSTR. BATH SLOPED CLG.
- HALL 8' CLG.
- BAR LEDGE
- KIT. 10X10 8' CLG.
- PANTRY
- DW
- W-I CLOS.
- UTL.
- ENT. 10' CLG.
- B.
- CLO
- HALL 8' CLG.
- BDRM.#3 10X11 8' CLG.
- DOUBLE GARAGE
- POR.
- BDRM.#2 10X12 9' CLG.
- CL.

MAIN FLOOR

Units	Single
Price Code	A
Total Finished	1,429 sq. ft.
Main Finished	1,429 sq. ft.
Basement Unfinished	1,472 sq. ft.
Garage Unfinished	438 sq. ft.
Dimensions	49'x53'
Foundation	Basement
	Crawlspace
	Slab
Bedrooms	3
Full Baths	2
Main Ceiling	8'
Max Ridge Height	23'
Roof Framing	Stick
Exterior Walls	2x4

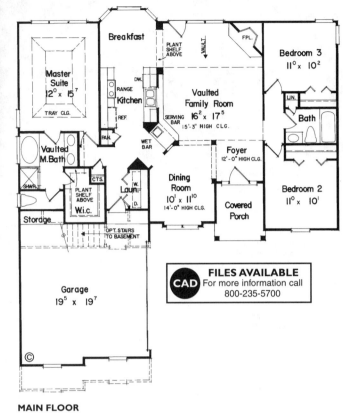

CAD FILES AVAILABLE
For more information call
800-235-5700

MAIN FLOOR

Units	Single
Price Code	A
Total Finished	1,432 sq. ft.
Main Finished	1,432 sq. ft.
Basement Unfinished	1,454 sq. ft.
Garage Unfinished	440 sq. ft.
Dimensions	49'x52'4"
Foundation	Basement
	Crawlspace
Bedrooms	3
Full Baths	2
Max Ridge Height	24'2"
Roof Framing	Stick
Exterior Walls	2x4

CAD FILES AVAILABLE
For more information call
800-235-5700

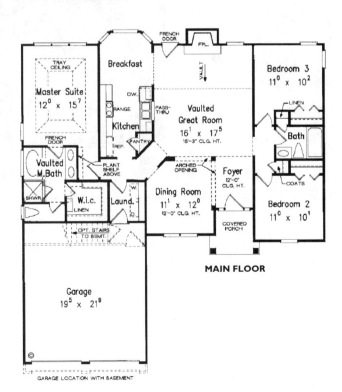

MAIN FLOOR

GARAGE LOCATION WITH BASEMENT

Design 97235

MAIN FLOOR

Covered Porch

Master Suite 12³ x 15⁵

Vltd. M. Bath

SHWR

W.i.c.

Foyer

Vaulted Great Room 14³ x 20³ 12'-10" HIGH CLG.

Kitchen 12'-10" HIGH CLG.

Vaulted Breakfast

Bedroom 2 11³ x 10⁰

Bath

LINEN

Dining Room 10⁰ x 11³

Bedroom 3 11³ x 10³

LOWER FLOOR

Unfinished Basement

Garage 21² x 21⁵

STAIRS UP

COATS

Units	Single
Price Code	B
Total Finished	1,609 sq. ft.
Main Finished	1,509 sq. ft.
Lower Finished	100 sq. ft.
Basement Unfinished	954 sq. ft.
Garage Unfinished	484 sq. ft.
Dimensions	49'x34'4"
Foundation	Basement
Bedrooms	3
Full Baths	2
Max Ridge Height	28'
Roof Framing	Stick
Exterior Walls	2x4

CAD FILES AVAILABLE For more information call 800-235-5700

Design 97207

SECOND FLOOR

Vaulted Great Room Below

Bath

Bedroom 3 12⁵ x 10⁷

Bedroom 2 12⁵ x 11⁵

W.i.c.

Foyer Below

FIRST FLOOR

Master Suite 12⁰ x 15³

Vaulted Master Bath

SHWR

W.i.c.

Vaulted Great Room 14⁶ x 19³

Dining Room 11⁵ x 10⁰

Covered Porch

Kitchen

Breakfast

Pantry

Two Story Foyer

Storage

Garage 20⁵ x 19⁹

Units	Single
Price Code	B
Total Finished	1,690 sq. ft.
First Finished	1,236 sq. ft.
Second Finished	454 sq. ft.
Basement Unfinished	1,236 sq. ft.
Garage Unfinished	462 sq. ft.
Dimensions	49'x46'10"
Foundation	Basement Crawlspace Slab
Bedrooms	3
Full Baths	2
Half Baths	1
Max Ridge Height	25'
Roof Framing	Stick
Exterior Walls	2x4

CAD FILES AVAILABLE For more information call 800-235-5700

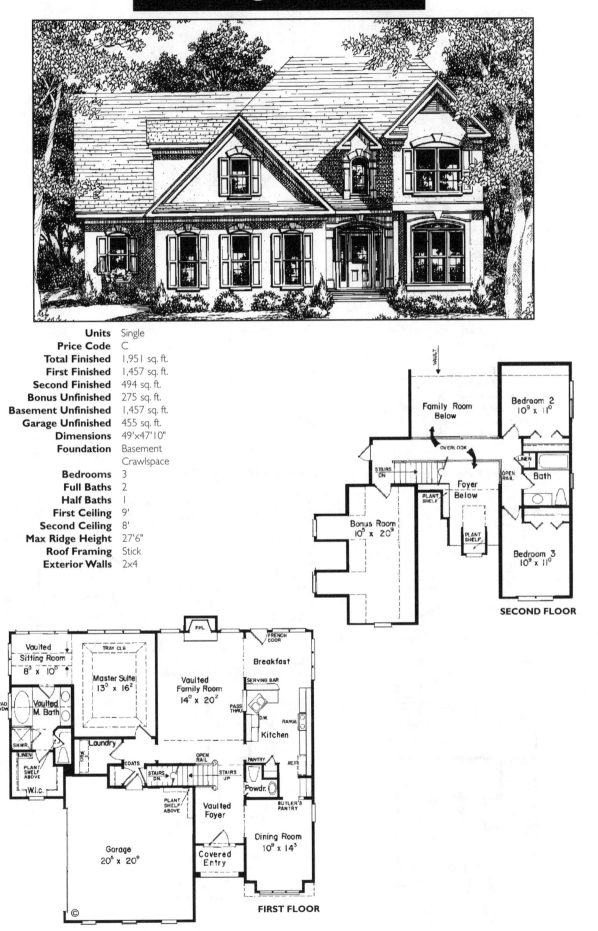

Units	Single
Price Code	C
Total Finished	1,951 sq. ft.
First Finished	1,457 sq. ft.
Second Finished	494 sq. ft.
Bonus Unfinished	275 sq. ft.
Basement Unfinished	1,457 sq. ft.
Garage Unfinished	455 sq. ft.
Dimensions	49'x47'10"
Foundation	Basement
	Crawlspace
Bedrooms	3
Full Baths	2
Half Baths	1
First Ceiling	9'
Second Ceiling	8'
Max Ridge Height	27'6"
Roof Framing	Stick
Exterior Walls	2x4

SECOND FLOOR

Bedroom 2
10⁹ x 11⁰

Bedroom 3
10⁹ x 11⁰

Family Room Below

Bonus Room
10⁵ x 20⁹

Foyer Below

Bath

VAULT

OVERLOOK

STAIRS DN

OPEN RAIL

LINEN

PLANT SHELF

FIRST FLOOR

Vaulted Sitting Room
8⁰ x 10⁰

Master Suite
13⁰ x 16²

TRAY CLG

Vaulted Family Room
14⁰ x 20²

Breakfast

SERVING BAR

PASS THRU

Kitchen

RANGE

D.W.

Vaulted M. Bath

Laundry

COATS

OPEN RAIL

PANTRY

REF.

Powdr.

BUTLER'S PANTRY

STAIRS DN.

STAIRS UP

Vaulted Foyer

Dining Room
10⁹ x 14³

Garage
20⁵ x 20⁹

Covered Entry

W.i.c.

PLANT SHELF ABOVE

SHWR.

LINEN

RAD WDW

FPL.

FRENCH DOOR

Units	Single
Price Code	E
Total Finished	2,472 sq. ft.
First Finished	1,802 sq. ft.
Second Finished	670 sq. ft.
Garage Unfinished	594 sq. ft.
Porch Unfinished	240 sq. ft.
Dimensions	49'x79'
Foundation	Slab
Bedrooms	3
Full Baths	2
Half Baths	I
First Ceiling	10'
Second Ceiling	8'
Max Ridge Height	33'
Roof Framing	Stick
Exterior Walls	2x4

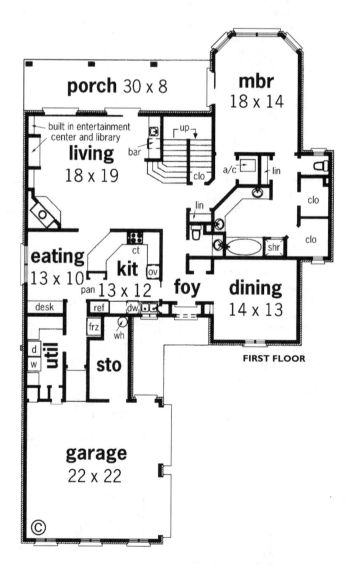

FIRST FLOOR

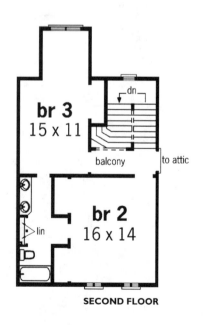

SECOND FLOOR

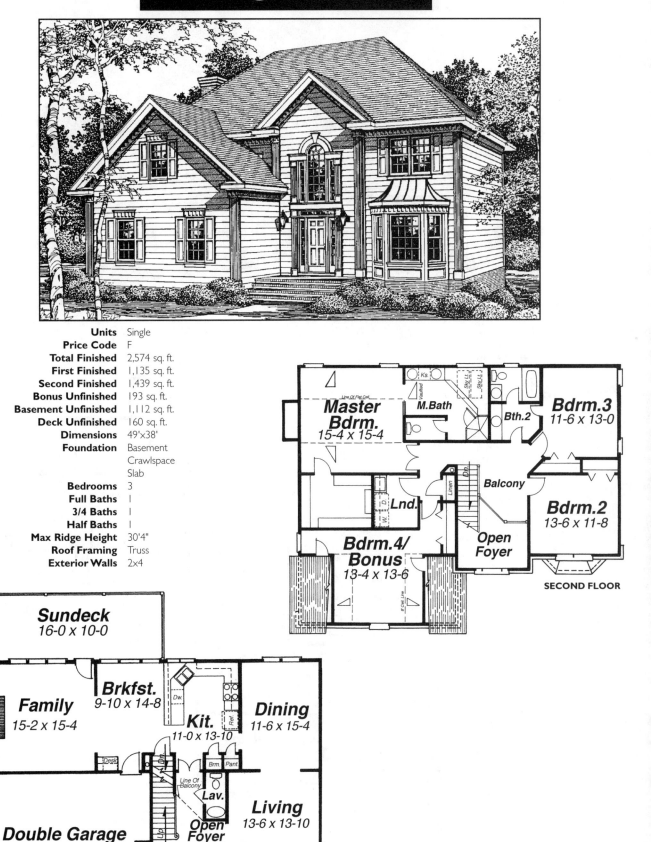

Units	Single
Price Code	F
Total Finished	2,574 sq. ft.
First Finished	1,135 sq. ft.
Second Finished	1,439 sq. ft.
Bonus Unfinished	193 sq. ft.
Basement Unfinished	1,112 sq. ft.
Deck Unfinished	160 sq. ft.
Dimensions	49'x38'
Foundation	Basement
	Crawlspace
	Slab
Bedrooms	3
Full Baths	1
3/4 Baths	1
Half Baths	1
Max Ridge Height	30'4"
Roof Framing	Truss
Exterior Walls	2x4

SECOND FLOOR

Master Bdrm. 15-4 x 15-4
M.Bath
Bth.2
Bdrm.3 11-6 x 13-0
Lnd.
Balcony
Bdrm.2 13-6 x 11-8
Open Foyer
Bdrm.4/ Bonus 13-4 x 13-6

FIRST FLOOR

Sundeck 16-0 x 10-0
Family 15-2 x 15-4
Brkfst. 9-10 x 14-8
Kit. 11-0 x 13-10
Dining 11-6 x 15-4
Living 13-6 x 13-10
Lav.
Open Foyer 10-10 x 7-0
Double Garage 23-4 x 21-8

Units	Single
Price Code	G
Total Finished	2,918 sq. ft.
First Finished	1,884 sq. ft.
Second Finished	1,034 sq. ft.
Garage Unfinished	566 sq. ft.
Porch Unfinished	240 sq. ft.
Dimensions	49'x79'
Foundation	Slab
Bedrooms	4
Full Baths	3
Half Baths	1
First Ceiling	10'
Second Ceiling	8'
Max Ridge Height	33'
Roof Framing	Stick
Exterior Walls	2x4

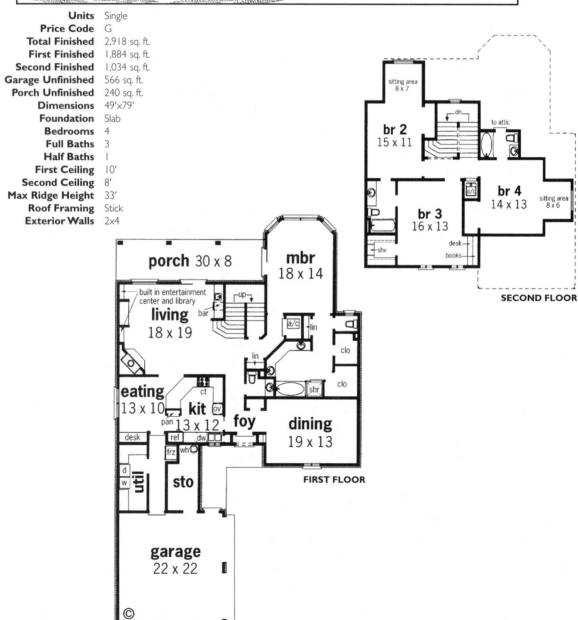

Win free blueprints!

2 Easy Ways to Enter

1. Log on to www.garlinghouse.com and fill out our questionnaire on-line

—OR—

2. Fill out the questionnaire below and mail to:
   Free Home Plans Contest
   Garlinghouse, LLC
   4125 Lafayette Rd. Ste. 100
   Chantilly, VA 20151

1. To Enter
No purchase necessary. Limit one entry per person per calendar month.

2. Contest Period
May 15, 2004 to May 15, 2005.

3. Selection of Winners
One drawing will be held on or near the last day of each month during the drawing period. One winner will be selected each month by a random drawing from all entries received during the previous month. Odds of winning depend on the number of entries received.

4. Prize
A four-copy set (our "Minimum 4-Set Construction Package") of the home plan of the winner's choice will be awarded to one winner per month during the contest period. Home plans not offered for sale by the Garlinghouse Company are not eligible.

5. Eligibility
This drawing is open to U.S. residents who are 18 years of age or older at the time of entry. Employees and consultants of Garlinghouse and its parent, affiliates, subsidiaries, advertising and promotion agencies and members of the immediate families of any Garlinghouse employee or consultant are not eligible to enter. Void where prohibited by law.

6. Terms & Conditions
The Garlinghouse Company is not responsible for taxes or shipping charges. *For complete rules, terms and conditions, additional fine print, and information regarding notification of winners, log on to* www.garlinghouse.com.

Name: _____

Address: _____

City: _____ **State:** _____ **Zip:** _____

Daytime telephone number: (___) _____   **Email:** _____

the **Garlinghouse** company

Where did you buy this publication?
- ❏ Newsstand
- ❏ Grocery store
- ❏ Pharmacy/Conv. store
- ❏ Lumberyard/Home Center
- ❏ Bookstore
- ❏ Other _____

Please specify store: _____

Why did you buy this publication?
- ❏ Value
- ❏ Number of plans
- ❏ Appealing cover photo
- ❏ Impulse
- ❏ Other _____

What style are you most interested in?
- ❏ Farmhouse or Country
- ❏ Colonial
- ❏ Rustic Cottage or Cabin
- ❏ Victorian
- ❏ European
- ❏ Traditional
- ❏ Other _____

When are you planning to build?
- ❏ Within 6 months
- ❏ 6-12 months
- ❏ 1-2 years
- ❏ More than 2 years
- ❏ Undecided

What is the approximate size of the home?
- ❏ Under 1,000 square feet
- ❏ 1,000 to 2,000
- ❏ 2,000 to 3,000
- ❏ 3,000 to 4,000
- ❏ Over 4,000

What type of home?
- ❏ One level
- ❏ Two story with all bedrooms on second floor
- ❏ Two story with one or two bedrooms on first floor
- ❏ Other _____

Have you bought land? ❏ Yes ❏ No

Please provide any other comments.
Let us know if you have special requirements (e.g. you want a great-room but no living room) or specific property features (e.g. you have a sloped or narrow lot).

_____

_____

_____

Design 97600

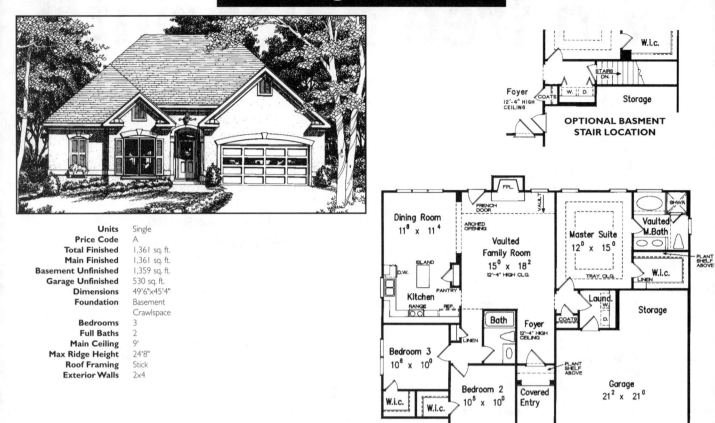

Units	Single
Price Code	A
Total Finished	1,361 sq. ft.
Main Finished	1,361 sq. ft.
Basement Unfinished	1,359 sq. ft.
Garage Unfinished	530 sq. ft.
Dimensions	49'6"x45'4"
Foundation	Basement
	Crawlspace
Bedrooms	3
Full Baths	2
Main Ceiling	9'
Max Ridge Height	24'8"
Roof Framing	Stick
Exterior Walls	2x4

OPTIONAL BASMENT STAIR LOCATION

MAIN FLOOR

Design 98431

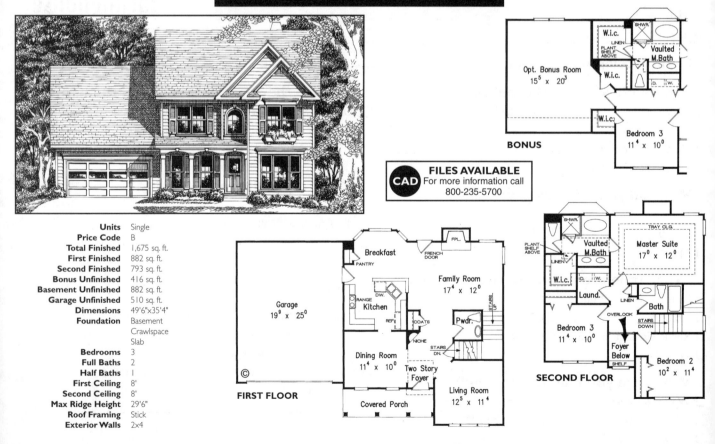

Units	Single
Price Code	B
Total Finished	1,675 sq. ft.
First Finished	882 sq. ft.
Second Finished	793 sq. ft.
Bonus Unfinished	416 sq. ft.
Basement Unfinished	882 sq. ft.
Garage Unfinished	510 sq. ft.
Dimensions	49'6"x35'4"
Foundation	Basement
	Crawlspace
	Slab
Bedrooms	3
Full Baths	2
Half Baths	1
First Ceiling	8'
Second Ceiling	8'
Max Ridge Height	29'6"
Roof Framing	Stick
Exterior Walls	2x4

FILES AVAILABLE
CAD For more information call
800-235-5700

BONUS

FIRST FLOOR

SECOND FLOOR

PHOTOGRAPHY: TIM MURPHY, PHOTO IMAGERY

Units	Single
Price Code	J
Total Finished	3,550 sq. ft.
First Finished	1,880 sq. ft.
Second Finished	1,670 sq. ft.
Basement Unfinished	1,780 sq. ft.
Garage Unfinished	444 sq. ft.
Deck Unfinished	599 sq. ft.
Dimensions	49'6"x75'2"
Foundation	Basement
Bedrooms	4
Full Baths	3
First Ceiling	9'
Second Ceiling	8'
Vaulted Ceiling	16'
Tray Ceiling	10'
Max Ridge Height	31'
Roof Framing	Stick
Exterior Walls	2x6

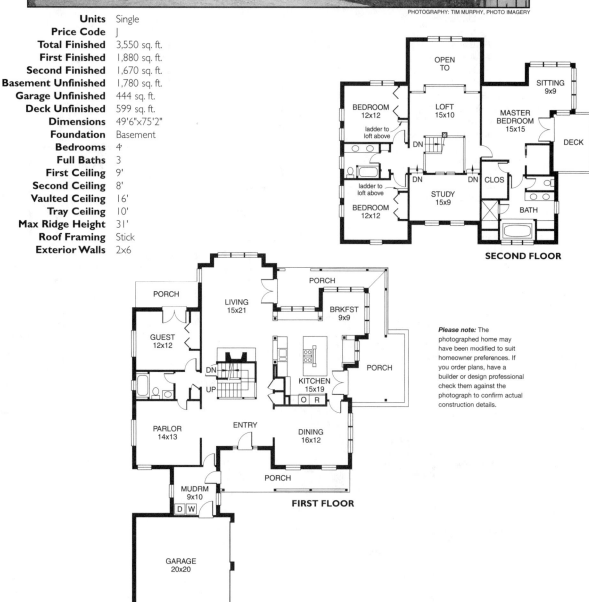

Please note: The photographed home may have been modified to suit homeowner preferences. If you order plans, have a builder or design professional check them against the photograph to confirm actual construction details.

SECOND FLOOR

FIRST FLOOR

Design 97698

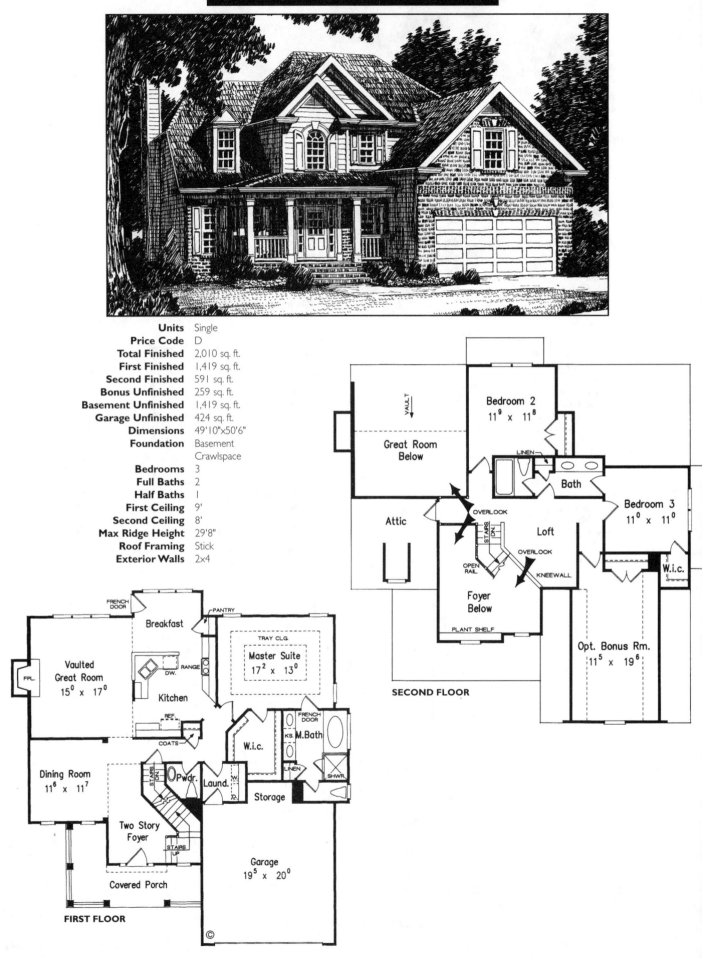

Units	Single
Price Code	D
Total Finished	2,010 sq. ft.
First Finished	1,419 sq. ft.
Second Finished	591 sq. ft.
Bonus Unfinished	259 sq. ft.
Basement Unfinished	1,419 sq. ft.
Garage Unfinished	424 sq. ft.
Dimensions	49'10"x50'6"
Foundation	Basement
	Crawlspace
Bedrooms	3
Full Baths	2
Half Baths	1
First Ceiling	9'
Second Ceiling	8'
Max Ridge Height	29'8"
Roof Framing	Stick
Exterior Walls	2x4

SECOND FLOOR

Bedroom 2
11⁹ x 11⁸

Great Room Below

Attic

Bath

Loft

Bedroom 3
11⁰ x 11⁰

W.i.c.

Foyer Below

PLANT SHELF

Opt. Bonus Rm.
11⁵ x 19⁶

OVERLOOK

OPEN RAIL

KNEEWALL

VAULT

STAIRS DN.

LINEN

FIRST FLOOR

Breakfast

PANTRY

FRENCH DOOR

Vaulted Great Room
15⁰ x 17⁰

FPL.

Kitchen

RANGE

DW.

REF.

COATS

Master Suite
17² x 13⁰

TRAY CLG.

W.i.c.

M.Bath

KS.

LINEN

SHWR.

FRENCH DOOR

Dining Room
11⁶ x 11⁷

Pwdr.

Laund.

W. D.

Storage

Two Story Foyer

STAIRS DN.

STAIRS UP

Covered Porch

Garage
19⁵ x 20⁰

To order blueprints, call **800-235-5700** or visit us on the web, **familyhomeplans.com**

Design 66054

Units	Single
Price Code	D
Total Finished	2,192 sq. ft.
Main Finished	2,192 sq. ft.
Bonus Unfinished	403 sq. ft.
Dimensions	49'10"x75'11"
Foundation	Slab
Bedrooms	3
Full Baths	2
Main Ceiling	10'
Max Ridge Height	26'
Roof Framing	Stick
Exterior Walls	2x4

Design 62036

Units	Single
Price Code	B
Total Finished	1,538 sq. ft.
Main Finished	1,538 sq. ft.
Dimensions	50'x56'
Foundation	Basement
	Crawlspace
	Slab
Bedrooms	3
Full Baths	2

MASTER SUITE
16'-10" X 11'-6"
9' PAN CEILING

GREAT RM.
20'-0" X 15'-6"
9' BOXED CEILING

BEDROOM 3
11'-10" X 11'-0"

M.BATH
16'-0" X 10'-6"
SKL
K.S.

LIN

LIN

KITCHEN
10'-0" X 10'-0"

DINING
10'-6" X 11'-10"

FOYER

BATH

LIN

DW
RG
REF

PAN

LAU.

HVAC

STORAGE
WH

D
W

COVERED PORCH

BEDROOM 2
11'-10" X 11'-0"
VAULTED CEILING

GARAGE
21'-0" X 21'-0"

MAIN FLOOR

Units	Single
Price Code	B
Total Finished	1,699 sq. ft.
Main Finished	1,699 sq. ft.
Dimensions	50'x51'
Foundation	Crawlspace
Bedrooms	3
Full Baths	2
Main Ceiling	9'
Max Ridge Height	23'
Roof Framing	Truss
Exterior Walls	2x6

MAIN FLOOR

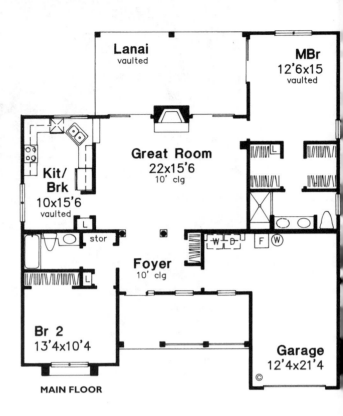

Units	Single
Price Code	A
Total Finished	1,275 sq. ft.
Main Finished	1,275 sq. ft.
Garage Unfinished	286 sq. ft.
Porch Unfinished	140 sq. ft.
Dimensions	46'x50'
Foundation	Slab
Bedrooms	2
Full Baths	1
3/4 Baths	1
Main Ceiling	8'
Max Ridge Height	17'4"
Roof Framing	Truss
Exterior Walls	2x4

Lanai vaulted

MBr 12'6x15 vaulted

Kit/ Brk 10x15'6 vaulted

Great Room 22x15'6 10' clg

stor

Foyer 10' clg

Br 2 13'4x10'4

Garage 12'4x21'4

MAIN FLOOR

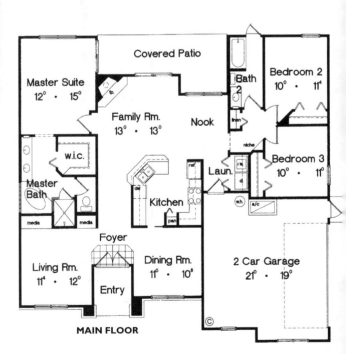

Units	Single
Price Code	B
Total Finished	1,558 sq. ft.
Main Finished	1,558 sq. ft.
Garage Unfinished	413 sq. ft.
Dimensions	50'x45'
Foundation	Slab
Bedrooms	3
Full Baths	2
Main Ceiling	10'-14'6"
Max Ridge Height	21'
Roof Framing	Truss
Exterior Walls	2x4

Covered Patio

Master Suite 12⁰ . 15⁰

Family Rm. 13⁰ . 13⁰

Nook

Bath 2

Bedroom 2 10⁴ . 11⁴

w.i.c.

Master Bath

Laun.

niche

Bedroom 3 10⁰ . 11⁰

media media

Kitchen

pan

Foyer

Living Rm. 11⁴ . 12⁰

Dining Rm. 11⁰ . 10⁸

2 Car Garage 21⁰ . 19⁰

Entry

MAIN FLOOR

Design 65476

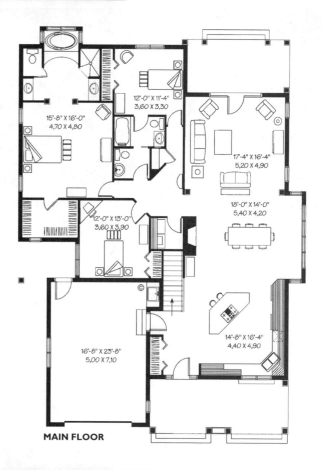

Units	Single
Price Code	C
Total Finished	2,118 sq. ft.
Main Finished	2,118 sq. ft.
Dimensions	50'x67'
Foundation	Basement
Bedrooms	3
Full Baths	2
Half Baths	1

MAIN FLOOR

Design 65308

SECOND FLOOR

Units	Single
Price Code	C
Total Finished	1,840 sq. ft.
First Finished	980 sq. ft.
Second Finished	860 sq. ft.
Dimensions	49'8"x32'
Foundation	Basement
Bedrooms	3
Full Baths	1
3/4 Baths	1
Half Baths	1

FIRST FLOOR

Design 98461

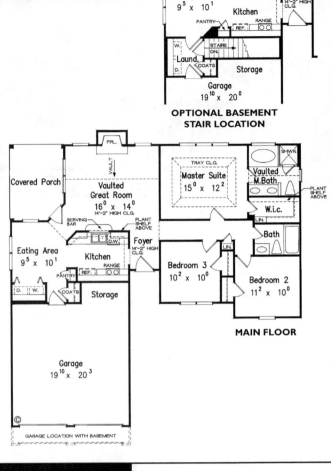

OPTIONAL BASEMENT STAIR LOCATION

Eating Area 9⁵ x 10¹
Kitchen
Foyer 14'-2" HIGH CLG.
PANTRY
REF.
RANGE
W.
Laund.
D.
STAIRS DN.
COATS
Storage
Garage 19¹⁰ x 20⁰

Units	Single
Price Code	A
Total Finished	1,185 sq. ft.
Main Finished	1,185 sq. ft.
Basement Unfinished	1,185 sq. ft.
Garage Unfinished	425 sq. ft.
Dimensions	50'x49'4"
Foundation	Basement
	Crawlspace
Bedrooms	3
Full Baths	2
Max Ridge Height	22'
Roof Framing	Stick
Exterior Walls	2x4

CAD FILES AVAILABLE For more information call 800-235-5700

FPL.
VAULT
Covered Porch
Vaulted Great Room 16⁰ x 14⁰ 14'-2" HIGH CLG.
SERVING BAR
PLANT SHELF ABOVE
TRAY CLG.
Master Suite 15⁰ x 12²
SHWR.
Vaulted M.Bath
PLANT SHELF ABOVE
W.i.c.
LIN.
Bath
Eating Area 9⁵ x 10¹
D.W.
Kitchen
RANGE
REF.
Foyer 14'-2" HIGH CLG.
PANTRY
COATS
D. W.
Storage
LIN.
Bedroom 3 10² x 10⁰
Bedroom 2 11² x 10⁰

MAIN FLOOR

Garage 19¹⁰ x 20³

GARAGE LOCATION WITH BASEMENT

Design 19491

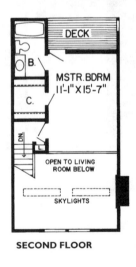

DECK
B.
MSTR. BDRM 11'-1" X 15'-7"
C.
DN
L
OPEN TO LIVING ROOM BELOW
SKYLIGHTS

SECOND FLOOR

Please note: The photographed home may have been modified to suit homeowner preferences. If you order plans, have a builder or design professional check them against the photograph to confirm actual construction details.

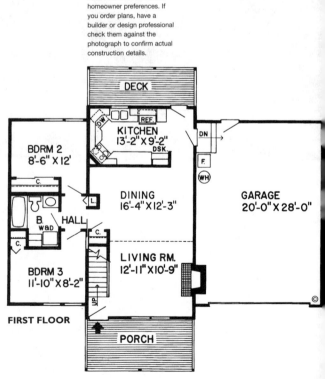

DECK
DW
REF.
KITCHEN 13'-2" X 9'-2"
DSK.
DN
BDRM 2 8'-6" X 12'
C.
F.
WH
DINING 16'-4" X 12'-3"
GARAGE 20'-0" X 28'-0"
B.
HALL
W&D
C.
BDRM 3 11'-10" X 8'-2"
LIVING RM. 12'-11" X 10'-9"
UP

FIRST FLOOR

PORCH

Units	Single
Price Code	A
Total Finished	1,220 sq. ft.
First Finished	920 sq. ft.
Second Finished	300 sq. ft.
Garage Unfinished	583 sq. ft.
Dimensions	50'x46'8"
Foundation	Crawlspace
Bedrooms	3
Full Baths	2
Max Ridge Height	25'
Roof Framing	Stick
Exterior Walls	2x6

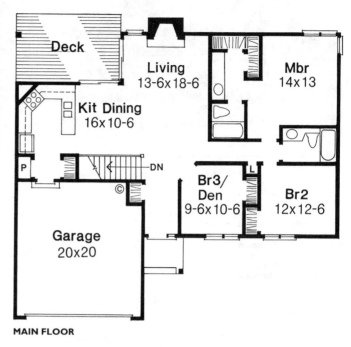

Units	Single
Price Code	A
Total Finished	1,223 sq. ft.
Main Finished	1,223 sq. ft.
Garage Unfinished	440 sq. ft.
Porch Unfinished	36 sq. ft.
Dimensions	50'x42'
Foundation	Basement
Bedrooms	3
Full Baths	2

MAIN FLOOR

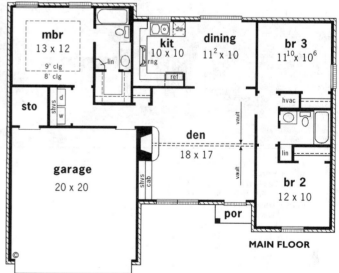

Units	Single
Price Code	A
Total Finished	1,237 sq. ft.
Main Finished	1,237 sq. ft.
Garage Unfinished	436 sq. ft.
Dimensions	50'x38'
Foundation	Crawlspace
	Slab
Bedrooms	3
Full Baths	2
Main Ceiling	8'
Max Ridge Height	18'6"
Roof Framing	Stick
Exterior Walls	2x4

MAIN FLOOR

Units	Single
Price Code	A
Total Finished	1,267 sq. ft.
Main Finished	1,267 sq. ft.
Basement Unfinished	1,267 sq. ft.
Garage Unfinished	467 sq. ft.
Dimensions	50'x46'
Foundation	Basement
Bedrooms	3
Full Baths	1
3/4 Baths	1

MAIN FLOOR

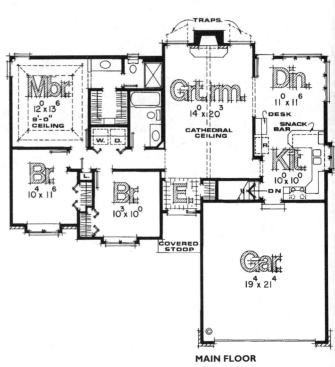

Units	Single
Price Code	A
Total Finished	1,271 sq. ft.
Main Finished	1,271 sq. ft.
Garage Unfinished	433 sq. ft.
Dimensions	50'x46'
Foundation	Basement
	Slab
Bedrooms	3
Full Baths	1
3/4 Baths	1
Max Ridge Height	16'
Roof Framing	Stick
Exterior Walls	2x4

* Alternate foundation options available at an additional charge.
  Please call 1-800-235-5700 for more information.

MAIN FLOOR

Design 97614

Units	Single
Price Code	A
Total Finished	1,287 sq. ft.
Main Finished	1,287 sq. ft.
Bonus Unfinished	312 sq. ft.
Basement Unfinished	1,287 sq. ft.
Garage Unfinished	516 sq. ft.
Dimensions	50'x55'10"
Foundation	Basement
	Crawlspace
Bedrooms	3
Full Baths	2
Max Ridge Height	24'
Roof Framing	Stick
Exterior Walls	2x4

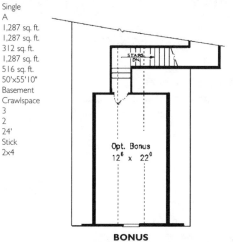

MAIN FLOOR

FILES AVAILABLE
CAD For more information call
800-235-5700

BONUS

Design 20161

PHOTOGRAPHY: JOHN EHRENCLOU

Units	Single
Price Code	A
Total Finished	1,307 sq. ft.
Main Finished	1,307 sq. ft.
Basement Unfinished	1,298 sq. ft.
Garage Unfinished	462 sq. ft.
Dimensions	50'x40'
Foundation	Basement
	Crawlspace
	Slab
Bedrooms	3
Full Baths	2
Main Ceiling	8'
Max Ridge Height	19'
Roof Framing	Stick
Exterior Walls	2x6

Please note: The photographed home may have been modified to suit homeowner preferences. If you order plans, have a builder or design professional check them against the photograph to confirm actual construction details.

OPTIONAL CRAWLSPACE/SLAB FOUNDATION

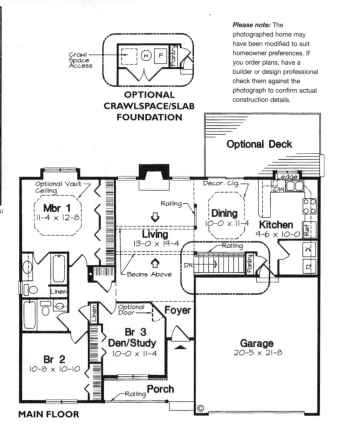

MAIN FLOOR

Units	Single
Price Code	A
Total Finished	1,312 sq. ft.
Main Finished	1,312 sq. ft.
Basement Unfinished	1,293 sq. ft.
Garage Unfinished	459 sq. ft.
Deck Unfinished	185 sq. ft.
Porch Unfinished	84 sq. ft.
Dimensions	50'x40'
Foundation	Basement
	Crawlspace
	Slab
Bedrooms	3
Full Baths	2
Main Ceiling	8'
Max Ridge Height	20'
Roof Framing	Stick
Exterior Walls	2x6

**OPTIONAL
CRAWLSPACE/SLAB
FOUNDATION**

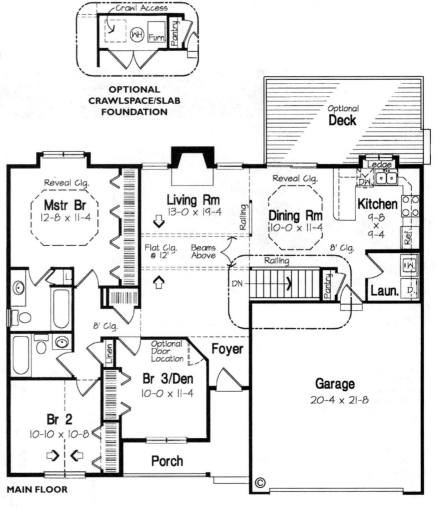

MAIN FLOOR

Design 60025

Units	Single
Price Code	B
Total Finished	1,744 sq. ft.
First Finished	884 sq. ft.
Second Finished	860 sq. ft.
Basement Unfinished	884 sq. ft.
Garage Unfinished	456 sq. ft.
Dimensions	50'×32'
Foundation	Basement
	Crawlspace
Bedrooms	4
Full Baths	2
Half Baths	1
First Ceiling	9'
Second Ceiling	8'
Max Ridge Height	30'
Roof Framing	Stick
Exterior Walls	2×4

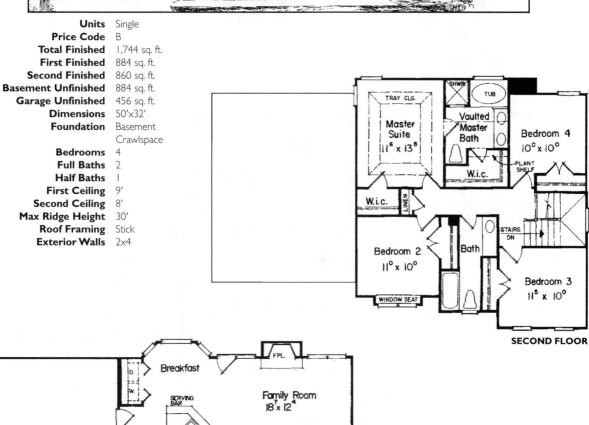

SECOND FLOOR

FIRST FLOOR

Units	Single
Price Code	A
Total Finished	1,314 sq. ft.
Main Finished	1,314 sq. ft.
Basement Unfinished	1,488 sq. ft.
Garage Unfinished	484 sq. ft.
Deck Unfinished	238 sq. ft.
Porch Unfinished	112 sq. ft.
Dimensions	50'x54'
Foundation	Basement
Bedrooms	3
Full Baths	1
3/4 Baths	1
Main Ceiling	8'
Max Ridge Height	16'
Roof Framing	Truss
Exterior Walls	2x6

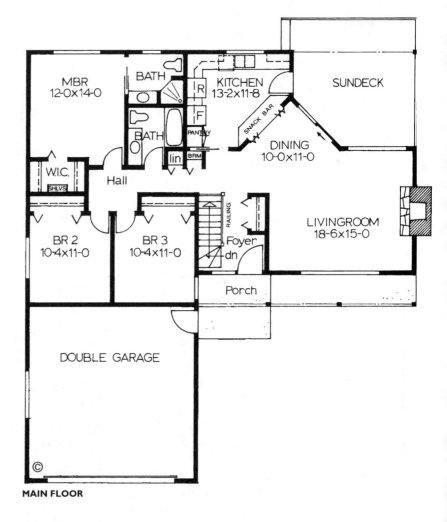

MAIN FLOOR

Units	Single
Price Code	A
Total Finished	1,315 sq. ft.
Main Finished	1,315 sq. ft.
Basement Unfinished	1,315 sq. ft.
Garage Unfinished	488 sq. ft.
Porch Unfinished	75 sq. ft.
Dimensions	50'x54'8"
Foundation	Basement
Bedrooms	3
Full Baths	2
Main Ceiling	8'
Max Ridge Height	18'
Roof Framing	Truss
Exterior Walls	2x4

MAIN FLOOR

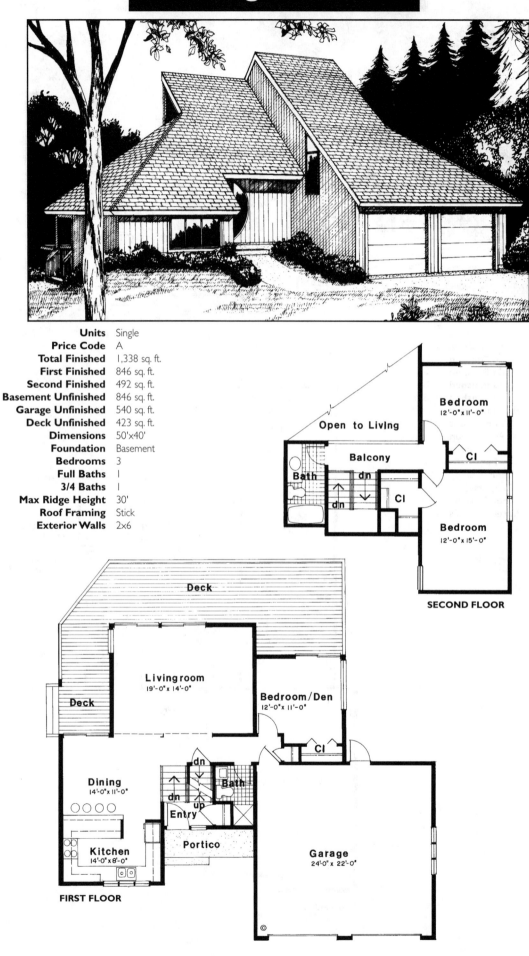

Units	Single
Price Code	A
Total Finished	1,338 sq. ft.
First Finished	846 sq. ft.
Second Finished	492 sq. ft.
Basement Unfinished	846 sq. ft.
Garage Unfinished	540 sq. ft.
Deck Unfinished	423 sq. ft.
Dimensions	50'x40'
Foundation	Basement
Bedrooms	3
Full Baths	1
3/4 Baths	1
Max Ridge Height	30'
Roof Framing	Stick
Exterior Walls	2x6

Bedroom 12'-0" x 11'-0"

Open to Living

Balcony

Bath

Cl

Bedroom 12'-0" x 15'-0"

dn / dn / dn

Cl

SECOND FLOOR

Deck

Living room 19'-0" x 14'-0"

Deck

Bedroom/Den 12'-0" x 11'-0"

Cl

Dining 14'-0" x 11'-0"

dn

Bath

Kitchen 14'-0" x 8'-0"

dn / up

Entry

Portico

Garage 24'-0" x 22'-0"

FIRST FLOOR

Design 10128

Units	Single
Price Code	A
Total Finished	1,344 sq. ft.
Main Finished	1,344 sq. ft.
Garage Unfinished	720 sq. ft.
Dimensions	50'x30'
Foundation	Slab
Bedrooms	3
Full Baths	2

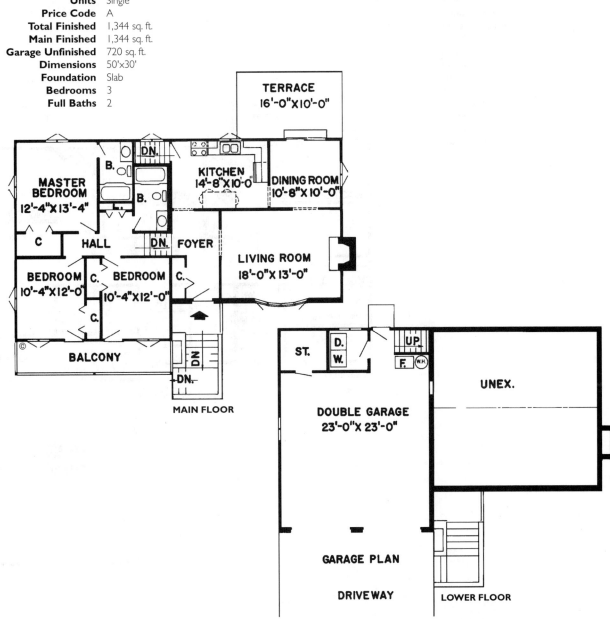

Design 99750

Units	Single
Price Code	A
Total Finished	1,349 sq. ft.
Main Finished	1,349 sq. ft.
Dimensions	50'x50'
Foundation	Crawlspace
Bedrooms	3
Full Baths	1
3/4 Baths	1
Max Ridge Height	15'
Roof Framing	Stick/Truss
Exterior Walls	2x6

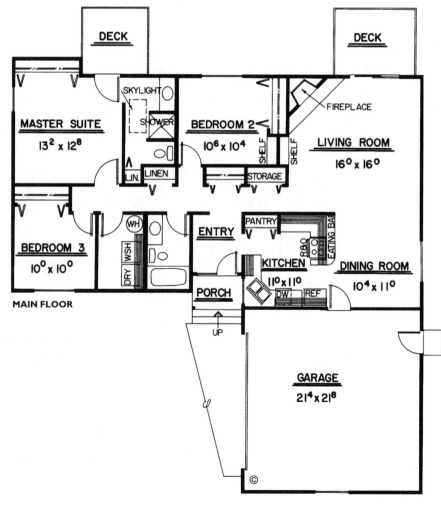

MAIN FLOOR

Units	Single
Price Code	A
Total Finished	1,350 sq. ft.
Main Finished	1,350 sq. ft.
Dimensions	50'x50'
Foundation	Crawlspace
Bedrooms	3
Full Baths	1
3/4 Baths	1
Roof Framing	Stick/Truss
Exterior Walls	2x6

Design 34054

Units	Single
Price Code	A
Total Finished	1,400 sq. ft.
Main Finished	1,400 sq. ft.
Basement Unfinished	1,400 sq. ft.
Garage Unfinished	528 sq. ft.
Dimensions	50'x28'
Foundation	Basement
	Crawlspace
	Slab
Bedrooms	3
Full Baths	2
Main Ceiling	8'
Max Ridge Height	17'
Roof Framing	Stick
Exterior Walls	2x4, 2x6

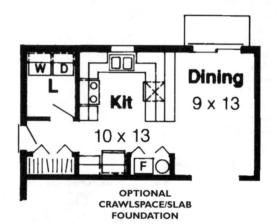

**OPTIONAL
CRAWLSPACE/SLAB
FOUNDATION**

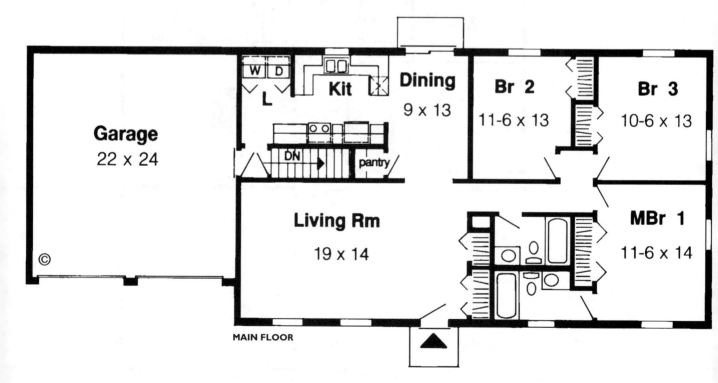

MAIN FLOOR

Design 90352

Units	Single
Price Code	A
Total Finished	1,418 sq. ft.
Main Finished	1,418 sq. ft.
Dimensions	50'x51'4"
Foundation	Slab
Bedrooms	2
Full Baths	2
Exterior Walls	2x4

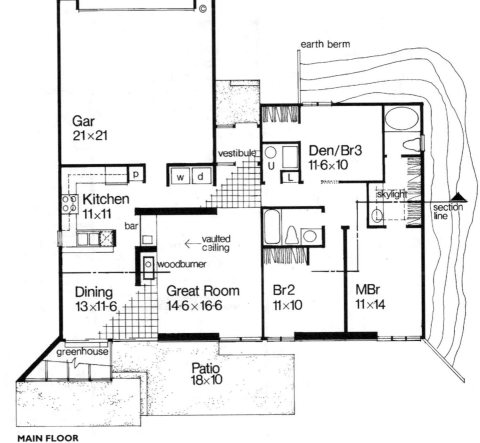

MAIN FLOOR

Units	Single
Price Code	A
Total Finished	1,421 sq. ft.
First Finished	1,046 sq. ft.
Second Finished	375 sq. ft.
Basement Unfinished	1,046 sq. ft.
Garage Unfinished	472 sq. ft.
Dimensions	50'x48'
Foundation	Basement
Bedrooms	3
Full Baths	2
Max Ridge Height	26'
Roof Framing	Stick
Exterior Walls	2x6

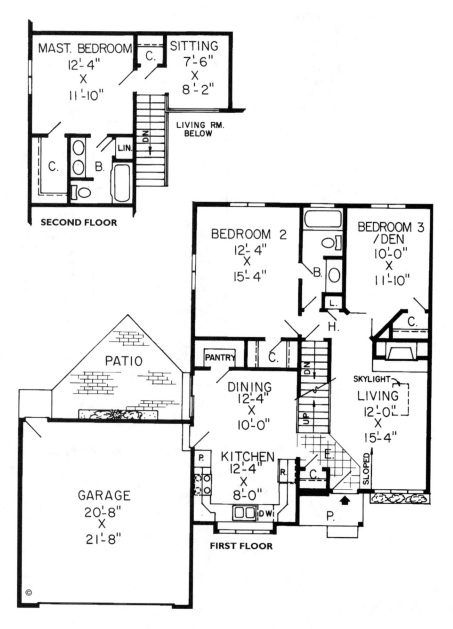

Design 93221

Units	Single
Price Code	A
Total Finished	1,438 sq. ft.
Main Finished	1,438 sq. ft.
Dimensions	50'x50'
Foundation	Crawlspace
	Slab
Bedrooms	3
Full Baths	2
Max Ridge Height	19'
Roof Framing	Stick/Truss
Exterior Walls	2x4

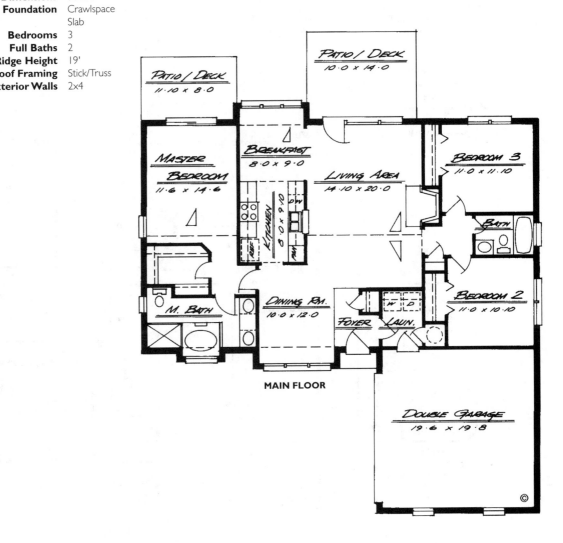

PATIO / DECK
11·10 x 8·0

PATIO / DECK
10·0 x 14·0

MASTER BEDROOM
11·6 x 14·6

BREAKFAST
8·0 x 9·0

LIVING AREA
14·10 x 20·0

BEDROOM 3
11·0 x 11·10

KITCHEN
8·0 x 9·10

BATH

DINING RM.
10·0 x 12·0

FOYER LAUN.

BEDROOM 2
11·0 x 10·10

M. BATH

MAIN FLOOR

DOUBLE GARAGE
19·6 x 19·8

Design 20164

PHOTOGRAPHY: GAUTHIER ROOFING AND SIDING

Units	Single
Price Code	A
Total Finished	1,456 sq. ft.
Main Finished	1,456 sq. ft.
Basement Unfinished	1,448 sq. ft.
Garage Unfinished	452 sq. ft.
Dimensions	50'x45'4"
Foundation	Basement
	Crawlspace
	Slab
Bedrooms	3
Full Baths	2
Main Ceiling	8'
Max Ridge Height	19'
Roof Framing	Stick
Exterior Walls	2x6

Please note: The photographed home may have been modified to suit homeowner preferences. If you order plans, have a builder or design professional check them against the photograph to confirm actual construction details.

(Optional) Deck

Dining 12-0 x 9-9

Living Rm 12-2 x 19-4

MBR #1 11-8 x 14-0

Decor. Clg. (Optional)

Plant Shelf Above

Desk

Kitchen 9-4 x 13-4

Sink

Range

Ref

W. D.

DN

Foyer

Railing

Garage 19-4 x 23-6

Den/BR #3 10-5 x 11-6

BR #2 10-5 x 10-5

MAIN FLOOR

Garage

Furn.

WH

Crawl Space Access

P

OPTIONAL CRAWLSPACE/SLAB FOUNDATION

Units	Single
Price Code	A
Total Finished	1,499 sq. ft.
Main Finished	1,499 sq. ft.
Dimensions	50'×60'
Foundation	Basement
	Crawlspace
Bedrooms	3
Full Baths	2
Max Ridge Height	20'
Roof Framing	Stick/Truss
Exterior Walls	2x6

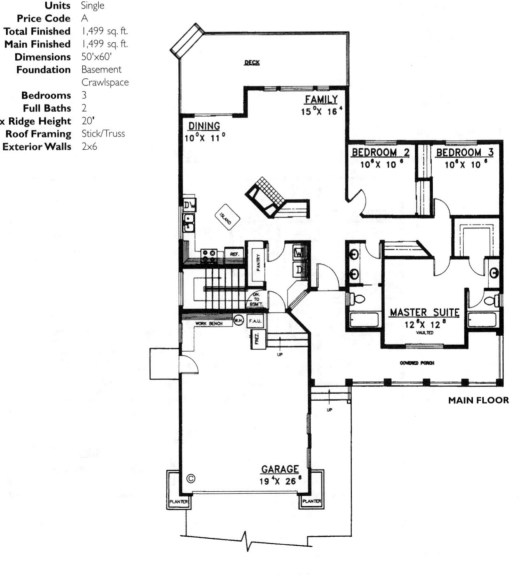

DECK

FAMILY
15⁰ X 16⁴

DINING
10⁰ X 11⁰

BEDROOM 2
10⁴ X 10⁶

BEDROOM 3
10⁴ X 10⁶

DW

ISLAND

REF.

PANTRY

W
D

DN.
TO
BSM'T.

MASTER SUITE
12⁶ X 12⁸
VAULTED

WORK BENCH

R.H. F.A.U.

FREZ.

UP

COVERED PORCH

UP

MAIN FLOOR

GARAGE
19⁴ X 26⁶

PLANTER

PLANTER

©

Units	Single
Price Code	A
Total Finished	1,499 sq. ft.
Main Finished	1,499 sq. ft.
Dimensions	50'x50'
Foundation	Crawlspace
Bedrooms	3
Full Baths	1
3/4 Baths	1
Half Baths	1
Max Ridge Height	18'
Roof Framing	Stick/Truss
Exterior Walls	2x6

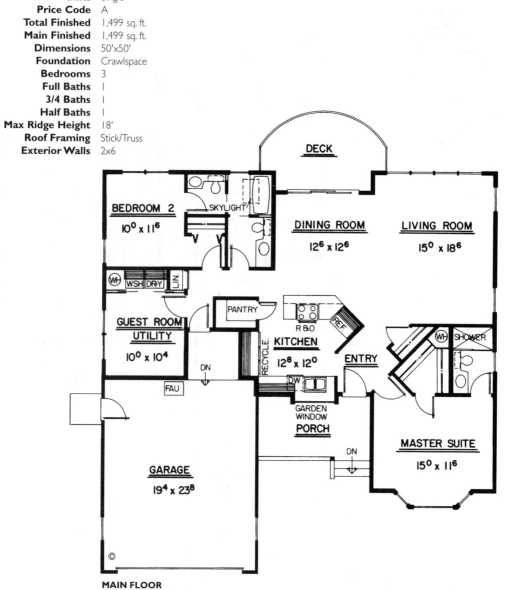

MAIN FLOOR

Units	Single
Price Code	B
Total Finished	1,539 sq. ft.
Main Finished	1,539 sq. ft.
Basement Unfinished	1,530 sq. ft.
Garage Unfinished	460 sq. ft.
Deck Unfinished	160 sq. ft.
Porch Unfinished	182 sq. ft.
Dimensions	50'x45'4"
Foundation	Basement
	Crawlspace
	Slab
Bedrooms	3
Full Baths	2
Main Ceiling	8'
Max Ridge Height	21'
Roof Framing	Stick
Exterior Walls	2x6

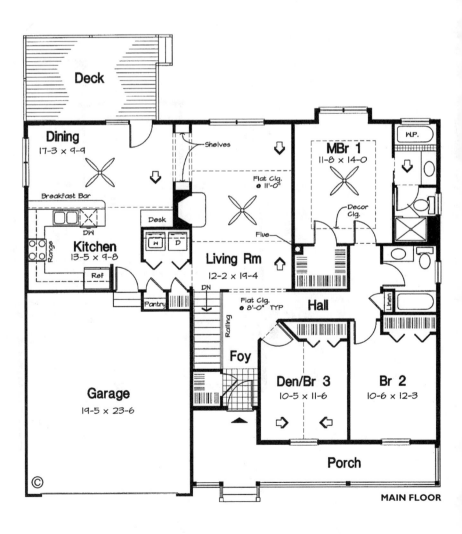

MAIN FLOOR

Units	Single
Price Code	B
Total Finished	1,545 sq. ft.
Main Finished	1,545 sq. ft.
Basement Unfinished	1,545 sq. ft.
Garage Unfinished	396 sq. ft.
Dimensions	50'x49'
Foundation	Basement
Bedrooms	3
Full Baths	2
Max Ridge Height	24'
Roof Framing	Stick
Exterior Walls	2x6

MAIN FLOOR

Design 94918

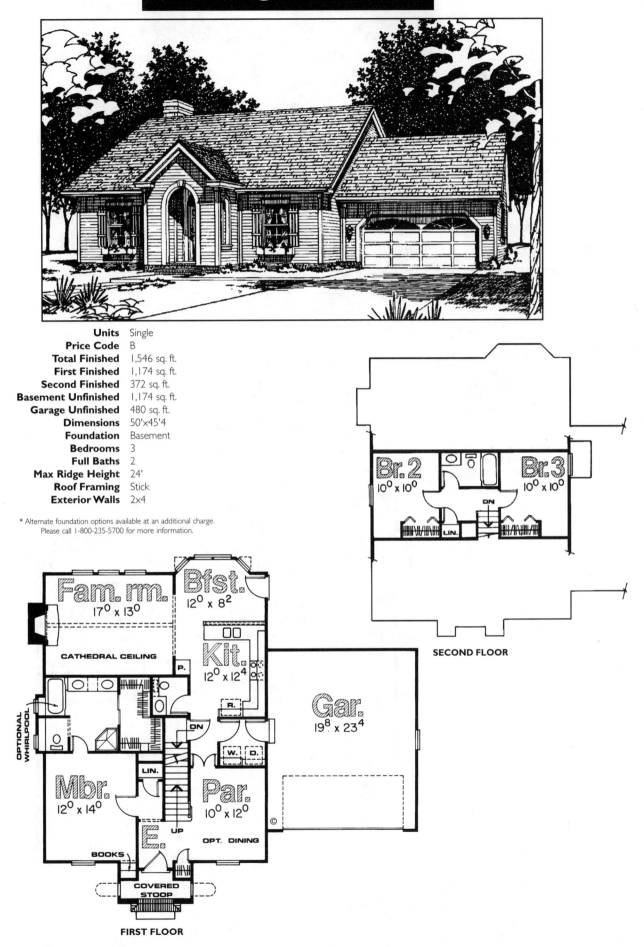

Units	Single
Price Code	B
Total Finished	1,546 sq. ft.
First Finished	1,174 sq. ft.
Second Finished	372 sq. ft.
Basement Unfinished	1,174 sq. ft.
Garage Unfinished	480 sq. ft.
Dimensions	50'x45'4
Foundation	Basement
Bedrooms	3
Full Baths	2
Max Ridge Height	24'
Roof Framing	Stick
Exterior Walls	2x4

* Alternate foundation options available at an additional charge.
  Please call 1-800-235-5700 for more information.

SECOND FLOOR

Br. 2
10⁰ x 10⁰

Br. 3
10⁰ x 10⁰

DN

LIN.

Fam. rm.
17⁰ x 13⁰

CATHEDRAL CEILING

Bfst.
12⁰ x 8²

Kit.
12⁰ x 12⁴

P.

R.

Gar.
19⁸ x 23⁴

DN

W. D.

OPTIONAL WHIRLPOOL

Mbr.
12⁰ x 14⁰

LIN.

UP

Par.
10⁰ x 12⁰

OPT. DINING

BOOKS

COVERED STOOP

FIRST FLOOR

Units	Single
Price Code	B
Total Finished	1,546 sq. ft.
Main Finished	1,546 sq. ft.
Dimensions	50'x50'
Foundation	Crawlspace
Bedrooms	3
Full Baths	1
3/4 Baths	1
Max Ridge Height	19'
Roof Framing	Truss
Exterior Walls	2x4

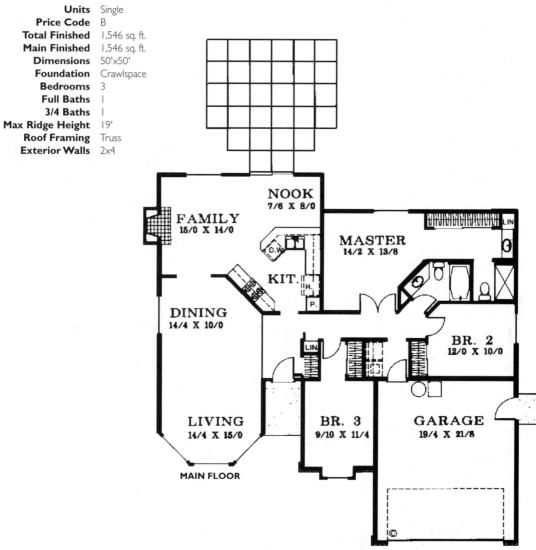

NOOK 7/6 X 8/0

FAMILY 15/0 X 14/0

MASTER 14/2 X 13/8

KIT.

DINING 14/4 X 10/0

BR. 2 12/0 X 10/0

LIVING 14/4 X 15/0

BR. 3 9/10 X 11/4

GARAGE 19/4 X 21/8

MAIN FLOOR

Design 99349

Units	Single
Price Code	B
Total Finished	1,549 sq. ft.
First & Second Finished	1,549 sq. ft.
Bonus Unfinished	700 sq. ft.
Garage Unfinished	640 sq. ft.
Dimensions	50'x34'4"
Foundation	Basement
Bedrooms	3
Full Baths	2
Max Ridge Height	75'
Roof Framing	Truss
Exterior Walls	2x4

Patio

Master Br
12x17

Living Rm
14x14

Brkfst
11x7-6

Br 2
12x11-6

Br 3
11x12

Dining
12-2x12-8

W
D

DN   UP

FIRST & SECOND FLOOR

Garage
23x27-6

Bonus Space

UP

LOWER FLOOR

Units	Single
Price Code	B
Total Finished	1,554 sq. ft.
First Finished	806 sq. ft.
Second Finished	748 sq. ft.
Garage Unfinished	467 sq. ft.
Dimensions	50'x40'
Foundation	Basement
	Crawlspace
	Slab
Bedrooms	3
Full Baths	2
Half Baths	1
First Ceiling	8'
Second Ceiling	8'
Max Ridge Height	29'
Roof Framing	Stick
Exterior Walls	2x4

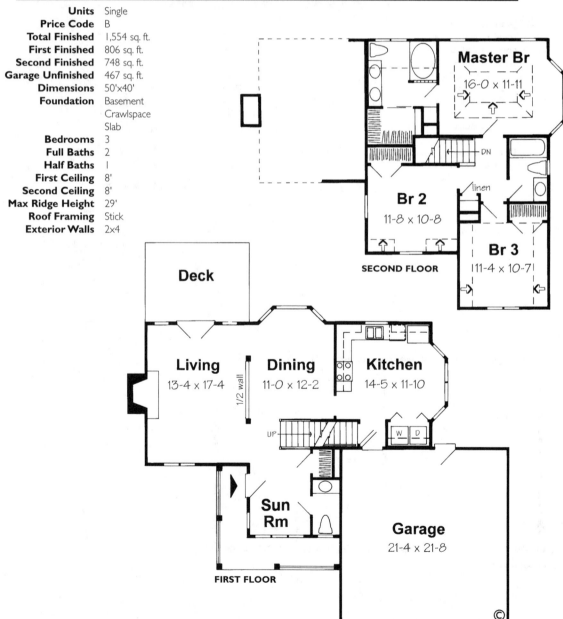

Design 94920

Units	Single
Price Code	B
Total Finished	1,554 sq. ft.
Main Finished	1,554 sq. ft.
Basement Unfinished	1,554 sq. ft.
Garage Unfinished	464 sq. ft.
Dimensions	50'x52'8"
Foundation	Basement
Bedrooms	3
Full Baths	2
Main Ceiling	8'
Max Ridge Height	24'
Roof Framing	Stick
Exterior Walls	2x4

* Alternate foundation options available at an additional charge. Please call 1-800-235-5700 for more information.

Please note: The photographed home may have been modified to suit homeowner preferences. If you order plans, have a builder or design professional check them against the photograph to confirm actual construction details.

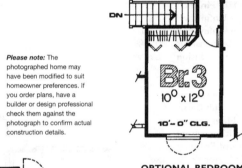

OPTIONAL BEDROOM

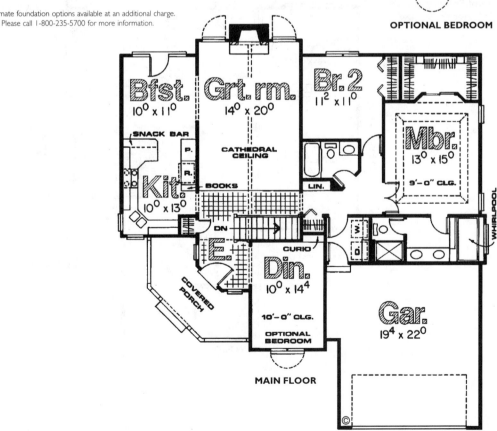

MAIN FLOOR

Units	Single
Price Code	B
Total Finished	1,557 sq. ft.
Main Finished	1,557 sq. ft.
Garage Unfinished	434 sq. ft.
Porch Unfinished	137 sq. ft.
Dimensions	50'×50'
Foundation	Basement
	Crawlspace
	Slab
Bedrooms	3
Full Baths	2
Main Ceiling	9'
Max Ridge Height	24'
Roof Framing	Truss
Exterior Walls	2×6

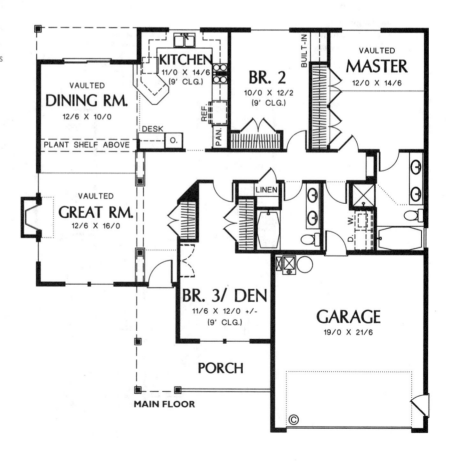

Design 65372

Units	Single
Price Code	B
Total Finished	1,564 sq. ft.
First Finished	983 sq. ft.
Second Finished	581 sq. ft.
Basement Unfinished	983 sq. ft.
Garage Unfinished	336 sq. ft.
Dimensions	50'x39'
Foundation	Basement
Bedrooms	2
Full Baths	1
3/4 Baths	1
Max Ridge Height	26'5"
Roof Framing	Truss
Exterior Walls	2x6

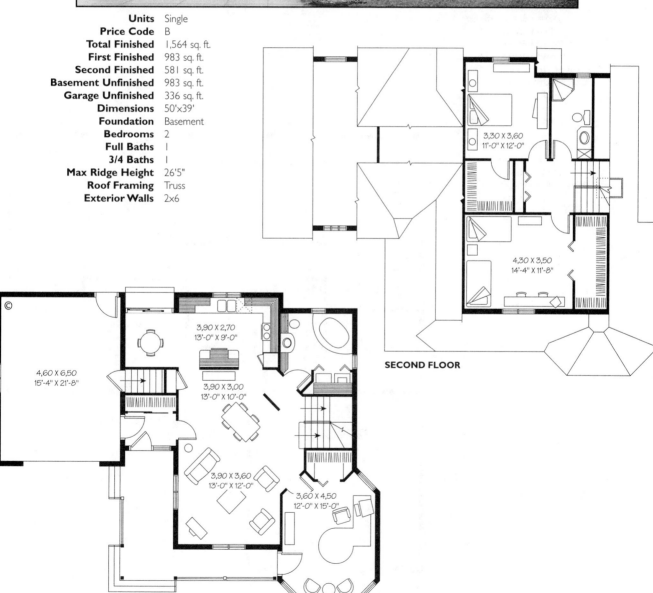

3,30 X 3,60
11'-0" X 12'-0"

4,30 X 3,50
14'-4" X 11'-8"

SECOND FLOOR

4,60 X 6,50
15'-4" X 21'-8"

3,90 X 2,70
13'-0" X 9'-0"

3,90 X 3,00
13'-0" X 10'-0"

3,90 X 3,60
13'-0" X 12'-0"

3,60 X 4,50
12'-0" X 15'-0"

FIRST FLOOR

Design 90975

Units	Single
Price Code	B
Total Finished	1,565 sq. ft.
Main Finished	1,565 sq. ft.
Basement Unfinished	1,546 sq. ft.
Garage Unfinished	441 sq. ft.
Porch Unfinished	24 sq. ft.
Dimensions	50'x52'6"
Foundation	Basement
Bedrooms	3
Full Baths	1
3/4 Baths	1
Main Ceiling	8'
Max Ridge Height	16'6"
Roof Framing	Truss
Exterior Walls	2x6

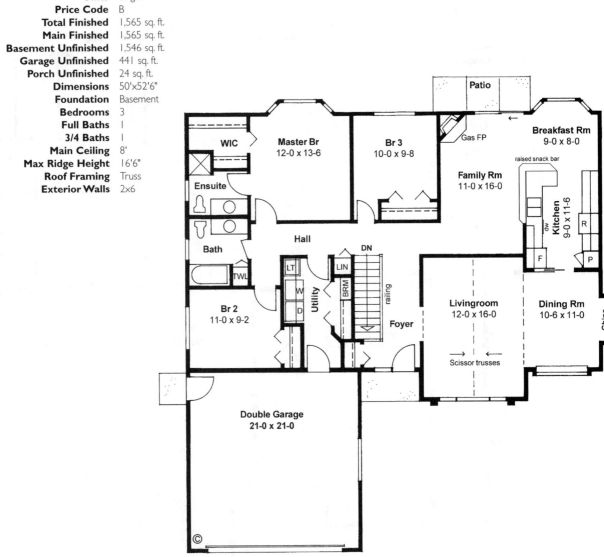

MAIN FLOOR

Units	Single
Price Code	B
Total Finished	1,565 sq. ft.
Main Finished	1,565 sq. ft.
Garage Unfinished	440 sq. ft.
Dimensions	50'x53'
Foundation	Crawlspace
Bedrooms	3
Full Baths	2
Max Ridge Height	23'
Roof Framing	Stick
Exterior Walls	2x6

MAIN FLOOR

Units	Single
Price Code	B
Total Finished	1,575 sq. ft.
Main Finished	1,575 sq. ft.
Basement Unfinished	1,658 sq. ft.
Garage Unfinished	459 sq. ft.
Dimensions	50'x52'6"
Foundation	Basement
	Crawlspace
Bedrooms	3
Full Baths	2
Main Ceiling	9'
Max Ridge Height	23'6"
Roof Framing	Stick
Exterior Walls	2x4

CAD **FILES AVAILABLE**
For more information call
800-235-5700

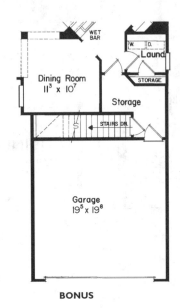

BONUS

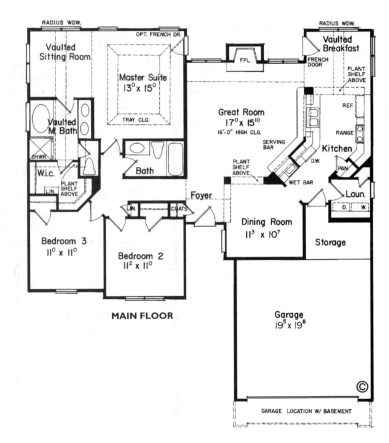

MAIN FLOOR

Units	Single
Price Code	B
Total Finished	1,596 sq. ft.
First Finished	1,191 sq. ft.
Second Finished	405 sq. ft.
Basement Unfinished	1,191 sq. ft.
Garage Unfinished	454 sq. ft.
Dimensions	50'x48'
Foundation	Basement
Bedrooms	3
Full Baths	2
Half Baths	1
Max Ridge Height	26'2"
Roof Framing	Stick
Exterior Walls	2x4

* Alternate foundation options available at an additional charge.
Please call 1-800-235-5700 for more information.

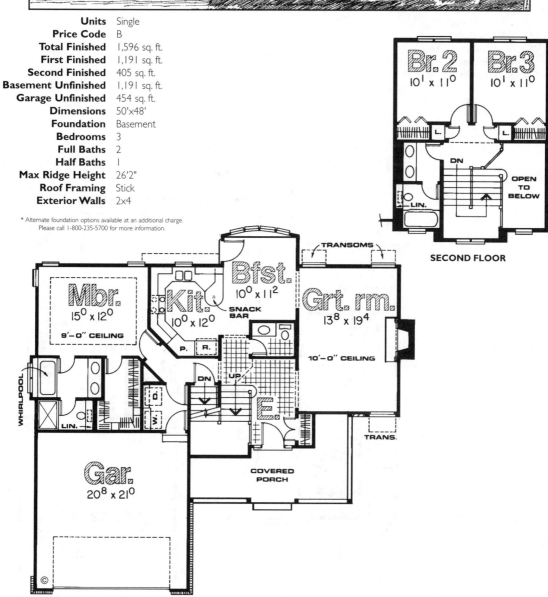

SECOND FLOOR

FIRST FLOOR

Units	Single
Price Code	B
Total Finished	1,611 sq. ft.
Main Finished	1,611 sq. ft.
Garage Unfinished	486 sq. ft.
Dimensions	50'x57'10"
Foundation	Slab
Bedrooms	3
Full Baths	2

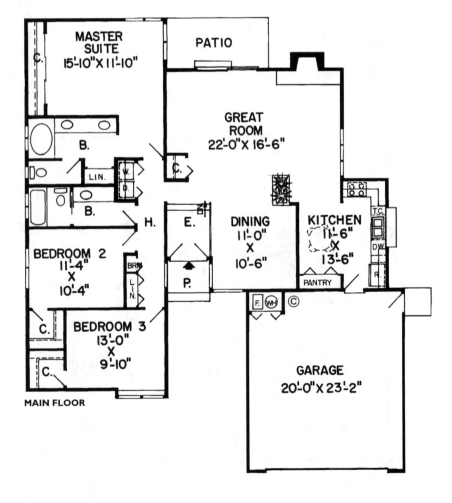

MAIN FLOOR

Design 94915

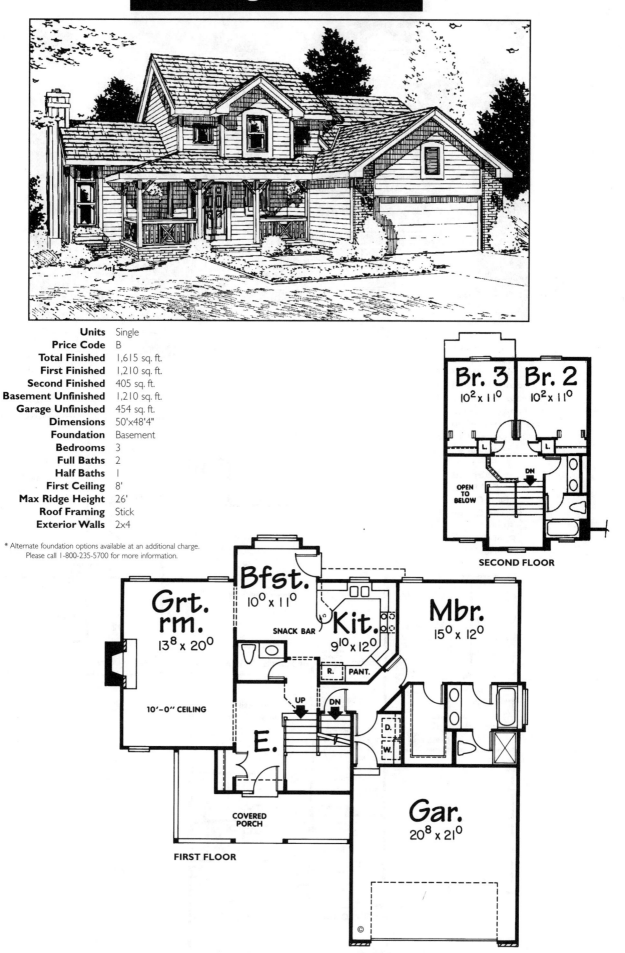

Units	Single
Price Code	B
Total Finished	1,615 sq. ft.
First Finished	1,210 sq. ft.
Second Finished	405 sq. ft.
Basement Unfinished	1,210 sq. ft.
Garage Unfinished	454 sq. ft.
Dimensions	50'x48'4"
Foundation	Basement
Bedrooms	3
Full Baths	2
Half Baths	1
First Ceiling	8'
Max Ridge Height	26'
Roof Framing	Stick
Exterior Walls	2x4

* Alternate foundation options available at an additional charge.
Please call 1-800-235-5700 for more information.

SECOND FLOOR

Br. 3
10² x 11⁰

Br. 2
10² x 11⁰

OPEN TO BELOW

DN

FIRST FLOOR

Grt. rm.
13⁸ x 20⁰
10'-0" CEILING

Bfst.
10⁰ x 11⁰

SNACK BAR

Kit.
9¹⁰ x 12⁰

Mbr.
15⁰ x 12⁰

R. PANT.

UP   DN

E.

COVERED PORCH

Gar.
20⁸ x 21⁰

Design 60056

Units	Single
Price Code	C
Total Finished	2,179 sq. ft.
First Finished	1,668 sq. ft.
Second Finished	511 sq. ft.
Bonus Unfinished	302 sq. ft.
Basement Unfinished	1,668 sq. ft.
Garage Unfinished	410 sq. ft.
Dimensions	50'x56'
Foundation	Basement
	Crawlspace
Bedrooms	4
Full Baths	3
First Ceiling	9'
Second Ceiling	8'
Max Ridge Height	29'6"
Roof Framing	Stick
Exterior Walls	2x4

CAD FILES AVAILABLE
For more information call
800-235-5700

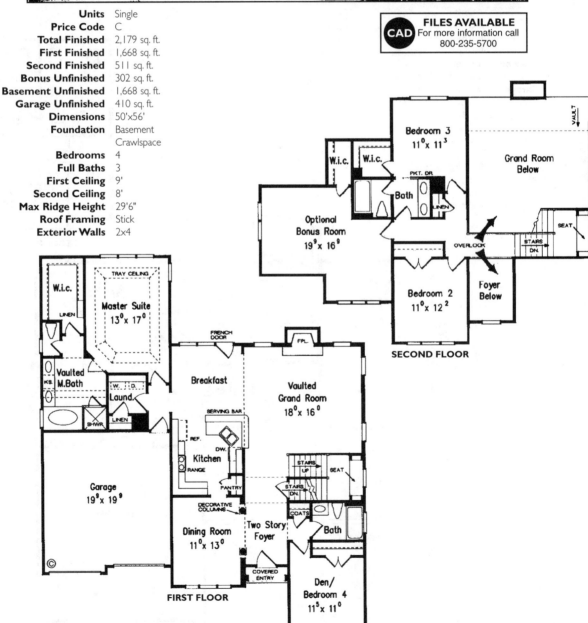

Units	Single
Price Code	B
Total Finished	1,620 sq. ft.
Main Finished	1,620 sq. ft.
Dimensions	50'x55'8"
Foundation	Basement
	Crawlspace
Bedrooms	3
Full Baths	1
3/4 Baths	1
Max Ridge Height	23'
Roof Framing	Stick
Exterior Walls	2x4

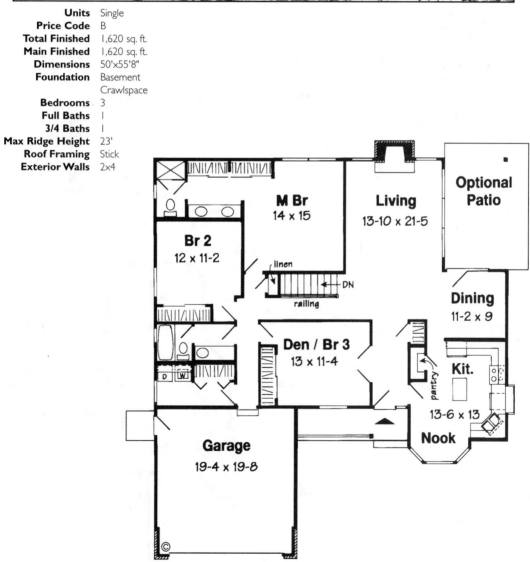

MAIN FLOOR

Design 98746

Units	Single
Price Code	B
Total Finished	1,630 sq. ft.
Main Finished	1,630 sq. ft.
Dimensions	50'x58'
Foundation	Crawlspace
Bedrooms	3
Full Baths	1
3/4 Baths	1
Max Ridge Height	21'3"
Roof Framing	Stick/Truss
Exterior Walls	2x6

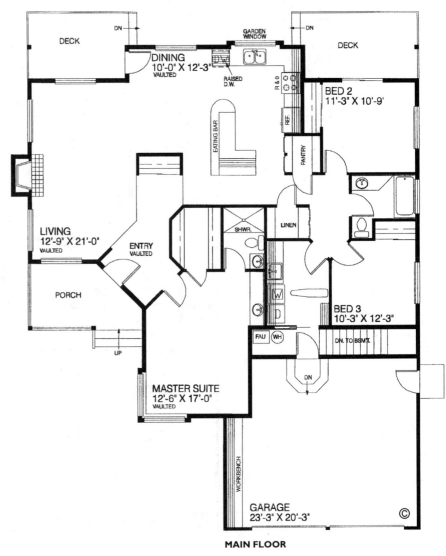

MAIN FLOOR

Design 20526

Units	Single
Price Code	B
Total Finished	1,633 sq. ft.
Main Finished	1,633 sq. ft.
Basement Unfinished	1,633 sq. ft.
Garage Unfinished	423 sq. ft.
Dimensions	50'x55'
Foundation	Basement
Bedrooms	3
Full Baths	2
Max Ridge Height	22'
Roof Framing	Stick
Exterior Walls	2x6

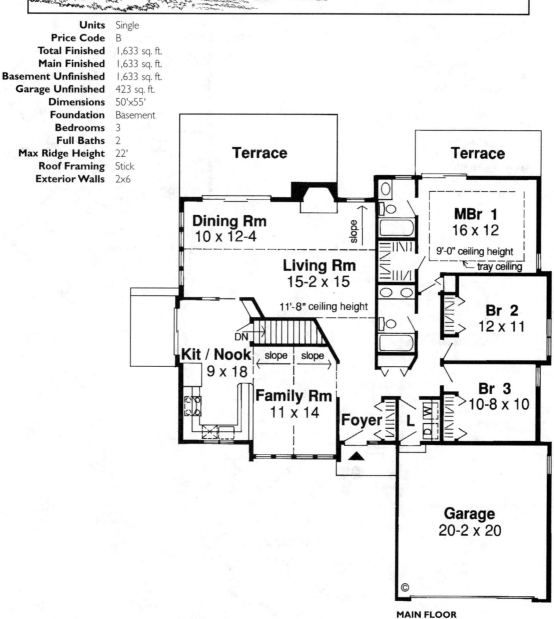

Terrace

Terrace

Dining Rm
10 x 12-4

slope

MBr 1
16 x 12

9'-0" ceiling height

tray ceiling

Living Rm
15-2 x 15

11'-8" ceiling height

Br 2
12 x 11

Kit / Nook
9 x 18

DN

slope   slope

Family Rm
11 x 14

Foyer   L

Br 3
10-8 x 10

D W

Garage
20-2 x 20

©

MAIN FLOOR

Design 98718

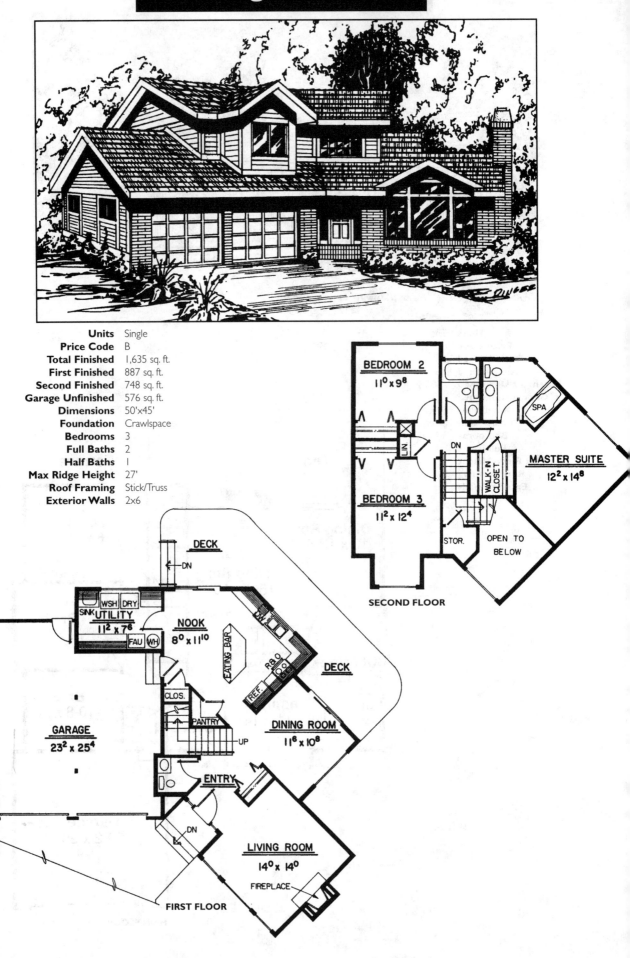

Units	Single
Price Code	B
Total Finished	1,635 sq. ft.
First Finished	887 sq. ft.
Second Finished	748 sq. ft.
Garage Unfinished	576 sq. ft.
Dimensions	50'x45'
Foundation	Crawlspace
Bedrooms	3
Full Baths	2
Half Baths	1
Max Ridge Height	27'
Roof Framing	Stick/Truss
Exterior Walls	2x6

BEDROOM 2
11⁰ x 9⁸

SPA

LIN

DN

WALK-IN CLOSET

MASTER SUITE
12² x 14⁸

BEDROOM 3
11² x 12⁴

STOR.

OPEN TO BELOW

SECOND FLOOR

DECK

DN

SNK WSH DRY
UTILITY
11² x 7⁶

FAU WH

NOOK
8⁰ x 11¹⁰

EATING BAR

DW

REF.

DECK

DINING ROOM
11⁶ x 10⁸

CLOS.

PANTRY

UP

GARAGE
23² x 25⁴

ENTRY

DN

LIVING ROOM
14⁰ x 14⁰

FIREPLACE

©

FIRST FLOOR

Units	Single
Price Code	B
Total Finished	1,640 sq. ft.
Main Finished	1,640 sq. ft.
Garage Unfinished	408 sq. ft.
Deck Unfinished	72 sq. ft.
Porch Unfinished	60 sq. ft.
Dimensions	50'x56'4"
Foundation	Slab
Bedrooms	3
Full Baths	2
Max Ridge Height	24'2"
Roof Framing	Stick
Exterior Walls	2x4

MAIN FLOOR

Units	Single
Price Code	B
Total Finished	1,641 sq. ft.
First Finished	831 sq. ft.
Second Finished	810 sq. ft.
Bonus Unfinished	280 sq. ft.
Basement Unfinished	816 sq. ft.
Garage Unfinished	484 sq. ft.
Deck Unfinished	180 sq. ft.
Dimensions	50'x28'6"
Foundation	Basement Crawlspace Slab
Bedrooms	3
Full Baths	2
Half Baths	1
Max Ridge Height	30'
Roof Framing	Stick
Exterior Walls	2x4

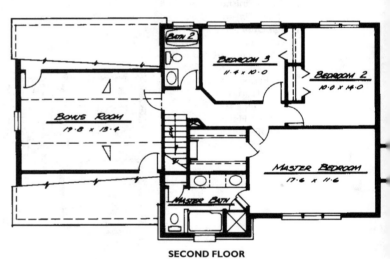

SECOND FLOOR

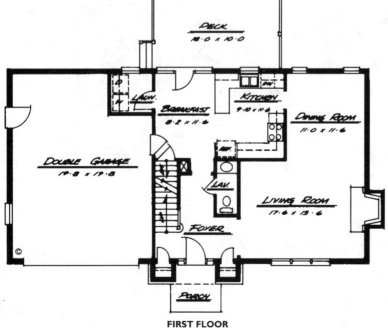

FIRST FLOOR

Design 98423

Units	Single
Price Code	B
Total Finished	1,671 sq. ft.
Main Finished	1,671 sq. ft.
Basement Unfinished	1,685 sq. ft.
Garage Unfinished	400 sq. ft.
Dimensions	50'x51'
Foundation	Basement
	Crawlspace
	Slab
Bedrooms	3
Full Baths	2
Main Ceiling	9'
Max Ridge Height	22'6"
Roof Framing	Stick
Exterior Walls	2x4

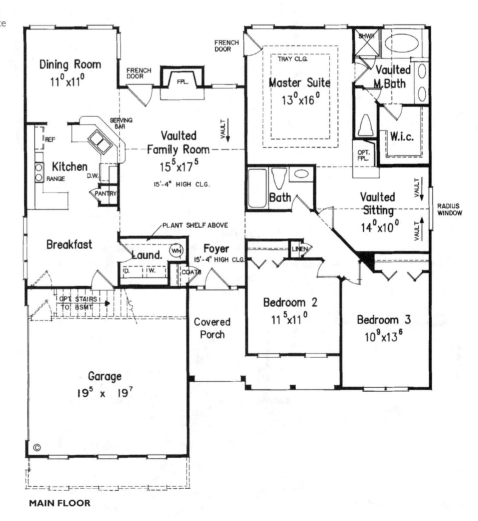

MAIN FLOOR

Design 93306

Units	Single
Price Code	B
Total Finished	1,672 sq. ft.
First Finished	884 sq. ft.
Second Finished	788 sq. ft.
Basement Unfinished	884 sq. ft.
Garage Unfinished	450 sq. ft.
Dimensions	50'x31'
Foundation	Basement
Bedrooms	3
Full Baths	2
Half Baths	1
Max Ridge Height	28'
Roof Framing	Stick/Truss
Exterior Walls	2x6

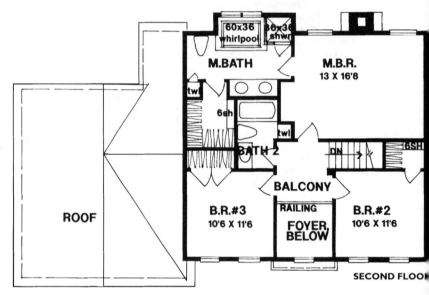

SECOND FLOOR

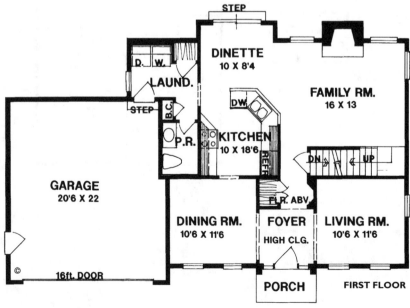

FIRST FLOOR

Units	Single
Price Code	B
Total Finished	1,674 sq. ft.
Main Finished	1,674 sq. ft.
Basement Unfinished	1,656 sq. ft.
Garage Unfinished	472 sq. ft.
Dimensions	50'x50'6"
Foundation	Basement
Bedrooms	3
Full Baths	2
Max Ridge Height	23'
Roof Framing	Stick
Exterior Walls	2x6

Units	Single
Price Code	B
Total Finished	1,683 sq. ft.
First Finished	969 sq. ft.
Second Finished	714 sq. ft.
Basement Unfinished	969 sq. ft.
Garage Unfinished	484 sq. ft.
Dimensions	50'x39'6"
Foundation	Basement
Bedrooms	3
Full Baths	2
Half Baths	1
Max Ridge Height	25'
Roof Framing	Truss
Exterior Walls	2x6

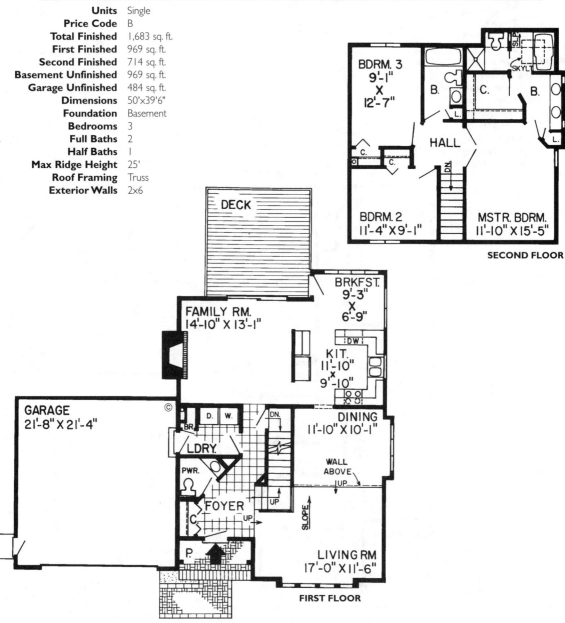

SECOND FLOOR

FIRST FLOOR

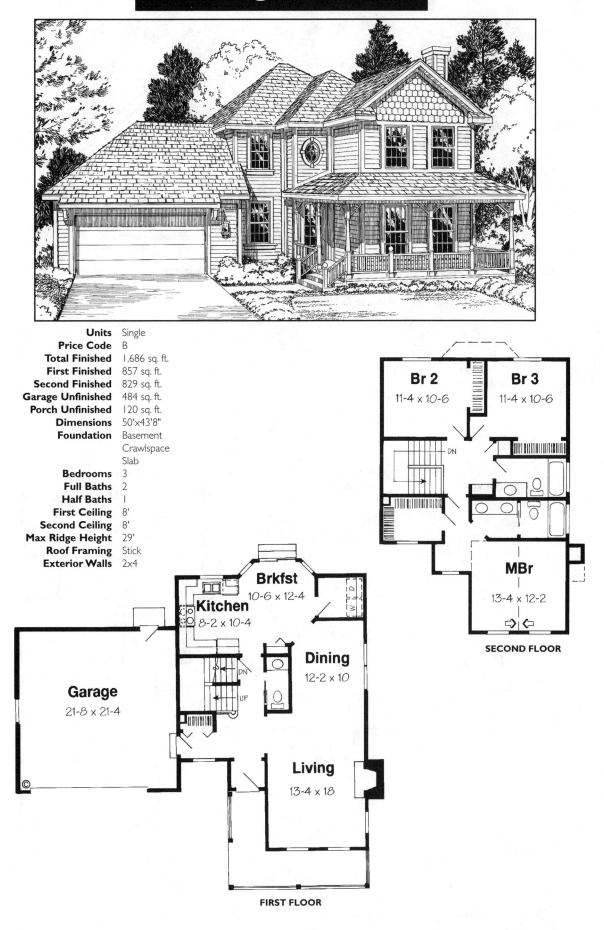

Units	Single
Price Code	B
Total Finished	1,686 sq. ft.
First Finished	857 sq. ft.
Second Finished	829 sq. ft.
Garage Unfinished	484 sq. ft.
Porch Unfinished	120 sq. ft.
Dimensions	50'x43'8"
Foundation	Basement
	Crawlspace
	Slab
Bedrooms	3
Full Baths	2
Half Baths	1
First Ceiling	8'
Second Ceiling	8'
Max Ridge Height	29'
Roof Framing	Stick
Exterior Walls	2x4

Br 2
11-4 x 10-6

Br 3
11-4 x 10-6

DN

MBr
13-4 x 12-2

SECOND FLOOR

Brkfst
10-6 x 12-4

Kitchen
8-2 x 10-4

Garage
21-8 x 21-4

DN

UP

Dining
12-2 x 10

Living
13-4 x 18

FIRST FLOOR

Units	Single
Price Code	B
Total Finished	1,687 sq. ft.
Main Finished	1,687 sq. ft.
Garage Unfinished	419 sq. ft.
Dimensions	50'x52'
Foundation	Basement
	Crawlspace
Bedrooms	3
Full Baths	2
Max Ridge Height	21'
Roof Framing	Stick
Exterior Walls	2x4

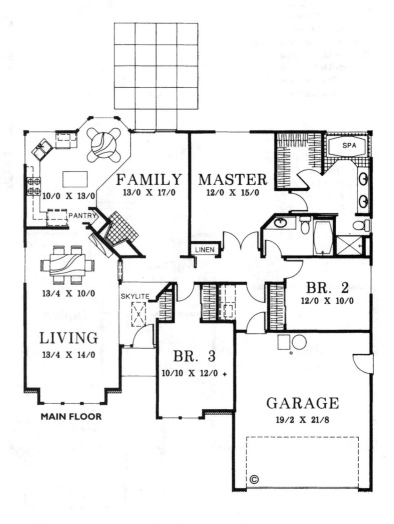

FAMILY
13/0 X 17/0

MASTER
12/0 X 15/0

10/0 X 13/0

PANTRY

SPA

LINEN

13/4 X 10/0

SKYLITE

BR. 2
12/0 X 10/0

LIVING
13/4 X 14/0

BR. 3
10/10 X 12/0 +

GARAGE
19/2 X 21/8

MAIN FLOOR

Units	Single
Price Code	B
Total Finished	1,689 sq. ft.
Main Finished	1,689 sq. ft.
Dimensions	50'x68'
Foundation	Basement
	Crawlspace
	Slab
Bedrooms	3
Full Baths	2
Exterior Walls	2x4

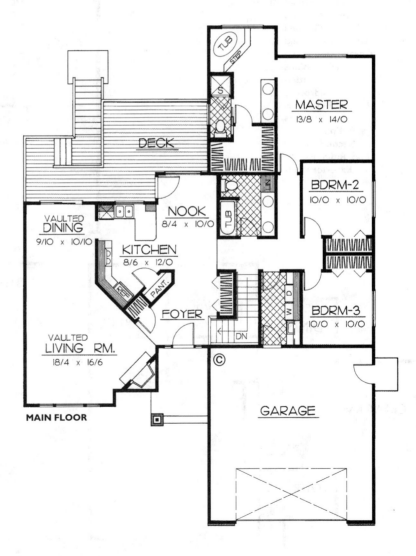

MASTER
13/8 x 14/0

BDRM-2
10/0 x 10/0

BDRM-3
10/0 x 10/0

DECK

NOOK
8/4 x 10/0

VAULTED
DINING
9/10 x 10/10

KITCHEN
8/6 x 12/0

PANT.

REF.

FOYER

VAULTED
LIVING RM.
18/4 x 16/6

DN

GARAGE

MAIN FLOOR

Units	Single
Price Code	B
Total Finished	1,698 sq. ft.
First Finished	951 sq. ft.
Second Finished	747 sq. ft.
Bonus Unfinished	254 sq. ft.
Garage Unfinished	703 sq. ft.
Dimensions	50'x44'6"
Foundation	Crawlspace
Bedrooms	3
Full Baths	2
3/4 Baths	1
First Ceiling	9'
Second Ceiling	8'
Max Ridge Height	28'
Exterior Walls	2x6

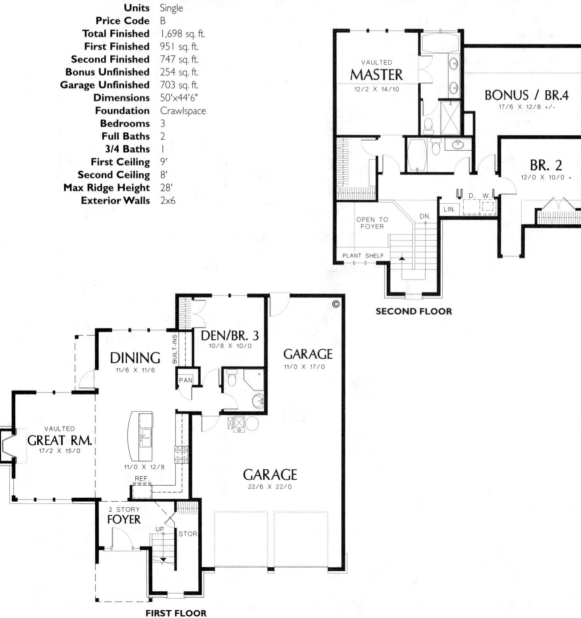

SECOND FLOOR

FIRST FLOOR

Design 93262

Units	Single
Price Code	B
Total Finished	1,708 sq. ft.
Main Finished	1,708 sq. ft.
Garage Unfinished	400 sq. ft.
Dimensions	50'x56'
Foundation	Crawlspace
	Slab
Bedrooms	3
Full Baths	2
Main Ceiling	8'
Max Ridge Height	24
Roof Framing	Stick/Truss
Exterior Walls	2x4

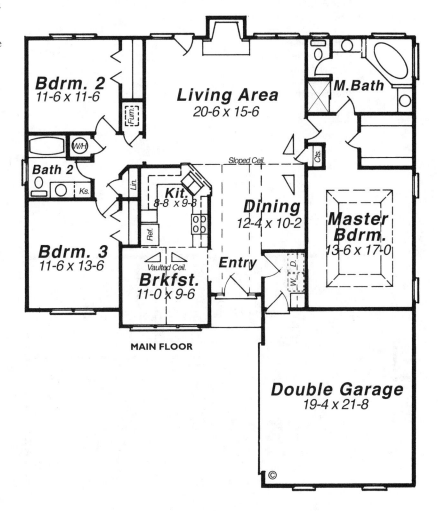

Bdrm. 2
11-6 x 11-6

Living Area
20-6 x 15-6

M. Bath

Bath 2

Kit.
8-8 x 9-8

Dining
12-4 x 10-2

Master Bdrm.
13-6 x 17-0

Bdrm. 3
11-6 x 13-6

Brkfst.
11-0 x 9-6

Entry

Vaulted Ceil.

Sloped Ceil.

MAIN FLOOR

Double Garage
19-4 x 21-8

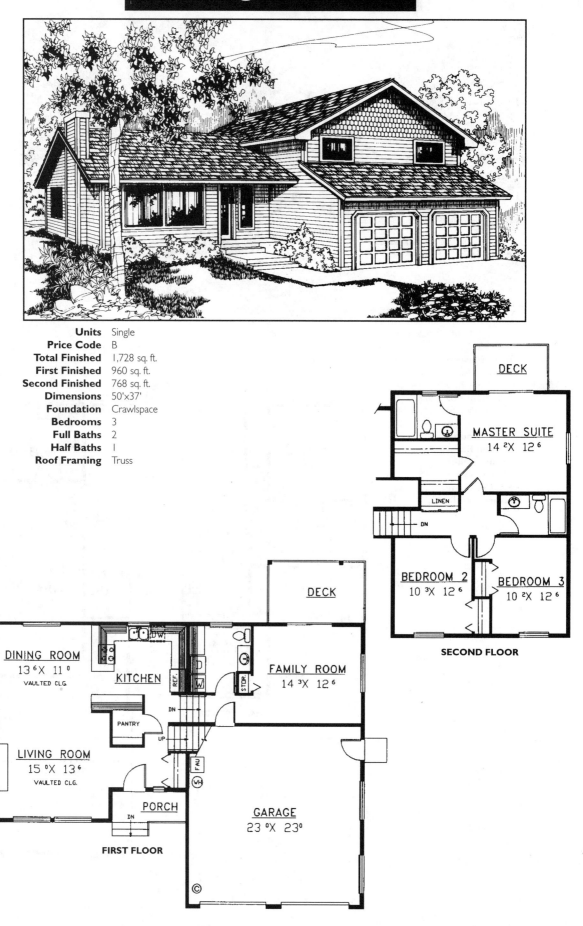

Units	Single
Price Code	B
Total Finished	1,728 sq. ft.
First Finished	960 sq. ft.
Second Finished	768 sq. ft.
Dimensions	50'x37'
Foundation	Crawlspace
Bedrooms	3
Full Baths	2
Half Baths	1
Roof Framing	Truss

DECK

MASTER SUITE
14 ²X 12 ⁶

LINEN

DN

BEDROOM 2
10 ³X 12 ⁶

BEDROOM 3
10 ²X 12 ⁶

SECOND FLOOR

DECK

DINING ROOM
13 ⁶X 11 ⁰
VAULTED CLG.

KITCHEN

FAMILY ROOM
14 ³X 12 ⁶

STOR.

REF.

DW

DN

PANTRY

UP

LIVING ROOM
15 ⁰X 13 ⁶
VAULTED CLG.

F.A.U.

W.H.

PORCH

DN

GARAGE
23 ⁰X 23 ⁰

FIRST FLOOR

Design 94991

Units	Single
Price Code	B
Total Finished	1,731 sq. ft.
First Finished	1,306 sq. ft.
Second Finished	425 sq. ft.
Basement Unfinished	1,306 sq. ft.
Garage Unfinished	434 sq. ft.
Dimensions	50'x52'
Foundation	Basement
Bedrooms	3
Full Baths	2
Half Baths	1
Max Ridge Height	25'7"
Roof Framing	Stick
Exterior Walls	2x4

* Alternate foundation options available at an additional charge.
Please call 1-800-235-5700 for more information.

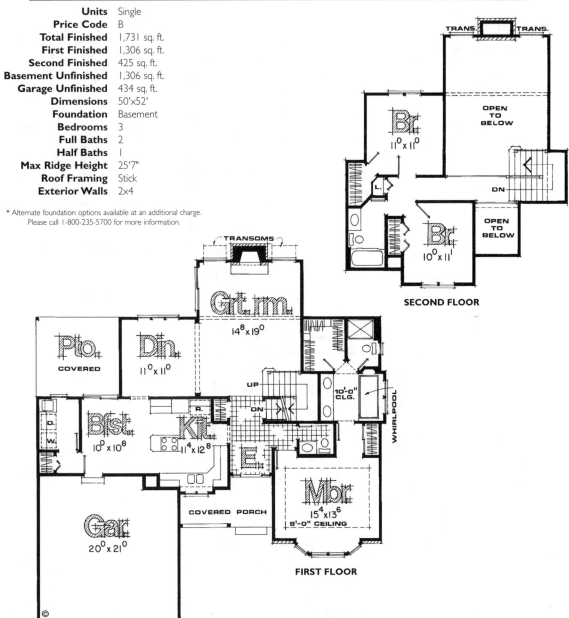

Design 92002

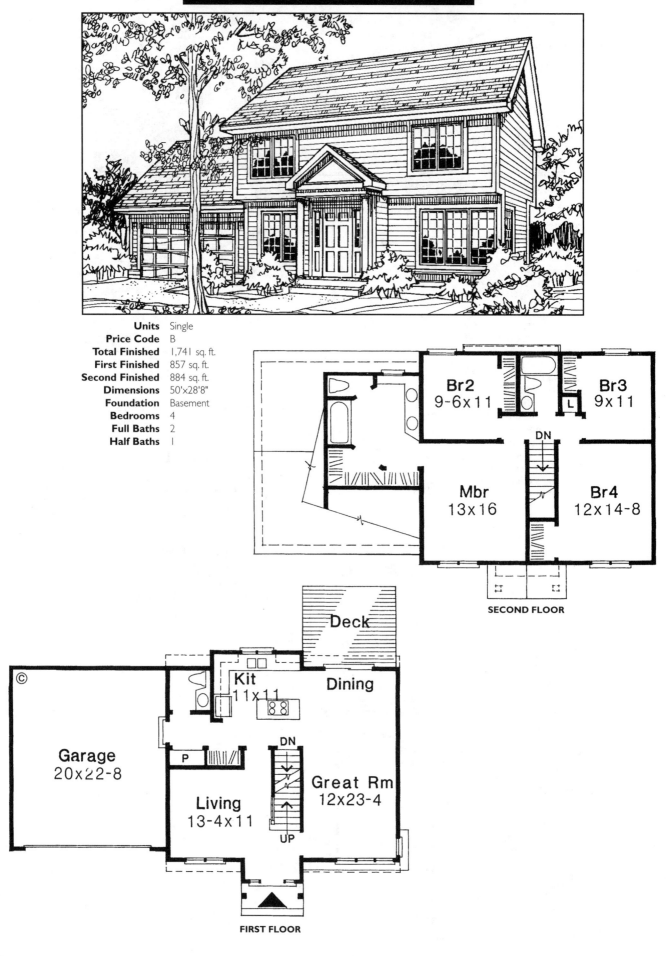

Units	Single
Price Code	B
Total Finished	1,741 sq. ft.
First Finished	857 sq. ft.
Second Finished	884 sq. ft.
Dimensions	50'x28'8"
Foundation	Basement
Bedrooms	4
Full Baths	2
Half Baths	I

Br2
9-6x11

Br3
9x11

DN

Mbr
13x16

Br4
12x14-8

SECOND FLOOR

Deck

Kit
11x11

Dining

Garage
20x22-8

P

DN

Great Rm
12x23-4

Living
13-4x11

UP

FIRST FLOOR

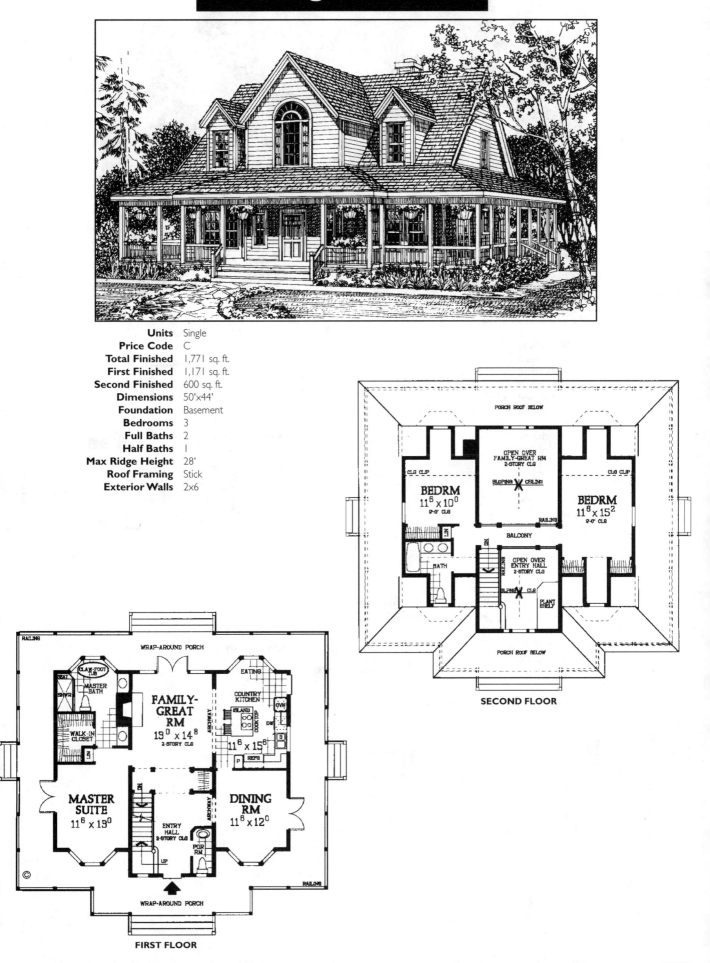

Units	Single
Price Code	C
Total Finished	1,771 sq. ft.
First Finished	1,171 sq. ft.
Second Finished	600 sq. ft.
Dimensions	50'x44'
Foundation	Basement
Bedrooms	3
Full Baths	2
Half Baths	1
Max Ridge Height	28'
Roof Framing	Stick
Exterior Walls	2x6

SECOND FLOOR

FIRST FLOOR

Units	Single
Price Code	C
Total Finished	1,788 sq. ft.
First Finished	1,191 sq. ft.
Second Finished	597 sq. ft.
Basement Unfinished	1,191 sq. ft.
Garage Unfinished	454 sq. ft.
Dimensions	50'x48'
Foundation	Basement
Bedrooms	4
Full Baths	2
Half Baths	1
First Ceiling	8'
Max Ridge Height	28'
Roof Framing	Stick
Exterior Walls	2x4

* Alternate foundation options available at an additional charge.
  Please call 1-800-235-5700 for more information.

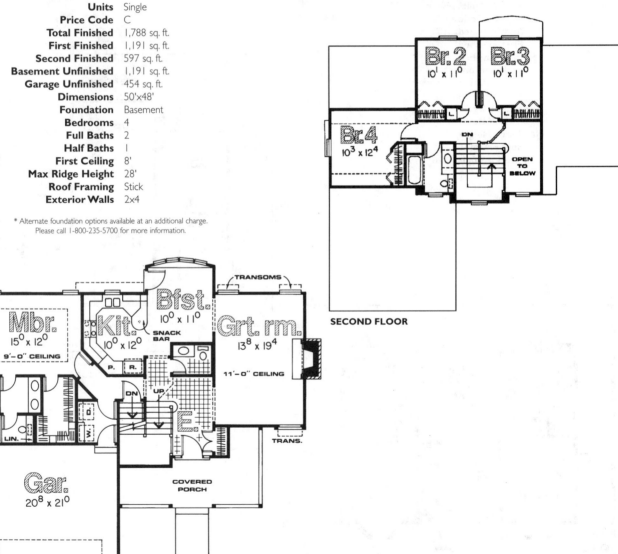

SECOND FLOOR

FIRST FLOOR

Units	Single
Price Code	C
Total Finished	1,792 sq. ft.
First Finished	1,047 sq. ft.
Second Finished	745 sq. ft.
Porch Unfinished	149 sq. ft.
Dimensions	50'x49'6"
Foundation	Crawlspace
Bedrooms	3
Full Baths	2
Half Baths	1
Max Ridge Height	26'
Roof Framing	Stick/Truss
Exterior Walls	2x6

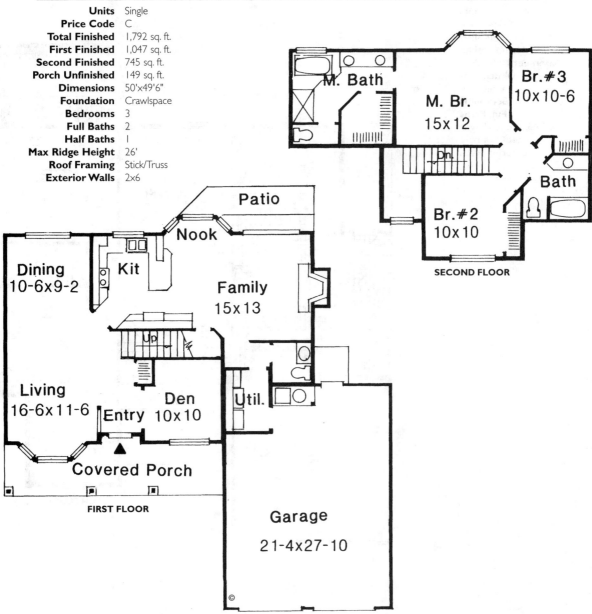

M. Bath

M. Br.
15x12

Br.#3
10x10-6

Dn.

Bath

Br.#2
10x10

SECOND FLOOR

Patio

Nook

Kit

Dining
10-6x9-2

Family
15x13

Up

Living
16-6x11-6

Den
10x10

Entry

Util.

Covered Porch

FIRST FLOOR

Garage
21-4x27-10

Units	Single
Price Code	C
Total Finished	1,796 sq. ft.
Main Finished	1,796 sq. ft.
Basement Unfinished	1,796 sq. ft.
Dimensions	50'x61'
Foundation	Basement
Bedrooms	3
Full Baths	2
Max Ridge Height	20'
Roof Framing	Stick
Exterior Walls	2x6

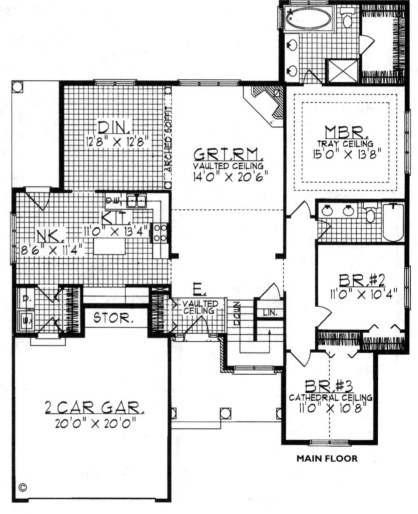

MAIN FLOOR

Design 98823

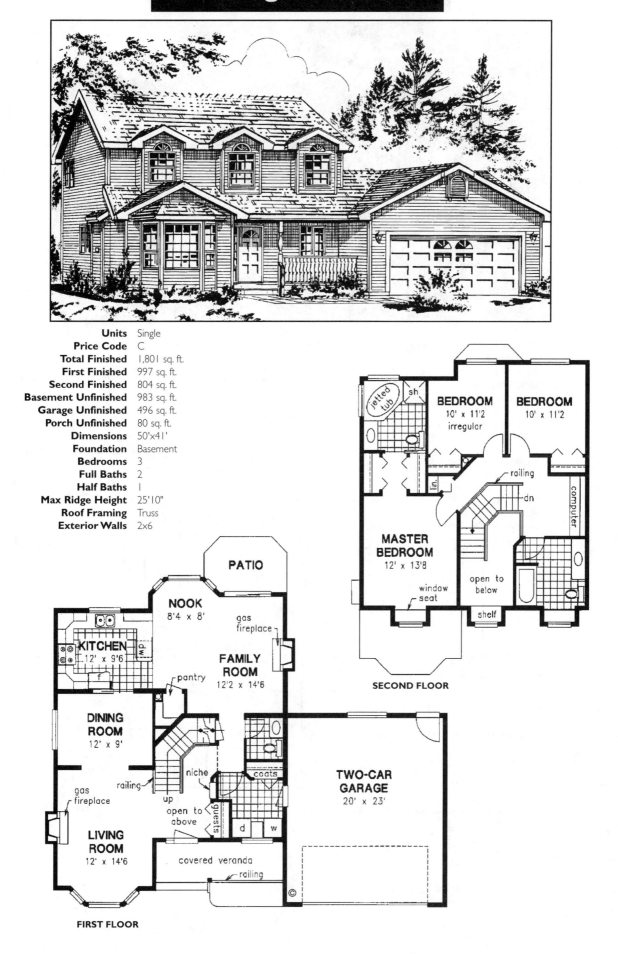

Units	Single
Price Code	C
Total Finished	1,801 sq. ft.
First Finished	997 sq. ft.
Second Finished	804 sq. ft.
Basement Unfinished	983 sq. ft.
Garage Unfinished	496 sq. ft.
Porch Unfinished	80 sq. ft.
Dimensions	50'x41'
Foundation	Basement
Bedrooms	3
Full Baths	2
Half Baths	1
Max Ridge Height	25'10"
Roof Framing	Truss
Exterior Walls	2x6

SECOND FLOOR

jetted tub
sh
BEDROOM 10' x 11'2 irregular
BEDROOM 10' x 11'2
lin.
railing
dn
computer
MASTER BEDROOM 12' x 13'8
open to below
window seat
shelf

FIRST FLOOR

PATIO
NOOK 8'4 x 8'
gas fireplace
KITCHEN 12' x 9'6
FAMILY ROOM 12'2 x 14'6
pantry
DINING ROOM 12' x 9'
niche
railing
coats
TWO-CAR GARAGE 20' x 23'
up
open to above
guests
d w
gas fireplace
LIVING ROOM 12' x 14'6
covered veranda
railing

Design 57011

Units	Single
Price Code	Please call for pricing
Total Finished	2,485 sq. ft.
First Finished	1,365 sq. ft.
Second Finished	1,120 sq. ft.
Bonus Unfinished	506 sq. ft.
Dimensions	49'8"x64'
Foundation	Combo Basement/Crawlspace
Bedrooms	3
Full Baths	2
Half Baths	1
Max Ridge Height	31'
Roof Framing	Stick
Exterior Walls	2x4

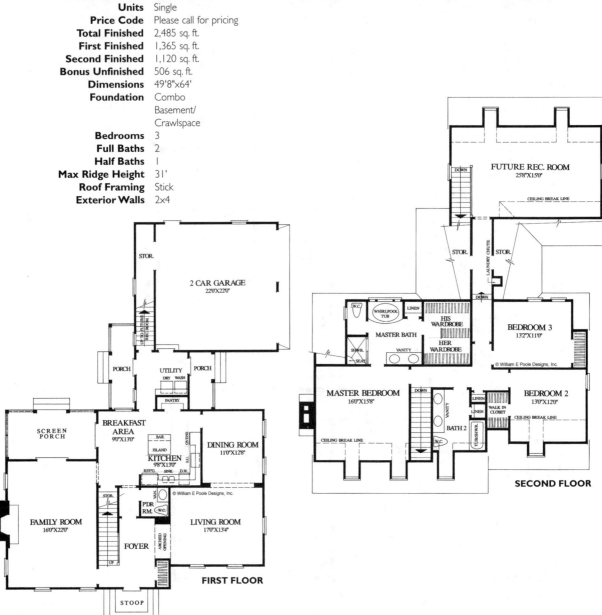

FIRST FLOOR

SECOND FLOOR

Units	Single
Price Code	B
Total Finished	1,704 sq. ft.
Main Finished	1,704 sq. ft.
Garage Unfinished	423 sq. ft.
Dimensions	50'x50'8"
Foundation	Slab
Bedrooms	3
Full Baths	2
Max Ridge Height	21'2"
Roof Framing	Truss

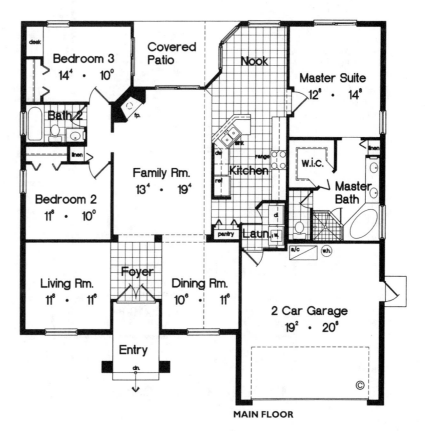

MAIN FLOOR

PHOTOGRAPHY: JOHN EHRENCLOU

Units	Single
Price Code	C
Total Finished	1,838 sq. ft.
First Finished	1,088 sq. ft.
Second Finished	750 sq. ft.
Basement Unfinished	750 sq. ft.
Garage Unfinished	517 sq. ft.
Dimensions	50'x36'8"
Foundation	Basement
	Crawlspace
	Slab
Bedrooms	3
Full Baths	2
Half Baths	1
Max Ridge Height	27'
Roof Framing	Stick
Exterior Walls	2x4, 2x6

Please note: The photographed home may have been modified to suit homeowner preferences. If you order plans, have a builder or design professional check them against the photograph to confirm actual construction details.

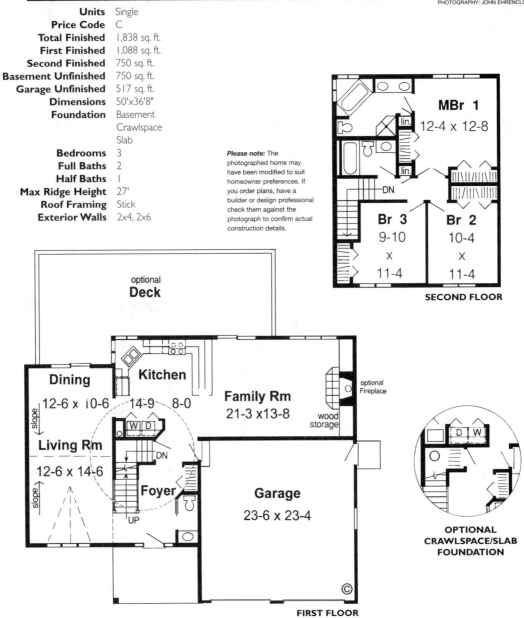

SECOND FLOOR

MBr 1
12-4 x 12-8

Br 3
9-10
x
11-4

Br 2
10-4
x
11-4

DN

optional
Deck

Dining
12-6 x 10-6

Kitchen
14-9   8-0

Family Rm
21-3 x13-8

optional
Fireplace

wood
storage

Living Rm
12-6 x 14-6

W D
DN

Foyer

UP

Garage
23-6 x 23-4

FIRST FLOOR

**OPTIONAL
CRAWLSPACE/SLAB
FOUNDATION**

D W

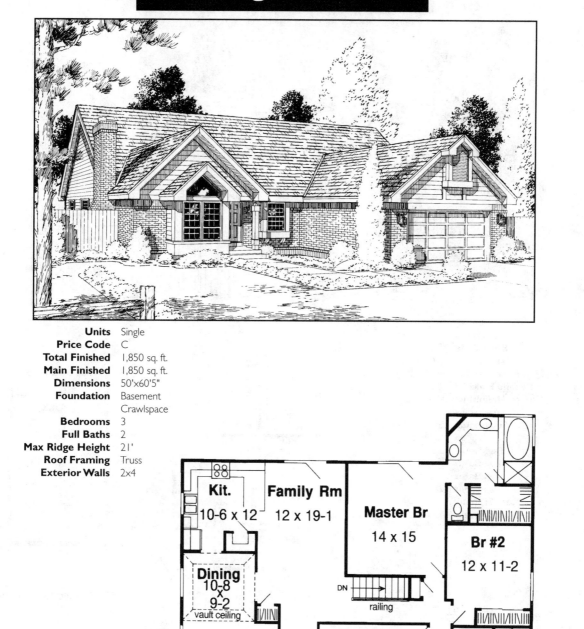

Units	Single
Price Code	C
Total Finished	1,850 sq. ft.
Main Finished	1,850 sq. ft.
Dimensions	50'x60'5"
Foundation	Basement
	Crawlspace
Bedrooms	3
Full Baths	2
Max Ridge Height	21'
Roof Framing	Truss
Exterior Walls	2x4

Kit. 10-6 x 12

Family Rm 12 x 19-1

Master Br 14 x 15

Br #2 12 x 11-2

Dining 10-8 x 9-2 vault ceiling

DN

railing

Living Rm 13-7 x 14-8

Br #3 / Den 13 x 11-4

Foyer

L'dry

W   D

slope   slope

vault clg.

MAIN FLOOR

Garage 18-10 x 19-8

©

Design 20223

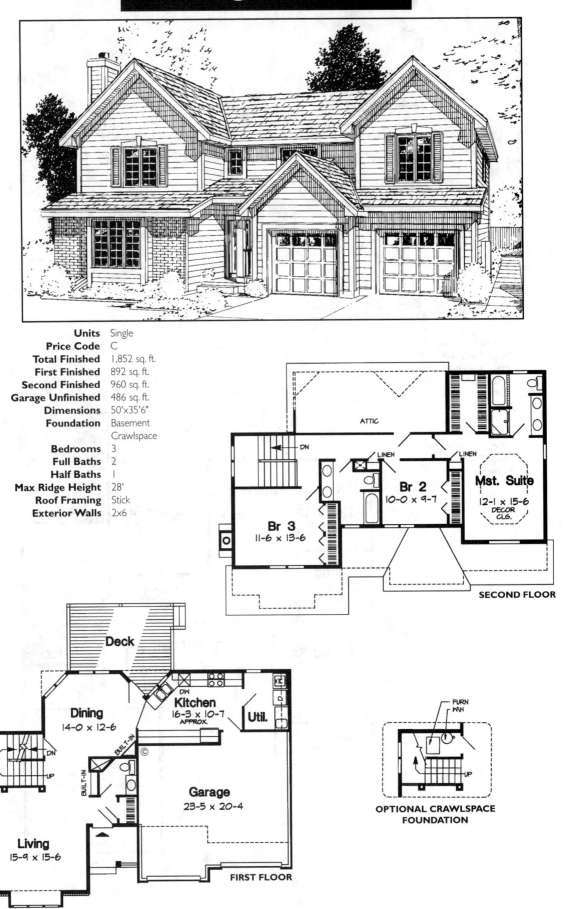

Units	Single
Price Code	C
Total Finished	1,852 sq. ft.
First Finished	892 sq. ft.
Second Finished	960 sq. ft.
Garage Unfinished	486 sq. ft.
Dimensions	50'x35'6"
Foundation	Basement
	Crawlspace
Bedrooms	3
Full Baths	2
Half Baths	1
Max Ridge Height	28'
Roof Framing	Stick
Exterior Walls	2x6

ATTIC

DN

LINEN

LINEN

Br 2
10-0 x 9-7

Mst. Suite
12-1 x 15-6
DECOR CLG.

Br 3
11-6 x 13-6

SECOND FLOOR

Deck

Dining
14-0 x 12-6

DW

Kitchen
16-3 x 10-7
APPROX.

Util.

DN

UP

BUILT-IN

BUILT-IN

©

Garage
23-5 x 20-4

Living
15-9 x 15-6

FIRST FLOOR

FURN
WH

UP

**OPTIONAL CRAWLSPACE
FOUNDATION**

Design 20059

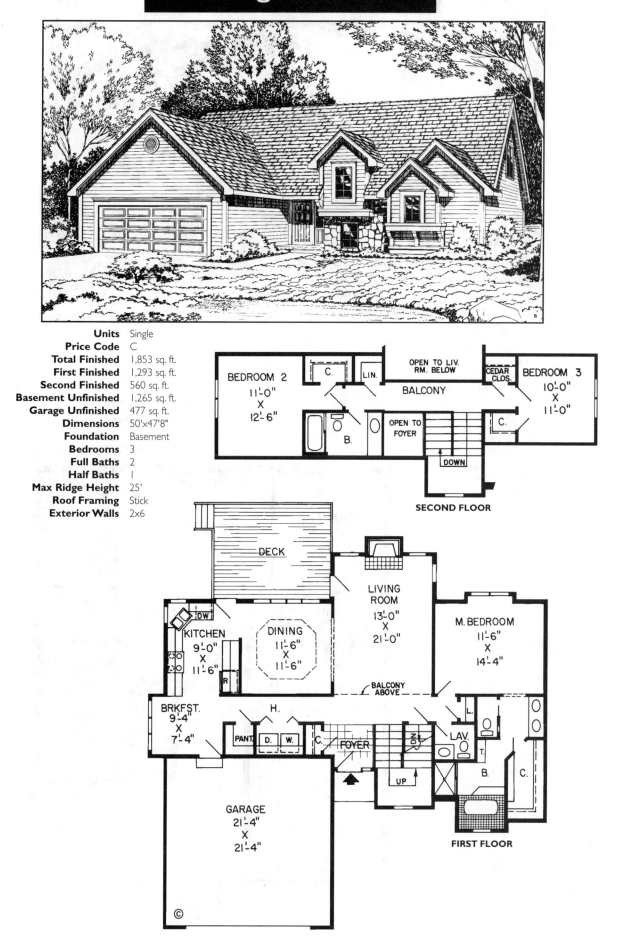

Units	Single
Price Code	C
Total Finished	1,853 sq. ft.
First Finished	1,293 sq. ft.
Second Finished	560 sq. ft.
Basement Unfinished	1,265 sq. ft.
Garage Unfinished	477 sq. ft.
Dimensions	50'x47'8"
Foundation	Basement
Bedrooms	3
Full Baths	2
Half Baths	1
Max Ridge Height	25'
Roof Framing	Stick
Exterior Walls	2x6

BEDROOM 2
11'-0"
X
12'-6"

C.
LIN.

OPEN TO LIV.
RM. BELOW

BALCONY

CEDAR
CLOS.

BEDROOM 3
10'-0"
X
11'-0"

C.

B.

OPEN TO
FOYER

DOWN

SECOND FLOOR

DECK

LIVING ROOM
13'-0"
X
21'-0"

M. BEDROOM
11'-6"
X
14'-4"

KITCHEN
9'-0"
X
11'-6"

DW

DINING
11'-6"
X
11'-6"

R

BALCONY
ABOVE

L.

BRKFST.
9'-4"
X
7'-4"

H.

PANT.

D.

W.

C.

FOYER

UP

LAV.

T.

B.

C.

GARAGE
21'-4"
X
21'-4"

©

FIRST FLOOR

Units	Single
Price Code	C
Total Finished	1,863 sq. ft.
Main Finished	1,863 sq. ft.
Garage Unfinished	442 sq. ft.
Deck Unfinished	162 sq. ft.
Dimensions	50'x61'2"
Foundation	Slab
Bedrooms	4
Full Baths	2
Max Ridge Height	28'6"
Roof Framing	Stick
Exterior Walls	2x4

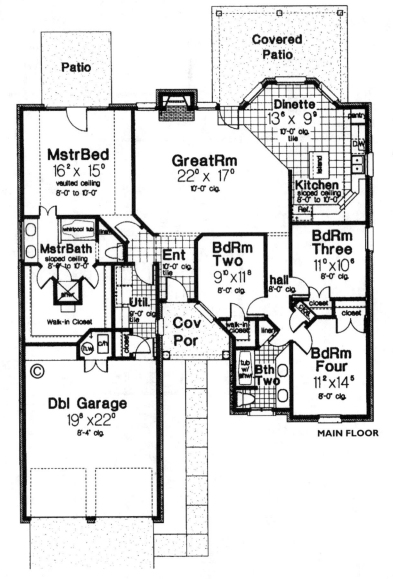

MAIN FLOOR

Units	Single
Price Code	C
Total Finished	1,865 sq. ft.
Main Finished	1,865 sq. ft.
Dimensions	50'x59'
Foundation	Crawlspace
Bedrooms	3
Full Baths	2
Max Ridge Height	24'
Roof Framing	Stick
Exterior Walls	2x6

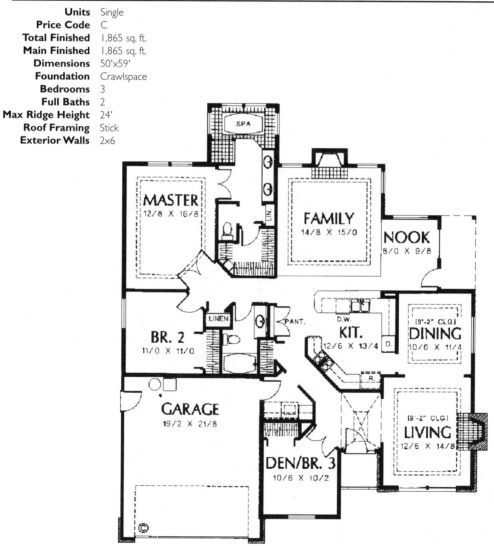

MAIN FLOOR

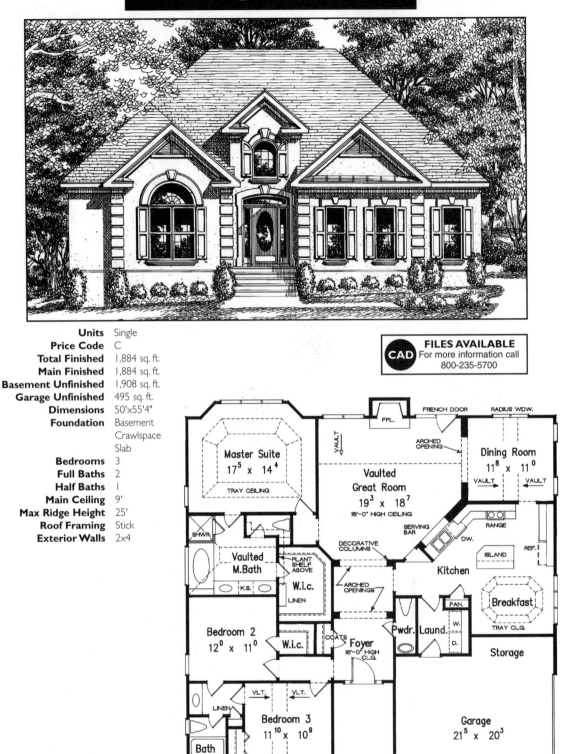

Units	Single
Price Code	C
Total Finished	1,884 sq. ft.
Main Finished	1,884 sq. ft.
Basement Unfinished	1,908 sq. ft.
Garage Unfinished	495 sq. ft.
Dimensions	50'x55'4"
Foundation	Basement
	Crawlspace
	Slab
Bedrooms	3
Full Baths	2
Half Baths	1
Main Ceiling	9'
Max Ridge Height	25'
Roof Framing	Stick
Exterior Walls	2x4

FILES AVAILABLE
For more information call
800-235-5700

MAIN FLOOR

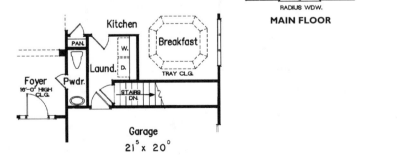

OPTIONAL BASEMENT STAIR LOCATION

GARAGE LOCATION W/ BASEMENT

Units	Single
Price Code	C
Total Finished	1,893 sq. ft.
First Finished	1,277 sq. ft.
Second Finished	616 sq. ft.
Basement Unfinished	1,265 sq. ft.
Garage Unfinished	477 sq. ft.
Deck Unfinished	265 sq. ft.
Porch Unfinished	32 sq. ft.
Dimensions	50'x49'
Foundation	Basement
	Crawlspace
	Slab
Bedrooms	3
Full Baths	2
Half Baths	1
Max Ridge Height	27'
Roof Framing	Stick
Exterior Walls	2x6

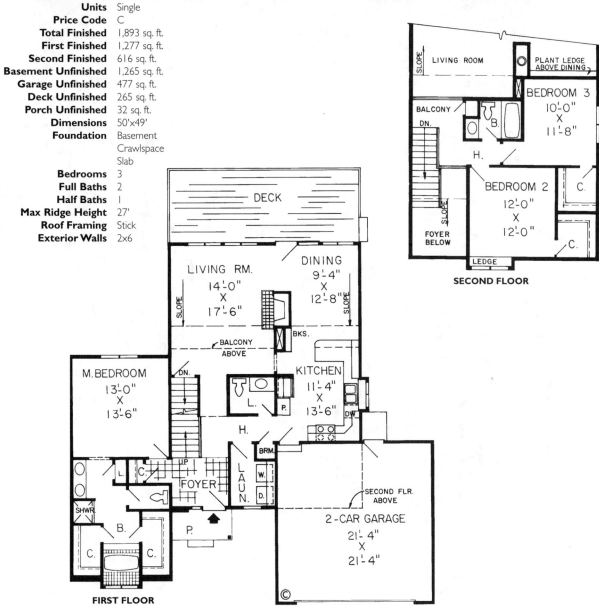

SECOND FLOOR

FIRST FLOOR

Units	Single
Price Code	C
Total Finished	1,895 sq. ft.
First Finished	1,295 sq. ft.
Second Finished	600 sq. ft.
Dimensions	50'x55'3"
Foundation	Basement
Bedrooms	3
Full Baths	2
Half Baths	1
Max Ridge Height	28'
Roof Framing	Truss
Exterior Walls	2x6

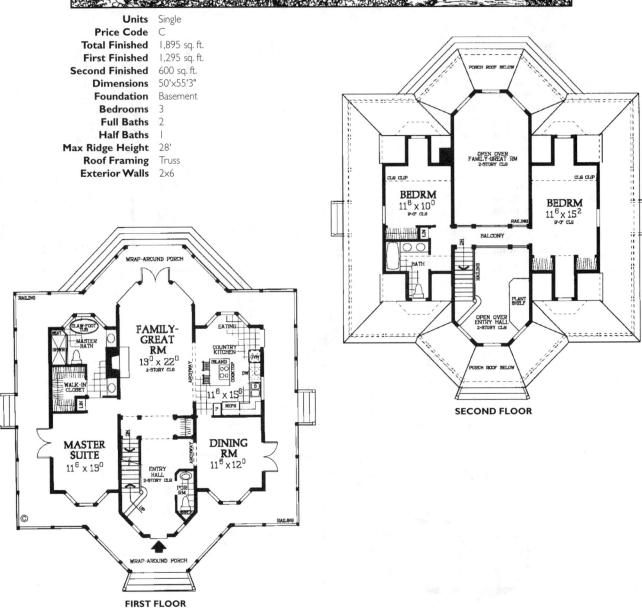

FIRST FLOOR

SECOND FLOOR

Units	Single
Price Code	C
Total Finished	1,917 sq. ft.
Main Finished	1,709 sq. ft.
Lower Finished	208 sq. ft.
Basement Unfinished	443 sq. ft.
Garage Unfinished	552 sq. ft.
Deck Unfinished	220 sq. ft.
Dimensions	50'x48'
Foundation	Basement
Bedrooms	3
Full Baths	2
Max Ridge Height	29'
Roof Framing	Stick
Exterior Walls	2x4

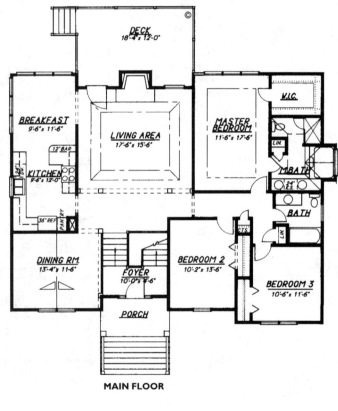

MAIN FLOOR

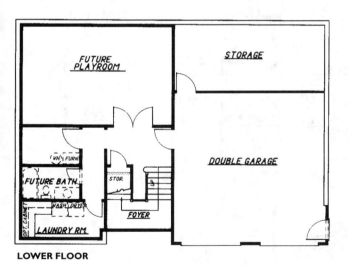

LOWER FLOOR

Design 91045

Units	Single
Price Code	C
Total Finished	1,919 sq. ft.
Main Finished	1,919 sq. ft.
Dimensions	50'x66'6"
Foundation	Crawlspace
Bedrooms	3
Full Baths	2
Max Ridge Height	22'
Roof Framing	Truss
Exterior Walls	2x6

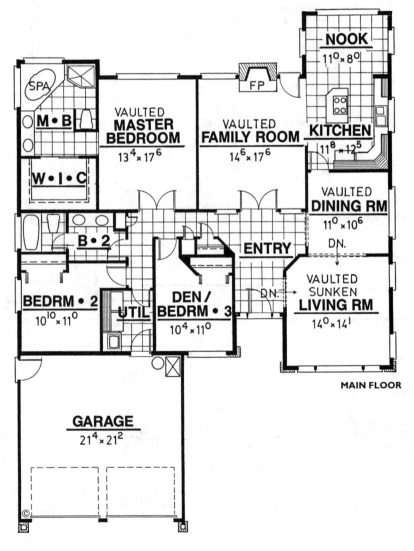

MAIN FLOOR

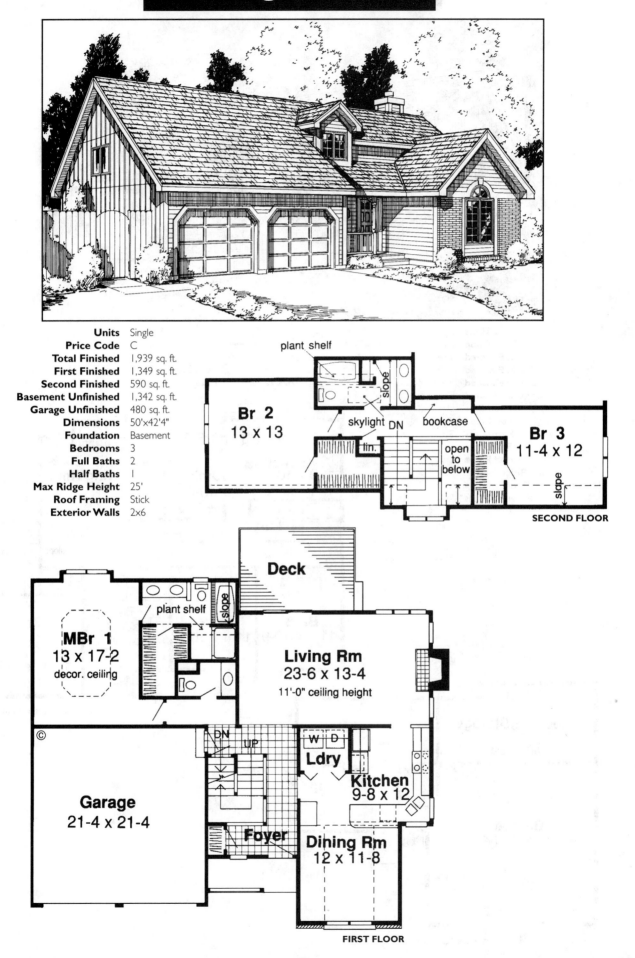

Units	Single
Price Code	C
Total Finished	1,939 sq. ft.
First Finished	1,349 sq. ft.
Second Finished	590 sq. ft.
Basement Unfinished	1,342 sq. ft.
Garage Unfinished	480 sq. ft.
Dimensions	50'x42'4"
Foundation	Basement
Bedrooms	3
Full Baths	2
Half Baths	1
Max Ridge Height	25'
Roof Framing	Stick
Exterior Walls	2x6

plant shelf

Br 2
13 x 13

skylight   DN

bookcase

fin.

open to below

Br 3
11-4 x 12

slope

slope

SECOND FLOOR

Deck

plant shelf

slope

MBr 1
13 x 17-2
decor. ceiling

Living Rm
23-6 x 13-4
11'-0" ceiling height

DN   UP

W   D

Ldry

Kitchen
9-8 x 12

Garage
21-4 x 21-4

Foyer

Dining Rm
12 x 11-8

FIRST FLOOR

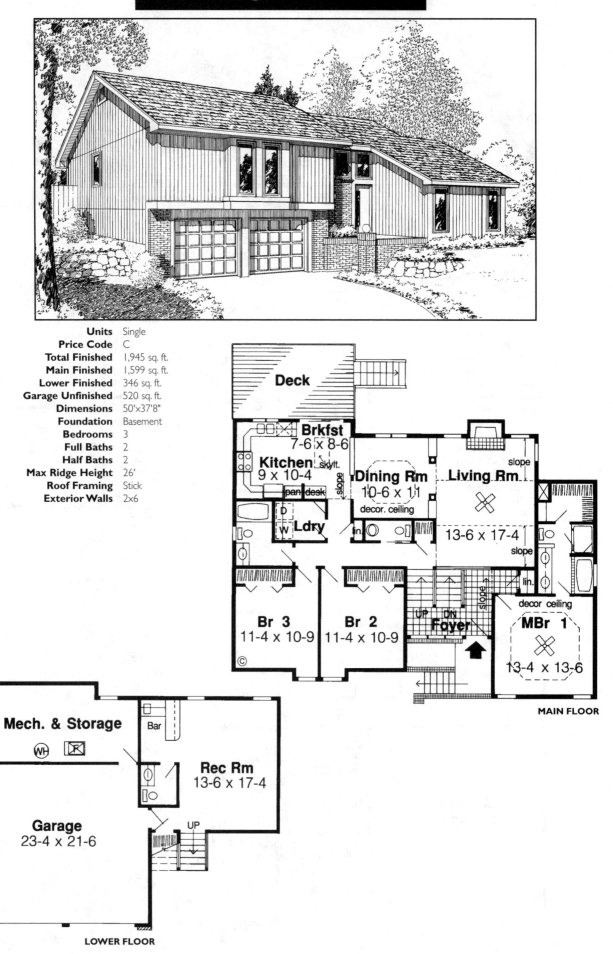

Units	Single
Price Code	C
Total Finished	1,945 sq. ft.
Main Finished	1,599 sq. ft.
Lower Finished	346 sq. ft.
Garage Unfinished	520 sq. ft.
Dimensions	50'×37'8"
Foundation	Basement
Bedrooms	3
Full Baths	2
Half Baths	2
Max Ridge Height	26'
Roof Framing	Stick
Exterior Walls	2x6

Deck

Brkfst 7-6 x 8-6

Kitchen 9 x 10-4 skylt.

pan desk

Dining Rm 10-6 x 11 decor. ceiling

Living Rm 13-6 x 17-4 slope

Ldry

Br 3 11-4 x 10-9

Br 2 11-4 x 10-9

UP DN **Foyer**

MBr 1 13-4 x 13-6 decor ceiling

MAIN FLOOR

Mech. & Storage WH

Bar

Rec Rm 13-6 x 17-4

Garage 23-4 x 21-6

UP

LOWER FLOOR

Design 93342

Units	Single
Price Code	C
Total Finished	1,950 sq. ft.
First Finished	1,004 sq. ft.
Second Finished	946 sq. ft.
Bonus Unfinished	200 sq. ft.
Basement Unfinished	1,004 sq. ft.
Garage Unfinished	450 sq. ft.
Porch Unfinished	28 sq. ft.
Dimensions	50'x34'
Foundation	Basement
Bedrooms	3
Full Baths	2
Half Baths	1
First Ceiling	9'
Second Ceiling	8'
Max Ridge Height	30'
Roof Framing	Stick/Truss
Exterior Walls	2x6

SECOND FLOOR

ROOF

WHIRLPOOL TUB

STEP

SEAT

M. BATH

SHWR.

TWL.

6 SH.

M.B.R.
18-0 X 12-6

W.I.C.

6 SH.

BONUS RM.
(UNFINISHED)
20-0 X 10-0
(FLAT CLG. AREA)

HALL

LIN.

B.R. 2
12-0 X 12-0

BATH 2

TWL.

6 SH.

B.R. 3
10-0 X 13-0

FIRST FLOOR

6 FT. S.G.D.

DINETTE
12-0 X 10-0

D. W.

LNDR.

STEP

FAM. RM.
18-0 X 12-6

D.W.

HOOD RANGE

KITCHEN
12-6 X 13-6

PANT.

REFR.

PDR.

DN.

UP.

GARAGE
20-0 X 24-0

DINING RM.
12-0 X 11-0

FOYER

LIV. RM.
11-0 X 13-0

16 FT. GAR. DOOR

PORCH

Units	Single
Price Code	C
Total Finished	1,964 sq. ft.
First Finished	1,156 sq. ft.
Second Finished	808 sq. ft.
Basement Unfinished	1,156 sq. ft.
Garage Unfinished	484 sq. ft.
Porch Unfinished	32 sq. ft.
Dimensions	50'x54'
Foundation	Basement
Bedrooms	3
Full Baths	2
Half Baths	1
First Ceiling	8'
Max Ridge Height	26'9"

SECOND FLOOR

BR 2 11-0x12-0
MBR 14-0x12-0
ENS
BATH
LOFT 13-4 x 8-10
dn
Hall
lin
BR 3 9-0x10-10
railing
Livingroom below
Foyer below

FIRST FLOOR

Sunken FAMILY ROOM 16-0x12-0
railing
NOOK
KITCHEN 17-0x12-0
dw
R
dn
Pantry
F
DINING 13-0x10-8
dn
Hall
d,n
open over
LAV
W I D
Utility
vlc sky-lite
Sunken LIVINGROOM 17-0x13-6
up
dn
FOYER
DOUBLE GARAGE 21-0 x 21-0
vaulted clg.

Units	Single
Price Code	C
Total Finished	1,990 sq. ft.
Main Finished	1,990 sq. ft.
Garage Unfinished	672 sq. ft.
Deck Unfinished	84 sq. ft.
Porch Unfinished	60 sq. ft.
Dimensions	50'x77'4"
Foundation	Slab
Bedrooms	4
Full Baths	2
Half Baths	1
Main Ceiling	8'-10'
Max Ridge Height	24'6"
Roof Framing	Stick
Exterior Walls	2x4

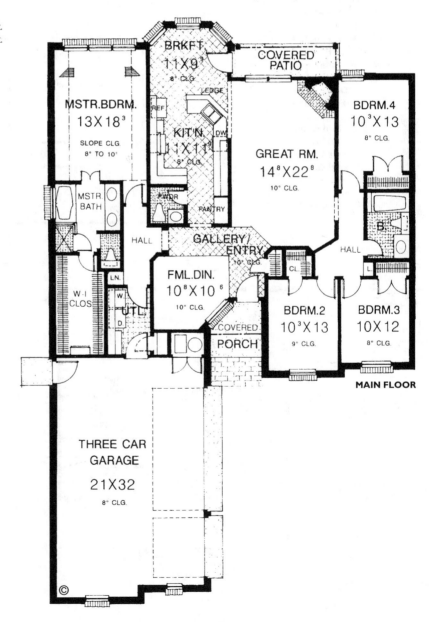

MAIN FLOOR

Design 98442

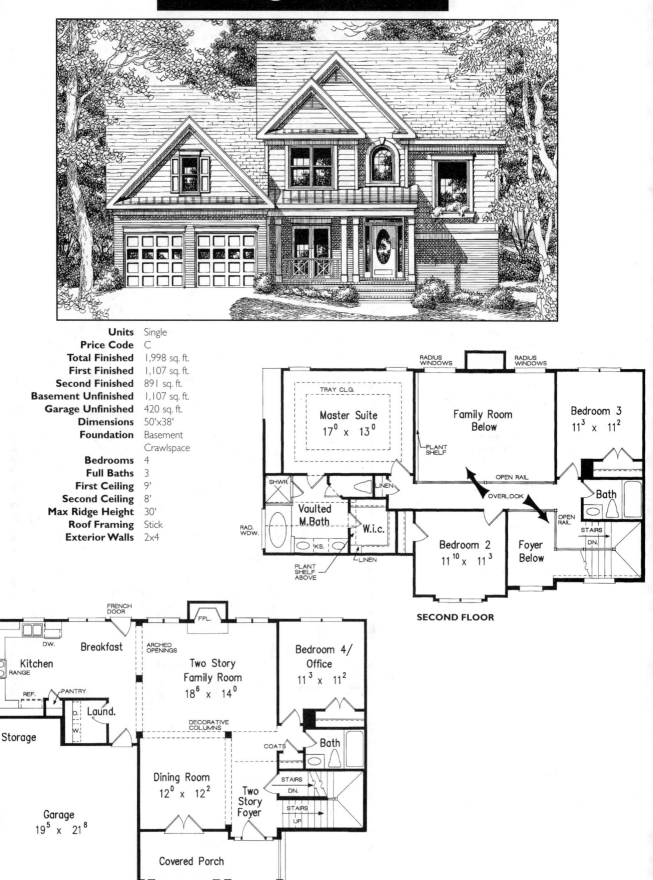

Units	Single
Price Code	C
Total Finished	1,998 sq. ft.
First Finished	1,107 sq. ft.
Second Finished	891 sq. ft.
Basement Unfinished	1,107 sq. ft.
Garage Unfinished	420 sq. ft.
Dimensions	50'x38'
Foundation	Basement
	Crawlspace
Bedrooms	4
Full Baths	3
First Ceiling	9'
Second Ceiling	8'
Max Ridge Height	30'
Roof Framing	Stick
Exterior Walls	2x4

SECOND FLOOR

RADIUS WINDOWS   RADIUS WINDOWS

TRAY CLG.

Master Suite
17⁰ x 13⁰

Family Room Below

Bedroom 3
11³ x 11²

PLANT SHELF

OPEN RAIL

SHWR.   LINEN

Vaulted M.Bath

OVERLOOK

Bath

RAD. WDW.

KS.

W.i.c.

LINEN

Bedroom 2
11¹⁰ x 11³

OPEN RAIL   STAIRS   DN.

Foyer Below

PLANT SHELF ABOVE

FIRST FLOOR

FRENCH DOOR

FPL.

DW.   Breakfast   ARCHED OPENINGS

Kitchen

RANGE

Two Story Family Room
18⁶ x 14⁰

Bedroom 4/ Office
11³ x 11²

REF.   PANTRY

D.   Laund.

W.

DECORATIVE COLUMNS

COATS   Bath

Storage

Dining Room
12⁰ x 12²

STAIRS   DN.

Two Story Foyer

STAIRS   UP

Garage
19⁵ x 21⁸

Covered Porch

Units	Single
Price Code	D
Total Finished	2,081 sq. ft.
Main Finished	2,081 sq. ft.
Dimensions	50'x51'
Foundation	Crawlspace
Bedrooms	3
Full Baths	2
Half Baths	I
Max Ridge Height	30'
Roof Framing	Stick
Exterior Walls	2x6

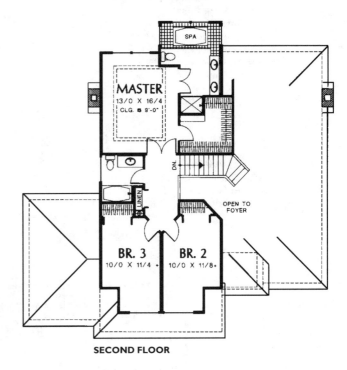

SECOND FLOOR

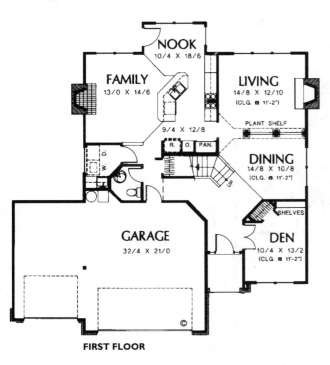

FIRST FLOOR

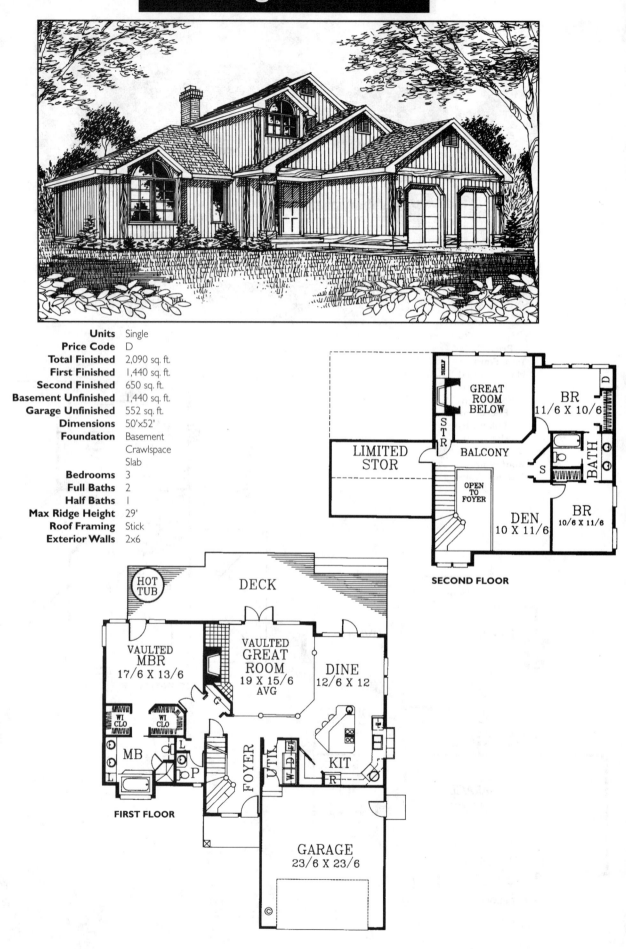

Units	Single
Price Code	D
Total Finished	2,090 sq. ft.
First Finished	1,440 sq. ft.
Second Finished	650 sq. ft.
Basement Unfinished	1,440 sq. ft.
Garage Unfinished	552 sq. ft.
Dimensions	50'x52'
Foundation	Basement
	Crawlspace
	Slab
Bedrooms	3
Full Baths	2
Half Baths	1
Max Ridge Height	29'
Roof Framing	Stick
Exterior Walls	2x6

SECOND FLOOR

GREAT ROOM BELOW

BR 11/6 X 10/6

LIMITED STOR

STR

BALCONY

OPEN TO FOYER

DEN 10 X 11/6

BR 10/6 X 11/8

BATH

FIRST FLOOR

HOT TUB

DECK

VAULTED MBR 17/6 X 13/6

VAULTED GREAT ROOM 19 X 15/6 AVG

DINE 12/6 X 12

WI CLO

WI CLO

MB

FOYER

UTIL

KIT

GARAGE 23/6 X 23/6

Units	Duplex
Price Code	G
Total Finished	2,092 sq. ft.
Main Finished	2,092 sq. ft.
Garage Unfinished	494 sq. ft.
Dimensions	50'x66'10"
Foundation	Slab
Bedrooms	4
Full Baths	4
Main Ceiling	8'
Max Ridge Height	15'
Roof Framing	Stick
Exterior Walls	2x4

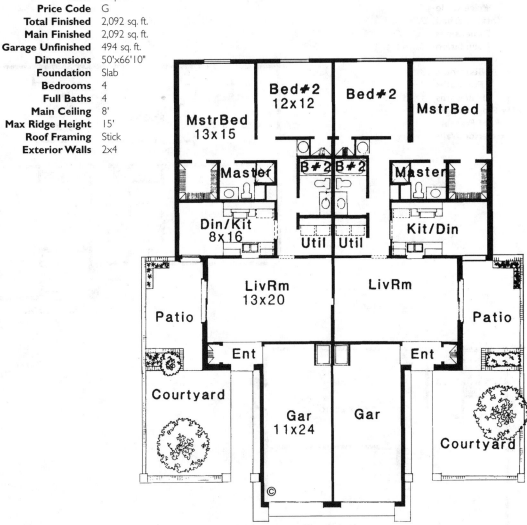

MAIN FLOOR

Units	Single
Price Code	D
Total Finished	2,097 sq. ft.
Dimensions	50'x32'6"
Foundation	Basement
	Slab
Bedrooms	3
Full Baths	2
Half Baths	1
Max Ridge Height	23'
Roof Framing	Stick
Exterior Walls	2x4

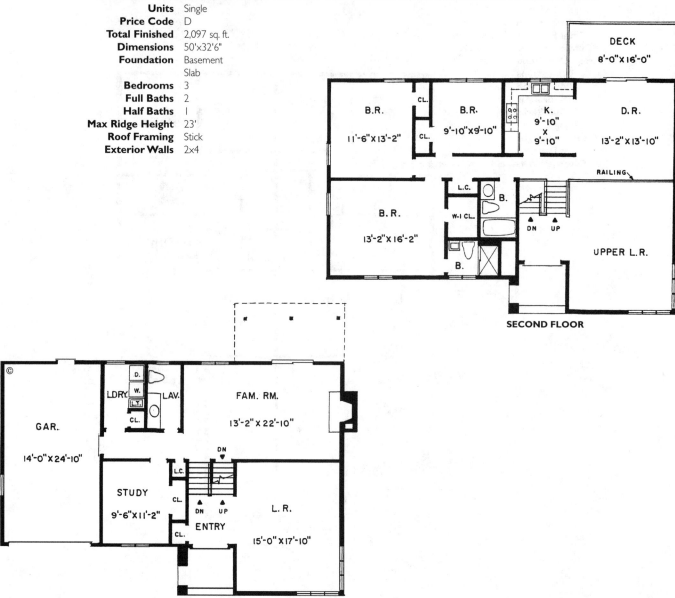

SECOND FLOOR

FIRST FLOOR

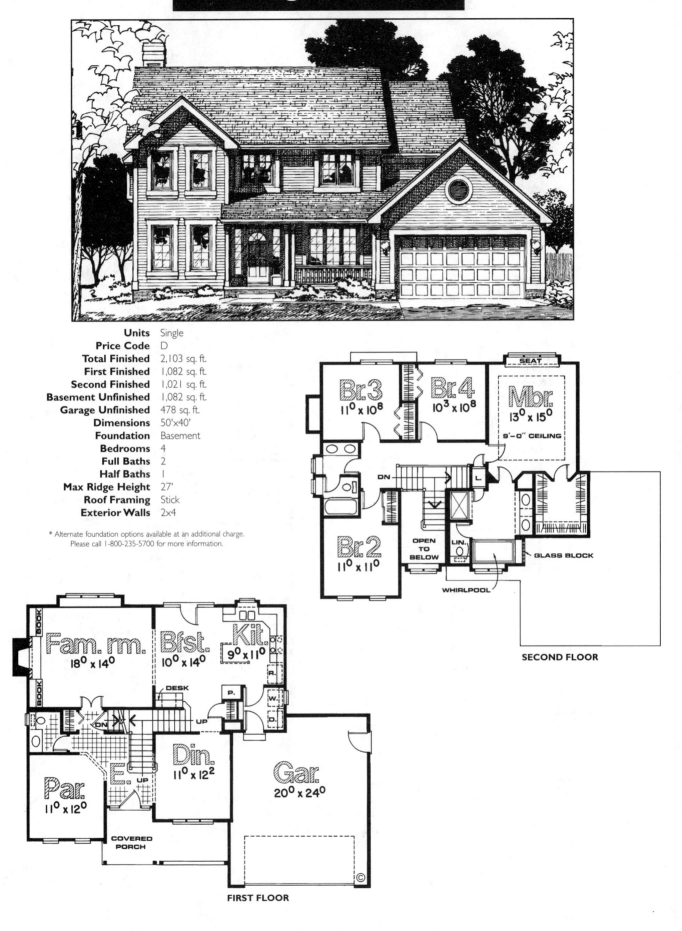

Units	Single
Price Code	D
Total Finished	2,103 sq. ft.
First Finished	1,082 sq. ft.
Second Finished	1,021 sq. ft.
Basement Unfinished	1,082 sq. ft.
Garage Unfinished	478 sq. ft.
Dimensions	50'x40'
Foundation	Basement
Bedrooms	4
Full Baths	2
Half Baths	1
Max Ridge Height	27'
Roof Framing	Stick
Exterior Walls	2x4

* Alternate foundation options available at an additional charge.
Please call 1-800-235-5700 for more information.

Br.3 11⁰ x 10⁸

Br.4 10³ x 10⁸

Mbr. 13⁰ x 15⁰
9'-0" CEILING
SEAT

DN

Br.2 11⁰ x 11⁰

OPEN TO BELOW

LIN.

GLASS BLOCK

WHIRLPOOL

SECOND FLOOR

Fam. rm. 18⁰ x 14⁰
BOOK
BOOK

Bfst. 10⁰ x 14⁰
DESK

Kit. 9⁰ x 11⁰
R.

P.
W.
D.

DN
UP

Par. 11⁰ x 12⁰

Din. 11⁰ x 12²
UP

Gar. 20⁰ x 24⁰

COVERED PORCH

FIRST FLOOR

Units	Single
Price Code	D
Total Finished	2,108 sq. ft.
Main Finished	2,108 sq. ft.
Dimensions	50'x66'
Foundation	Basement
	Crawlspace
	Slab
Bedrooms	3
Full Baths	2
Max Ridge Height	23'
Roof Framing	Stick
Exterior Walls	2x4

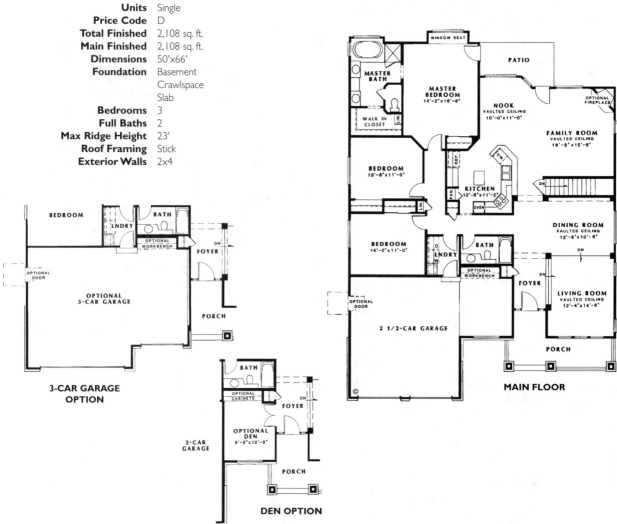

3-CAR GARAGE OPTION

DEN OPTION

MAIN FLOOR

Design 10202

Units	Single
Price Code	D
Total Finished	2,132 sq. ft.
First Finished	1,172 sq. ft.
Second Finished	960 sq. ft.
Garage Unfinished	408 sq. ft.
Dimensions	50'x40'
Foundation	Basement
Bedrooms	4
Full Baths	2
Half Baths	1

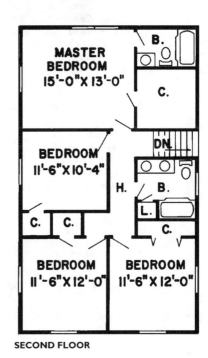

SECOND FLOOR

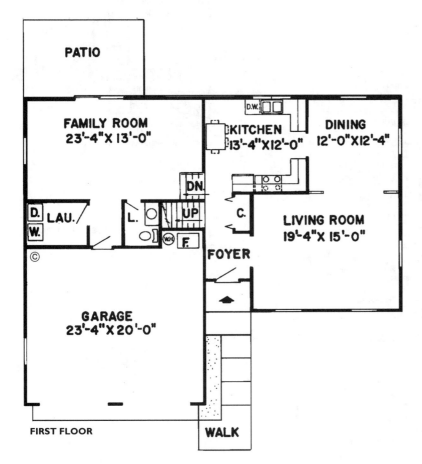

FIRST FLOOR

Design 91411

Units	Single
Price Code	D
Total Finished	2,139 sq. ft.
First Finished	1,249 sq. ft.
Second Finished	890 sq. ft.
Garage Unfinished	462 sq. ft.
Dimensions	50'x52'
Foundation	Basement
	Crawlspace
	Slab
Bedrooms	4
Full Baths	2
Half Baths	1
Max Ridge Height	27'
Roof Framing	Stick
Exterior Walls	2x6

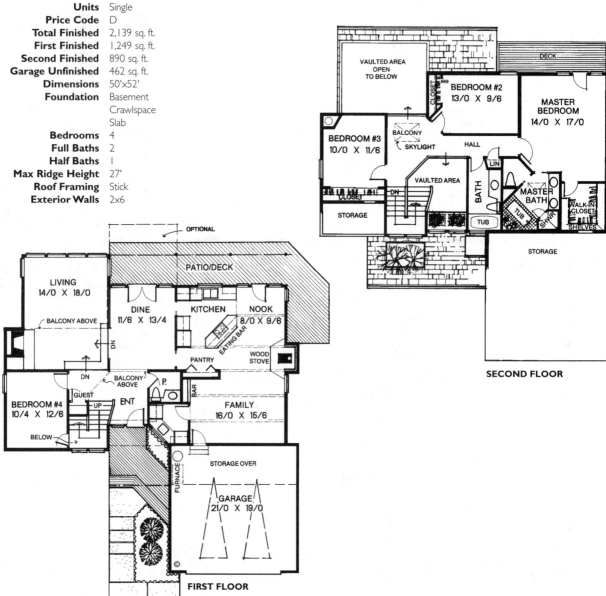

Design 61006

Units	Single
Price Code	D
Total Finished	2,143 sq. ft.
First Finished	1,400 sq. ft.
Second Finished	743 sq. ft.
Dimensions	50'x28'
Foundation	Slab
Bedrooms	3
Full Baths	2

SECOND FLOOR

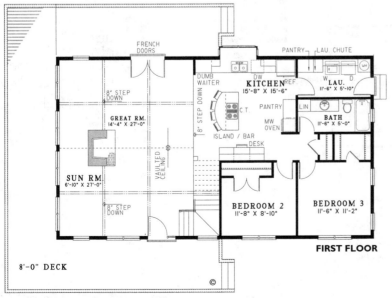

FIRST FLOOR

Design 10565

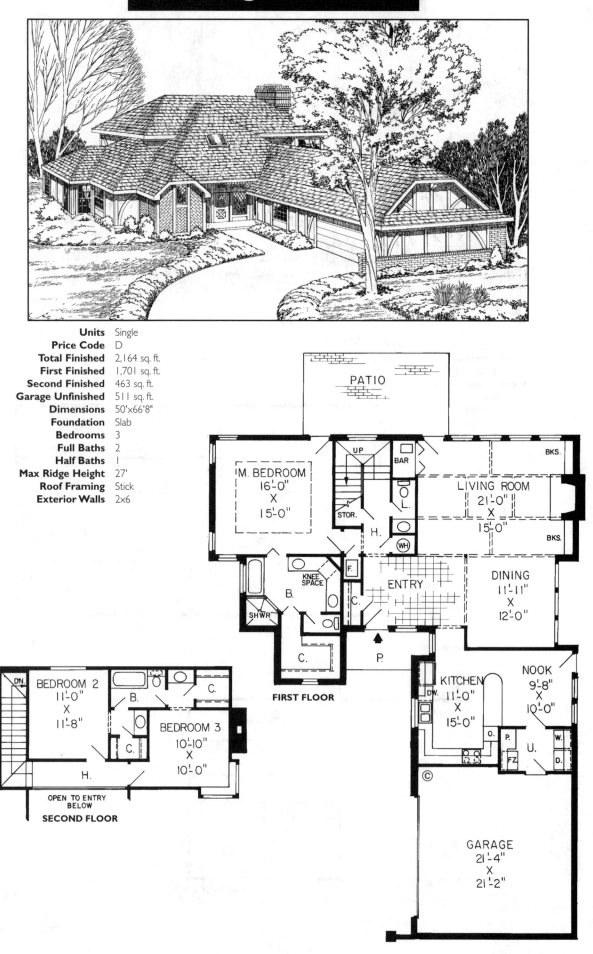

Units	Single
Price Code	D
Total Finished	2,164 sq. ft.
First Finished	1,701 sq. ft.
Second Finished	463 sq. ft.
Garage Unfinished	511 sq. ft.
Dimensions	50'x66'8"
Foundation	Slab
Bedrooms	3
Full Baths	2
Half Baths	1
Max Ridge Height	27'
Roof Framing	Stick
Exterior Walls	2x6

PATIO

UP

BAR

BKS.

M. BEDROOM
16'-0"
X
15'-0"

LIVING ROOM
21'-0"
X
15'-0"

STOR.

H.

L.

WH

BKS.

F.

KNEE
SPACE

B.

ENTRY

DINING
11'-11"
X
12'-0"

C.

SHWR

C.

P.

FIRST FLOOR

NOOK
9'-8"
X
10'-0"

DW.

KITCHEN
11'-0"
X
15'-0"

O.

P.

W.

FZ.

U.

D.

©

DN.

BEDROOM 2
11'-0"
X
11'-8"

B.

C.

C.

BEDROOM 3
10'-10"
X
10'-0"

C.

H.

OPEN TO ENTRY
BELOW

SECOND FLOOR

GARAGE
21'-4"
X
21'-2"

To order blueprints, call **800-235-5700** or visit us on the web, **family home plans.com**

Units	Single
Price Code	D
Total Finished	2,181 sq. ft.
First Finished	1,660 sq. ft.
Second Finished	521 sq. ft.
Dimensions	50'x69'6"
Foundation	Basement
	Crawlspace
	Slab
Bedrooms	3
Full Baths	2
Half Baths	1
Max Ridge Height	30'
Roof Framing	Stick
Exterior Walls	2x6

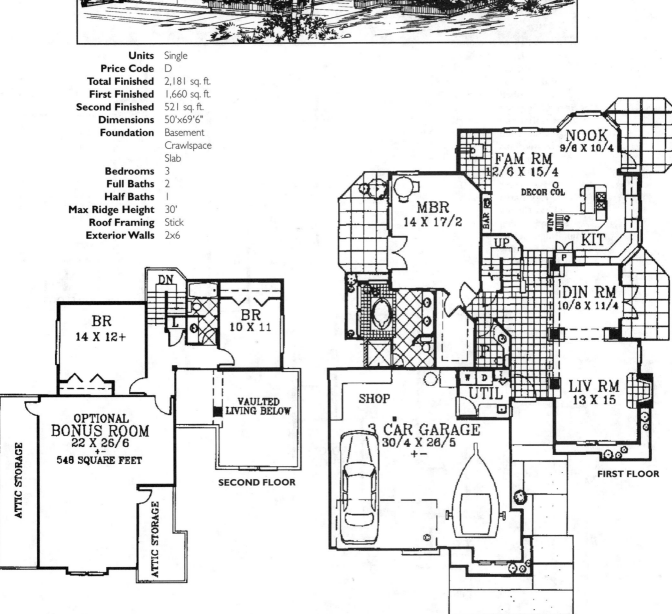

SECOND FLOOR

FIRST FLOOR

Units	Single
Price Code	D
Total Finished	2,196 sq. ft.
First Finished	1,658 sq. ft.
Second Finished	538 sq. ft.
Bonus Unfinished	496 sq. ft.
Garage Unfinished	608 sq. ft.
Dimensions	50'x56'
Foundation	Crawlspace
Bedrooms	4
Full Baths	2
Half Baths	1
First Ceiling	9'
Second Ceiling	8'
Max Ridge Height	28'
Roof Framing	Stick
Exterior Walls	2x6

Units	Single
Price Code	D
Total Finished	2,198 sq. ft.
First Finished	1,179 sq. ft.
Second Finished	1,019 sq. ft.
Basement Unfinished	1,179 sq. ft.
Garage Unfinished	466 sq. ft.
Dimensions	50'x44'
Foundation	Basement
	Slab
Bedrooms	4
Full Baths	2
3/4 Baths	1
Half Baths	1
Max Ridge Height	27'2"
Roof Framing	Stick
Exterior Walls	2x4

* Alternate foundation options available at an additional charge.
Please call 1-800-235-5700 for more information.

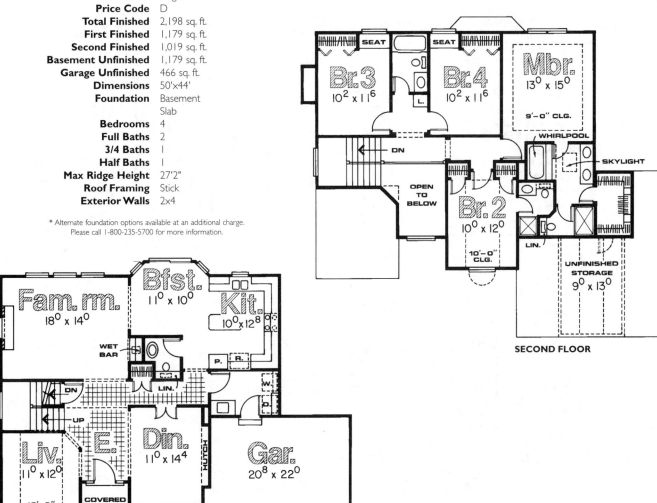

SECOND FLOOR

FIRST FLOOR

Units	Single
Price Code	D
Total Finished	2,224 sq. ft.
First Finished	1,392 sq. ft.
Second Finished	832 sq. ft.
Dimensions	50'x60'6"
Foundation	Basement
	Crawlspace
	Slab
Bedrooms	4
Full Baths	2
3/4 Baths	1
Max Ridge Height	25'
Roof Framing	Stick
Exterior Walls	2x6

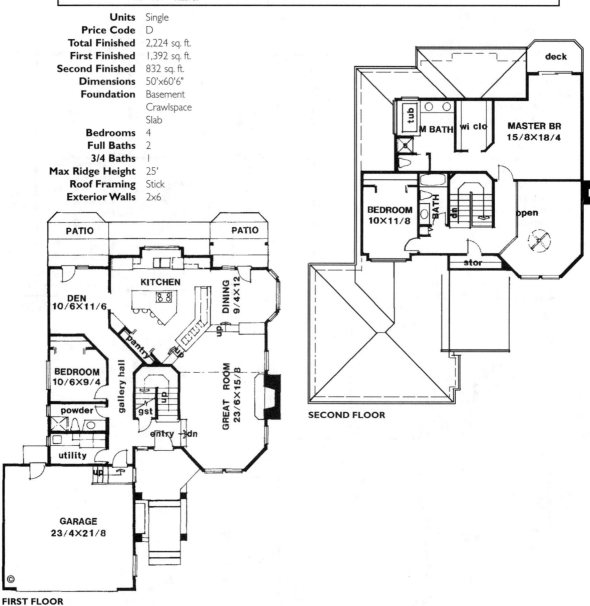

SECOND FLOOR

FIRST FLOOR

Units	Single
Price Code	A
Total Finished	997 sq. ft.
Main Finished	997 sq. ft.
Dimensions	49'6"x33'6"
Foundation	Crawlspace
Bedrooms	3
Full Baths	2
Max Ridge Height	16'
Roof Framing	Stick
Exterior Walls	2x4

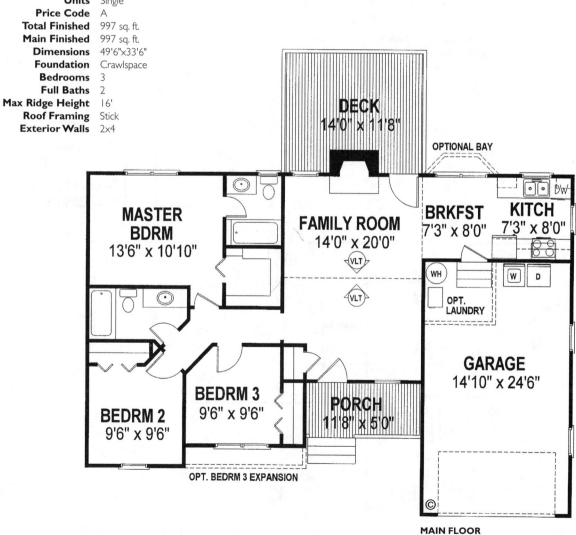

DECK
14'0" x 11'8"

OPTIONAL BAY

MASTER BDRM
13'6" x 10'10"

FAMILY ROOM
14'0" x 20'0"

BRKFST
7'3" x 8'0"

KITCH
7'3" x 8'0"

WH

OPT. LAUNDRY

W   D

BEDRM 2
9'6" x 9'6"

BEDRM 3
9'6" x 9'6"

PORCH
11'8" x 5'0"

GARAGE
14'10" x 24'6"

OPT. BEDRM 3 EXPANSION

MAIN FLOOR

Units	Single
Price Code	E
Total Finished	2,291 sq. ft.
First Finished	1,454 sq. ft.
Second Finished	837 sq. ft.
Dimensions	50'x46'
Foundation	Crawlspace
Bedrooms	3
Full Baths	2
Half Baths	I
Max Ridge Height	24'
Roof Framing	Stick/Truss
Exterior Walls	2x6

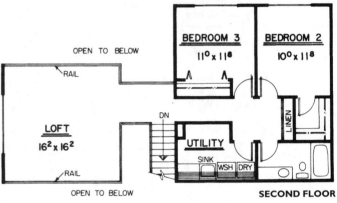

SECOND FLOOR

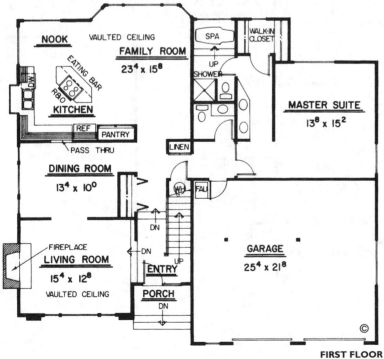

FIRST FLOOR

Units	Single
Price Code	E
Total Finished	2,322 sq. ft.
First Finished	1,322 sq. ft.
Second Finished	1,000 sq. ft.
Dimensions	50'x54'10"
Foundation	Crawlspace
Bedrooms	3
Full Baths	2
Half Baths	I
Max Ridge Height	30'
Roof Framing	Truss
Exterior Walls	2x6

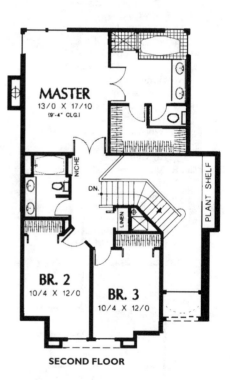

SECOND FLOOR

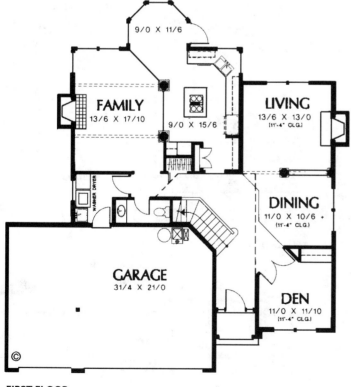

FIRST FLOOR

Units	Single
Price Code	E
Total Finished	2,330 sq. ft.
Main Finished	2,330 sq. ft.
Basement Unfinished	2,330 sq. ft.
Garage Unfinished	416 sq. ft.
Deck Unfinished	196 sq. ft.
Dimensions	50'x70'
Foundation	Crawlspace
Bedrooms	3
Full Baths	3
Main Ceiling	9'
Tray Ceiling	14'
Max Ridge Height	32'
Roof Framing	Stick
Exterior Walls	2x4

MAIN FLOOR

Units	Single
Price Code	E
Total Finished	2,349 sq. ft.
First Finished	1,106 sq. ft.
Second Finished	1,147 sq. ft.
Lower Finished	96 sq. ft.
Basement Unfinished	1,010 sq. ft.
Garage Unfinished	515 sq. ft.
Deck Unfinished	224 sq. ft.
Dimensions	50'x56'4"
Foundation	Basement
Bedrooms	4
Full Baths	2
Half Baths	1
Max Ridge Height	29'
Roof Framing	Stick
Exterior Walls	2x4

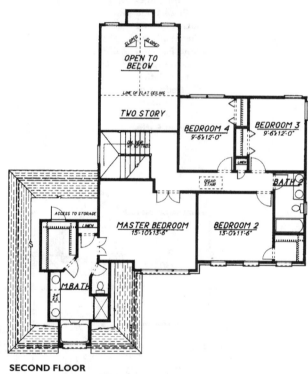

SECOND FLOOR

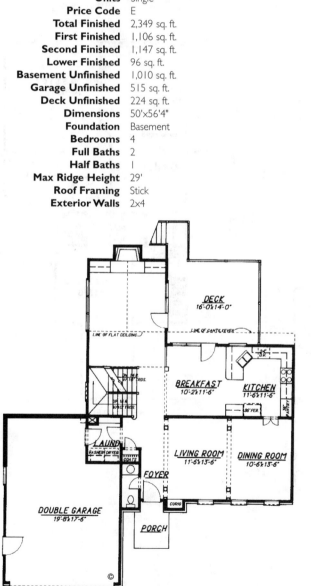

FIRST FLOOR

Design 90543

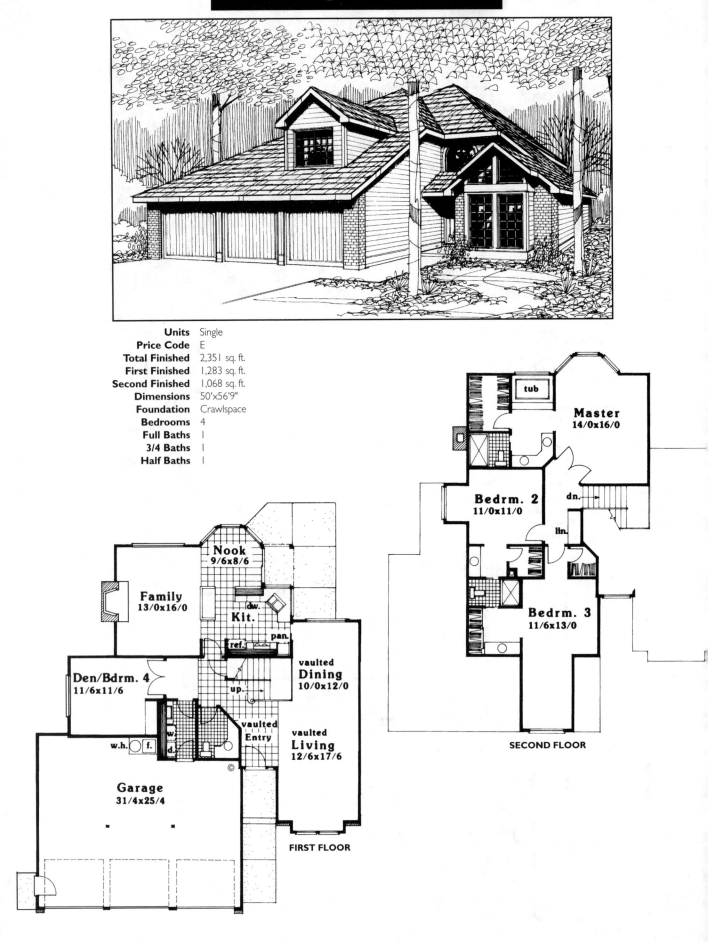

Units	Single
Price Code	E
Total Finished	2,351 sq. ft.
First Finished	1,283 sq. ft.
Second Finished	1,068 sq. ft.
Dimensions	50'x56'9"
Foundation	Crawlspace
Bedrooms	4
Full Baths	1
3/4 Baths	1
Half Baths	1

Nook
9/6x8/6

Family
13/0x16/0

Kit.

dw.

pan.

ref.

Den/Bdrm. 4
11/6x11/6

up.

vaulted
Dining
10/0x12/0

vaulted
Entry

vaulted
Living
12/6x17/6

w.h. f. w. d.

Garage
31/4x25/4

FIRST FLOOR

tub

Master
14/0x16/0

Bedrm. 2
11/0x11/0

dn.

lin.

Bedrm. 3
11/6x13/0

SECOND FLOOR

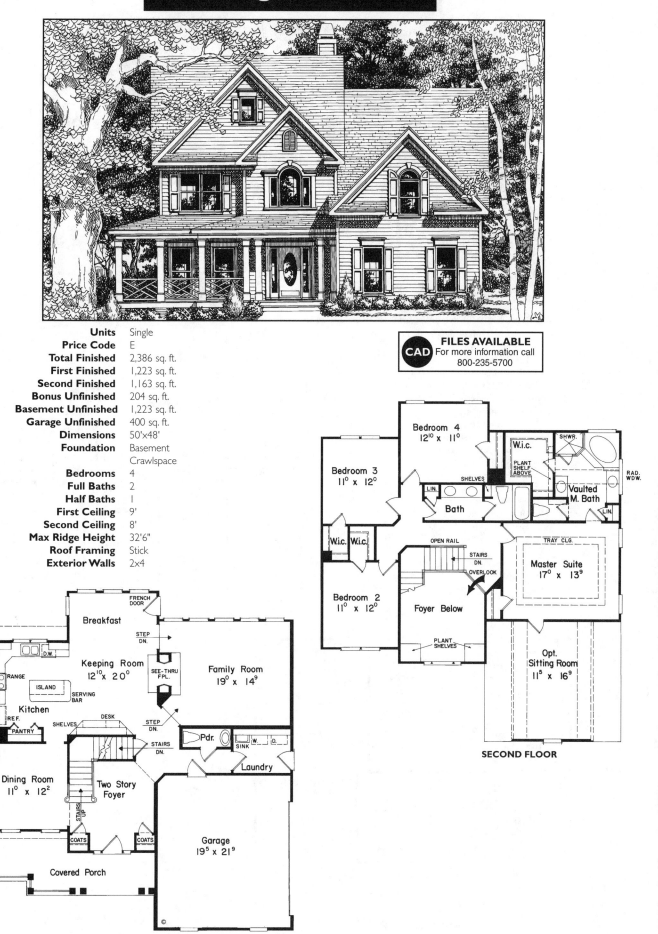

Units	Single
Price Code	E
Total Finished	2,386 sq. ft.
First Finished	1,223 sq. ft.
Second Finished	1,163 sq. ft.
Bonus Unfinished	204 sq. ft.
Basement Unfinished	1,223 sq. ft.
Garage Unfinished	400 sq. ft.
Dimensions	50'x48'
Foundation	Basement Crawlspace
Bedrooms	4
Full Baths	2
Half Baths	1
First Ceiling	9'
Second Ceiling	8'
Max Ridge Height	32'6"
Roof Framing	Stick
Exterior Walls	2x4

CAD FILES AVAILABLE
For more information call
800-235-5700

FIRST FLOOR

SECOND FLOOR

PHOTOGRAPHY: COURTESY OF THE DESIGNER

Units	Single
Price Code	E
Total Finished	2,394 sq. ft.
First Finished	1,560 sq. ft.
Second Finished	834 sq. ft.
Basement Unfinished	772 sq. ft.
Garage Unfinished	760 sq. ft.
Deck Unfinished	192 sq. ft.
Dimensions	50'x47'
Foundation	Basement
Bedrooms	4
Full Baths	2
Half Baths	1
First Ceiling	8'
Max Ridge Height	27'
Roof Framing	Stick
Exterior Walls	2x4

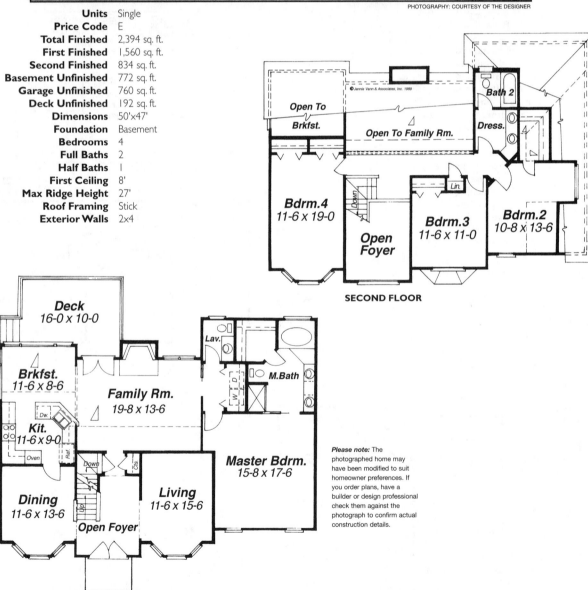

© Jannis Vann & Associates, Inc. 1989

SECOND FLOOR

Open To Brkfst.

Open To Family Rm.

Bath 2

Dress.

Bdrm.4
11-6 x 19-0

Open Foyer

Bdrm.3
11-6 x 11-0

Bdrm.2
10-8 x 13-6

Lin.

Down

FIRST FLOOR

Deck
16-0 x 10-0

Brkfst.
11-6 x 8-6

Family Rm.
19-8 x 13-6

Lav.

M.Bath

Kit.
11-6 x 9-0

Dw.

Oven

Ref.

Down

Up

W D

Cls.

Master Bdrm.
15-8 x 17-6

Dining
11-6 x 13-6

Living
11-6 x 15-6

Open Foyer

Please note: The photographed home may have been modified to suit homeowner preferences. If you order plans, have a builder or design professional check them against the photograph to confirm actual construction details.

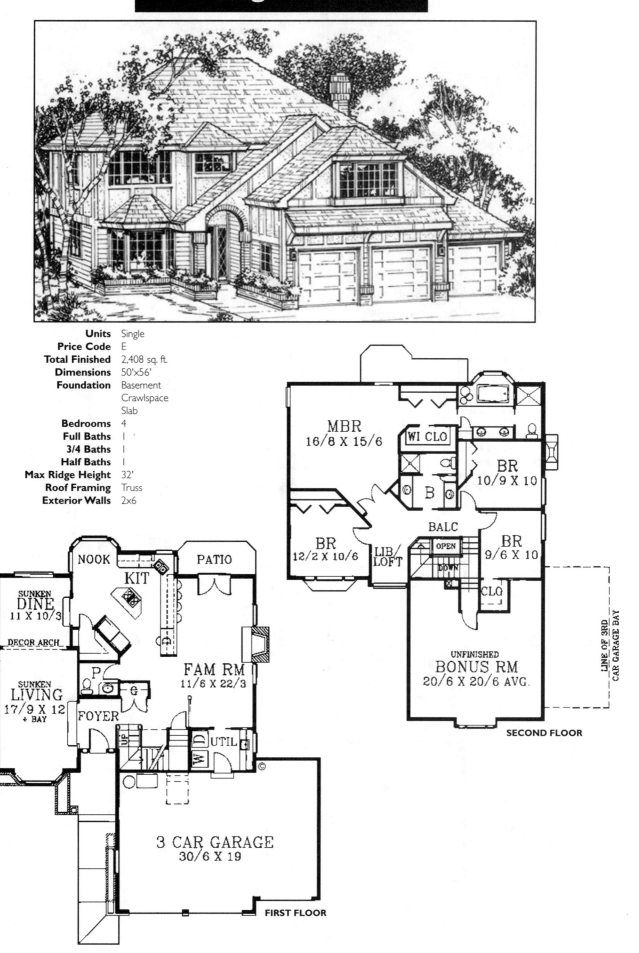

Units	Single
Price Code	E
Total Finished	2,408 sq. ft.
Dimensions	50'x56'
Foundation	Basement
	Crawlspace
	Slab
Bedrooms	4
Full Baths	1
3/4 Baths	1
Half Baths	1
Max Ridge Height	32'
Roof Framing	Truss
Exterior Walls	2x6

MBR
16/8 X 15/6

WI CLO

BR
10/9 X 10

B

BALC

BR
12/2 X 10/6

LIB/
LOFT

OPEN

BR
9/6 X 10

DOWN

CLO

LINE OF 3RD
CAR GARAGE BAY

UNFINISHED
BONUS RM
20/6 X 20/6 AVG.

SECOND FLOOR

NOOK

PATIO

KIT

SUNKEN
DINE
11 X 10/3

DECOR ARCH

SUNKEN
LIVING
17/9 X 12
+ BAY

FAM RM
11/6 X 22/3

P

FOYER

UP

W D

UTIL

3 CAR GARAGE
30/6 X 19

FIRST FLOOR

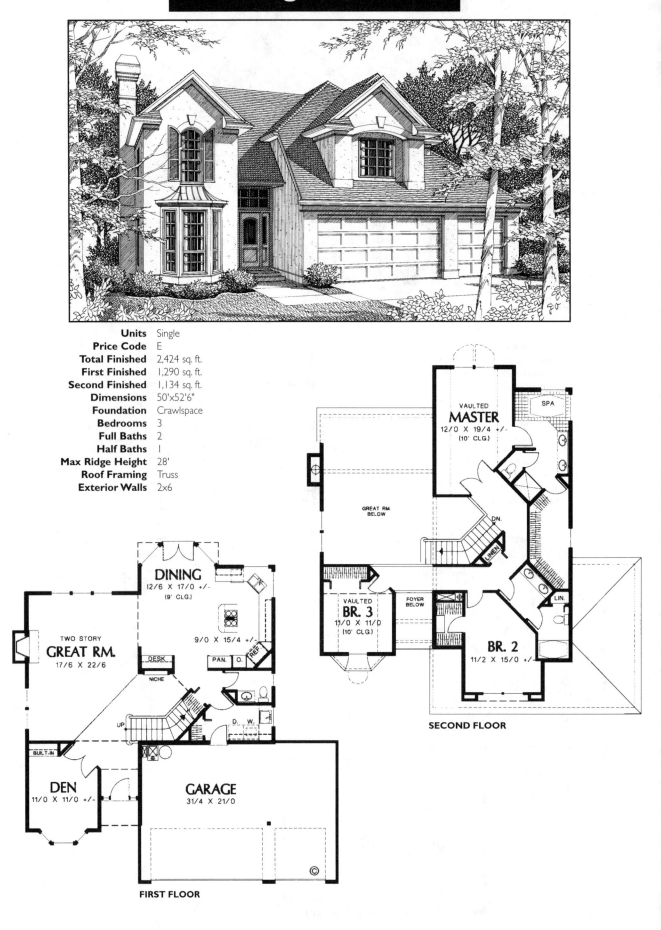

Units	Single
Price Code	E
Total Finished	2,424 sq. ft.
First Finished	1,290 sq. ft.
Second Finished	1,134 sq. ft.
Dimensions	50'x52'6"
Foundation	Crawlspace
Bedrooms	3
Full Baths	2
Half Baths	1
Max Ridge Height	28'
Roof Framing	Truss
Exterior Walls	2x6

VAULTED
MASTER
12/0 X 19/4 +/-
(10' CLG.)

SPA

GREAT RM.
BELOW

DN.

LINEN

VAULTED
BR. 3
11/0 X 11/0
(10' CLG.)

FOYER
BELOW

LIN.

BR. 2
11/2 X 15/0 +/-

SECOND FLOOR

DINING
12/6 X 17/0 +/-
(9' CLG.)

9/0 X 15/4 +/-

PAN.

O.

REF

TWO STORY
GREAT RM.
17/6 X 22/6

DESK

NICHE

UP

D. W.

BUILT-IN

DEN
11/0 X 11/0 +/-

GARAGE
31/4 X 21/0

FIRST FLOOR

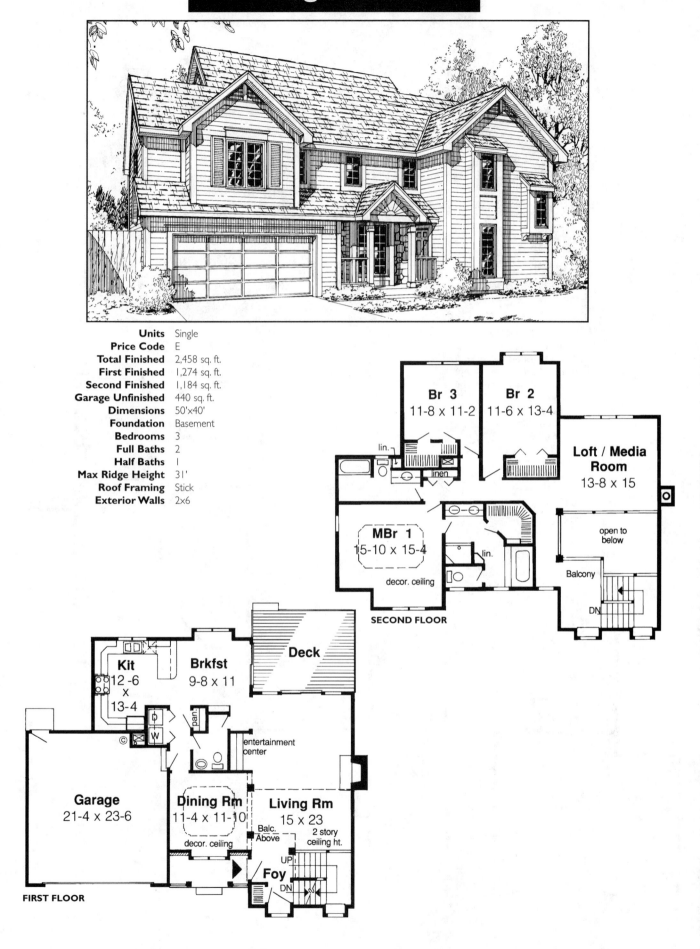

Units	Single
Price Code	E
Total Finished	2,458 sq. ft.
First Finished	1,274 sq. ft.
Second Finished	1,184 sq. ft.
Garage Unfinished	440 sq. ft.
Dimensions	50'x40'
Foundation	Basement
Bedrooms	3
Full Baths	2
Half Baths	1
Max Ridge Height	31'
Roof Framing	Stick
Exterior Walls	2x6

SECOND FLOOR

Br 3
11-8 x 11-2

Br 2
11-6 x 13-4

Loft / Media Room
13-8 x 15

lin.

linen

MBr 1
15-10 x 15-4
decor. ceiling

lin.

open to below

Balcony

DN

FIRST FLOOR

Kit
12-6 x 13-4

Brkfst
9-8 x 11

Deck

pan.

entertainment center

Garage
21-4 x 23-6

Dining Rm
11-4 x 11-10
decor. ceiling

Living Rm
15 x 23
2 story ceiling ht.

Balc. Above

UP

Foy

DN

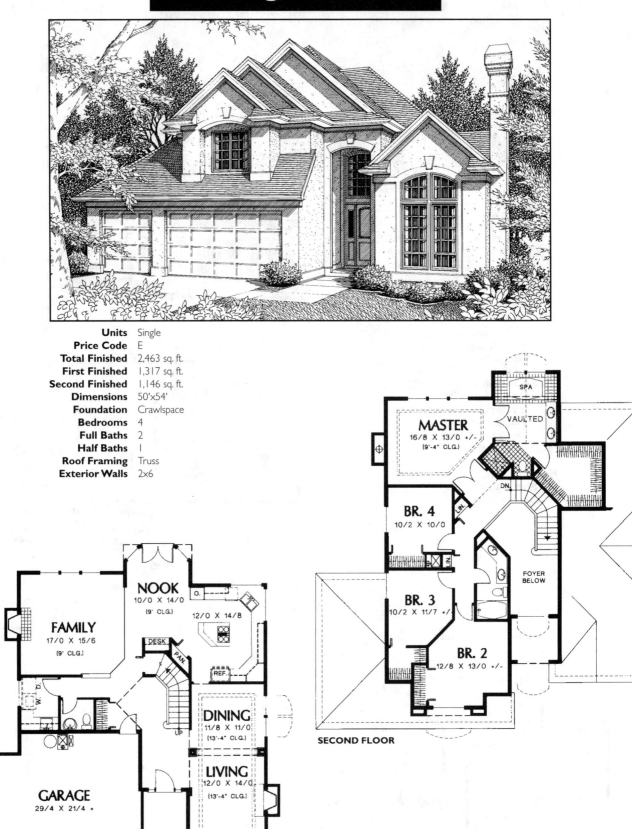

Units	Single
Price Code	E
Total Finished	2,463 sq. ft.
First Finished	1,317 sq. ft.
Second Finished	1,146 sq. ft.
Dimensions	50'x54'
Foundation	Crawlspace
Bedrooms	4
Full Baths	2
Half Baths	1
Roof Framing	Truss
Exterior Walls	2x6

SECOND FLOOR

MASTER
16/8 X 13/0 +/-
(9'-4" CLG.)

SPA

VAULTED

BR. 4
10/2 X 10/0

DN.

BR. 3
10/2 X 11/7 +/-

FOYER
BELOW

BR. 2
12/8 X 13/0 +/-

FAMILY
17/0 X 15/6
(9' CLG.)

NOOK
10/0 X 14/0
(9' CLG.)

12/0 X 14/8

DESK

PAN.

REF.

UP

DINING
11/8 X 11/0
(13'-4" CLG.)

LIVING
12/0 X 14/0
(13'-4" CLG.)

GARAGE
29/4 X 21/4 +

W. D.

FIRST FLOOR

Units	Single
Price Code	F
Total Finished	2,663 sq. ft.
First Finished	1,351 sq. ft.
Second Finished	1,312 sq. ft.
Basement Unfinished	1,351 sq. ft.
Garage Unfinished	466 sq. ft.
Dimensions	50'x41'4"
Foundation	Basement
	Crawlspace
Bedrooms	5
Full Baths	3
First Ceiling	9'
Second Ceiling	8'
Max Ridge Height	33'
Roof Framing	Stick
Exterior Walls	2x4

CAD FILES AVAILABLE
For more information call
800-235-5700

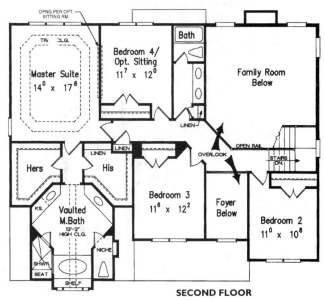

SECOND FLOOR

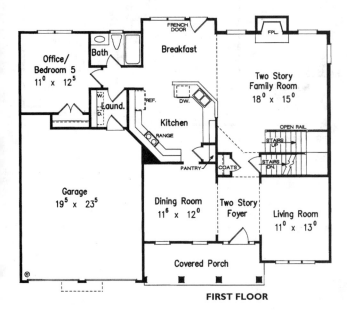

FIRST FLOOR

Design 90575

Units	Single
Price Code	E
Total Finished	2,489 sq. ft.
First Finished	1,927 sq. ft.
Second Finished	562 sq. ft.
Garage Unfinished	1,008 sq. ft.
Porch Unfinished	27 sq. ft.
Dimensions	50'x46'
Foundation	Crawlspace
Bedrooms	3
Full Baths	2
Half Baths	1

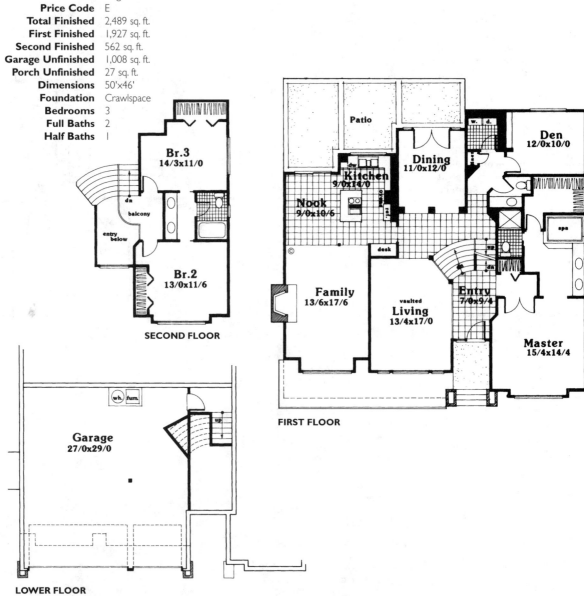

SECOND FLOOR

Br.3
14/3x11/0

Br.2
13/0x11/6

dn

balcony

entry
below

FIRST FLOOR

Patio

Kitchen
9/0x14/0

Dining
11/0x12/0

w. d.

Den
12/0x10/0

Nook
9/0x10/6

Family
13/6x17/6

Living
13/4x17/0
vaulted

desk

Entry
7/0x9/4

up

dn

spa

Master
15/4x14/4

©

LOWER FLOOR

Garage
27/0x29/0

wh. fum.

up

To order blueprints, call **800-235-5700** or visit us on the web, **familyhomeplans.com**

Design 91556

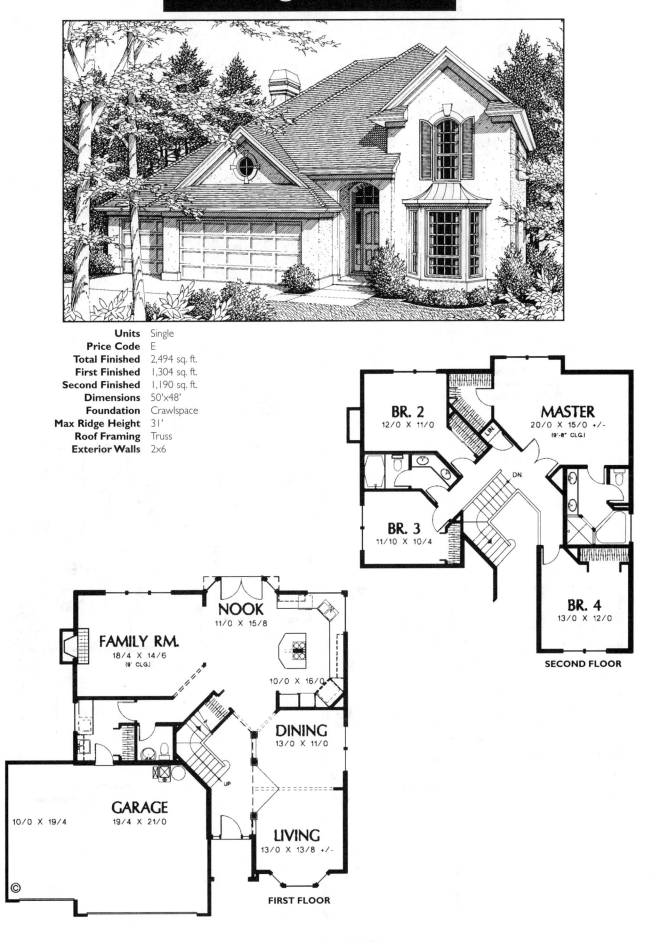

Units	Single
Price Code	E
Total Finished	2,494 sq. ft.
First Finished	1,304 sq. ft.
Second Finished	1,190 sq. ft.
Dimensions	50'x48'
Foundation	Crawlspace
Max Ridge Height	31'
Roof Framing	Truss
Exterior Walls	2x6

BR. 2
12/0 X 11/0

MASTER
20/0 X 15/0 +/-
(9'-8" CLG.)

LIN.

DN.

BR. 3
11/10 X 10/4

BR. 4
13/0 X 12/0

SECOND FLOOR

FAMILY RM.
18/4 X 14/6
(9' CLG.)

NOOK
11/0 X 15/8

10/0 X 16/0

DINING
13/0 X 11/0

UP

GARAGE
19/4 X 21/0

10/0 X 19/4

LIVING
13/0 X 13/8 +/-

FIRST FLOOR

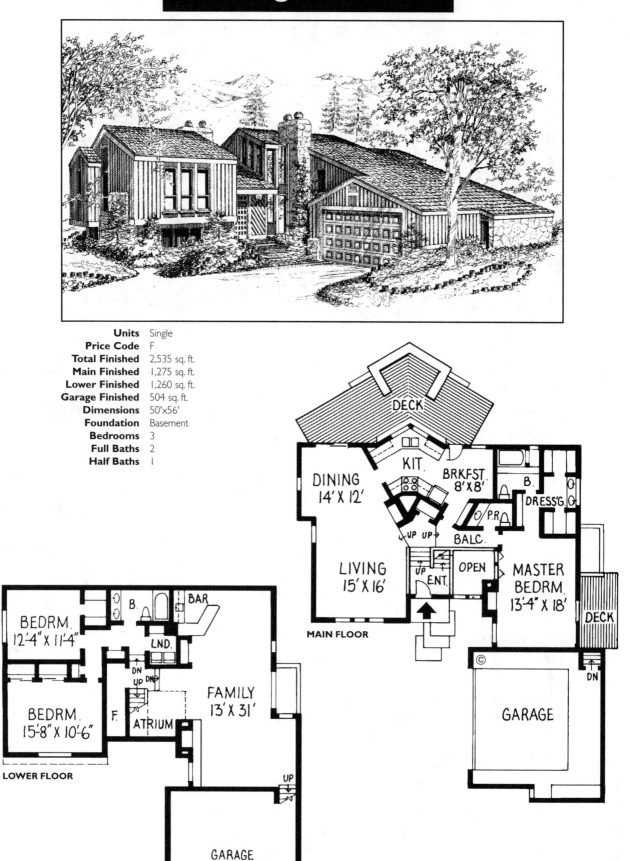

Units	Single
Price Code	F
Total Finished	2,535 sq. ft.
Main Finished	1,275 sq. ft.
Lower Finished	1,260 sq. ft.
Garage Finished	504 sq. ft.
Dimensions	50'x56'
Foundation	Basement
Bedrooms	3
Full Baths	2
Half Baths	1

DECK

KIT.

DINING
14' X 12'

BRKFST.
8' X 8'

B.
DRESS'G.

P.R.

BALC.

LIVING
15' X 16'

UP UP

OPEN

MASTER
BEDRM.
13'-4" X 18'

UP
E.NT.

DECK

MAIN FLOOR

BEDRM.
12'-4" X 11'-4"

B.

BAR

LND.

DN
UP DN

BEDRM.
15'-8" X 10'-6"

F.

ATRIUM

FAMILY
13' X 31'

GARAGE

DN

LOWER FLOOR

UP

GARAGE
FOUNDATION

Design 24653

Units	Single
Price Code	F
Total Finished	2,578 sq. ft.
First Finished	1,245 sq. ft.
Second Finished	1,333 sq. ft.
Bonus Unfinished	192 sq. ft.
Basement Unfinished	1,245 sq. ft.
Garage Unfinished	614 sq. ft.
Dimensions	50'x46'
Foundation	Basement
	Crawlspace
	Slab
Bedrooms	3
Full Baths	2
Half Baths	1
First Ceiling	9'
Second Ceiling	8'
Max Ridge Height	35'
Roof Framing	Stick
Exterior Walls	2x4

SECOND FLOOR

Br 2
11-8 x 12-4

Br 3
11-8 x 12-5

Mstr. Suite
18-4 x 13-4

optional skylight

DN   railing

Common
9-5 x 13-8

linen

open to below

Bonus
11-4 x 15-8

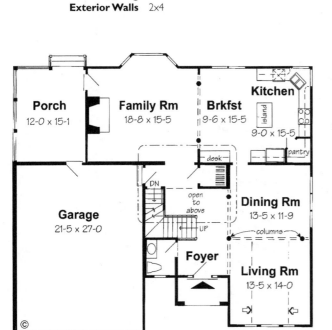

FIRST FLOOR

Porch
12-0 x 15-1

Family Rm
18-8 x 15-5

Brkfst
9-6 x 15-5

Kitchen
island
9-0 x 15-5

pantry

desk

DN

open to above

UP

Garage
21-5 x 27-0

Dining Rm
13-5 x 11-9

Foyer

columns

Living Rm
13-5 x 14-0

crawl access

w/h

furn.

**OPTIONAL
CRAWLSPACE/SLAB
FOUNDATION**

Units	Single
Price Code	F
Total Finished	2,578 sq. ft.
First Finished	1,395 sq. ft.
Second Finished	1,183 sq. ft.
Garage Unfinished	487 sq. ft.
Dimensions	50'x60'10"
Foundation	Crawlspace
Bedrooms	4
Full Baths	2
Half Baths	I
Max Ridge Height	31'
Roof Framing	Stick
Exterior Walls	2x6

SECOND FLOOR

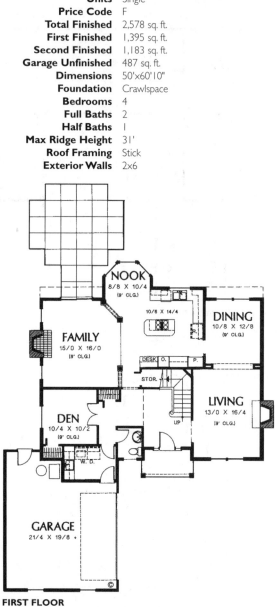

FIRST FLOOR

Units	Single
Price Code	F
Total Finished	2,632 sq. ft.
First Finished	1,183 sq. ft.
Second Finished	1,351 sq. ft.
Lower Finished	98 sq. ft.
Basement Unfinished	1,085 sq. ft.
Deck Unfinished	280 sq. ft.
Dimensions	50'x38'
Foundation	Basement
Bedrooms	4
Full Baths	3
Half Baths	1
Max Ridge Height	35'4"
Roof Framing	Truss
Exterior Walls	2x4

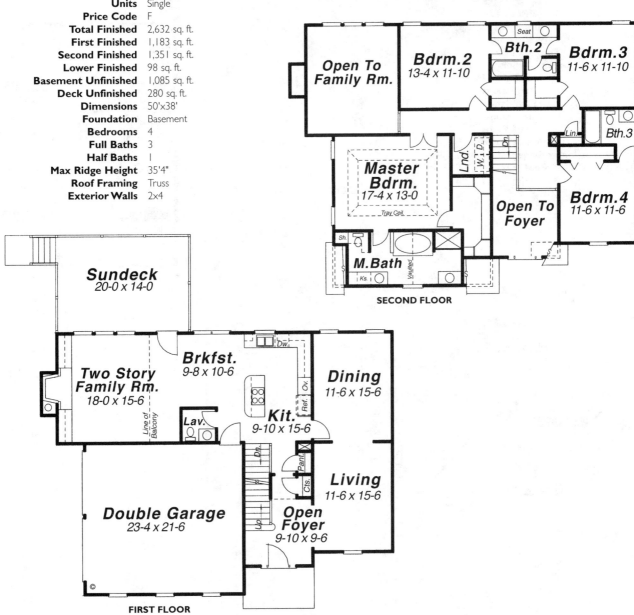

SECOND FLOOR

Open To Family Rm.

Bdrm.2
13-4 x 11-10

Bth.2
Seat

Bdrm.3
11-6 x 11-10

Bth.3
Lin.

Master Bdrm.
17-4 x 13-0
Tray Ceil.

Lnd.
W.I.D.
Dn

Open To Foyer

Bdrm.4
11-6 x 11-6

M.Bath
Sh.
Vaulted
Ks.

FIRST FLOOR

Sundeck
20-0 x 14-0

Two Story Family Rm.
18-0 x 15-6
Line of Balcony

Brkfst.
9-8 x 10-6

Dw.

Dining
11-6 x 15-6

Kit.
9-10 x 15-6
Ref.
Ov.

Lav.

Living
11-6 x 15-6
Pant.
Dn

Double Garage
23-4 x 21-6

Open Foyer
9-10 x 9-6
Up
Cts.

Units	Single
Price Code	F
Total Finished	2,652 sq. ft.
First Finished	1,532 sq. ft.
Second Finished	1,120 sq. ft.
Garage Unfinished	660 sq. ft.
Deck Unfinished	496 sq. ft.
Dimensions	50x66'10"
Foundation	Crawlspace
Bedrooms	3
Full Baths	2
3/4 Baths	1
Max Ridge Height	22'6"
Roof Framing	Stick/Truss
Exterior Walls	2x6

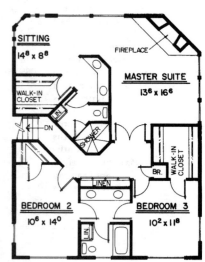

SECOND FLOOR

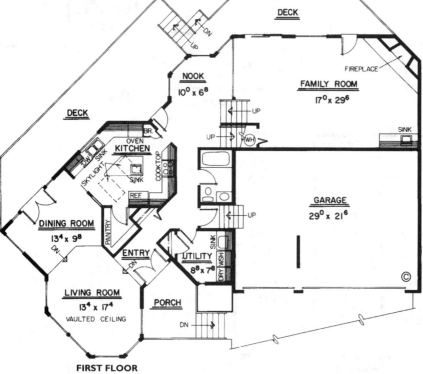

FIRST FLOOR

Units	Single
Price Code	F
Total Finished	2,662 sq. ft.
First Finished	1,540 sq. ft.
Second Finished	1,122 sq. ft.
Garage Unfinished	626 sq. ft.
Dimensions	50'x54'8"
Foundation	Slab
Bedrooms	4
Full Baths	3
Max Ridge Height	24'
Roof Framing	Stick
Exterior Walls	2x6

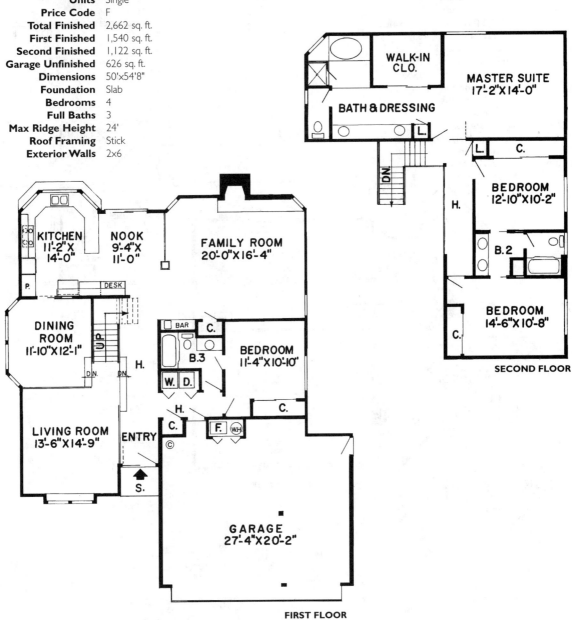

SECOND FLOOR

FIRST FLOOR

Units	Single
Price Code	F
Total Finished	2,691 sq. ft.
First Finished	1,539 sq. ft.
Second Finished	1,152 sq. ft.
Garage Unfinished	660 sq. ft.
Dimensions	50'x66'6"
Foundation	Crawlspace
Bedrooms	4
Full Baths	2
3/4 Baths	1
Max Ridge Height	23'
Roof Framing	Stick/Truss
Exterior Walls	2x6

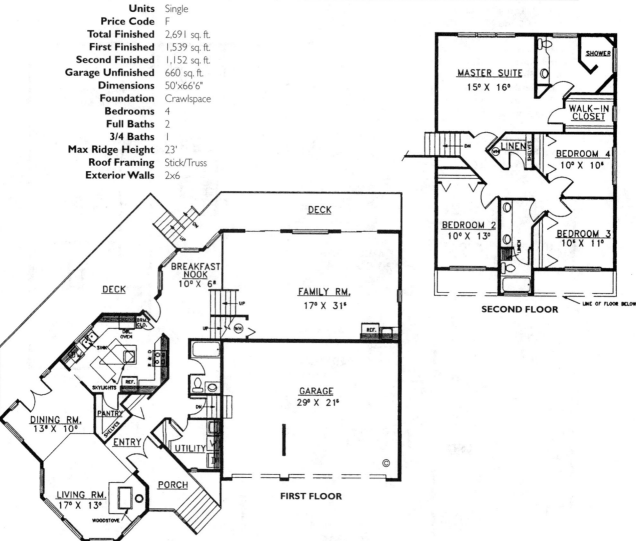

SECOND FLOOR

FIRST FLOOR

Design 93612

Units	Single
Price Code	G
Total Finished	2,864 sq. ft.
First Finished	2,062 sq. ft.
Second Finished	802 sq. ft.
Garage Unfinished	400 sq. ft.
Dimensions	50'x53'
Foundation	Slab
Bedrooms	4
Full Baths	2
Half Baths	1
Max Ridge Height	32'
Roof Framing	Stick
Exterior Walls	2x4

SECOND FLOOR

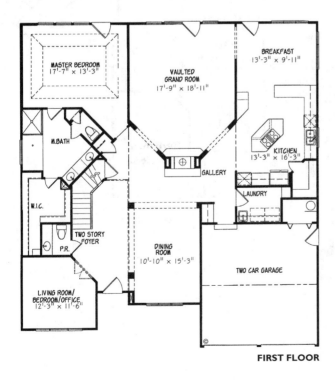

FIRST FLOOR

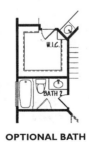

OPTIONAL BATH

Units	Single
Price Code	G
Total Finished	2,892 sq. ft.
First Finished	1,525 sq. ft.
Second Finished	1,367 sq. ft.
Dimensions	50'x57'
Foundation	Basement
	Crawlspace
Bedrooms	3
Full Baths	2
Half Baths	1

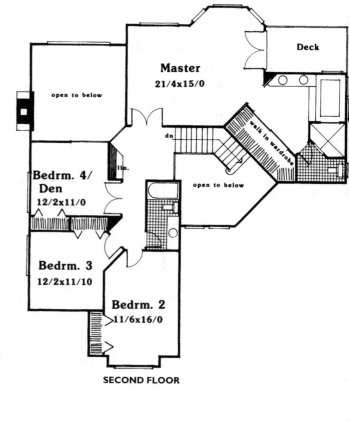

SECOND FLOOR

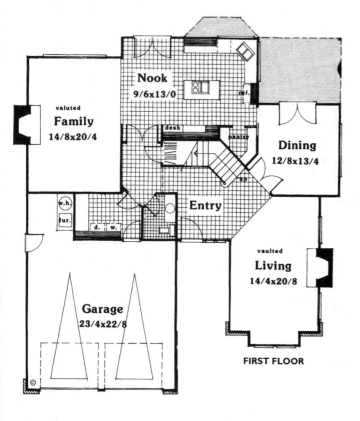

FIRST FLOOR

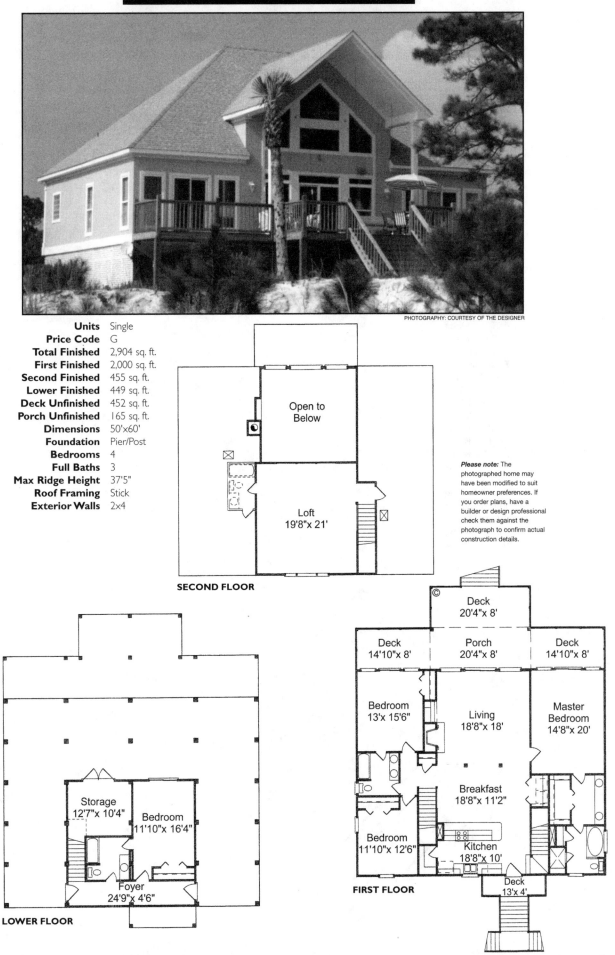

PHOTOGRAPHY: COURTESY OF THE DESIGNER

Units	Single
Price Code	G
Total Finished	2,904 sq. ft.
First Finished	2,000 sq. ft.
Second Finished	455 sq. ft.
Lower Finished	449 sq. ft.
Deck Unfinished	452 sq. ft.
Porch Unfinished	165 sq. ft.
Dimensions	50'x60'
Foundation	Pier/Post
Bedrooms	4
Full Baths	3
Max Ridge Height	37'5"
Roof Framing	Stick
Exterior Walls	2x4

SECOND FLOOR

Open to Below

Loft
19'8"x 21'

Please note: The photographed home may have been modified to suit homeowner preferences. If you order plans, have a builder or design professional check them against the photograph to confirm actual construction details.

LOWER FLOOR

Storage
12'7"x 10'4"

Bedroom
11'10"x 16'4"

Foyer
24'9"x 4'6"

FIRST FLOOR

Deck
20'4"x 8'

Deck
14'10"x 8'

Porch
20'4"x 8'

Deck
14'10"x 8'

Bedroom
13'x 15'6"

Living
18'8"x 18'

Master Bedroom
14'8"x 20'

Breakfast
18'8"x 11'2"

Bedroom
11'10"x 12'6"

Kitchen
18'8"x 10'

Deck
13'x 4'

Design 32352

PHOTOGRAPHY: LAURIE BLACK

Units	Single
Price Code	F
Total Finished	3,211 sq. ft.
First Finished	1,952 sq. ft.
Second Finished	1,259 sq. ft.
Garage Unfinished	468 sq. ft.
Dimensions	50'x77'
Foundation	Crawlspace
Bedrooms	2
Full Baths	2
3/4 Baths	1
Half Baths	1
First Ceiling	9'
Second Ceiling	8'
Vaulted Ceiling	23'3"
Max Ridge Height	29'
Roof Framing	Stick
Exterior Walls	2x6

SECOND FLOOR

MASTER BEDROOM 27x15

CLOS

BEDROOM 13x15

BALC OPEN

CLOS

FIRST FLOOR

KIT 14x20 R

PORCH

DINING 19x15

LIVING 15x23

ENTRY

TV

LDRY

PORCH

STOR

OFFICE 13x13

GARAGE 17x25

Please note: The photographed home may have been modified to suit homeowner preferences. If you order plans, have a builder or design professional check them against the photograph to confirm actual construction details.

Design 97863

Units	Single
Price Code	E
Total Finished	3,246 sq. ft.
First Finished	2,475 sq. ft.
Second Finished	771 sq. ft.
Garage Unfinished	432 sq. ft.
Deck Unfinished	102 sq. ft.
Dimensions	50'x56'9"
Foundation	Slab
Bedrooms	4
Full Baths	1
3/4 Baths	1
Half Baths	1
First Ceiling	9'4"
Second Ceiling	8'
Max Ridge Height	28'
Roof Framing	Stick
Exterior Walls	2x4

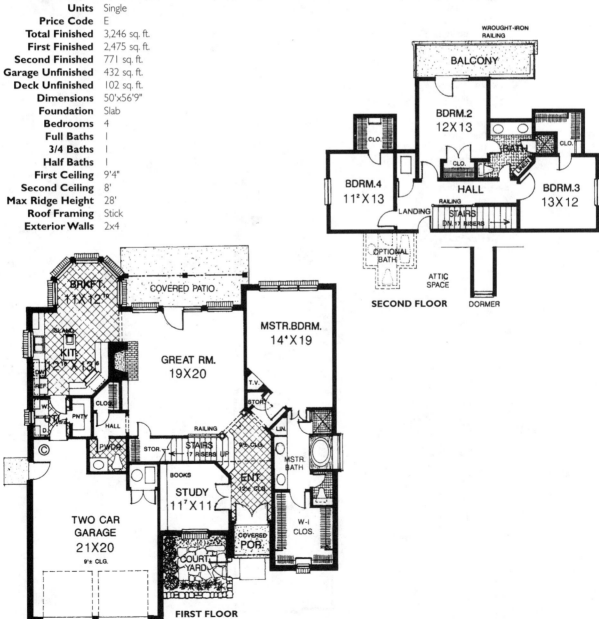

Design 32113

PHOTOGRAPHY: JENIFER JORDAN

Units	Single
Price Code	K
Total Finished	3,837 sq. ft.
First Finished	2,091 sq. ft.
Second Finished	1,746 sq. ft.
Garage Unfinished	641 sq. ft.
Deck Unfinished	228 sq. ft.
Porch Unfinished	46 sq. ft.
Dimensions	50'x81'
Foundation	Slab
Bedrooms	3
Full Baths	2
Half Baths	2
First Ceiling	10'
Second Ceiling	9'
Vaulted Ceiling	20'6"
Max Ridge Height	31'
Roof Framing	Stick
Exterior Walls	2x4

Please note: The photographed home may have been modified to suit homeowner preferences. If you order plans, have a builder or design professional check them against the photograph to confirm actual construction details.

SECOND FLOOR

DECK

BATH

CLOS

CLOS

OPEN TO LIVING

MASTER BEDROOM 18x18

CLOS

COMP RM

DN

OPEN

BEDROOM 14x12

EXERCISE 15x14

CLOS

BATH

BEDROOM 11x14

CLOS

FIRST FLOOR

COVERED PATIO

FAMILY 17x12

BAR R

BREAKFAST 15x13

LIVING 25x25

DINING 12x17

KIT 15x19

R O

ENTRY

UP

GARAGE 9x19

P

F

UTILITY

D W

GARAGE 20x21

Exterior Elevations

These front, rear, and sides of the home include information pertaining to the exterior finish materials, roof pitches, and exterior height dimensions.

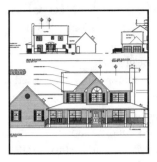

Cabinet Plans

These plans, or in some cases elevations, will detail the layout of the kitchen and bathroom cabinets at a larger scale. Available for most plans.

Typical Wall Section

This section will address insulation, roof components, and interior and exterior wall finishes. Your plans will be designed with either 2x4 or 2x6 exterior walls, but if you wish, most professional contractors can easily adapt the plans to the wall thickness you require.

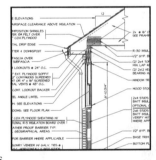

Fireplace Details

If the home you have chosen includes a fireplace, a fireplace detail will show typical methods of constructing the firebox, hearth, and flue chase for masonry units, or a wood frame chase for zero-clearance units. Available for most plans.

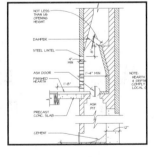

Foundation Plan

These plans will accurately show the dimensions of the footprint of your home, including load-bearing points and beam placement if applicable. The foundation style will vary from plan to plan. **(Please note: There may be an additional charge for optional foundation plan. Please call for details.)**

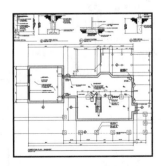

Roof Plan

The information necessary to construct the roof will be included with your home plans. Some plans will reference roof trusses, while many others contain schematic framing plans. These framing plans will indicate the lumber sizes necessary for the rafters and ridgeboards based on the designated roof loads.

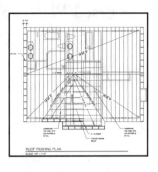

Typical Cross Section

A cut-away cross section through the entire home shows your building contractor the exact correlation of construction components at all levels of the house. It will help to clarify the load bearing points from the roof all the way down to the basement. Available for most plans.

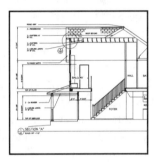

Detailed Floor Plans

The floor plans of your home accurately depict the dimensions of the positioning of all walls, doors, windows, stairs, and permanent fixtures. They will show you the relationship and dimensions of rooms, closets, and traffic patterns. The schematic of the electrical layout may be included in the plan.

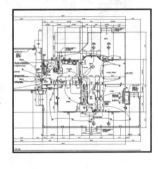

Stair Details

If the design you have chosen includes stairs, the plans will show the information that you need in order to build them— either through a stair cross section or on the floor plans.

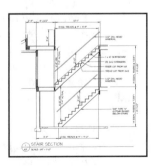

Garlinghouse Options & Extras

Reversed Plans can Make Your Dream Home Just Right!

You could have exactly the home you want by flipping it end-for-end. Simply order your plans "reversed." We'll send you one full set of mirror-image plans (with the writing backwards) as a master guide for you and your builder.

The remaining sets of your order will come as shown in this book so the dimensions and specifications are easily read on the job site. Most plans in our collection come stamped "reversed" so there is no construction confusion.

We can only send reversed plans with multiple-set orders. There is a $50 charge for this service.

Some plans in our collection are available in "Right Reading Reverse." Right Reading Reverse plans will show your home in reverse. This easy-to-read format will save you valuable time and money. Please contact our Sales Department at 800-235-5700 to check for Right Reading Reverse availability. There is a $135 charge for this service. **RRR**

Remember to Order Your Materials List

Available at a modest additional charge, the Materials List gives the quantity, dimensions, and specifications for the major materials needed to build your home. You will get faster, more accurate bids from your contractors and building suppliers—and avoid paying for unused materials and waste. **Materials Lists are available for all home plans except as otherwise indicated, but can only be ordered with a set of home plans.** Due to differences in regional requirements and homeowner or builder preferences, electrical, plumbing and heating/air conditioning equipment specifications are not designed specifically for each plan. **ML**

What Garlinghouse Offers

Home Plan Blueprint Package

By purchasing a multiple-set package of blueprints or a Vellum from Garlinghouse, you not only receive the physical blueprint documents necessary for construction, but you are also granted a license to build one (and only one) home. You can also make simple modifications, including minor non-structural changes and material substitutions, to our design as long as these changes are made directly on the blueprints purchased from Garlinghouse and no additional copies are made.

Home Plan Vellums

By purchasing Vellums for one of our home plans, you receive the same construction drawings found in the blueprints, but printed on vellum paper. Vellums can be erased and are perfect for making design changes. They are also semi-transparent, making them easy to duplicate. But most importantly, the purchase of home plan Vellums comes with a broader license that allows you to make changes to the design (i.e., create a hand drawn or CAD derivative work), to make copies of the plan, and to build one home from the plan.

License to Build Additional Homes

With the purchase of a blueprint package or Vellums, you automatically receive a license to build one home and only one home. If you want to build more homes than you are licensed to build through your purchase of a plan, then additional licenses must be purchased at reasonable costs from Garlinghouse. Inquire for more information.

Modifying Your Favorite Design Made Easy

MODIFICATION PRICING GUIDE

CATEGORIES	AVERAGE COST
Adding or removing living space (square footage)	Quote required
Adding or removing a garage	Starting at $400
Garage: Front entry to side load or vice versa	Starting at $300
Adding a screened porch	Starting at $280
Adding a bonus room in the attic	Starting at $450
Changing full basement to crawlspace or vice versa	Starting at $220
Changing full basement to slab or vice versa	Starting at $260
Changing exterior building materials	Starting at $200
Changing roof lines	Starting at $360
Adjusting ceiling height	Starting at $280
Adding, moving or removing an exterior opening	$65 per opening
Adding or removing a fireplace	Starting at $90
Modifying a non-bearing wall or room	$65 per room
Changing exterior walls from 2"x4" to 2"x6"	Starting at $200
Redesigning a bathroom or a kitchen	Starting at $120
Reverse plan right reading	Quote required
Adapting plans for local building code requirements	Quote required
Engineering and Architectural stamping and services	Quote required
Adjust plan for handicapped accessibility	Quote required
Interactive Illustrations (choices of exterior materials)	Quote required
Metric conversion of home plan	$400

* Please remember that figures shown are average costs. Your quote may be higher or lower depending upon your specific requirements.

#1 Modifying Your Garlinghouse Home Plan

Simple modifications to your dream home, including minor non-structural changes and material substitutions, can be made by you and your builder with the consent of your local building official, by marking the changes directly on your blueprints. However, if you are considering making significant changes to your chosen design, we recommend that you use the services of The Garlinghouse Design Staff. We will help take your ideas and turn them into a reality, just the way you want. Here's our procedure:

Call 800-235-5700 and order your modification estimate. The fee for this estimate is $50. We will review your plan changes and provide you with an estimate to draft your specific modifications before you purchase the vellums. *Please note: A vellum must be purchased to modify a home plan design.*

After you receive your estimate, if you decide to have Garlinghouse do the changes, the $50 estimate fee will be deducted from the cost of your modifications. If, however, you chose to use a different service, the $50 estimate fee is non-refundable. *(Note: Personal checks cannot be accepted for the estimate.)*

A 75% deposit is required before we begin making the actual modifications to your plans.

Once the design changes have been completed to your vellum plan, a representative will call to inform you that your modified vellum plan is complete and will be shipped as soon as the final payment has been made. For additional information, call us at 1-800-235-5700. Please refer to the Modification Pricing Guide for estimated modification costs.

#2 Reproducible Vellums for Local Modification Ease

If you decide not to use Garlinghouse for your modifications, we recommend that you follow our same procedure of purchasing vellums. You then have the option of using the services of the original designer of the plan, a local professional designer, or an architect to make the modifications.

With a vellum copy of our plans, a design professional can alter the drawings just the way you want, then you can print as many copies of the modified plans as you need to build your house. And, since you have already started with our complete detailed plans, the cost of those expensive professional services will be significantly less than starting from scratch. Refer to the price schedule for vellum costs.

Ignoring Copyright Laws Can Be A $100,000 MISTAKE

U.S. copyright laws allow for statutory penalties of up to $100,000 per incident for copyright infringement involving any of the copyrighted plans found in this publication. The law can be confusing. So, for your own protection, take the time to understand what you can and cannot do when it comes to home plans.

What You Can't Do

You Cannot Duplicate Home Plans
Purchasing a set of blueprints and making additional sets by reproducing the original is illegal. If you need more than one set of a particular home plan, you must purchase them.

You Cannot Copy Any Part of a Home Plan to Create Another
Creating your own plan by copying even part of a home design found in this publication without permission is called "creating a derivative work" and is illegal.

You Cannot Build a Home Without a License
You must have specific permission or a license to build a home from a copyrighted design, even if the finished home has been changed from the original plan. It is illegal to build one of the homes found in this publication without a license.

How to obtain a construction cost calculation based on labor rates and building material costs in your zip code area.

What will your dream home cost? ZIP QUOTE has the answer!

How does Zip Quote actually work? When you call to order, you must choose from the options available for your specific home in order for us to process your order. Once we receive your Zip Quote order, we process your specific home plan building materials list through our Home Cost Calculator which contains up-to-date rates for all residential labor trades and building material costs in your zip code area. The result? A calculated cost to build your dream home in your zip code area. This calculation will help you (as a consumer or a builder) evaluate your building budget.

All database information for our calculations is furnished by Marshall & Swift, L.P. For over 60 years, Marshall & Swift L.P. has been a leading provider of cost data to professionals in all aspects of the construction and remodeling industries.

Zip Quote can be purchased in two separate formats, either an itemized or a bottom-line format.

Option 1 The **Itemized Zip Quote** is a detailed building materials list. Each building materials list line item will separately state the labor cost, material cost, and equipment cost (if applicable) for the use of that building material in the construction process. This building materials list will be summarized by the individual building categories and will have additional columns where you can enter data from your contractor's estimates for a cost comparison between the different suppliers and contractors who will actually quote you their products and services.

Option 2 The **Bottom-Line Zip Quote** is a one line summarized total cost for the home plan of your choice. This cost calculation is also based on the labor cost, material cost, and equipment cost (if applicable) within your zip code area. Bottom-Line Zip Quote is available for most plans. Please call for availability.

Cost The price of your Itemized Zip Quote is based upon the pricing schedule of the plan you have selected, in addition to the price of the materials list. Please refer to the pricing schedule on our order form. The price of your initial Bottom-Line Zip Quote is $29.95. Each additional Bottom-Line Zip Quote ordered in conjunction with the initial order is only $14.95. A Bottom-Line Zip Quote may be purchased separately and does NOT have to be purchased in conjunction with a home plan order.

FYI An Itemized Zip Quote Home Cost Calculation can ONLY be purchased in conjunction with a Home Plan order. The Itemized Zip Quote can not be purchased separately. If you find within 60 days of your order date that you will be unable to build this home, then you may apply the price of the plans and the materials list towards the price of a new set of plans (see order info pages for plan exchange policy). The Itemized Zip Quote and the Bottom-Line Zip Quote are NOT returnable. The price of the initial Bottom-Line Zip Quote order can be credited toward the purchase of an Itemized Zip Quote order, only if available. Additional Bottom-Line Zip Quote orders, within the same order can not be credited. Please call our Sales Department for more information.

An Itemized Zip Quote is available for plans where you see this symbol. **ZIP**

A Bottom-Line Zip Quote is available for all plans under 4,000 sq. ft. or where you see this symbol. **BL** Please call for current availability.

Some More Information The Itemized and Bottom-Line Zip Quotes give you approximated costs for constructing the particular house in your area. These costs are not exact and are only intended to be used as a preliminary estimate to help determine the affordability of a new home and/or as a guide to evaluate the general competitiveness of actual price quotes obtained through local suppliers and contractors. **Land, landscaping, sewer systems, site work, contractor overhead and profit, and other expenses are not included in our building cost figures. Excluding land and landscaping, you may incur an additional 20% to 40% in costs from the original estimate.** Garlinghouse and Marshall & Swift L.P. cannot guarantee any level of data accuracy or correctness in a Zip Quote and disclaim all liability for loss with respect to the same, in excess of the original purchase price of the Zip Quote product. All Zip Quote calculations are based upon the actual blueprints and do not reflect any differences or options that may be shown on the published house renderings, floor plans, or photographs.

CAD Files Now Available

A CAD file is available for plans where you see this symbol.

Cad files are available in .dc5 or .dxf format or .dwg formats (R12, R13, R14, R2000). Please specify the file format at the time of your order. You will receive one bond set along with the CAD file when you place your order. **NOTE: CAD files are NOT returnable and can not be exchanged.**

Your Blueprints Can Be Sealed by A Registered Architect

We can have your home plan blueprints sealed by an architect that is registered in most states. Please call our Order Department for details. Although an architect's seal will not guarantee approval of your home plan blueprints, a seal is sometimes required by your state or local building department in order to get a building permit. Please talk to your local building officials, before you order your blueprints, to determine if a seal is needed in your area. You will need to provide the county and state of your building site when ordering an architect's seal on your blueprints, and please allow additional time to process your order (an additional five to fifteen working days, at least). Seals are available for plans numbered 0-15,999, 17,000-18,999, 20,000 - 31,999, and 34,000 - 34,999.

State Energy Certificates

A few states require that an energy certificate be prepared for your new home to their specifications before a building permit can be issued. Again, your local building official can tell you if one is required in your state. You will first need to fill out the energy certificate checklist available to you when your order is placed. This list contains questions about type of heating used, siding, windows, location of home, etc. This checklist provides all the information needed to prepare your state energy certificate. **Please note: energy certificates are only available on orders for blueprints with an architect's seal.** Certificates are available for plans numbered 0-15,999, 17,000-18,999, 20,000 - 31,999, and 34,000 - 34,999.

Specifications & Contract Form

We send this form to you free of charge with your home plan order. The form is designed to be filled in by you or your contractor with the exact materials to use in the construction of your new home. Once signed by you and your contractor it will provide you with peace of mind throughout the construction process.

Detail Plans
Valuable Information About Construction Techniques—Not Plan Specific

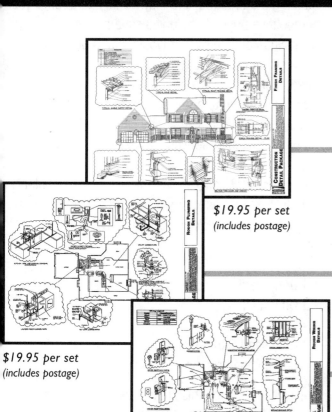

$19.95 per set
(includes postage)

$19.95 per set
(includes postage)

$19.95 per set
(includes postage)

PLEASE NOTE: The detail plans are not specific to any one home plan and should be used only as a general reference guide. Because local codes and requirements vary greatly, we recommend that you obtain drawings and bids from licensed contractors to do your mechanical plans. However, if you want to know more about techniques — and deal more confidently with subcontractors — we offer these remarkably useful detail sheets. These detail sheets will aid in your understanding of these technical subjects.

RESIDENTIAL CONSTRUCTION DETAILS

Ten sheets that cover the essentials of stick-built residential home construction. Details foundation options — poured concrete basement, concrete block, or monolithic concrete slab. Shows all aspects of floor, wall and roof framing. Provides details for roof dormers, overhangs, chimneys and skylights. Conforms to requirements of Uniform Building code or BOCA code. Includes a quick index and a glossary of terms.

RESIDENTIAL PLUMBING DETAILS

Eight sheets packed with information detailing pipe installation methods, fittings, and sized. Details plumbing hook-ups for toilets, sinks, washers, sump pumps, and septic system construction. Conforms to requirements of National Plumbing code. Color coded with a glossary of terms and quick index.

RESIDENTIAL ELECTRICAL DETAILS

Eight sheets that cover all aspects of residential wiring, from simple switch wiring to service entrance connections. Details distribution panel layout with outlet and switch schematics, circuit breaker and wiring installation methods, and ground fault interrupter specifications. Conforms to requirements of National Electrical Code. Color coded with a glossary of terms.

Questions?
Call our customer service number at 1-800-235-5700.

the Garlinghouse company

Order Form

BEST PLAN VALUE IN THE INDUSTRY!

Order Code No. **H4HNL**

_____ foundation

____ set(s) of blueprints for plan # _____ $_____

____ Vellum for plan # _____ $_____

____ Additional set(s) @ $50 each for plan # _____ $_____
(Not available for 1 set-study set)

____ Mirror Image Reverse @ $50 each $_____

____ Right Reading Reverse @ $135 each $_____

____ Materials list for plan # _____ $_____

____ Detail Plans (Not plan specific) @ $19.95 each

    ❑ Construction ❑ Plumbing ❑ Electrical $_____

____ Bottom-Line Zip Quote @ $29.95 for plan # _____ $_____

____ Additional Bottom-Line Zip Quotes

    @ $14.95 for plan(s) # _____ $_____

    Zip code where building _____

____ Itemized Zip Quote for plan(s) # _____ $_____

    Shipping $_____

    Subtotal $_____

    Sales Tax (VA residents add 4.5%. Not required for other states.) $_____

TOTAL AMOUNT ENCLOSED $_____

Send your check, money order, or credit card information to:
(No C.O.D.'s Please)

Please submit all United States & other nations orders to:

The Garlinghouse Co.
Attn: Order Fulfillment Dept.
4125 Lafayette Rd. Ste. 100
Chantilly, VA. 20151
CALL: (800) 235-5700

VISA **MasterCard**

Please Submit all Canadian plan orders to:
Garlinghouse Company
102 Ellis Street
Penticton, BC V2A 4L5
CALL: (800) 361-7526 FAX: (250) 493-7526

ADDRESS INFORMATION:

NAME: _____

STREET: _____

CITY: _____

STATE: _____ ZIP: _____

DAYTIME PHONE: _____

E-MAIL ADDRESS: _____

Credit Card Information

Charge To: ❑ Visa   ❑ Mastercard

Card # | | | | | | | | | | | | | | | |

Signature _____ Exp. ____ / ____

To order your plan on-line now using our secure server, visit:
www.garlinghouse.com

CUSTOMER SERVICE	**TO PLACE ORDERS**
Questions on existing orders?	• To order your home plans • Questions about a plan
➡ **1-800-895-3715**	➡ **1-800-235-5700**

Privacy Statement (please read)

Dear Valued Garlinghouse Customer,

Your privacy is extremely important to us. We'd like to take a little of your time to explain our privacy policy.

As a service to you, we would like to provide your name to companies such as the following:

- Building material manufacturers that we are affiliated with, who would like to keep you current with their product line and specials.
- Building material retailers that would like to offer you competitive prices to help you save money.
- Financing companies that would like to offer you competitive mortgage rates.

In addition, as our valued customer, we would like to send you newsletters to assist in your building experience. *We* would also appreciate *your* feedback by filling out a customer service survey aimed to improve our operations.

You have total control over the use of your contact information. You let us know exactly how you want to be contacted. Please check all boxes that apply.
Thank you.

❑ Don't mail
❑ Don't call
❑ Don't E-mail
❑ Only send Garlinghouse newsletters and customer service surveys

In closing, we hope this shows Garlinghouse's firm commitment to providing superior customer service and protection of your privacy. We thank you for your time and consideration.

Sincerely,

The Garlinghouse Company

For Our **USA** Customers:
Order Toll Free: 1-800-235-5700
Monday-Friday 8:00 a.m. to 8:00 p.m. Eastern Time

CUSTOMER SERVICE	TO PLACE ORDERS
Questions on existing orders?	• To order your home plans • Questions about a plan
➡ 1-800-895-3715	➡ 1-800-235-5700

For Our **Canadian** Customers:
Order Toll Free: 1-800-361-7526
Monday-Friday 8:00 a.m. to 5:00 p.m. Pacific Time
or FAX your Credit Card order to 1-250-493-7526
Customer Service: 1-250-493-0942

Please have ready: 1. Your credit card number 2. The plan number 3. The order code number ⇨ **H4HNL**

Garlinghouse 2004 Blueprint Price Code Schedule

*Prices subject to change without notice.

	1 Set Study Set	4 Sets	8 Sets	Vellums	ML	Bottom-Line ZIP Quote	CADD Files
A	$395	$435	$485	$600	$60	$29.95	$1,250
B	$425	$465	$515	$630	$60	$29.95	$1,300
C	$450	$490	$540	$665	$60	$29.95	$1,350
D	$490	$530	$580	$705	$60	$29.95	$1,400
E	$530	$570	$620	$750	$70	$29.95	$1,450
F	$585	$625	$675	$800	$70	$29.95	$1,500
G	$630	$670	$720	$850	$70	$29.95	$1,550
H	$675	$715	$765	$895	$70	$29.95	$1,600
I	$700	$740	$790	$940	$80	$29.95	$1,650
J	$740	$780	$830	$980	$80	$29.95	$1,700
K	$805	$845	$895	$1,020	$80	$29.95	$1,750
L	$825	$865	$915	$1,055	$80	$29.95	$1,800

Shipping — (Plans 1-35999)	1-3 Sets	4-6 Sets	7+ & Vellums
Standard Delivery (UPS 2-Day)	$25.00	$30.00	$35.00
Overnight Delivery	$35.00	$40.00	$45.00

Shipping — (Plans 36000-99999)	1-3 Sets	4-6 Sets	7+ & Vellums
Ground Delivery (7-10 Days)	$15.00	$20.00	$25.00
Express Delivery (3-5 Days)	$20.00	$25.00	$30.00

International Shipping & Handling	1-3 Sets	4-6 Sets	7+ & Vellums
Regular Delivery Canada (10-14 Days)	$30.00	$35.00	$40.00
Express Delivery Canada (7-10 Days)	$60.00	$70.00	$80.00
Overseas Delivery Airmail (3-4 Weeks)	$50.00	$60.00	$65.00

Additional sets with original order $50

IMPORTANT INFORMATION TO READ BEFORE YOU PLACE YOUR ORDER

How Many Sets of Plans Will You Need?

The Standard 8-Set Construction Package

*Our experience shows that you'll speed up every step of construction and avoid costly building errors by ordering enough sets to go around. Each tradesperson wants a set—the general contractor and all subcontractors: foundation, electrical, plumbing, heating/air conditioning, and framers. Don't forget your lending institution, building department, and, of course, a set for yourself. * Recommended For Construction **

The Minimum 4-Set Construction Package

*If you're comfortable with arduous follow-up, this package can save you a few dollars by giving you the option of passing down plan sets as work progresses. You might have enough copies to go around if work goes exactly as scheduled and no plans are lost or damaged by subcontractors. But for only $60 more, the 8-set package eliminates these worries. * Recommended For Bidding **

The 1 Set-Study Set

We offer this set so you can study the blueprints to plan your dream home in detail. They are stamped "study set only—not for construction" and you cannot build a home from them. In pursuant to copyright laws, it is illegal to reproduce any blueprint. 1 set-study sets cannot be ordered in a reversed format.

To Reorder, Call 800-235-5700

If you find after your initial purchase that you require additional sets of plans, a materials list, or other items, you may purchase them from us at special reorder prices (please call for pricing details) provided that you reorder within six months of your original order date. There is a $28 reorder processing fee that is charged on all reorders. For more information on reordering plans, please contact our Sales Department.

Customer Service/Exchanges Call 800-895-3715

If for some reason you have a question about your existing order, please call 800-895-3715. Your plans are custom printed especially for you once you place your order. For that reason we cannot accept any returns. If for some reason you find that the plan you have purchased from us does not meet your needs, then you may exchange that plan for any other plan in our collection. We allow you 60 days from your original invoice date to make an exchange. At the time of the exchange, you will be charged a processing fee of 20% of the total amount of your original order, plus the difference in price between the plans (if applicable), plus the cost to ship the new plans to you. Call our Customer Service Department for more information. Please Note: Reproducible Vellums can only be exchanged if they are unopened.

Important Shipping Information

Please refer to the shipping charts on the order form for service availability for your specific plan number. Our delivery service must have a street address or Rural Route Box number—never a post office box. (PLEASE NOTE: Supplying a P.O. Box number will only will delay the shipping of your order.) Use a work address if no one is home during the day. Orders being shipped to APO or FPO must go via First Class Mail. Please include the proper postage.

For our International Customers, only Certified bank checks and money orders are accepted and must be payable in U.S. currency. For speed, we ship international orders Air Parcel Post. Please refer to the chart for the correct shipping cost.

Important Canadian Shipping Information

To our friends in Canada, we have a plan design affiliate in Penticton, BC. This relationship will help you avoid the delays and charges associated with shipments from the United States. Moreover, our affiliate is familiar with the building requirements in your community and country. We prefer payments in U.S. currency. If you however are sending Canadian funds, please add 45% to the prices of the plans and shipping fees.

An Important Note About Building Code Requirements

All plans are drawn to conform to one or more of the industry's major national building standards. However, due to the variety of local building regulations, your plan may need to be modified to comply with local requirements—snow loads, energy loads, seismic zones, etc. Do check them fully and consult your local building officials.

A few states require that all building plans used be drawn by an architect registered in that state. While having your plans reviewed and stamped by such an architect may be prudent, laws requiring non-conforming plans like ours to be completely redrawn forces you to unnecessarily pay very large fees. If your state has such a law, we strongly recommend you contact your state representative to protest.

The rendering, floor plans, and technical information contained within this publication are not guaranteed to be totally accurate. Consequently, no information from this publication should be used either as a guide to constructing a home or for estimating the cost of building a home. Complete blueprints must be purchased for such purposes.

Index

Option Key

| BL | Bottom-Line Zip Quote | ML | Materials List BL/ML | ZIP | Itemized Zip Quote | RRR | Right Reading Reverse | DUP | Duplex |

* Call 1-800-235-5700 for pricing information.

Index

Option Key

BL	Bottom-Line Zip Quote	**ML**	Materials List BL/ML	**ZIP**	Itemized Zip Quote	**RRR**	Right Reading Reverse	**DUP**	Duplex

TOP SELLING
GARAGE PLANS

Save money by Doing-It-Yourself using our Easy-To-Follow plans. Whether you intend to build your own garage or contract it out to a building professional, the Garlinghouse garage plans provide you with everything you need to price out your project and get started. Put our 90+ years of experience to work for you. Order now!!

No. 06016C $24.95

Cape Cod Style Apartment Garage With One Bedroom

- 28' x 24' Overall Dimensions
- 544 Square Foot Apartment
- 12/12 Gable Roof with Dormers
- Slab or Stem Wall Foundation Options

No. 06015C $24.95

Apartment Garage With Two Bedrooms

- 28' x 26' Overall Dimensions
- 728 Square Foot Apartment
- 4/12 Pitch Gable Roof
- Slab or Stem Wall Foundation Options

No. 06012C $16.95

30' Deep Gable &/or Eave Entry Jumbo Garages

- 4/12 Pitch Gable Roof
- Available Options for Extra Tall Walls, Garage & Personnel Doors, Foundation, Window, & Sidings
- Package contains 4 Different Sizes
- 30' x 28'   • 30' x 32'   • 30' x 36'   • 30' x 40'

No. 06013C $16.95

Two-Car Eave Entry Garage With Mudroom/Breezeway

- Attaches to Any House
- 36' x 24' Eave Entry
- Available Options for Utility Room with Bath, Mudroom, Screened-In Breezeway, Roof, Foundation, Garage & Personnel Doors, Window, & Sidings

No. 06001C $14.95

12', 14' & 16' Wide-Gable Entry 1-Car Garages

- Available Options for Roof, Foundation, Window, Door, & Sidings
- Package contains 8 Different Sizes
- 12' x 20' Mini-Garage • 14' x 22' • 16' x 20' • 16' x 24'
- 14' x 20'   • 14' x 24' • 16' x 22' • 16' x 26'

No. 06003C $14.95

24' Wide-Gable Entry 2-Car Garages

- Available Options for Side Shed, Roof, Foundation, Garage & Personnel Doors, Window, & Sidings
- Package contains 5 Different Sizes
- 24' x 22'   • 24' x 28'   • 24' x 36'
- 24' x 24'   • 24' x 32'

No. 06007C $16.95

Gable 2-Car Gable Entry Gambrel Roof Garages

- Rear Stairs to Loft Workshop
- Front Loft Cargo Door With Pulley Lift
- Available Options for Foundation, Garage & Personnel Doors, Window, & Sidings
- Package contains 5 Different Sizes
- 22' x 26' • 22' x 28' • 24' x 28' • 24' x 30' • 24' x 32'

No. 06006C $16.95

22' & 24' Deep Eave Entry 2 & 3-Car Garages

- Can Be Built Stand-Alone or Attached to House
- Available Options for Roof, Foundation, Garage & Personnel Doors, Window, & Sidings
- Package contains 6 Different Sizes
- 22' x 28'   • 22' x 32'   • 24' x 32'
- 22' x 30'   • 24' x 30'   • 24' x 36'

No. 06002C $14.95

20' & 22' Wide-Gable Entry 2-Car Garages

- Available Options for Roof, Foundation, Garage & Personnel Doors, Window, & Sidings
- Package contains 7 Different Sizes
- 20' x 20'   • 20' x 24'   • 22' x 22'   • 22' x 28'
- 20' x 22'   • 20' x 28'   • 22' x 24'

No. 06008C $16.95

Eave Entry 2 & 3-Car Clerestory Roof Garages

- Interior Side Stairs to Loft Workshop
- Available Options for Engine Lift, Foundation, Garage & Personnel Doors, Window, & Sidings
- Package contains 4 Different Sizes
- 24' x 26'   • 24' x 28'   • 24' x 32'   • 24' x 36'

Order Code No: **H4HNL**

Garage Order Form

Please send me 1 complete set of the following
GARAGE PLAN BLUEPRINTS:

Item no. & description _____ Price

$ _____

Additional Sets

    (@ $10.00 EACH) $ _____

Garage Vellum

    (@ $200.00 EACH) $ _____

Shipping Charges: **UPS Ground (3-7 days within the US)** $ _____
    1-3 plans $7.95
    4-6 plans $9.95
    7-10 plans $11.95
    11 or more plans $17.95

Subtotal: $ _____

Resident sales tax: $ _____
(VA residents add 4.5%. Not required for other states.)

Total Enclosed: $ _____

My Billing Address is:

Name: _____

Address: _____

City: _____

State: _____ Zip: _____

Daytime Phone No. (   ) _____

My Shipping Address is:

Name: _____

Address: _____
    (UPS will not ship to P.O. Boxes)

City: _____

State: _____ Zip: _____

For Faster Service...Charge It!
U.S. & Canada Call
1(800)235-5700

MASTERCARD, VISA

Card # | | | | | | | | | | | | | | | |

Signature _____ Exp. ___ / ___

If paying by credit card, to avoid delays:
billing address must be as it appears on credit card statement

---

Here's What You Get

- One complete set of drawings for each plan ordered
- Detailed step-by-step instructions with easy-to-follow diagrams on how to build your garage (not available with apartment garages)
- For each garage style, a variety of size and garage door configuration options
- Variety of roof styles and/or pitch options for most garages
- Complete materials list
- Choice between three foundation options: Monolithic Slab, Concrete Stem Wall or Concrete Block Stem Wall
- Full framing plans, elevations and cross-sectionals for each garage size and configuration

Garage Plan Blueprints

All blueprint garage plan orders contain one complete set of drawings with instructions and are priced as listed next to the illustration. **These blueprint garage plans can not be modified.** Additional sets of plans may be obtained for $10.00 each with your original order. UPS shipping is used unless otherwise requested. Please include the proper amount for shipping.

Garage Plan Vellums

By purchasing vellums for one of our garage plans, you receive one vellum set of the same construction drawing found in the blueprints, but printed on vellum paper. Vellums can be erased and are perfect for making design changes. They are also semi-transparent making them easy to duplicate. But most importantly, the purchase of garage plan vellums comes with a broader license that allows you to make changes to the design (ie, create hand drawn or CAD derivative work), to make copies of the plan and to build one garage from the plan.

Send your order to:
(With check or money order payable in U.S. funds only)
The Garlinghouse Company
Attn: Order Fulfillment Dept.
4125 Lafayette Rd. Ste. 100
Chantilly, Va. 20151

No C.O.D. orders accepted; U.S. funds only. UPS will not ship to Post Office boxes, FPO boxes, APO boxes, Alaska or Hawaii.

Canadian orders:
UPS Ground (5-10 days within Canada)
1-3 plans $15.95
4-6 plans $17.95
7-10 plans $19.95
11 or more plans $24.95
Prices subject to change without notice.